Violent Delights, Violent Ends

D1260588

Love moderately; long love doth so; Too swift arrives as tardy as too slow.

Fondest Regards,

Mircee von Henne

VIOLENT Delights, VIOLENT Ends

SEX, RACE, & HONOR IN
COLONIAL CARTAGENA
DE INDIAS

Nicole von Germeten

University of New Mexico Press | Albuquerque

LIBRARY OF CONGRESS CATALOGING-IN-PUBLICATION DATA

Germeten, Nicole von.
Violent delights, violent ends : sex, race, and honor in colonial Cartagena de Indias /
Nicole von Germeten.
pages cm
Includes bibliographical references and index.
ISBN 978-0-8263-5395-5 (pbk. : alk. paper) — ISBN 978-0-8263-5396-2 (electronic)
1. Sex—Colombia—Cartagena—History. 2. Cartagena (Colombia)—Race relations—History.
3. Violence—Colombia—Cartagena—History. 4. Honor—Colombia—Cartagena—History.
I. Title.
HQ18.C65G47 2013
303.609861—dc23
2013019963

TYPESET BY LILA SANCHEZ

BOOK DESIGN
Composed in 10.25/13.5 Minion Pro Regular
Display type is Minion Pro

For my friends and mentors, Robert and Mary Jo Nye.

CONTENTS

ACKNOWLEDGMENTS

THE RESEARCH FOR THIS BOOK WAS ORIGINALLY FUNDED BY A COLLEGE of Liberal Arts Research Grant from Oregon State University. Thank you to the History Department chair at that time, Paul Farber, for supporting my application and my sabbatical time off from teaching, which I used to begin this project. The American Philosophical Society also supported my research with a small grant in 2011. I made great progress in my research while in residence as a visiting scholar at the Center for Latin American Studies at Stanford University on and off from 2008 to 2010. Thank you to Herbert Klein and Megan Gorman for your hospitality there and to Ben Vinson for initially introducing me to the Center faculty.

I appreciate the assistance of the staff at the Archivo General de la Nación in Bogota, the Archivo General de Indias in Seville, and the Archivo Nacional in Madrid. I offer my warmest gratitude and affection to the distinguished historian padre Tulio Aristizábal of the San Pedro Claver Church and Museum in Cartagena, as well as to the other kind, learned, and hospitable padres of the Society of Jesus who reside there.

Many thanks to Kristen Block, Rebecca Earle, and Linda Curcio Nagy for their scholarly support and collegial input on this project. Kristen encouraged this book idea in its infancy at the Latin American Studies Association conference in Rio in 2009. Linda participated with me in panels at Rocky Mountain Conference of Latin American Studies and LASA while I worked on the project. Rebecca kindly read a chapter in one of her many areas of expertise, the history of clothing in the Viceroyalties. Thanks to Karen Melvin for inviting me to air some initial ideas on this project to the History Department at Bates College. Michelle McKinley also gave me two opportunities to present at the University of Oregon at conferences supported by the Center for Latino and Latin American Studies, as well as included me in panels at RMCLAS. I appreciate her superb scholarship and personal warmth and kindness. Rachel Moore quickly provided a great translation for a difficult eighteenth-century note. Dain Borges, George Reid Andrews, and Ramon Gutierrez kindly hosted my presentation of early analysis of this material at an event on Race and Sexuality in Latin America at the University of Chicago. Frank Proctor helped me organize my ideas by offering me the opportunity to write an article on sexuality and witchcraft for *History Compass*.

Thank you to my Oregon State University students in HST 350, HST 310, and HST 407 for reading and commenting on the rough drafts of these chapters. Members of the History Faculty at Oregon State University, including Anita Guerrini, Chris Nichols, Ben Mutschler, Paul Kopperman, and Marisa Chappell, were kind enough to read and closely critique a chapter of this book in the fall of 2012. My colleague William Husband provided an especially helpful analysis, although all of the history faculty in attendance offered useful and challenging advice on improving chapter 10. Thank you to Robert Peckyno for your encouraging marketing ideas. Robert and Mary Jo Nye carefully read and edited several chapters. I would not have written this book or known anything about honor and violence if it had not been for Bob Nye's outstanding mentorship over the last ten years. I hope that my scholarly and generous colleagues can take some pride in their contributions to the finished product.

Kris Lane, Kathryn Sloane, and two anonymous readers provided insightful, helpful comments and close readings of very rough drafts of this book. Kris Lane made an extra effort to reread the introduction and greatly increased my confidence in the final result. Although their input significantly improved the final product, I am responsible for any remaining errors.

I gratefully acknowledge the amazing patience and fantastic support I enjoyed from University of New Mexico Press's editor-in-chief, W. Clark Whitehorn.

I remain grateful to Sarah Cline and William B. Taylor for their guidance during my time as a graduate student in history. James Lockhart has also been a scholarly inspiration and provided specific advice regarding personal letters quoted in this book.

Kasia Cichowicz, I appreciate your humor, irrepressible enthusiasm, and positive predictions for this book. Collin English, I hope there will be many more intellectually stimulating discussions to come. I am so grateful to Ricardo Raul Salazar Rey for his unstinting friendship, constant advice, and humor over the past few years. Martin Nesvig has also extended his welcome friendship and perceptive historical expertise. Brent Ayrey helped me find the records of the criminal cases at the heart of this book in Bogota almost a decade ago. Thank you to my parents, Joan and Jim von Germeten, and my sister, Ann von Germeten, for tolerantly reading early chapter drafts. I appreciate how Matthew Stinger took an interest in the topic of love magic and lessened my anxiety in the final phases of this project.

To the sweetest, kindest, funniest lady I know, Inez: I am looking forward to our conversations about history, life, and scholarship in the future.

Doña Lorenzana, doña Manuela, Paula, and doña Luisa have become my intellectual and emotional *comadres*. Although William Shakespeare never visited the sixteenth-century Caribbean, his works communicate an understanding of violent passions, like the ones that Cartagena provoked in the seventeenth century, and continue to inspire in the present day. Whenever you are in this city, you forget at your peril that:

> These violent delights have violent ends
> And in their triumph die, like fire and powder,
> Which as they kiss consume. The sweetest honey
> Is loathsome in its own deliciousness
> And in the taste confounds the appetite.
> Therefore love moderately; long love doth so;
> Too swift arrives as tardy as too slow.
> (*Romeo and Juliet*, act 2, scene 6)

INTRODUCTION

PERHAPS THE MOST USEFUL WAY TO INTRODUCE THE THEMES EX-
plored in this book is to plunge directly into a case in the historical record
that illustrates them in a succinct way. In the 1640s, Cartagena de India's
authorities were not only dealing with the tail end of dozens of witch trials and extended attacks on the local Portuguese slave traders, but they also
faced a scandal involving a young *doña* who used sex to manipulate a lustful,
corrupt inquisitor. In 1643, Lorenzo Martinez de Castro presented a complaint before the Holy Office against the inquisitor Juan Ortiz, calling him a
"bad administrator of the tribunal," with an "evil conscience" and "no fear of
god" who committed acts "against the holy sacraments of the church, especially matrimony."[1] It was publicly known that Castro's wife doña Rufina
de Rojas, a seventeen-year-old *sevillana*, had gone to Ortiz's house one evening while her husband was away from home and had not left until the next
morning. Castro claimed that he had a right to kill his wife to avoid further
scandal resulting from her adulterous betrayal of the marriage sacrament.
But instead, he denounced the ungodliness of the inquisitor and started
the process of an annulment. Lorenzo said that his own slaves, as well as
those in Ortiz's household, witnessed the adultery between the doña and
the inquisitor.

In the inquisitorial investigation, five domestic slaves confessed that
doña Rufina had told them to put herbs called *berenjena de monte* ("mountain eggplant," the popular name for a plant in the nightshade family) or
chamiza (a kind of wild cane or reed used for medicinal purposes) in her
husband's food to make him lose his senses temporarily so she could "do
whatever she wanted."[2] She told the slaves not to bother confessing that they
tampered with his food because she declared that these acts were not sins.

1

While the adultery was not their concern, and minor use of herbal medicine usually did not spark an investigation, this kind of amateur religious advice especially infuriated inquisitors. This case summary derives from the words of two enslaved witnesses who testified to the Holy Office that they accompanied doña Rufina when she went to visit the inquisitor Ortiz during the day and night.

A twenty-nine-year-old *mulato* carpenter called Pedro Suárez escorted doña Rufina to Ortiz's house on four different occasions. Suárez was enslaved to another man, but he labored as a carpenter with doña Rufina's husband. Suárez acted as a kind of bodyguard for Rufina and the two conversed on a very personal level. Suárez said that the first visit to Ortiz's house took place on the very day that Rufina began her testimonies before the tribunal. After her audience with the Holy Office, doña Rufina returned home and consulted her grandmother doña Inés, who advised her to "dress well and adorn herself and go to Juan Ortiz's house and fall at his feet as a beautiful negotiator." Later that evening, doña Rufina went to Ortiz's house accompanied by Suárez and her slave Ana Criolla. The two women entered through the front door and climbed the main staircase to chat with Ortiz in his *sala*, in the presence of his black page. Suárez waited on the patio for a half hour. On the walk home, he asked doña Rufina how the negotiations (over lessening the accusations the slaves had made regarding tampering with her husband's food) had progressed, and she replied that Ortiz reassured her that giving her husband the herb was not of concern to the tribunal.

Doña Rufina's dress on these visits stuck in Suárez and Ana's minds. On the night after her first visit, the three returned again to discuss the case. On this occasion, Ortiz told doña Rufina to return to speak before the tribunal in a few days, but to wear a veil and "very modest black" instead of the colorful dress she wore the first time.[3] Doña Rufina followed these orders. When she went back for her second official interrogation, she entered Holy Office building by a small side door at 5 a.m. When she returned home, upset but apparently not overly worried about her case, doña Inés told her that she should return to Ortiz's house again to thank him for his help. Doña Rufina protested that she was "not a woman who went out at night," but in a few days she sent the inquisitor a note and returned to his house for a third visit at 7 p.m. with Ana and Suárez. After this visit, Rufina told Suárez that she had "negotiated very well" with Ortiz.[4] The terms of receiving a lighter punishment, as doña Rufina reported to Suárez, were spending a night with Ortiz. Doña Rufina put him off until the night of the fiesta for Saint John.

Doña Rufina's twenty-five-year-old slave Ana Criolla knew a few more details about her mistress's encounters with Ortiz, since she actually accompanied Rufina into the house. Ana at first refused to confess to her involvement in the affair, until the inquisitors put her in solitary confinement in the *calabozo* (cell, possibly underground) for one night. Unable to tolerate her uncomfortable cell, Ana admitted to going to Ortiz's house with Rufina and added that her mistress wore a white bodice and a green wool overskirt lined in pink taffeta, with the lining showing through the top layer.[5] When Suárez and Ana accompanied Rufina to the inquisitor's house a final time, Suárez observed that she was "well perfumed and dressed."[6] In her defense, doña Rufina said that she wore the same clothes as she would inside her house, a white bodice and a serge skirt lined in green taffeta.[7] On this occasion, the page had the women enter through a private, hidden door at around 10 p.m. Doña Rufina instructed Suárez not to return until 3 a.m. On this visit, Ortiz took Rufina into a bedroom. Ana slept in the sala until Rufina woke her up in the morning, and they exited through the back door.

When he picked up the two women, Suárez said Rufina was "very happy, because the inquisitor said he would help and favor her." A few days later, Ortiz kindly sent her some pastries (empanadas and pasteles). By this stage, Suárez decided he would no longer be a party to corruption—he refused to participate in any more nighttime outings and even asked if he could work for a different master.[8] Doña Rufina also admitted that she had sex with the inquisitor (she used the words *acostándose con el*, or "sleeping with him," and not the more formulaic *acto carnal* or *relaciones ilícitas*). As a result of her sex acts with Ortiz, as well as her age and her elite status, doña Rufina did not suffer imprisonment in the secret prisons of the Holy Office, but was granted the privilege of occupying the rooms normally inhabited by the jailer's daughter. However, despite the sexual negotiations, the inquisitors fined her fifty pesos and warned her to avoid witchcraft in the future or risk a harsher punishment.[9]

Doña Rufina's suppressed sex scandal illustrates the central thesis of this book: women in colonial Cartagena de Indias took control of their own sex lives and used sex and rhetoric connected to sexuality to plead their cases when they had to negotiate with colonial bureaucrats. Our general understanding of patriarchy and unequal gender roles present in this society were often mitigated in practice in a variety of courts and legal proceedings. But this was a double-edged sword; Cartagena women could be sexually assertive, but they also had to be acutely aware of the danger inherent in disregarding the restricted, highly judgmental outlook on female sexuality set by Counter Reformation Catholicism and the precepts of the Hispanic honor code. Of course, ideas about honor adapted to a culturally diverse and demographically unstable colonial reality.

This case also brings to life the common occurrence of intimate ties formed between slaves and elite women who explored sex outside marriage. Women such as doña Rufina found themselves interrogated by the Holy Office because they trusted their slaves to help them use magical methods to find nonmarital sexual satisfaction. Love magic, a popular method for seducing men in seventeenth-century Cartagena, mixed indigenous, African, Creole, and European ingredients and methods and often played a role in women's illicit sexuality.[10] If secret sexual machinations and the use of spells and potions turned into a public scandal, domestic slaves became extremely useful witnesses in a criminal or inquisitorial investigation.

In the husband's reaction here, we see aggressive, litigious posturing and threats of violence in line with the Hispanic honor code, a reaction doña Rufina risked when she stepped outside the bounds of marital sex. Castro effectively presented his case by complaining about female sexuality in the vocabulary of male honor. In this discourse, women play a crucial role in the honor code but are not always victims of it. While men frequently presented themselves as full of righteous anger at affronts to their honor, women cast themselves in the role of sexual victims. Since the courts ostensibly functioned as a gesture to protect the weaker members of society, elite, honorable men often portrayed themselves in defensive legal positions, content to defend themselves by asserting their honor. In contrast, women appeared as humble petitioners. Both roles were strategically designed to produce favorable outcomes in the litigation. We will see a continuous dynamic between men asserting honor and women struggling to assert their sexual agency through the use of effective litigating techniques.

This book analyzes these court cases through the testimony reported to judicial authorities. We should acknowledge what everyone knew at this time—stories told in court were a rhetorical tool meant to improve one's chances of a favorable judicial outcome. For colonial women, sexuality was a competitive, tense, and vibrant part of their lives, but this was not usually the persona they presented in court. Litigating men knew that anger and the violence provoked by outraged honor justified various kinds of crimes. An honorable man had a right to act violently in response to slights, and in their view, this did not really have anything to do with the authorities and official litigation; men of honor should not suffer judicial consequences for acting according to essential Spanish values. A persona based on sexual aggressiveness was more common and acceptable for men, but as the above example proves, women had their own version of sexual agency regardless of the rhetoric of passivity that they presented to judges.

Competing political factions sparred constantly in Cartagena. This case follows the norm for how factions used female sex and the language of honor as weapons or a means of settling scores. Men often took advantage of the courts' function as protectors of the weak to exploit instances of sexual insults for political purposes. Non-elite women also took part in some of these campaigns, though surviving documentation suggests they used their sexuality more for economic survival than for political ends. Lastly, doña Rufina's example suggests the importance clothing possessed for determining judgments about public reputation and adherence to conventional sexual morality.

As an important Spanish port city and the site of an Inquisition high court, a slave market, a leper colony, a military base, and a prison colony, Cartagena sat at the center of a web of colonial institutions that imposed order upon local residents by enforcing Catholicism, cultural and religious boundaries, and prevailing race and gender hierarchies. Embedded in these institutions were the Hispanic values of sexual honor and blood purity. Despite an expanding city wall as Cartagena increased its fortifications throughout the colonial period, this remained a port city open to international influences. The encircling walls and fortifications worked like a lid raising the temperature on a mixture ready to boil over at any moment. Cartagena resembled New Orleans in their shared experience of "rogue colonialism."[11] The city simmered with illegal activity, ranging from contraband trade, to prostitution, to heretical religious practice. Even the supposedly untouchable tenets of the honor code were open to interpretation in this port city.

As was the case in nearly all population centers in viceregal Spanish America, residents of Cartagena maintained tense working relationships with colonial institutions and values as they negotiated their daily life. This especially applies to the wide array of people who were not native to Cartagena but had settled there either willingly or unwillingly.[12] Throughout the city's history, Cartagena's authorities struggled to deal with a wide variety of either non-Spanish and/or non-Catholic residents, as well as various groups of people sent to the city specifically for the purpose of incarceration, including condemned criminals and lepers. Other transient groups in Cartagena were barely tolerated Protestants, as well as the sailors and soldiers common to every bustling port. Sick travelers hoping to get out as soon as possible populated Cartagena's hospitals.

Spaniards first settled in this region in 1533, led by Cartagena's official founding father, Pedro de Heredia. They were drawn by the promise of gold buried in the tombs of the Sinu indigenous civilization. Gold-hungry men came quickly: 800 by 1534 and 2,000 by 1535. This early boom soon declined, but by 1565, around 4,000 people lived in Cartagena. In the first third of the seventeenth century, Cartagena had only 1,500 *vecinos*, and an estimated 6,000 residents.[13] By 1630, 184 foreigners resided in the city, and over 80 percent of these individuals were Portuguese. Thousands of slaves passing through the city added to the city's temporary inhabitants.[14] By 1684, 7,341 people lived in Cartagena, with slaves adding 25 percent to that number. In the wake of the destructive 1697 French invasion, Cartagena was virtually depopulated, but the city gradually recovered to 4,556 inhabitants in 1708. The city's population increased dramatically in the late eighteenth century and early nineteenth century: a detailed census calculated 13,690 residents in 1777, growing to 17,600 by 1809. Racially-mixed and enslaved women numerically dominated the population. In 1777, nearly 20 percent of local residents were unmarried free women of color.[15]

By the early seventeenth century, Cartagena possessed a complete compliment of Spanish religious institutions. The city was the seat of a bishop, and from 1610, the location of one of three Holy Office tribunals of the Spanish Inquisition in the Americas. Wealthy local Spaniards sponsored the foundations of several convents and friaries representing the Dominican order (with a rudimentary convent in 1534), the Franciscans (eventually in the convent of San Diego, with the earliest local foundation in 1555, although the Franciscans were deterred by the pirate attacks described later), as well as the friars of Saint Augustine (1582) and Our Lady of Mercy. The outlying barrio of Getsemaní had its own Franciscan convent and parish churches. The Jesuits established themselves in the city in 1606. The nunneries included one occupied by Discalced Carmelites and another with nuns dedicated to Saint Clare. Three local hospitals treated charity cases: San Sebastian (dating to 1537), Espíritu Santo (founded by the town council in 1595), and the leper hospital, San Lázaro, in formation in the late sixteenth century. Lastly, outside the city on the small mountain called La Popa, was a convent dedicated to Nuestra Señora de la Candelaria.[16] In the secular realm, the most important local authorities were the governor and his appointed lieutenant general. A sergeant major oversaw internal military judicial issues. Underneath these offices were a town council and several *alcaldes* and *alguaciles* with judicial functions. Litigants in local court cases could appeal to the *audiencia* or high court in Bogota.[17] In 1741, the crown created a new viceregal seat in Bogota, which had jurisdiction over Cartagena.

Cartagena's walled city enclosed most of these Spanish institutions and many of the events discussed in this book took place within these walls. For much of the colonial era, the mainland was only accessible via the Puerta de Media Luna or Half Moon Gate. For many decades, the San Lázaro leprosarium stood just outside this entranceway. Slave markets and barracks also bustled near the docks adjacent to the city center. The local slave trading economy and its infrastructure spilled over into the humble structures of the Getsemaní barrio, heavily populated by Africans and their children and grandchildren. This less prestigious neighborhood served as the setting for critical events in the lives of some of the more intriguing women discussed in the chapters that follow. As noted in 1620 by the local bishop, "the most scandalous people in this city live in Getsemaní."[18] In the same year, the authorities surveyed this neighborhood, observing that nearly 20 percent of the plots of land were owned by single women (usually of African descent), many of whom rented them out to male tenants, including slaves and passing travelers.[19] While some of the single women who lived in Getsemaní were recognized as prostitutes, many other female residents "fit into a gray area between marriage and prostitution," living with men in serial monogamy or juggling several lovers at once.[20] In eighteenth-century Cartagena, at least one-third of all residences had a woman as head of household and in charge of a small family group. These women were single, widowed, or subject to an absent husband, and most of them were nonwhite.[21] These are the intriguing, active women who populate many of the pages that follow.

This book begins its story just as Cartagena began to recover from decades of regular attacks by English and French corsairs, who "hovered about every Caribbean port like flocks of vultures."[22] They attacked regularly in the sixteenth century, first in 1543 with the invasion of Jean François de la Roque (sieur de Roberval), known as Roberto Baal in Spanish histories. Helped by a Spaniard, Baal and his men robbed the city of 35,000 pesos worth of gold and silver, as well as 2,500 pesos from the royal treasury.[23] Three hundred *corsarios* led by the Frenchman Martin Cote burned Cartagena in

1559, although they considered the small city hardly worth their efforts, ransoming it for 4,000 pesos.[24] The threat of the French raiders compelled local residents to petition the crown to build up the city's defensives, beginning over two centuries of nearly continuous militarization in Cartagena. With only two pieces of artillery, the city defended itself from John Hawkins in 1568, after rejecting his efforts to trade in contraband goods and slaves.[25]

The town's physical structure architecturally expressed its fears of pirate attacks and broader imperial insecurities. Starting in 1569, the crown, via its representative the Viceroy of Peru don Francisco de Toledo, began to take a more careful interest in Cartagena's fortifications. Construction was well underway by the time Francis Drake turned his ambitions to Cartagena in the 1580s.[26] With twenty-three ships and three thousand men, Drake easily sacked Cartagena in 1586. Drake made a mockery of the rudimentary fortifications, which included a chain across the entrance to the harbor, and the minor resistance offered by an undisciplined defense force mixing Spanish, Indian, and African combatants. The Spanish authorities fled the city as Drake burned a hundred of the humbler houses and part of the cathedral. The corsarios stayed in the city for fifty-three days and received over 100,000 ducats from the local residents. Precisely at the time of Drake's occupation of the city, the Council of the Indies in Spain was working on Cartagena's ambitious fortification project, which ultimately resulted in a wall around the city, masterminded by the talented engineer Bautista Antonelli.[27] Despite building walls, harbor defenses, and bulwarks around the city, the city again fell to an attack by five thousand French buccaneers led by the Baron de Pointis in 1697.[28] Finally, in 1741, Spanish forces led by the heroic Blas de Lezo (a grizzled veteran who had lost a leg, an arm, and an eye in previous battles) defeated thousands of English invaders led by Admiral Vernon. With its strong ties to the Atlantic world, including Haiti, in 1810, Cartagena was one of the first cities to declare independence from Spain, although over a decade of struggles followed.

Colonial archives are quite limited in Cartagena. Local criminal records have not survived. Only the scantiest remnants recording baptisms, marriages, ecclesiastical divorces, and deaths before the mid- to late-nineteenth century survived, either in parishes or the cathedral. Unlike many important cities in Spanish America, in Cartagena, researchers will not find copies of deeds of sale, powers of attorney, last wills and testaments, dowries, and all the other minutia of buying, selling, and exchanging property customarily filed away by colonial notaries. All secular court cases presented here were appealed to the high court in Bogota and have been preserved in the Colombian national archives. Complete inquisition records also have not survived the centuries: only a handful of complete cases involving religious belief exist for the seventeenth century, although historians can find thousands of pages of other kinds of Holy Office records (documenting dozens of criminal, financial, clerical, and jurisdictional disputes) stored in the Spanish national historic archives in Madrid.[29] In the absence of notarial records or more complete criminal files, the documents drawn up in inquisition trials "provide an overview of colonial life not available from other sources. The way in which social institutions react to the rebel, the nonconformist . . . yields all manner of data."[30] Only the most notorious cases have survived the centuries, but these cases hint at a pervasive practice of sexual magic, female sexual agency, and violence committed in the name of honor. The authorities took particular notice in public infractions, or when someone chose to litigate over sexual matters, especially women's sex acts or reputation of sexual activity, in order to demolish a political rival.[31]

The sparse surviving material with content related to sex, honor, race, and violence is not well-served by a statistical analysis as opposed to the narrative approach I employ here. Even if the surviving cases were plentiful, Robert Darnton argued decades ago against counting in favor of simply reading the stories told in archives, to search for an interpretation or understanding "not manufactured by the historian but by the people he studies."[32] This book will not contain "any quantitative estimates of, say, the kinds of weapons people used in sixteenth-century homicide," but will instead discuss the stories told about the homicides and the justifications given by historical actors for resorting to violence.[33] Natalie Zemon Davis's concern with the narratives presented by petitioners for royal pardon and how they adhered to or diverged from accepted templates, informs this book's approach to presenting archival evidence. Petitioners before courts shaped their stories to positively affect the outcome of their case. These stories were not necessarily fictions or malicious deceptions, however cruel or manipulative some criminal perpetrators might appear to us. Instead, the narratives were constructed to fit the values of the time and display each speaker's desired self-presentation and his or her understanding of how stories should be told.

Decades ago, Asunción Lavrin questioned the effectiveness of official attempts to control Spanish viceregal sexuality. At least as far back as Alfonso X's thirteenth-century code known as the *Siete partidas*, Spanish

rulers used religious morality as a template for social and gender hierarchies, as well as government and judicial systems.[34] However, there is a
great difference between models of sexual comportment and actual on-the-
ground modification of behavior, something that would be very difficult to
measure in any case. Recently, a number of scholars of early modern Spain
have proven that women both effectively used the courts to mitigate patriarchal domination *and* actually succeeded in enjoying sexual agency.[35] But
in the Americas, the Black Legend of Spanish conquistadors' rapaciousness is still popular and continues to be applied to the longer arc of colonial history. In effect, historians of Spanish America have not yet engaged
fully with the interpretations common in the historiography of Spain. Early
modern Spanish prescriptive literature, especially the often cited works of
Juan Luis Vives and Fray Luis de León, placed female sexual modesty at the
pinnacle of all virtues and married it to men's obligation to commit violent
acts to protect weak and susceptible women from their own sexuality.[36]
Literary and clerical sources support this view, but archival cases remain
full of raunchy, explicit, and irreverent witness testimonies.[37] Historians
such as Richard Boyer and Ann Twinam correctly warn against putting too
much credence in the practical applicability of literary sources for understanding sex and honor in colonial Spanish America.[38]

An emphasis on official decrees and cases when the secular or religious
authorities investigated or punished individuals involved in acts officially
viewed as illicit (such as practicing love magic, prostitution, or cohabitation)
often leads historians to interpret colonial sexuality only as a manifestation
of power and domination, influenced by the work of Michel Foucault.[39] This
approach especially tempts historians who draw on sexuality to make arguments about race in the colonial era. To give an example, in his 2009 book
Colonial Blackness: A History of Afro-Mexico, Herman Bennett entitled a
chapter on cohabitation, "Discipline and Culture." This chapter uses evidence from a handful of ecclesiastical crackdowns on unmarried lovers of
African descent in late sixteenth- and early seventeenth-century Mexico City
to argue for the existence of strict control over sex in daily life. In contrast, in
her analysis of the same kinds of cases for seventeenth-century Lima, María
Emma Mannarelli came to the exact opposite conclusion, noting a "com-
placency with regard to sex outside of marriage" and "a high level of acceptance for these unions."[40] Mannarelli rightly foregrounds the fact that the
authorities generally did not make the effort to prosecute people who violated unrealistically strict moral regulations, only taking an interest when

they uncovered a more serious crime. The rest of the time, the authorities did not survey or effectively suppress sexuality. As Guido Ruggiero wrote in 1985, "with apologies to Foucault, sexuality was not a discovery of the modern world."[41] It is not uncommon to find historians embracing opposing interpretations of sexual control: for Cartagena, the Colombian historian Jaime Humberto Borja Gómez stresses sexual/racial oppression in his publications, while María Cristina Navarette tends toward seeing the possibility of non-coercive relationships between lovers of different races.

When they focus exclusively on power, historians are liable to forget that sex is and was a pleasurable experience. Contrary to the most basic physiological facts, we seem to want colonial sex to be "nasty, brutish and short."[42] An emphasis on male judicial codes or masculinized literary rhetoric in regards to female sexuality can erase the existence of female desire. Jacqueline Murray notes that even feminist scholars tend "to privilege the social relations of the sexes at the expense of the sexual."[43] In 2002, Karen Viera Powers criticized the persistent focus in Latin American historiography on "gloryify[ing] male sexual domination and ascrib[ing] to women the constricted role of passive sexual objects."[44] Although Viera Powers concluded her essay with a sense of hope that the work of current and future scholars will complicate the age old "discourse of sexual conquest" and the slightly newer "totalizing discourse of rape and victimhood that is equally disempowering," these paradigms still attract historians, even those who are deeply invested in the history of sexuality. Through analyzing how men and women presented themselves in several different kinds of courts, this book seeks to answer Viera Power's call for a new perspective on colonial sex.

Honor and sexuality are inseparable areas of investigation for Spanish America. Theoretically, many of the men discussed throughout this book, such as military and church officials, represented paragons of honor. These men assessed their honor in contrast to other men who lacked the appropriate lineage, marital status, or wealth.[45] Honor required pure Spanish and Christian lineage (known as *limpieza de sangre* or "clean blood"). This guaranteed exclusive access to most professions and encouraged an obsessive concern for precedence and a lavish display of wealth whenever possible.[46] Soldiers, sailors, and bureaucrats often asserted their honor by making claims to loyal and extensive service to the king, but any man, regardless of his occupation, based his personal sense of honor on his reputation for carefully protecting the sexual reputation/activity of all his dependents, including both female relatives and slaves who lived under his roof. The values of

honor, status, and reputation were embedded in different registers in different levels of society but were felt to some degree by all Carthaginians, and
they expressed them in manners appropriate to their race, station, and class.
Thus, love, jealousy, status, authority, and sexuality were regulated at least in
part by socially differentiated versions of the honor code, according to which
some things were appropriate and tolerated and others were not. This gave
rise to emotional outbursts that individuals experienced as legitimate reactions to violations of the code.

The archives of the secular courts in Spain and the Americas show
that men offered only lip service to moral codes. Instead, they based their
sense of honor more on lineage, outward appearances, and reputation.[47] The
importance of one's personal appearance meant that clothing, jewelry and
other signs of wealth could reveal the subtle ways that individuals performed
honor on the city streets. A critical facet of understanding Spanish and
Spanish American honor is the concept of "public and notorious." Nearly
every witness interrogation in the cases cited here ends with a question asking if all the information provided by the deponent is "public and notorious,"
discussed and known publicly (*publico y notorio, de publica voz y fama*).
This public world contrasted with a private domain inhabited only by family, the most intimate friends, and domestics. If either side of a case wanted
to make any point regarding an individual's honor, the prosecution or the
defense had to call on the judgments of the "public and notorious" world
outside the home because it was a person's commonly known reputation,
not their private deeds, that determined their honor.[48] If only small group
of intimate friends, relatives, and servants knew about an illicit act, in terms
of honor and reputation, the act was irrelevant. Due to the malleability of
personal honor, Twinam stresses that lost honor could be regained, especially with the late eighteenth century introduction of the *gracias a sacar*, a
royal pronouncement on one's legitimacy. On the other hand, Tamar Herzog
shows that in some cases reputation, once lost, could not be regained because
Castilian law codified "public and notorious" information (i.e., gossip) as
the most damning evidence of criminal acts. According to Herzog, if an act
or behavior was "public and notorious," there was no evidence that could
stand against it: rumor conquered facts.[49]

However, Twinam argues that men and women defined honor at the
local level and thus, it fluctuated depending on an individual's life stage and
the shifting dynamic between his or her public persona and private behavior.
Twinam's subtle and flexible view of honor contrasts with that of another

scholar, Ramon Gutiérrez, who stresses that this culture rewarded male sexual aggression as a critical factor in colonial domination. Gutiérrez argues that men increased their honor through violating women, writing, "male honor was . . . secured and enhanced through displays of virility, notably the corruption of other men's women" and "in terms of honor it was the adulterer's conquest of another man's woman that made him the paragon of virtue."[50] This conclusion would have sexually passive women trapped between repressive institutions, families, and aggressive men, whereas evidence found for Cartagena suggests that honor was more often a rhetorical weapon deployed before the courts than the inspiration of male sexual aggression.[51]

While Twinam would certainly agree that men's sexual activity did not necessarily harm an honorable reputation, as was more frequently the case for women, her sources suggest that a sense of conscience based on ethics and religion did influence men. Twinam shows that men sincerely desired to pass on their honor to their illegitimate children, recognizing them legally even if they did not fit the strictest definitions of having a "pure" Spanish, legitimate lineage. Twinam observes that a moral code of behavior was a concept distinct from the idea of honor. She found that irresponsible fathers (presumably the kind of men who would act as sexually aggressive "machos") often lacked local ties that would influence them to recognize and help their children. This kind of man was marginal in a local society and did not represent a behavioral ideal for the men who had established their reputations locally.[52] Communities took a role in curbing seducers through gossip: wagging tongues of both genders guaranteed that men could not seduce women or girls of good reputation without consequences.[53] On occasion, men even claimed that more experienced women seduced them. These male victims received community support for their assertions of sexual innocence, turning the tables on the classic narrative of aggressive male sexuality.[54]

Love magic and illicit sex often went hand in hand in colonial Cartagena, and through this link, the Holy Office investigated and documented male and female, white and nonwhite sexuality. The first tribunal of the Spanish Inquisition came to the Americas in 1572, less than a century after the Catholic monarchs Ferdinand and Isabel founded this court in their Spanish dominions in an effort to stamp out what they viewed as heretical backsliding, most particularly the continued secret practice of Judaism by recent converts. Crypto Jews were not the most important target of the American tribunals (based in Mexico City, Lima, and Cartagena), as they had been for the first few decades of inquisitorial persecutions in Iberia, although there were a few major persecutions in sixteenth-century and seventeenth-century New Spain and South America. Instead, inquisitors over the course of the seventeenth and eighteenth centuries investigated what can be called "sin-crimes": bigamy, heretical statements, blasphemy, solicitation in the confessional, various clerical sins, and sodomy, sorcery, and witchcraft.[55] The Holy Office depended on accusations of these acts made by the populace in general, prompting individuals to make denunciations by reading aloud and posting an Edict of Faith, a statement exhorting the public to declarations of other people's sins before the Tribunal.[56] Self-denunciations and voluntary confessions were not uncommon. Through this process, individuals could use the Holy Office to further their side of personal conflicts or political rivalries, as the inquisition was far from monolithic, unified, or omnipotent.[57]

Scholars can use the records of the Holy Office to effectively illuminate some very private parts of colonial history, from couples' explicit erotic practices done in their bedrooms to the herbal concoctions that women cooked up in their kitchens. The most well-known analysis of colonial love magic is still Ruth Behar's 1989 essay, "Sexual Witchcraft, Colonialism, and Women's Powers."[58] Behar interprets very intimate acts, such as a woman serving a husband or master food ensorcelled with her own bodily fluids in order to *amansar* (tame) or *ligar* (bind) him, as a form of political resistance. In Behar's view, this demonstration of female power overturns gender and racial hierarchies. In the decades since the publication of Behar's article, scholars have continued to analyze love magic cases as reversals of colonial hierarchies, emphasizing cases where female (especially nonwhite) bodies, effluences, and physicality controlled and intimidated men, who were enraged at their loss of personal discipline or potency.[59] Behar's conclusions might work for the three cases cited in her article, but this kind of analysis does not work for all cases of sexual witchcraft, especially those presented in this book. Joan Bristol effectively breaks with Behar's approach, arguing that Afro-Mexican sorceresses were probably not seeking to disrupt colonial hierarchies through witchcraft, realizing that their powers were limited and to some degree monitored.[60] Nora Jaffary also turns away from an interpretation fixated on conscious rebellion, hierarchy subversion, and the unswerving focus on the symbolism of the female body and its effluences in her discussion of Mexican mystics prosecuted by the Holy Office. She points out that recent scholars who doggedly seek subversive tendencies in women tried by the Holy Office perpetuate misogynistic fears common in the viceroyalties. Instead Jaffary trusts that women believed their own claims and practices, and with practicality in mind, sought an income derived from preaching or mysticism.[61] Bristol and Jaffary's interpretations of mysticism, witchcraft, and sorcery as disconnected from grand narratives of rebellion and power make sense for the many poor women cited in this book, who simply pursued a bit of economic security through selling their skills as healers and erotic magic experts. They also used their expertise to find sexual pleasure for themselves.

I have not followed Behar's analysis here for two reasons: her essay is not about a larger witch craze involving Satanic pacts, and it derives from male complaints to inquisitors. In Cartagena, alleged witches pointed fingers at their own peers and colleagues, a pattern that follows European models.[62] European ideas about Satan, derived from sources on demonology, also come up in my case studies. The difference in who made the accusations shifts the focus away from a gender-based power struggle to an emphasis on a social and occupational circle where women competed for access to limited resources, depending on men willing to support them or clients for their spells and concoctions. My perception is that Behar paradoxically deemphasizes the sexual by presenting women (despite her assertions that their power derived from sexuality) as victims simply reacting to male abuse. In contrast, women in Spain and Cartagena initiated the use of love magic to control their husbands and spend time with their lovers, thus to some degree forging their own sexual experiences.

Martha Few also emphasizes racial hierarchies, framing her accounts of Guatemala witch persecutions as taking place in eras of especially stressful colonial racial tension and conflict. Few focuses on the female body as a conduit for love magic but does not concentrate on female sexuality or the desires that probably motivated many of the women mentioned in her book. However, in contrast to Behar, Few argues that many non-elite colonial women already had a stronger and more permanent grasp on certain kinds of power, including as business women or healers, even outside of their reputations as notorious witches. This power represents a critical aspect of ongoing cultural and ethnic resistance, if one chooses to view love magic practice as a rejection of colonial norms. Few effectively devotes much attention to the love magic marketplace and the extensive and diverse social ties that connected women involved in love magic.[63]

In line with Jaffary, Bristol, and Twinam's more subtle analysis of the Spanish court system, Kimberly Gauderman argues that Hispanic women successfully litigated against their husbands due to a crown policy of "de-centralized power relations. . . . Authority was produced within a network that prevented any individual or group from consolidating a position of absolute control." The Spanish imperial system is a masterful example of "multiply and diversify" to foster constantly competing bureaucracies.[64] Legal opportunities, community pressure, and surveillance actually prevented men from centralizing their patriarchal control, despite the fact that honor and patriarchy were key cultural values. Women's manipulations of their sexuality in the colonial courts could have a political component, alongside with contributing to poor women's sheer survival.

Each chapter in this book highlights the political nature of female sexuality in Cartagena de Indias, focusing on a different aspect of this vibrant and dynamic facet of colonial life. The chapters are roughly chronological, covering the period from approximately 1600 to 1800, with an emphasis on the first half of the seventeenth century. The first chapter looks at a late sixteenth-century woman who chose to use her virginity and its loss to bring down a local leader. The second chapter introduces the racially-charged aspects of Cartagena women's sexuality in exploring how an elite doña contributed to the downfall of another government official through her affair with him and her practice of love magic, with the aid of a diverse group of women and one male slave. The next two chapters present men and their expressions of righteous anger sparked by insults directed at their wives or slaves. These outbursts could lead to horrible acts of calculated anger. Here we see how seemingly petty disputes over honor had broad implications in this international entrepôt. A central theme is that honor was a powerful value, but it was extremely pliable within Cartagena's particular political context and the circumstances of each case. The ubiquitous presence of honor as critical to self-defense or in attacks on others meant sexual activity and reputation played an essential role in the rhetoric of these cases. Chapter 5 investigates one man's reaction to the sexual agency of two women (one enslaved, the other a doña) in his house and their very different experiences of love, sex, and marriage, again following from an effort to weaken a political rival. Chapters 6 through 8 turn to inquisitorial inquiries into the local practice of love magic in the 1630s, with an emphasis on freedwomen as leaders in the competitive sorcery/healing community. These chapters strive to bring to life sexual experiences, the racially-mixed social milieu of magical practice, and even how these nonwhite sorceresses presented themselves in terms of dress and appearance. Chapter 9 returns to male violence, honor as a rhetorical tool, and the shocking fate of an elite Spanish prostitute.

The last two chapters move into the eighteenth century, with an exploration of marriage, honor, women's agency, and how Cartagena doñas and freedwomen took serious risks to forge their own sexual experiences, seeking a very delicate and hard-to-find mix of love, companionship, and economic support from men. All of the themes introduced in the opening story of doña Rufina and her attempts at sorcery and seduction persist in these later cases but with slight differences in perceptions of race, honor, marriage, and which institutions will involve themselves in sexual conflicts. While it is challenging to establish a precisely calibrated sense of change over time in terms of private life from the early seventeenth century to the end of the eighteenth century, surviving documentation does suggest subtle changes in how Carthaginians understood love, sex, marriage, and honor as these forces interacted with local institutions and the preoccupations of the crown and local bureaucracies. Until the wars of independence, a diverse range of local women continued to use the courts to protect themselves from men's overweening authority over their personal lives. The Holy Office's loss of power from the mid-1600s to the late 1700s ended investigations of erotic magic and fears of the Satan's influence in day-to-day life. The local numeric domination of Afro-descendants continued to define Spanish ideas of sexuality, but exchanges between women appear less intimate and more competitive toward the close of the colonial era. Instead of inquisitors, new crown bureaucrats and the military dominated Cartagena society after 1750, affecting the kinds of personal disputes that came before the governor or the bishop. Fortunately for historians, sexuality appears in the archives due to the Spanish courts' paternalistic functions and the tense factionalism in this sexually-charged port city.

CHAPTER ONE

DEBATABLE VIRGINITY

Doña María de Montemayor

FROM THE SIXTEENTH CENTURY AND THROUGHOUT THE COLONIAL ERA, Cartagena women exposed their sex lives to judicial scrutiny for both political and personal reasons. In 1598, the parents of doña María de Montemayor, age eighteen, accused don Juan Ramírez, Cartagena's thirty-six-year-old *alguacil mayor* (constable), of *estupro*, meaning ravishment or defloration. This was not an accusation of violent rape but, instead, the seduction of a virgin. It was a precise, clearly defined legal allegation in this time period and the centuries to follow.[1] Jumping to the end of the story, Governor Pedro de Acuña did order Ramírez to compensate doña María for her lost virginity. However, after reading all of the evidence, today's investigator is inclined to believe don Juan's defense and his claim that he was framed by María and her parents. If we project modern emotions on the case presented by the alleged female victim and her family, we will sympathize with doña María, naturally falling for the good and evil characters as they develop in the trial documents, a narrative familiar in many cases of this kind found throughout the history of early modern Spain and Spanish America. However, these narrations were formulaic and were modeled on a generic template. And in this particular case, the accusers did not even do a good job filling in the details necessary to make the familiar formulas believable. Since doña María's reputation could not stand up to scrutiny and the evidence against don Juan was quite weak, one wonders why her parents risked publicizing her damaged reputation by making the accusation of defloration. The most likely reasons were financial gain and putting forward a publicly acceptable story to explain her pregnancy. The written record focuses on honor, in this example, as manifested by sexual behavior and its repercussions, but as we will see often in this book, the motivations behind exposing sex acts often relate to local political rivalries. Doña María's case is the first in a set of bookends—I will conclude this book with a mid-eighteenth century example of another woman defending her sexual reputation in a very different era and context.

Early modern Iberian and Latin American women and their families had several judicial options available to them if they chose to litigate over issues regarding sexual activity, marriage, or female reputation.[2] The alleged victims of male sexual aggression effectively used the secular or ecclesiastical court systems and often won their lawsuits, resulting in either the public disgrace or bankrupting of their seducers. In litigation over sex before marriage that did not result in official matrimony, the surviving cases for Cartagena derive from complaints made to the local governor, the highest regional military and political representative of the Spanish crown. Some cases moved higher up the bureaucratic and judicial hierarchy to the viceroy and audiencia judges in Bogota.

Regardless of the cause or the court involved, all litigation involving female sexuality depended on asserting or defaming women's moral character and sexual reputation. Testimonies from highly biased witnesses regarding a woman's actions and the public understanding of her behavior fill pages and pages in these files. Over the course of this book, a template will emerge for both sides of the coin: what specific actions or gossip could ruin a woman's reputation, and conversely, what represented the moral ideal for women? It should come as no surprise that women ideally possessed virginity before marriage and maintained fidelity to husbands during marriage.[3] However, the common practice of women choosing sex outside marriage, "strongly challenges the two major frameworks for understanding early modern Spanish sexuality: the Mediterranean honor code and the Catholic Reformation."[4] Some women actively maneuvered witness statements to define their own personal honor based not on chastity, but on their character traits, marital status, occupation, social lives, businesses, and reputation among their peers. Married women and widows especially had access to a legal status granted in Spanish law that allowed them a chance to run their own financial and business affairs, opportunities that some took as a chance to create their own successful ventures without the constant supervision of their husbands.[5] Of course, all women had to declare, prove, and defend their honorable and virtuous status in order to receive the full protection of the law.

Elite men asserted their honor in court cases through their noble, Christian lineage and service to the crown, but even plebeian, nonwhite women found ways to claim honorable status and a good reputation. Poor women, even those obligated to work in the streets as servants or market sellers, argued that they behaved demurely in public and retained their sexual purity in their work-related interactions with men. Poor women might also claim a status of responsible, faithful wives and mothers to prove their honor. Women also perpetuated the honor code's focus on female sexuality by gossiping and publicly slandering each other through the use of insults relating to sex, especially words such as *puta*, or whore.[6] Since plebeian honor could not derive from claims to noble lineage, it was even more sensitive than elite status to public criticism and constant negotiation, along with violent defensiveness, even among women. In fact, public insults and beatings done by women represent the most effective way to ensure the continuation of a status system revolving around female sexuality.[7] What woman could endure public defamation or ostracizing by her peers, the women she had to deal with daily in the market and on the streets?

Women who adjudicated their sex lives in colonial Cartagena based their claims on the regulation of Catholic marriage set down in the sixteenth century at the Council of Trent and Spanish legal codes in the tradition of King Alfonso X's thirteenth-century *Siete partidas*. The fourth partida, or section, defined marriage in a religious context as dating back to Adam and Eve and of great benefit to both the individual members of a family and the society at large.[8] These traditional formulations reinforced the sexual activity of women as key to their status and fate. At the same time, the code supported women if they decided to sue for compensation or child support in the event they were seduced, impregnated, and abandoned by a single man. If the seducer was married, the unfortunate woman most likely had no hopes of financial support.[9]

To return to the case at hand, although María's father don Francisco de Montemayor was generally absent from his home (a situation that often led to seductions),[10] in February of 1598 he appeared to make a complaint against don Juan to Governor Acuña. Following a rhetorical pattern expected for this kind of accusation, the father narrated an account emphasizing his daughter's nobility, virtue, and innocence, which were violently overcome by her rapacious and unrelenting attacker.

> I am making a criminal complaint against don Juan Ramírez alguacil mayor before Your Mercy. . . . I say that in my house my daughter, an honest and secluded maiden [*doncella recogida*], in the company of her mother, my legitimate wife doña María de Adame, was raised with great honor, virtue, and seclusion as the daughter of noble and important parents. . . . She was commonly known as a maiden of good reputation. What happened was that the accused offender, with little fear of God our Lord, adding a great burden on his soul and conscience, in disdain for royal justice, with the power and hand of a constable, which should stimulate him to live an exemplary life and refrain from evil deeds, for four years solicited my daughter day and night. Wherever she went with her mother in the streets, he signaled them and other times he sent her messages with his servants, giving them to the black women in my house.[11]

According to her father, don Juan's plan to seduce doña María escalated as he began to circle her house at night, calling out passionate and flirtatious words to the shuttered windows, to the scandal of neighbors and passersby, in an attempt to "attract and deceive" the girl.[12] Francisco said doña María ignored the advances until August of 1597, when don Juan came to the window of the room where she slept with a slave. Don Juan woke up doña María, assailing her with promises and seductive words, saying that he would serve her and give her gifts all his life because he wanted to marry her. Doña María's father alleged that she continued to object, saying that she could not surrender without her parents' knowledge and consent. Don Juan broke off part of her room's window covering, but doña María allegedly still resisted, calling on her status as a virgin daughter of noble and honorable parents.

Don Juan returned a few days later at midnight, forcefully breaking open the shutters. He then entered the room and grabbed doña María, who again allegedly resisted and defended herself. Don Juan dragged her from her room (apparently through the second-story window), covering her in his cape, and carried her to another house, where he "corrupted" her, then later returned her to her own bedroom.[13] After this initial encounter, Don Juan continued to climb into Francisco's home through the bedroom window, acting as if he were doña María's husband and even boldly saying that he was.

By the time of the complaint, María was pregnant, and her father wanted full compensation and support for her child. Doña María's mother also made a complaint, demanding don Juan's imprisonment for breaking into the house and "robbing" her daughter.[14]

As the case unfolded, it appeared that this compelling account may have been nothing more than a neglectful father's desperate attempt to give his impregnated and disgraced daughter financial security and provide an explanation for why he failed in his honor-bound duty to protect the sexuality of the women in his family. The father was perhaps even caught up in a political plot organized in his absence. Despite Francisco's emotional defense of his daughter, the family could scarcely muster up credible witnesses to support their accusations. The witnesses for the prosecution came from the most marginal, distrusted group in Iberian society: criminals punished by a sentence of rowing for the king.[15] Three galley slaves claimed they saw don Juan entering and leaving the house at all times of the night and day. The lack of support from neighbors proved that doña María, for whatever reason, justified or not, lacked a reputation as a protected, virginal doncella. Nobody with honor publicly spoke in her favor, so in local Cartagena society she had no honor.

To testify to the events that took place in private, the prosecution called on two household slaves. One twenty-year-old household slave named María said she saw don Juan entering the house at will. As a domestic insider, this woman noted that don Juan entered doña María's room several times while her mother attended mass. Generally the couple had the door closed, but once María observed them in bed together. Don Juan also visited many times to chat with the mother and daughter. Neither María nor the galley slaves reported hearing marriage promises, a fundamental element in a defloration narrative necessary to assert the female victim's innocence in the seduction. The slave María only heard about the seduction through the window second hand. Information about the alleged marriage promise came from another slave, eighteen-year-old Lucia Çape, whose last name was the word used to refer to an African ethnic group from the region of modern Sierra Leone.[16] Lucia Çape said she witnessed firsthand the conversation at the window, including her mistress's protests and how don Juan took her through the window to his lodgings. Lucia was the only person able to provide the critical piece of evidence: that don Juan said "he would marry her [doña María]" just before he dragged her through the window. Lucia also admitted that, on later occasions, doña María asked her to leave the street door open so that don Juan could enter.[17]

The offended doncella narrated a similar story to her father's version, testifying that don Juan had been flirting with her for around five years, since she was thirteen years old. Although some older men did have sexual contact with elite Cartagena girls shortly after they reached puberty,[18] in doña María's case her youthful age when don Juan allegedly seduced her might have been exaggerated. In early modern Basque territory, one father claimed his forty-year-old daughter was only twenty-seven. Lying about a woman's age to further condemn her deflowerer or to object to a marriage was a common deception in early modern Spain and nineteenth-century Latin America. In one nineteenth-century case, for example, a girl was said to be fourteen and the man (known as the "ugly suitor") forty, but baptism records indicated the two were actually twenty-two and twenty-six.[19] Since the highly biased authorities chose not to investigate doña María's baptismal records, her actual age (alleged as only eighteen in 1598) remains a matter of pure speculation.

The conventions for these kinds of denunciations demanded that a woman present her seducer as persistently tempting her for a long period of time, meeting years of rejections.[20] Doña María's father claimed don Juan seduced her with these words, conventionally emphasizing the attacker's determination:

> He would serve her until death, that she should not be so scornful of him, how he swore he had to sell his house and leave Cartagena just because she would not look at him. . . . [He said] she made him serve her seven years before and seven years after in order to overcome her.[21]

Doña María said that don Juan publicly solicited her, but, unfortunately, she could not provide a witnesses to testify to any of his public pronouncements, except her own slave. According to custom, publicly stated marriage promises combined with sex bound don Juan to marry doña Maria. Predictably, the family's narrative of the seduction consistently used the vocabulary of female sexual passivity, despite doña María's eventual consistent affair with don Juan. In contrast to her rhetoric and her father's claims of her sexual purity, during the course of their affair doña María left her door open to don Juan and climbed out of her second floor window to the street numerous times. No testimony mentions any kind of violent struggle in her room. The rhetorical structures or "gendered . . . verbal performances where men and women played out traditional expectations of masculinity and femininity" employed by victims in defloration cases purposefully disguised women's agency in sexual acts in order to stress their innocence and to curry judicial favor.[22] These well-worn formulas should not obscure the fact that early modern women did make choices, however constrained, to engage in sexual activity and to present the repercussions to the court for compensation.[23]

On the August night in question, doña María said that don Juan repeatedly seduced her with promises of marriage as he gradually broke down the shutters in front of her window. He took her hands and kissed them before taking her to his house for two hours, where he took her virginity; on later occasions he continued to have "carnal access" with her many times, especially while her mother was at mass. When she became pregnant, doña María tried to insist on making their marriage official, but don Juan put her off. To help bolster her case, Maria presented several witnesses who visited her in her home, including a scribe and a midwife. After an examination, they testified that she looked five to seven months pregnant and that the mother already felt the unborn child's quickening.[24] Although they unequivocally proved she was pregnant, these witnesses did not provide any more evidence regarding the course of doña María's seduction.

Upon initially hearing this evidence, the governor ordered don Juan imprisoned and all of his possessions confiscated and auctioned off. By this time, the accused had already taken refuge in the Santo Domingo friary after being checked for weapons that might facilitate his escape; later, he would be transferred to the municipal jail. At this particular moment, Cartagena's authorities were embroiled in another more serious conflict sparked by the murder of the Spanish official Tristan del Uribe Salazar. Don Juan was implicated in the Salazar trial, so Governor Acuña, supported by a petition from Salazar's widow, ordered that two guards stand on duty outside his cell, with the prisoner paying their wages. Juan had other ongoing disputes with the governor, which encouraged him in his theory that his enemies in local government had doña María and her parents set him up with a false accusation. In his statements, don Juan explained that he considered the governor his "capital enemy" and suggested that doña María's mother and the governor's wife worked together to hatch the plot against him.[25] Don Juan believed the governor could not fairly judge the case so he appealed to the high court in Bogota. Their final decision on the defloration accusation is unclear, although it seems likely that they agreed with the governor's decision to compensate doña María, as will be explained later.

After his release on a *fianza* (a system of financially guaranteeing arrested criminals, similar to bail) of 20,000 ducats, don Juan began to argue his case in earnest before the Cartagena governor. He used the most obvious strategies for defending an accusation based on private sexual activity but also added some innovative investigative techniques. Don Juan concentrated on tearing down doña María's character, her witnesses, and her evidence, as well as gathering proof that the whole scheme was part of a plot to ruin him.[26] He also explored the basic judicial theories regarding defloration accusations. Don Juan argued that this entire case lacked validity because legal conventions held that only "honest and secluded virgins with good lives and reputations" could make accusations of estupro.[27] In theory, if a man could successfully cast doubt on a woman's virginity, according to basic logic and the legal conventions defining the concept of estupro, she could not accuse him of seducing and deflowering her.

Even taking into account the motives that might have led the accused to falsely besmirch doña María's character, don Juan presented a convincing case. It is certainly possible that don Juan may have lied about doña María's activities and bribed witnesses to do the same; however, if doña María had truly been a secluded doncella, it is hard to believe that in this society, where public persona meant everything, so many witnesses would make up gossip about María's tarnished and scandalous reputation and no one but her parents would speak up to disagree. Witnesses did not necessarily make up stories out of whole cloth, though they could dramatically exaggerate or misrepresent a woman's actions. On the other hand, in her self-defense, an elite doña of reputable status, even one with a little scandal attached to her name, could easily find a handful of witnesses to testify to her good name in the context of litigation. This entire system was based on character witnesses testifying to assert the litigants' personal reputation. As we will see in chapter 9, even a well-known seventeenth-century prostitute had friends that showed some restraint in discussing her occupation in the presence of judicial authorities.

It is hard to believe doña María's story because no one but her own parents said anything positive about her virtue. Other than their household slaves and condemned criminals, the parents did not provide any viable witnesses to testify to don Juan's persistent seductions, nor could they find any credible witnesses to admit to hearing his offer of marriage. By simply testifying that doña María was a woman who publicly socialized with men in compromising settings, the witnesses damaged her reputation. If don Juan was right and the seduction accusation was a setup organized by his local adversaries, they could not have convinced a truly virginal girl to frame don Juan and make up the accusation. His political rivals and personal enemies had to find someone who already had nothing to lose.

Even so, don Juan and his friends may have gone too far in the opposite direction by painting a lurid picture of doña María and her mother's behavior. Don Juan claimed that since the age of twelve, doña María had lived a promiscuous and dishonest life, engaged in "illicit friendship and communication . . . with different people in this city without her parents' consent, receiving anyone who desired her at her door or window at all hours of the day and night."[28] Doña María's mother also acted suspiciously by going to single men's homes to eat at odd hours with her daughter. Since both women dressed with suspect luxury considering their humble income, don Juan suggested that men gave them gifts, including clothing and jewels. Apparently, doña María's local nickname was the *doncella desenfadada*, an oxymoronic sobriquet translatable as the carefree, licentious, or loose virgin, and everyone in the city knew of her wanton shamelessness. Don Juan said María's father Francisco was hardly ever at home, suggesting that he could not protect the honor of his wife or his daughter.[29] Don Juan advanced his own honorable reputation as proof of his personal ethics and morality, denied seducing or soliciting doña María, and claimed that he interacted with the household only as a good neighbor.

Don Juan presented several different kinds of evidence to disprove María's accusations, appearing the very simulacrum of a sixteenth-century Sherlock Holmes with his emphasis on science, reason, and fact to support his arguments. Juan had a third party examine doña María's front door and found that there was no bolt, latch, cross bar, or lock securing the entryway, nor was there any evidence that these protections had been removed recently. Therefore, anyone could enter her house and thereby gain entry to the doncella desenfadada herself.[30] According to don Juan, it defied reason to accept the testimony of condemned criminals such as the three galley slaves who made contradictory and inconclusive reports of seeing him at doña María's window. He had no doubt that these men would lie under an oath on the Christian crucifix, especially one known to be a recent convert from Islam. Don Juan had the rowers' supervisor come to the court to read out their crimes and sentences from his log to emphasize their untrustworthy, criminal characters. Their biographies were underwhelming and did not give credit to their statements: one of the slaves was a forty-eight-year-old man from Asturias who had been a galley slave for half of his life and the other two were men of African descent, condemned to row for the king in Lima and Potosi. One of the prisoners testified that he had seen don Juan by the bright light of a full moon at 2 a.m., but on that particular night, don Juan noted that there had been no moon visible. To prove his accuracy regarding the phases of the moon, don Juan cited page 124 of a book called *Repertorio del mundo particular de las spheras del cielo y orbes*, published in Madrid in 1584.[31] Don Juan also asked a few local navigators to confirm this indisputable astronomical fact. The domestic slaves presented another easy target, as they were both women and minors (under age twenty-five).[32] Lucia Çape, the only person who actually heard don Juan make a promise of marriage, was most likely not even a native speaker of Spanish.

Don Juan framed his questions for witnesses around all of the facts relating to the case mentioned above, starting with doña María's character and ending with a query about the moon on the night in question. All of his witnesses were interrogated with the same queries, but they chose which questions to answer in their statements according to their area of expertise. As always, the questions contained prompts designed to push each witness to provide the replies that don Juan desired, but each person also added their own commentary.[33] The responses reveal how don Juan and his cronies defined a dishonorable woman. Juan de Palma, age nineteen and doña María's neighbor, said that María and her mother lived

> freely, admitting single men as visitors and chatting with them day and night at their house, speaking through their windows and responding to dishonest comments, dressing ostentatiously in bright colors, even though they are poor and lacking any fortune.

Palma, along with several other men who testified, including a Franciscan friar, confirmed that all of Cartagena mocked doña María as the "loose virgin." Witnesses agreed that she "did not live in seclusion and modestly as a virtuous and honorable doncella" and this was known and discussed widely in the city. Rich and poor knew of her shamelessness and some reputably honorable women did not admit mother or daughter into their houses.[34] Another man said the women kept their doors open past ten or eleven at night and neighbors heard music coming from their parties. It was opined that Doña María dressed indecently, especially considering her family's poverty, wearing colored sashes and the loose jackets typically worn by cowboys.

Several witnesses said that they had seen one man undressed, down to his taffeta and linen breeches, in the house and heard that the mother and daughter had late suppers with another man. Male and female gossips alike spread rumors that doña María seduced this man by displaying her breasts and legs from her window.

Although these witnesses had introduced the possibility that another man had corrupted doña María, in the end her family received 5,000 pesos in gold bars to help toward her dowry, and don Juan was obliged to pay all of the costs associated with his trial.[35] Generally in crimes of this kind, the judicial authorities sought to reestablish order through marriage, if possible.[36] In this case, it was apparently deemed unnecessary or undesirable to force don Juan to marry doña María. The point of the accusations was to thoroughly disgrace don Juan and ruin his political standing in Cartagena, not tie him to doña María for life. The authorities either sympathized with doña María despite her tainted reputation, or they were willing partners in a plot to bring down don Juan.

We may never know the truth behind this complaint of defloration, but in the end doña María's rhetoric of subjugated and abused innocence trumped don Juan's character bashing and aggressive investigation, two usually very effective judicial techniques. This fits with the thesis that the courts served as effective channels for weaker members of Hispanic society, who were theoretically the usual victims of male aggressive sexuality and gender inequalities. Perhaps don Juan was correct in arguing he would never receive a fair trial in Cartagena, where his enemies held the reins of power. This chapter gives one example of colonial women's sexual manipulations moving from the private to the public realm and how sexual passivity was the central narrative device, despite copious evidence (perhaps equally exaggerated to paint a picture of immorality and untrustworthiness) to the contrary. Regardless of the fact that there may have been a political motivation for starting litigation, the sexuality of doña María, impregnated and unmarried, who was still, if only weakly, under the influence of her parents, was directly at the center of judicial procedures. Her family actively exposed her sexuality to achieve their specific goals, despite knowing that a defloration case (by necessity centered on establishing a previous state of virginity) would bring any suspect activity into widespread public awareness. When considered alongside the popularity of love magic and the undisguised existence of prostitution, this suggests that seventeenth-century Carthaginians did not view female sexuality as simply something that could only be hidden or surrendered. In this instance, exposing her sexuality to sympathetic judicial authorities was one very effective way for a woman to control her fate. The next chapter introduces another sexually proactive woman. In this case, it is one who sought help from enslaved and European love magic experts, sparking a public scandal and an inquisitorial investigation.

CHAPTER TWO

LOVE MAGIC AND A MARRIED WOMAN

Doña Lorenzana de Acereto

THE CARTAGENA HOLY OFFICE STAGED ITS FIRST *AUTO DE FE* ON February 2, 1614, four years after Phillip III founded this branch of the Spanish Inquisition. Among the twenty *penitenciados*, four individuals marched as a punishment for practicing love magic.[1] The alleged sorcerers included the mulato slave Juan Lorenzo, born and raised in Lima; María Ramírez, born in Córdoba, Spain in 1573 and married to a Spanish soldier; Isabel Noble, the forty-eight-year-old wife of a Portuguese man; and a forty-year-old free *mulata* named Francisca Mejía, born in Extremadura, Spain. A casual observer of the auto de fe would not have known that these four plebeian penitenciados were linked to three elite Spanish women also recently tried by the Holy Office. The three wealthy *españolas* did not take part in the auto de fe, but instead enjoyed the privilege of lighter punishments in a smaller, more subdued private ceremony. These women were all given the honorific title doña: Ana María de Olarriaga, Isabel de Carvajal, and, at the center of this turbulent circle, the young Lorenzana de Acereto.

We know about doña Lorenzana's personal life and sexuality due to her dealings with these six plebeian love magic practitioners. The story begins with summaries of the evidence presented against doña Lorenzana by other witnesses, then moves on to her own statements, and concludes with her husband's contributions to the investigation. Although the religious authorities viewed love magic as illicit, disruptive, and even devilish, Cartagena's elite women took part in these practices. Their interests in the occult motivated highly personal interactions with a diverse range of the local population. These strange, defensive, explicit testimonies prove that married Spanish women knew nonmarital sex in all of its forms: prostitution, cohabitation, adultery, promiscuity, and the desperate and dangerous search for lovers and husbands. But their unbridled desires led to serious consequences as women disrupted their supposedly respectable and sexually controlled social milieu by crossing over the boundary of licit sex into the realm of affairs and illicit sex, which frequently involved magic. The repercussions included scandal, violence, shame, and official prosecution by the Holy Office or other courts. However, in every case the elite women (and to a lesser degree the plebeian women) successfully manipulated the Spanish courts and judicial authorities, often diffusing the problem or at least lessening their punishments and the long term effects of their disreputable acts.

Doña Lorenzana's story also reveals a moment in the early seventeenth century when Carthaginians turned to European women of various races as the most skilled and effective sources for erotic spells and incantations. At this time, no particular race or gender had a monopoly on love magic expertise. Even the arrival of the mulato slave Juan Lorenzo did not lead to a turn away from methods practiced in Iberia. In the early seventeenth century, love magic, including spoken incantations, ensorcelled food, and divination often arrived in Cartagena via the memories and experiences of women of either European or African ancestry who were born and raised in Spain or Portugal before coming to the Americas. They learned the European traditions of folk magic, handed down as popular folk knowledge through generations and influenced by the centuries of Islamic cultural domination over the Iberian Peninsula. Regardless of their race label or skin color, these women were Spanish or Portuguese in both birth and cultural background. Numerous inquisition case records from Catalonia, the Canary Islands, Andalucía, Valencia, and Castile contain spells with similar wording to those recorded in doña Lorenzana's trial.[2] Spanish sorceresses typically were marginalized women such as gypsies, who traveled constantly and practiced love magic as their occupation. In later cases, this information and expertise came via Cuba and Santo Domingo, carried by free women of color. Spanish widows and Afro-Caribbean freedwomen lived very similar itinerant lives in the seventeenth century, picking up incantations and recipes from knowledgeable women born all over the Atlantic world. These women used their knowledge of love magic to earn a living by selling/sharing that knowledge with a clientele of African, European, and Creole women. Although different populations became magic specialists in the New World, Iberians placed them within their own ancient cultural traditions.

The most common phrase used by Cartagena women to explain the goals of their magic practice was to "make men love me well." Black and white women both aspired for this "good love." The targeted men were their husbands, their lovers, or even, as they said themselves, "all men" or "every man." A few women directed magic toward their husbands in an effort to improve their marriages or possibly even to kill these men through *maleficio*, although no proven examples of damage to men's health have been found in Cartagena. No men complained or confessed that they were victims of these women's powers; the accusers were always other women, often competitors in the market for love magic or the women's clients who felt that they had been conned. The Cartagena women investigated by the Holy Office in the seventeenth century were motivated to practice love magic by a mixture of emotional concerns and a desire for more control and economic stability in their lives. Generally, Spanish sorceresses working in Iberia also lacked male protectors.[3] Despite the passionate longing expressed in their incantations, the need for financial support and stability inspired most women who ended up on trial for practicing love magic.

In Cartagena's Creole, Caribbean context, African and indigenous beliefs and practices (especially in the use of American plants) had a strong influence on the practice of love and sexual magic. Identifying the non-European influences on Latin American sorcery and witchcraft has been a focus for scholars studying inquisition records relating to magic and healing practices.[4] Afro Creole healing and magic practices used indigenous and European folk magic within the context of a West African world view, but practitioners of love magic in Cartagena did not live separately from their clientele of Spanish ancestry or birth.[5] Doña Lorenzana did not turn to only nonwhite love magic experts in the early seventeenth century. Although in Cartagena and elsewhere a client had to find a way to get in contact with someone she believed could help her, there was only one "world of witchcraft," and that was normal daily life, where people sought remedies for problems they viewed as insurmountable. Men and women of African, European, and racially-mixed descent might end up as the consulted experts. As Joan Bristol observes for New Spain, "consultations with indigenous and Afro-Mexican curers (curanderos/as) were routine events for colonial residents, regardless of caste." These interactions were entirely commonplace. Bristol accurately views Afro-Mexican use of love magic as "squarely in the mainstream of colonial curing practices" and concludes that Afro-Mexican healers and love magicians could gain income, status, and some improvement in living conditions.[6] Bristol's conclusions apply very well to Cartagena, where doña Lorenzana moved in a social circle of elite and plebeian women, all of whom very openly practiced divination, erotic magic, incantations, and potions designed to improve their love life and encourage sex that would lead them to happiness and economic gain.

Although Lorenzana was an enticing doña, the subject of a book about passionate women in history, a muse to novelists, and a lady whom academic historians have described as *bella*, we can scarcely discern that she was the focus of these investigations because of the many influences and different voices swirling around her.[7] The events of dona Lorenzana's youth inspire understanding and sympathy with her desire to take power over her life by means of sorcery. Although Lorenzana was born in Cartagena, she had few relatives in the city.[8] She lived a lonely childhood after her mother, a Spanish woman from outside Toledo, died when she was four years old.[9] Her father was a merchant from Genoa living in Porto Belo. He abandoned his daughter after the death of her mother, leaving doña Lorenzana to be raised by her maternal uncle. This uncle was a priest who, by the time of her trial, resided in Seville. In the oral autobiography she presented to inquisitors, doña Lorenzana said she married the notary Andrés de Campo at age sixteen. At that time, Andrés was forty-three years old. Although the honorific doña always precedes Lorenzana's name in all records, her husband did not merit the equivalent title of don. She claimed that she married at sixteen, but by age twenty-seven she had a thirteen-year-old daughter and a twelve-year-old son, as well as a four-year-old son and an infant of two months; this suggests that she began a sexual relationship with Andrés when she was no older than fourteen and he was already in his forties.[10] Doña Lorenzana's clergyman uncle did not protect her from early pregnancy, but he did provide for her education, because she could read and write. Likely, the uncle welcomed a suitor to whom he could pass on his responsibilities for his niece.

Unsurprisingly, a couple of years after the birth of her two older children, while doña Lorenzana was still younger than twenty years old, the life she was leading with her far older husband started to chafe at her. Like many other women in this book, she looked to an affair for sexual and emotional satisfaction. Around this time, a new sergeant major named Francisco Santander arrived in Cartagena.[11] Although he was conscientious in his job overseeing Cartagena's fortifications, Santander quickly made serious enemies, including the audiencia judge don Francisco de Herrera and members of the Cartagena city council. Santander also had supporters who viewed him as an honorable military leader. These contrary opinions led to factionalism and street violence. In order to bring down his enemies, Santander's defenders even resorted to accusations of the *pecado nefando*, or sodomy.[12] During Santander's time in prison, rumors circulated widely that doña Lorenzana supported him, presumably with gifts of food, money, and other items to make him more comfortable. The fact that doña Lorenzana's lover was such a prominent local Spaniard suggests that her Holy Office trial, saturated in sex and magic, was another attempt to bring down Santander. As we have seen with doña María Montemayor, Carthaginians combated their political rivals by exposing female sexuality in judicial cases.

Among the charges against Santander were his scandalous public affair with doña Lorenzana and his involvement in sorcery. At first, the diocesan court dealt with these public scandals because the Holy Office had not yet set up its local tribunal. In 1609, doña Lorenzana voluntarily called a *provisor*, or a representative of the bishop, to her house, confessing that she took part in a divination ritual involving a glass of water. Of course, she chose to present the relatively benign end of love magic practices, and whether or not she confessed in order to control the public scandal or because she feared the wages of sin is pure speculation. María Ramírez, the manager of a local brothel, and doña Ana Matienzo, the widow of a treasury official and Lorenzana's close friend, sat in on the provisor's visit to doña Lorenzana's house. The three women showed the cleric various spells they knew. He later told inquisitors that he did not keep a record of this informal investigation, because he feared doña Lorenzana's husband would harm her if he knew about it. Apparently, it was common local knowledge that the couple were having serious fights, and it was no surprise considering the fact that her affair with the sergeant major was public information. As a punishment for her sorcery, the provisor commanded doña Lorenzana to give fifteen pounds of candles to altars in churches around Cartagena.[13] The scandal had not diminished by the following year, so doña Lorenzana left her home to live in a discalced Carmelite convent, where she remained for two years. After this time in hiding, the Holy Office arrested and imprisoned her.

Like the bishop, Cartagena's first generation of inquisitors did not immediately concern themselves with this outbreak of sorcery. The inquisitors disembarked in Cartagena in late September 1610. Among them was the zealot Juan de Mañozca, who came from an appointment as the secretary of the Mexico City tribunal and would later serve the Lima starting in 1622, finally returning to a position as an archbishop in Mexico in 1643.[14] Two months later, the inquisitors brought together nearly all of the city's residents to hear a sermon in the cathedral, where the inquisitors explained their desire to seek out a variety of heresies. They demanded cooperation from all local officials.[15] Even before they published their first Edict of the Faith, a handful of women with guilty consciences voluntarily came before the Tribunal, confessing to participating in doña Lorenzana's circle of love magic practitioners. Although the Holy Office knew about the sorcery practice of all three doñas in 1610, they did not imprison the women for over two years. It is true that in 1610, the Inquisition prison facilities were not yet available, but on the other hand, the inquisitors did not fear the women's activities. All three of the women who voluntarily confessed to the bishop were españolas indulging in popular practices common in contemporary Spain. The resulting investigation reveals that love magic in early seventeenth-century Cartagena had an Iberian aspect reflected in the activities of non-elite Spanish and Portuguese women who had interacted with the three doñas. Despite the disparity in social status, these women (and one man) collaborated to influence men's sexuality and their own intimate lives. The tribunal's decisions on punishment conformed to extant colonial social and racial hierarchies, but its presence also increased the social tension and underlying violence inherent in these inequalities.

The first person to testify against doña Lorenzana was the forty-year-old widow doña Isabel de Carvajal, who had arrived in Cartagena from Seville five years earlier. She was not the only widow involved in this social circle of sorceresses, and the Holy Office often investigated widows in Spain for similar activities. Widows made a useful income from clients who wanted spells to influence their own affairs, or they called on magic in hopes of remarrying for the financial support a husband might offer. The widows involved in the Cartagena cases were not young, which limited their options for remarriage and increased their desperation, as we can see in doña Isabel's confessions regarding her practice of love magic. Isabel said that in 1605, doña Lorenzana had taught her the "Star Prayer," one version of numerous very similar star invocations popular in early modern Spain.[16] The widow confessed that she said the following invocation more than fifteen times, in an attempt to make a certain man love her:

> Highest and most beautiful star, I conjure you.
> I conjure you with one, with two, with three . . . [count to nine]
> In the name of Mount Olivet he enters,
> You enter in the name of Mount Olivet . . .
> You will bring me so-and-so bound and caught in my love and
>   my command.
> This is my will

In her desperate need for a man's emotional and financial support, doña Isabel took even more extreme measures to make this man love her: she confessed to repeating another spell forty times over several days, in this case invoking three demons. Doña Isabel had been involved in love magic for many years in Seville, regularly saying numerous spells (learned from different individuals, including a Catholic priest) to force her lover to desire her enough to marry her.[17] The fact that doña Isabel's spells occasionally employed Latin or sacred objects, such as a chrism or a bit of powder made from ground-up altar stone (*ara*), especially perturbed the Tribunal. The inquisitors initially sentenced her to perpetual banishment from the Indies and a fine of 200 reales. But swayed by her claims that she was a simply a weak woman influenced by sorceresses, that she did not believe that the devil could influence free will, nor that sacred objects could be used for bad ends, they later reduced her punishment to six years' banishment from the jurisdiction of Cartagena and a fine of one hundred reales. She also did not have to join the public auto de fe but instead had to attend a mass in the Holy Office chapel.

Another widowed doña, Ana María de Olarriaga, also voluntarily confessed shortly after the inquisitors' arrival. Several witnesses testified against her to the tribunal only a few hours later.[18] According to doña Ana María, her social circle said spells to make people fall in love and practiced divination to pass the time, and it potentially helped realize more urgent personal desires. Several women in this group, including doña Isabel, the Portuguese woman Isabel Noble, the procuress María Ramírez, and the free mulata Francisca Mejia, all confessed to practicing the *suerte de habas*, a conjuration involving beans.[19] As was also common in Spain in this era, the Cartagena circle of sorcerers wanted to go beyond learning about lovers' inclinations to actually influencing their behavior. Doña Ana María explained that one night, a group of men and women gathered at her house to help one man who was in love with a reluctant woman. To achieve their goal, they recited spells calling on the Devil, made a doll dressed in a woman's clothing, burned tree sap or gum mixed with sulfur over some embers, and then made a slave waft the smoke over the desired lady's doorway.[20]

Though only a few years older than doña Lorenzana, doña Ana María knew virtually every spell in the arsenal of an early modern Spanish enchantress. One of these was the famous "Prayer for the Lord of the Street," which compelled a man to appear. In this case, doña Lorenzana used the incantation on her lover, Francisco de Santander.[21] It was spoken as follows:

> So-and-so [insert name], you are in my house,
> And three real devils have just arrived
> Who will not let you rest until you are in my power.

Another version went:

> Lord of the street, lord of the street, *señor compadre*, crippled
>   lord,[22]
> Make so-and-so mine, make him [or her] love me and love me,
> And it is true that he [or she] must love me.
> Bark like a dog, bray like a donkey, cluck like a chicken

Doña Ana María confessed that one night, shortly after they uttered this spell, Santander came walking up to the house. To the fearful Inquisitors this outcome suggested that doña Lorenzana had made a pact with the devil, since he fulfilled her demands so quickly. In her defense, doña Lorenzana said that after the women invoked the Lord of the Street, they had eaten supper and she had hidden when Francisco appeared. She did not believe the spell made him come to see her but instead argued that it was a normal, routine event for him to visit her at this time. Doña Ana María also confessed that two men tried this spell at her house.[23]

As an expert in love magic, doña Ana María tried some of the more advanced spells in the Spanish tradition, using sacred, gruesome, and sexually explicit matériel to control men's actions. She confessed to collecting her lover's semen and burning it in an oil lamp because an unnamed woman told her this piqued a man's desire and love.[24] Women who enacted this spell in Castile, Valencia, and the Iberian Peninsula used a cloth to clean themselves after sex and then twisted it into a wick, which they burned in an oil lamp while chanting "as this wick burns, so shall so-and-so's heart burn."[25] Doña Ana María wanted to push her luck even further; on another occasion, she burned the semen of four men while chanting, "I conjure you with three [devils] from the bridge, three from the fountain," in hopes of marrying one of the men. She did not volunteer how she managed to collect the semen of so many men. In another ritual that must have required a willing male participant, doña Ana María said she coated her hands with unguent from a plant, possibly citronella, and spread it over his nude body. She did not explain why she did this, but most likely it was believed to be temporarily effective in "making a man love one well." Undoubtedly, these female sexual practices functioned as erotic and seductive techniques designed to promote pleasure (and perhaps continued male devotion), as opposed to magic rituals, and they open a window into what sensuality meant for these early modern women.

In one incident that far exceeded the realm of sensual enjoyment, doña Ana María helped doña Lorenzana in the most macabre spell mentioned in these testimonies.[26] While chatting one day in the San Francisco church, doña Lorenzana complained about all the problems she faced with her husband. The older widowed doña instructed her to "[s]end me a black cat's head," so doña Lorenzana went home, killed a black cat living at her house, and had it delivered to her friend's house. A few days later, doña Ana María sent back some powders, meant to go in her husband's food or drink in order to give him a "better disposition." However, doña Lorenzana claimed she had misgivings about using the powders, so she hid them in her desk.

The inquisitors viewed spells that took advantage of sacred words and objects to achieve earthly, physical desires as especially offensive. Early modern sorcerers commonly used these methods, invoking saints in incantations and incorporating Latin phrases in imitation of prayers or the words of the mass. Doña Ana María found many uses for *ara*, a stone broken off a church's altar. She purchased this substance from a priest and ground it into a powder, then mixed the powder into a cake and gave the cake to a man that she wished to marry. She also passed on the ara to doña Lorenzana to give to her husband in another effort to promote peace in their household. Doña Ana Maria believed ara could help more generally in bringing good luck or in warding off the effects of magic spells, so she put it in a small bag that she wore around her neck. The bag also contained a bit of a magnet and a scrap of paper with a prayer written on it.[27] Though she was clearly a key figure in the circle of local witches, the Holy Office punished doña Ana María very lightly, despite the fact she had no husband to protect her reputation. At first, the inquisitors fined her 1,000 reales and two years' banishment from the Cartagena region, along with hearing a penitential mass in the private tribunal chapel. Later, inquisitors in Spain told the Cartagena tribunal to return doña Ana María's money.

The Cartagena inquisitors did not even bring charges against another elite woman, forty-year-old doña Ana Matienzo, who was just as involved in love magic as the other three doñas. Doña Ana had been married to a Spanish treasury official, so although she was a widow by the time of her friends' inquisition trials, her elite status protected her from arrest by the Holy Office. She had a secure position that the plebeian members of the circle did not enjoy. Before doña Lorenzana retreated to the Carmelite convent, she lived with doña Ana and they passed their time practicing magic and consulting other experts, including the mulato sorcerer Juan Lorenzo and María Ramírez, the manager of a local brothel. The two doñas shared the house with the Portuguese healer Isabel Noble, whom they called on to cure doña Ana's *mal de madre* (or mother's sickness, most likely related to menstruation; midwives and experts in women's illnesses often crossed the line into sorcery).[28]

Let us turn now to the plebeians caught up in doña Lorenzana's group. Born in Lisbon, Isabel Noble knew a wide range of traditional Iberian divination rituals, including using scissors and a sieve to predict marriages and whether men would return on the next *flota*.[29] She also confessed to several incantations using the words of the Catholic mass. In her late forties, Isabel must have seemed old to her wealthy Spanish roommates. The inquisitors described her as weak and sickly since she required treatment in the hospital two times during her imprisonment. Her husband Manuel Cuaresma did not reside in Cartagena, so Isabel was obliged to live off her meager income as an itinerant curer and sorceress. Owing to her lowly status, the inquisitors had no qualms forcing her to shamefully walk the streets in the 1614 auto de fe. They did not bother to fine her but instead sentenced her to perpetual banishment from the Indies, because they undoubtedly suspected that, together with being a diviner, she also was a New Christian or a practicing Jew. Mysteriously, the Spanish *suprema* revoked the sentence of banishment, possibly because this self-declared "weak woman" did not present a threat to the social hierarchy.

Another member of this circle of love magic practitioners was María Ramirez, a brothel keeper in her early forties at the time of her trial. María was married to a soldier working in Cartagena's presidio. Low ranking soldiers were paid very little, so it is not surprising that she had to support herself, even with a husband working nearby. María was born near Córdoba and, like other Spanish sorceresses, knew numerous divination rituals and spells involving sacred objects and words. María, along with the Extremadura-born mulata Francisca Mejia, who was also harshly punished by the Cartagena Holy Office, used spells involving alum to predict if lovers would return.[30] One of María's most suspect incantations included these lines invoking a frighteningly large number of devils:

> I carry three companions on my shoulders,
> One is shadow, one is Sodom, and the other is my sister Marta . . .
> The plaza devils will take me to the dance;
> The notaries' devils and the fishing devils;
> The crossroad devils, the bridge devils,
> The fountain devils and the brothel devils,
> The mountain devils and the valley devils,
> You will all gather together.[31]

Given that their income depended on promoting male desire, early modern prostitutes readily sought expertise in love magic. Only four years after María Ramirez's trial, Mexico City authorities prosecuted a *mestiza* woman named Isabel de San Miguel for both procuring and sorcery because she gave men potions in the form of drinks that made them "go crazy and lose their wits, in order to make them desire" her employees.[32] Early modern Spaniards equated procuresses with *hechiceras*, a viewpoint solidified in the *siglo de oro* classic *La Celestina*.[33]

As a self-confessed entrepreneur in the local sex trade, María Ramírez certainly did not have an honorable reputation to protect, so the notoriously cruel inquisitor Juan de Mañozca felt justified in sentencing her to a hundred public lashes and perpetual banishment from the Indies. Physical punishment and public humiliation were usually reserved for nonwhite sorcerers and witches, not married women born in Spain. As a zealot of the Counter-Reformation, Mañozca probably objected to María's profession as a procuress—a despised occupation—despite the fact that Spanish monarchs regulated legal prostitution until 1621.[34] Though Mañozca viewed her as a "teacher of sorcery" corrupting other women including doñas, such as Lorenzana and Ana Matienzo, the more compassionate inquisitor Pedro Mateo de Salcedo wanted María to hear her sentence privately and suffer only banishment. Salcedo deemed lesser punishment appropriate because she had taken part in the confession made before the local bishop before the Holy Office had a court in Cartagena.[35] The bishop had sentenced her to nothing more than buying four pesos in candles to light the Holy Sacrament. It is unclear how the suprema in Spain decided the dispute.

María Ramírez seems an unlikely companion for respectable married and widowed doñas. But doña Lorenzana's marital woes drew a diverse crowd of conjurers and healers to her side, whether she was at home, visiting friends such as a doña Tomasa or a doña Luisa Manuela, or staying with doña Ana, the widow of the Spanish treasury official.[36] The circle surrounding doña Lorenzana also included women in their fifties who passed on a few harmless spells. The Holy Office did not bother to imprison one of these older women, a *beata* named Barbola de Esquivel, who wore a Carmelite habit and had a reputation for "knowing many things." When Barbola confessed to inquisitors, she deemphasized her willingness to pass on magic knowledge and the seriousness of her formulas. According to the beata, doña Lorenzana had complained to Barbola in 1610 about her constant fights with her husband. The doña fervently begged the beata for a remedy to calm or subdue (amansar) Andrés. After much pleading, Barbola taught her an innocuous ritual to "bring peace between two angry people."[37] One simply had to break a hazelnut in half, rejoin the two halves in the shape of a cross, and adhere them with blood drawn from a pinprick to the left middle finger, known as the "dedo del corazon," or heart finger. The nut cross should then sit on top of one's heart, sewn into an undershirt. After nine days, Barbola advised removing the nut, grinding it up, and serving it to the angry person in his eggs or stew. The beata said she had learned this trick from a cleric in Bogota many years before. Barbola seemed nervous when she confessed this conjuration to the inquisitors, and she did her best to explain the procedure in a benign way. In her own confessions, doña Lorenzana added that the beata feared giving her information about love magic because the inquisition was coming to town and that Barbola dreaded punishment. Her account did make Barbola seem more suspicious, because she said the beata asked her for five hazelnuts and a bit of menstrual blood so the older woman could prepare the crosses.[38] In her incessant efforts to improve her personal life, doña Lorenzana associated both with brothel keepers and women with saintly reputations.[39]

Another of Lorenzana's confidants, Catalina de los Ángeles, who was born in Seville and described as a free, unmarried mulata woman in her fifties, voluntarily appeared before the Tribunal only a few months after its arrival, confessing to strange events that took place at doña Lorenzana's house. Around 1608, Catalina said that she had visited Lorenzana almost every day as an intimate friend of the doña and her husband. Once, when Andrés was out, Lorenzana confessed to her husband's displeasure with her "liberties," presumably her affair with Santander.[40] Catalina learned from Lorenzana's slaves that Andrés's wife tried to force him to drink a cup of ensorcelled water that came from beatas affiliated with the Carmelite nuns. Catalina's strangest story was that Lorenzana, in the presence of her clerical uncle, had conjured up a demon. When the two stood on the balcony, they saw a large, black figure approaching the house, though this entity did not enter, because Lorenzana did not feel like waiting any longer.

Perhaps even more surprising than all of these events and social interactions was doña Lorenzana's relationship with the twenty-six-year-old mulato slave Juan Lorenzo, a notorious sorcerer who came to live in Cartagena from Lima along with his master, an Augustinian friar. Juan Lorenzo voluntarily appeared before the Holy Office only a few weeks after the inquisitors disembarked, willingly confessing his practice of divinations, conjurations, and love magic. Doña Lorenzana and her friends, who by this time were all dissatisfied customers and viewed him as a threatening swindler and imposter, provided the evidence for the inquisitors to build a case against Juan Lorenzo. Lorenzana's servants also testified to their mistress's interactions with the hechicero. The inquisitors judged him to be a master sorcerer who instructed and corrupted this group of elite Spanish women, so Juan Lorenzo received a harsh sentence of two hundred lashes and ten years banishment.[41] But from Juan Lorenzo's perspective, his female clients had involved themselves in magic long before they enthusiastically called on his services.

After his imprisonment in the city jail (since the Holy Office had not yet built their own official prison), Juan Lorenzo described his first encounter with doña Lorenzana to the inquisitors. Their initial meeting took place when he passed near her balcony and she called out to him, asking him to find her an *alquitara*, or alembic.[42] He assumed she appreciated his reputation that he "knew many things."[43] As their conversation progressed, doña Lorenzana asked Juan Lorenzo for a skull, so he arranged to acquire one at the church cemetery, assuming she would use it for an altar in her house.

Two days later, he passed the house again and saw doña Lorenzana in the corridor smashing up the skull, with a servant guarding the street entrance. Doña Lorenzana asked him if powder made from the skull would be a good thing to give to her husband, and Juan Lorenzo said yes. Later she brought him the powders and he made crosses and said incantations over them. At this stage in their relationship, doña Lorenzana passed on the spells that she knew, including the traditional Spanish conjuration of the *anima sola*. Once when Juan Lorenzo went to borrow some flour to make a cake, he saw doña Lorenzana wearing a man's shirt with several pieces of folded paper stuck in it. Lorenzana said the papers contained herbs that would "make her husband love her well."

Juan Lorenzo also confessed that a few months later, doña Lorenzana began to request ever more dangerous information. One day she called to him from a window at the treasurer's house where Lorenzana often visited her friend doña Ana and brought him into a private room so the servants would not hear what she was about to say. Juan Lorenzo claimed Lorenzana said he could not refuse to help her kill her husband, and in return, she would give him her best jewel, as well as money adding up to half of her fortune. Although in his account he at first denied her request, she pressured him to help her. Juan Lorenzo asked for a jar and money to buy a toad. Lorenzana told him that she already knew about an herb that grew near Tolú that, when rubbed on a woman's body, would kill a man. She desired to kill her husband and longed to strengthen sergeant major don Francisco's love, so Juan Lorenzo suggested the Star Prayer and another popular Spanish prayer dedicated to Santa Marta that might help influence her lover's emotions. Juan Lorenzo accused Lorenzana of maleficio to distract the inquisitors' attention away from his own sins, a common, though not always successful, strategy.

Although their relationship soon grew very tense, Juan Lorenzo's testimony suggests that at first he and doña Lorenzana willingly exchanged information about love magic, including the conjurations mentioned above and others such as the "Prayer to the Just Judge." He claimed she told him of remedies she was using to make her husband see less (presumably of her involvement in an affair) and be less jealous. One incident highlights Lorenzana's frustration with Andrés and points to a moment when her interchanges with the sorcerer went sour. At her request, Juan Lorenzo gave doña Lorenzana an herb to make her husband sleep heavily so she could remove his keys from under his pillow, allowing her to go out to visit her lover. The next morning, Juan Lorenzo checked in with Lorenzana and found her enraged because Andrés had not slept all night, obliging her to stay home. At this point, Lorenzana openly accused Juan Lorenzo of fakery.

After gathering evidence from Juan Lorenzo and doña Lorenzana's friends, the inquisitors turned to servants and others in intimate contact with the household, including Lorenzana's young niece, also named Lorenzana. This girl was only twelve years old in 1612, and she testified in seclusion as a novice in the Carmelite convent, where her aunt was also in retreat.[44] The niece described many strange events that took place in her aunt's house, where she lived when she was age ten and younger, especially the practice of "Water Divination." She claimed to see human figures and ships in a glass of water, in a ritual that took place in the presence of her aunt, servants, and other women. The young Lorenzana also knew about her aunt's love for the sergeant major Francisco Santander, heard about dangerous herbs put in Andrés's food, and witnessed Andrés find a small piece of paper in her aunt's desk. After this incident, she heard him say to a slave, "I can use this paper to make your mistress burn." The niece testified that various ensorcelled drinks and food items, including some that the lover Francisco ordered slaves to make, had harmed others in the household. The girl also said her aunt made a doll, drawing on facial features with a bit of damp coal. She sent the doll with her slave to Juan Lorenzo's house, and the next day, the sorcerer said the doll walked in the street during the night and smelled of sulfur.

Andrés de Campo's statements clearly hint at the household tensions that led his wife doña Lorenzana to flee to her friend's house and later to take refuge in a convent. Confessing voluntarily before the inquisitors, he said that one day he saw one of his slaves on the street looking nervous and fearful so he stopped her to question her. Andrés took a piece of paper from her and had her wait for him under guard in a house. Then he went home to find his wife wearing her cloak, packed and ready to leave the house with one of her daughters, her jewels, and three of her slaves. Enraged, he searched her trunks and found a small piece of dirty paper stuck in with her dresses. Someone with messy handwriting had written this incantation:

Francisco, with two I see you,
With five I draw you in,
I drink the blood the heart spills
So that you want me,
That you love me,
That you die for me.

However many women you see,
All will seem old and ugly.[45]

He also found a few handfuls of dried herbs. In his rage, Andrés burned
everything (apparently after memorizing it) and did not mention it to the
Holy Office until several months after Lorenzana's imprisonment. Andrés
confessed not to incriminate his wife further, which would harm his children's future, but to demonstrate that he still held some patriarchal authority in his house, despite his wife's known love affair.[46]

Doña Lorenzana herself presented a different view of their marriage.
As a very young adolescent, she had married into a large and complicated
household and lacked any close relatives to help her navigate this challenge,
so she trusted her slaves and her friends to carry out her efforts to influence
Andrés through magic. Doña Lorenzana asserted her innocence and denied
many of the accusations, especially the information that came from Juan
Lorenzo's testimony. She admitted to active involvement in love magic, but
she claimed all of it was to help her marriage and to "make peace" with her
husband. She disputed Juan Lorenzo's account of their relationship, claiming her friends told her to contact the slave because he knew all about "lies
and sorcery." In view of this reputation, doña Lorenzana argued that he
also lied in his confessions to the inquisitors. Lorenzana minimized her
own guilt by claiming that she resisted completing spells because of her
"scruples and fear." She argued that nothing she did should be taken seriously because she did not believe that magic was anything more than "the
tricks and inventions of women and conmen."[47]

Perhaps because he served a friar, Juan Lorenzo's spells had a very
religious tone, as did several of the other spells carried out by women who
claimed clergymen schooled them in love magic. Doña Lorenzana said
Juan Lorenzo instructed her to appeal to Saint Mark and Saint Martha,
even requesting a mass to be said for the latter. His advice to say five "Our
Fathers" and five "Hail Marys" hardly seemed something the Holy Office
would find objectionable. An oil that Juan Lorenzo gave Lorenzana and
doña Ana, which was meant for their faces with the goal of attracting their
husbands' love, was nothing more than makeup, although perhaps it was
oil used in baptisms. However, Juan Lorenzo also mixed in conjurations
involving a skull and a wax doll that Lorenzana believed he used to invoke
demons. She could not use the face oil because "her body trembled simply
from looking at it."[48]

While some of doña Lorenzana's involvement in magic might have seemed to her like a diverting way to pass the time, in truth, the young wife and mother only brought more worry and conflict into her life with her actions. Doña Lorenzana's relationship with the *sargento mayor* had created many of her personal difficulties, but she preferred to trace the origins of her problems to her husband's affairs. After her imprisonment by the Holy Office, Lorenzana admitted that after two years of marriage she had begun to fight with her husband because he told her about his ties to two married women.[49] Given that Andrés was twenty-seven years older than his wife, it is no surprise that he had a storied sexual past, a previous marriage, and older children.[50] As her marriage descended into conflict, corresponding to a period when she bore no children, doña Lorenzana drifted toward adultery and love magic. Meanwhile, she ineffectively tried to control the sexual relationships between her slaves and her husband's office employees. Many witnesses presented information about sexual activities within Lorenzana's household that revealed her failed attempts to control her servants.[51] Doña Lorenzana vociferously objected to sex between members of her household, but her opposition did nothing more than increase the number of her enemies. The witnesses encouraged the inquisitors to divert their investigations from the social circle of love magic practitioners to questions about sorcery in her domestic life.

When the slave women working in doña Lorenzana's house testified to the inquisitors, they presented themselves as following orders and described their actions as harmless, claiming they refused to do anything that could harm their master, at the price of disobeying doña Lorenzana. For example, Polonia Bioho, at her mistress's command, traveled to Turbaco, about one day's walk inland, to collect some herbs from an Indian. The herbs went under her master's pillow to "improve his disposition."[52] In her capacity as cook, Polonia received a white powder made from toasted donkey brains to improve Andres's mood, but she refused to put it in his food.[53] The slave Catalina often served as a messenger between Lorenzana and Juan Lorenzo, transporting the doll, candles, sulfur, and firecrackers to Governor Diego Fernandez de Velasco's house, where the sorcerer lived with his master.[54]

Part of Lorenzana's dissatisfaction with her marriage to the notary Andrés de Campo derived from her weak position in her household, especially her lack of authority over family slaves and her husband's employees. Andrés had several men working for him in his notarial office, and some of these retainers also lived in his home. Lorenzana struggled to gain the respect of older male scribes. Her efforts caused even more tension in her household. Rumors of her love affairs and that she used her slaves to help her practice love magic drastically weakened her position as a respectable *ama de casa*. One scribe employed by her husband, Sebastian Pacheco, age fifty-nine, testified against doña Lorenzana before the inquisitors in May of 1613. As Lorenzana's boarder, Pacheco said he saw many women who had bad reputations as herbalists and sorceresses coming and going from the house.[55] Pacheco also claimed that he, along with Andrés, ate an eggplant dish Lorenzana ordered her servants to poison with powders, causing them severe fevers that required a barber to bleed them.[56] On another occasion, Pacheco saw Lorenzana's stepdaughter María warn her father not to eat from a dish. In response, the food was removed, and Andrés lamented to his wife, "Am I such a bad man that you seek out spells to kill me?" Pacheco expressed the opinion that doña Lorenzana fed Andrés food that made him sleepy all the time so she could carry on her affair with the sergeant major don Francisco Santander.

Although Pacheco's testimony was neither conclusive nor particularly damning in terms of her sorcery, doña Lorenzana passionately defended herself against his accusations. With the help of her advocate Domingo de Argos (at this time a cathedral canon, later an important local inquisitor), Lorenzana attacked Pacheco's character and illuminated their tense relationship. She explained that Pacheco was her enemy because they fought over his affair with her slave Catalina Jolofa. She forbade Pacheco to sleep "below" (presumably where the resident domestic servants and slaves slept) with Catalina, but he ignored her, resulting in Catalina's birth of a mulata daughter, tellingly named Sebastiana. Lorenzana also claimed that Pacheco was a known drunkard who frequently spoke poorly of all kinds of people, even saying that he would happily lie if given ten pesos.[57] Other household slaves, including Catalina herself, confirmed doña Lorenzana's statements about the affair. A mulata slave named Antonia witnessed fights between Pacheco and Lorenzana and testified that her mistress tried very hard to prevent him from having sex with Catalina.[58] Antonia even claimed that she saw Sebastian running after Lorenzana holding his unsheathed sword. Doña Lorenzana saved herself by running toward her friend doña Ana, the treasurer's wife.

Unfortunately for Lorenzana, her advocate Argos could not find anyone else who would testify that Pacheco was a drunkard, but two other clerks employed by Andrés characterized Sebastian as an immature and embarrassing man who freely insulted others, including his boss. Within their office, Pacheco made a mockery of Andrés by holding up two fingers behind the chief notary's head to show his officemates that Andrés "had horns" (was a cuckold). On another occasion, when Andrés walked toward the office, Pacheco rudely said to his fellow clerks, "Here comes the *cabrón*."[59] Clearly, both husband and wife lost authority over their underlings due to their inability to control their sexuality, which resulted in diminished honor for both of them.

Pacheco was not the only enemy that doña Lorenzana dealt with inside the walls of her own home. She also rejected the validity of the testimony of a slave named Margarita because this woman was Andrés's lover and the mother of his illegitimate child. Their relationship had caused many of the couple's fights and may have led to Lorenzana fleeing the house, since Margarita bore Andres's child while his wife sheltered in the Carmelite convent.[60] According to the patriarchal model, men guarded household sexuality in the early modern Iberian world, but this case shows that women also took on this role. However, since doña Lorenzana had little authority in her own home, her efforts to control her own slaves' sexuality largely failed. Although violence is not mentioned in the documentation, if Pacheco had raped Catalina, doña Lorenzana would have failed to protect her slaves as a benevolent mistress, a moral role encouraged by the local Jesuit Alonso de Sandoval. If Pacheco and Catalina had a consensual relationship, a possibility that cannot be entirely ruled out, Lorenzana would have failed in the promotion of official moral standards among her dependents. Her own notorious affair undermined any influence she might have had over her slaves, servants, and employees.

When she could no longer live at home, Lorenzana fled to the Carmelite convent, but the nunnery did not protect her from the danger of her association with Juan Lorenzo. Doña Lorenzana and Juan Lorenzo were around the same age; they met when they were in their early twenties and both were imprisoned around age twenty-seven. They maintained a relationship that was at times patron/client, master/student, and/or cooperating friends. When threatened by the Spanish Inquisition, their interactions descended into manipulation and threats. This tension and struggle makes sense given the presence of a repressive imperial institution that clearly favored elite Spaniards over African-descended slaves. Juan Lorenzo, although much more experienced and sophisticated then doña Lorenzana, was more vulnerable to the inquisitors' wrath. He succumbed to his fear when he found out that Lorenzana took refuge in the convent after the Holy Office came to the city. Just before she entered the convent, Juan Lorenzo desperately played his best card, offering doña Lorenzana methods to kill her husband in exchange for one hundred pesos to buy his freedom. When she refused, he left, but he soon came to visit Lorenzana at the convent. In the presence of the sixty-year-old prioress and speaking through the *torno*, or turnstile, that protected the nuns' privacy, Juan Lorenzo asked doña Lorenzana what she planned to tell the inquisitors about him. She replied that she had much to confess, but he "earnestly" told her it was all lies. Doña Lorenzana's response was that "she valued her soul more than anything in the world," so Juan Lorenzo stormed out, after saying something threatening along the lines of "Go ahead and tell them then." In response to Lorenzana's agitation about this encounter, the prioress comforted her by saying that if he came back, Lorenzo would be beaten, a crude threat that highlighted Juan Lorenzo's presumptuous relationship with a doña. On another visit, the slave asked Lorenzana not to mention the skull, but she again insisted on telling everything, so he left with another threat, saying that great harm would come to her.[61] Juan Lorenzo had to both hide his sorcery and protect his reputation as a sorcerer, which was certainly an important source of his income.

Of course, Juan Lorenzo had far more to fear from the Holy Office than doña Lorenzana. Despite her lack of local family ties, her Genoese father, and her well-publicized affair, Lorenzana enjoyed the status and the privileges of an elite Spanish woman. Her marital and social position sheltered her from inquisitorial wrath and whatever crimes she had committed, because the inquisitors did not want to shame a fellow countryman and peer by degrading his legitimate spouse.[62] The Tribunal was new in town and not popular, especially in the opinion of other local bureaucrats and clerics. For the sake of their children's honor, Andrés protected and defended his wife. For more personal reasons, Lorenzana's lover don Francisco Santander also tried to help her case. He interrogated a friar about how the Holy Office might decide to punish someone involved in spells and sorcery. This friar reported local gossip to inquisitors about how Francisco was trying to influence slaves not to speak against doña Lorenzana when the inquisitors questioned them. Stories circulated about Francisco's rage in not being able to find out more about Lorenzana's case, since his inquiries to friars did not bear fruit, in light of the secrecy of inquisitorial proceedings. Doña Lorenzana protected her lover in return by not mentioning his name in her testimony so the inquisitors would not call him in as a witness and delay his return to Spain.[63]

For those involved in this case, and many of the others presented in this book, negotiating imprisonment was common, although prisoners did not always achieve success in their efforts to gain concessions. Doña Lorenzana tried to improve her own incarceration through complaints about her physical and mental wellbeing. After living a year in the local discalced Carmelite convent, she probably hoped that she would enjoy a similarly easy imprisonment after her arrest by the Holy Office in early 1613. After a short stop in the common cells, inquisitors moved doña Lorenzana to a cell where she began to complain about prison conditions.[64] She said she felt "heartsick and sorrowful" from being alone in her cell and asked for company. The common cells were on the lower floor, were very damp, and were open to passersby in the public plaza.

In response to her complaints, the inquisitors put her in cell number ten and called a doctor to help her. The doctor reported that doña Lorenzana was *melancolía y congoja* (melancholic and anxious) and had two incidences of *mal de corazón* in the night.[65] Lorenzana claimed that she might be pregnant and was suffering a hemorrhage, but also said she had given birth to her fourth child less than two months before. The doctor was not overly worried because she did not have a fever, but he continued to visit her after several more attacks of the mal de corazón and ongoing complaints about her anxious reaction to her incarceration. Doña Lorenzana also begged for a larger cell. After discussing her condition, one inquisitor sympathetically suggested that Lorenzana move to the convent under a fianza (an arrangement similar to paying bail) of 1,000 ducats. But the fearsome Mañozca dismissed this idea, not acknowledging that mal de corazón was a serious illness. Mañozca decided that since she did not have a fever, this was just ordinary "heart sickness" that made her depressed. He argued that she would have the same experience every time she entered the jail if she went to stay in the convent, and all the coming and going would detract from the supposed secrecy maintained in inquisition investigations. Futilely, doña Lorenzana persevered in asking for the inquisitors' mercy and permission to serve her sentence under house arrest, saying her heart sickness was worsening.[66] Nonetheless, she turned her full attention to the numerous accusations made against her.

With the help of her husband and lover, the inquisitors eventually sentenced doña Lorenzana to a very light penance. After the Cartagena Holy

Office punished doña Lorenzana with a 4,000 ducat fine, along with attending a private penitential mass, Andrés successfully convinced the suprema in Spain to refund the monetary penalty and clear his wife's name for the sake of their children. He made two conventional arguments justifying his request in typical rhetoric that stressed the value of lineage and status. First, he asked the Holy Office with its "accustomed mercy" to erase any stains on the honor of his family, simply because he was a noble of honorable blood (although he was not given the honorific don anywhere in these documents). Second, he observed that, as a woman born in Cartagena, Lorenzana was raised and nursed by Indian and black women who could not comprehend that there was anything wrong with using powders or spells, especially because doña Lorenzana grew up before the arrival of the local inquisition tribunal. This implied that his young wife was a child of a land new to the Christian faith. These self-serving arguments fit well with the inquisitors' views on the corrupting influence of Africans and Native Americans. Lorenzana suffered little official punishment, in contrast to her unfortunate plebeian associates such as Juan Lorenzo, who received two hundred lashes, and the Spanish procuress María Ramírez, who was sentenced to one hundred lashes.

Because there were elite Spanish women at its center, this early investigation of local sorcery did not grow as large as the witch hunt that pursued a few dozen Afro-Caribbean women in the 1630s, who are the subjects of chapters 6, 7, and 8. Doña Lorenzana was able to return to her status as a respectable local matron, while Cartagena-based inquisitors turned their attention to fears of African religious practice in the Zaragoza mining regions. Even with the involvement of Juan Lorenzo and other Afro-Iberians and the clear references to demons in the various incantations used by this group, the inquisitors did not frame this activity according to the demonological conventions of Satanic pacts and witches' Sabbaths.[67] All of the incantations and rituals—even those that mixed Catholic prayers with invoking demons—practiced by the early seventeenth-century Cartagena witches fit into Iberian folkways that the inquisitors did not find overly shocking, despite Andrés blaming the moral decline of the elite Spanish women on non-Europeans. At this point in Cartagena, the Holy Office did not fear a widespread African presence and influence enough to directly tie them to the devil. These attitudes would change in the 1630s.

Doña Lorenzana's case demonstrates that Cartagena women actively sought sexual satisfaction, even taking serious risks of inciting their husbands' jealous, honor-fueled rages. Women used magic to achieve their sexual goals, especially when they felt a desperate need for male economic support or, in doña Lorenzana's life, an ardent desire for pleasure outside her combative marriage and unbearably stressful domestic setting. They gathered together socially: elite doñas shared their intimate lives and illicit desires with a diverse group of nonwhite plebeians and slaves, from beatas to brothel keepers. When doña Lorenzana failed to control the sex between Spanish men and slave women in her own house, she turned the gendered tables on this power differential and looked to an enslaved man as a solution, causing many more problems for herself. While Juan Lorenzo was smarter and more sophisticated than doña Lorenzana, his race and enslaved status ultimately weakened his efforts to bring down doña Lorenzana and her elite friends with him. Clearly, nonwhite women did not hold a monopoly on love magic in early 1600s Cartagena, and doña Lorenzana's slaves even presented themselves as innocent victims in their mistress's plans to poison and enchant her husband. Whether consciously or not, doña Lorenzana chose to have an affair with the military leader Francisco Santander and therefore helped the local faction that wanted to bring him down and weaken his power. She did her best to negotiate within the system (with the help of don Francisco and her husband), but ultimately her race and social status were perhaps the best weapons against the harsh and humiliating punishment suffered by her plebeian cohort. She also effectively presented herself as piously afraid of the inquisitors' wrath. The Holy Office's involvement late in the game hints at the competitiveness between all the various church and state bureaucracies present in this city. Although their auto de fe confirmed the local expression of imperial race and status hierarchies, surprisingly, the inquisitors did not see this investigation as a good opportunity to highlight an especially non-European affiliation with the devil and bring more serious charges against Juan Lorenzo and the mulata women who marched in the procession with him. The next chapter continues the theme of honor and sex connecting to political, racial, and even international tensions, turning the focus to men's acts.

CHAPTER THREE

VIOLENCE, SEX, AND HONOR

MEN'S ACTIONS IN DEFENSE OF THEIR HONOR GENERATED MANY COURT cases involving sexuality in the early modern Iberian world. In seventeenth-century Cartagena, defending one's personal, familiar, and household honor sometimes led to public acts of violence and even homicide. This chapter explores cases where men asserted their dominance through their control over their dependents' sexuality. While the Spanish crown attempted to reign in ideas of private vengeance in the late medieval era by promoting an expanded judicial infrastructure, in early modern Spain and colonial Spanish America, enemies continued to carry out vendettas publicly on the street or in hidden locations in the countryside.[1] Though continued references to honor in many different kinds of legal disputes indicate an attempted transition from personal and familial to governmental jurisdiction over sexuality, this transition never fully succeeded. However, the courts did function as effective outlets to soften ingrained societal gender inequalities. Perceived insults or disrespectful behavior sparked the three cases of violence in this chapter, pitting men against men or men against women. In all cases the insults related to sex, sexual reputation, and establishing who held power over sexual options. The slights or offensives targeted the violent men themselves, as well as members of their households, whose sexual reputations were of a piece with the men's sense of honor and public reputation. Of course, any public statement questioning a man's wife's sexuality usually caused a violent reaction, but men also reacted aggressively when other men questioned or violated their control over their slaves' sexuality.[2]

In these cases, private sexual acts became public disputes, with the court mediating male violence justified by patriarchal prerogatives. In each case, violence sparked by trivial concerns over betrayed honor then provoked reactions, tying these seemingly petty local fights to imperial political issues, competing jurisdiction, threats from foreign powers, and important choices about how Spain wanted to rule its empire. The men discussed here viewed violence as an appropriate response to disrespect that they perceived as directed at the facets of their lives that contributed to their personal honor: their wives, their slaves, or their control over these dependents. Their reactions ranged from the normal and expected street sword fights to the more shameful secret torture of slaves.

The stories told in this chapter prove that Cartagena men often displayed their righteous anger in street brawls or in court as they defended their violent acts, or they allowed themselves to cruelly vent their rage on slaves and others they considered socially and racially inferior.[3] This is not to say that the brutal, homicidal acts described in this book were a product of an emotionally immature Spanish society peopled by violent, uncontrolled men.[4] The public display of anger by a man who perceived himself as dishonored was instead choreographed to maintain or confirm his lost status and reputation.[5] One man introduced here perpetrated domestic abuse of an enslaved woman who supposedly sexually betrayed him, her master, with full knowledge that sooner or later gossips would spread reports of the manly, masterful assertion of sexual control over dependents. Claims of offended honor effectively justified an angry, violent, or even homicidal outburst to judges, because in contrast to love and lust, early modern Spaniards viewed rage as an appropriate masculine emotional response to particular situations. In fact, neglecting to respond with rage to insults touching on honor was viewed as bizarre, immoral, and personally discrediting. European "lords could be—indeed, were often supposed to be—angry: expressing anger was intimately bound up with their status and honor."[6] This posture was so appealing that even Cartagena plebeians strove to carry out this model of lordly behavior. Calculated angry public reactions to insults clarified both the boundaries of relationships between equals and the rankings and expected treatment that inferiors should give superiors, an important demonstration of social hierarchies. In the case of men of equal status who engaged in street brawls, the perpetrators carefully constructed narratives of a gradual escalation to violence. Men claimed that they calmly told their opponent at least once to "Go with God" before drawing their swords. But there were some limits to anger and the blood-shed that might soon follow. Spaniards did not encourage or condone mis-directed, excessive fury, viewing it as unacceptable in a civilized society. However, given that Carthaginians generally tolerated anger and violence, such extreme displays did not necessarily lead to harsh judicial punish-ments for the perpetrators.

One seventeenth-century Spaniard residing in Cartagena chose to fight to the death to protect his reputation as the sole authority over his own slaves' sex lives. As a result of framing his rage as righteous defense of his patriarchal domestic privileges, he received the full protection of the judicial authorities. This eventually murderous conflict began at the start of Lent in 1602, when the bishop of Cartagena posted an edict demanding infor-mation about slaves in the diocese who were cohabitating.[7] Upon hearing about the edict, Jerónimo de Serpa, a poor but zealous Sevillian hatter living in Cartagena with one of his children, decided to investigate certain slaves owned by a thirty-six-year-old merchant named Francisco Luis. Serpa sus-pected that two of Luis's slaves were cohabitating, so he went early one morn-ing in March to the merchant's street, asking neighbors the slaves' names so he could report them to the bishop. By asking around, Serpa made public his concerns and his attempts to police Luis. In doing so, he publicly insulted Luis's honor by questioning his household authority, a fundamental aspect of his honorable identity.

When Luis heard about these inquiries, he was deeply offended that anyone would publicly undermine his patriarchal authority by daring to openly suggest that members of his household did not live honorably. When Serpa next passed by Luis's general store, the men argued in the street. Luis asserted that friends should not inform on each other and claimed that he had already turned in one of his slaves, following the bishop's edict.[8] Serpa responded in turn by saying that Luis insulted him with his statement that an honorable man did not peek in other men's windows. Serpa angrily yelled a very serious insult to honor a few times, saying, "What I did was right, and anyone who says differently is a lying scoundrel!" A total of nine merchants working in different stores witnessed this loud argument in front of Luis's store. Each storekeeper explained that at the time of the dispute they were either dressing or standing in their doorways. Those who were inside ran to their windows or doors to witness the altercation. In an instant, a mundane moment turned into a public performance of violence sparked by asper-sions against honor, transforming a familiar morning routine into the most beloved form of early modern Spanish drama. To get rid of Serpa and de-escalate the potential violence, Luis dismissively said, "Go with God," several times. At this point, the other merchants no longer watched passively but became involved in the conflict, advising Serpa to quiet himself and go home. Serpa did run back to his own nearby store but quickly returned brandishing his unsheathed sword, which he thrust into the arch over Luis's doorway, again calling Luis a scoundrel or rogue (*bellaco*) and demanding a fight.[9] Luis grabbed his sword and the men began to parry and thrust in the street, attracting an even larger crowd. Within minutes, Luis dealt Serpa a fatal blow to the head, which cut deeply to the bone. After a huge loss of blood, the hatter died six hours later. Moments before he died, Serpa recounted the argument to the arresting authorities, remembering that he and Luis exchanged heated words about each other's honor and honesty.

The authorities pursued this case in the name Antonio, Serpa's son who lived with him in Cartagena. They stressed that due to Serpa's death, the boy, his mother, and his siblings in Seville would be left in poverty, so the case served as an attempt to garner monetary compensation for the loss of a husband and father who had provided their livelihood. When the alcaldes imprisoned Luis, they confiscated and auctioned off the inventory of his store, which included items ranging from scissors and rosaries to clothing and tools. Serpa's son's advocate stressed that Serpa had behaved as any good Christian should, and Luis's insults prompted him to grab his sword and start the fight. Luis's initial sentence was to serve ten years as a galley slave and pay a 2,000 peso fine, with half of the money going to Serpa's family. He also had to compensate the court costs.[10] Luis appealed this judgment to the high court in Bogota because he claimed he acted in self-defense. He argued that he only reacted to the fact that Serpa ran at him carrying an unsheathed sword. Luis's advocate asserted that his client had only spoken calmly and quietly, despite the serious insults Serpa shouted at him.[11] Luis said he fought only to defend himself as Serpa entered his store thrusting his sword and calling him names.

Ultimately, the central point of argumentation in this case was the debate over whether or not Serpa had acted within reason in questioning Luis about his slaves' sexuality, in view of the fact that the entire scuffle was a result of Serpa's efforts to carry out the bishop's orders to report cohabitating slaves. The documentation reveals no firm conclusion or final judgment, because the audiencia judges in Bogota ultimately decided that Serpa's wife, not his underage son, had to prosecute Luis. This exalted regional court decided not prosecute a death that took place during a fight sparked by challenges to honor. In this case, the bishop's attempt to intervene in private sexual matters resulted in a pointless death and most likely no change whatsoever in Luis' slaves' sexual behavior and partnerships. Luis's reaction to Serpa's surveillance indicates that Luis situated control over slave sexuality in the domestic realm and therefore ruled over it as the man of the house. Authority figures, such as the bishop, ineffectively increased the violence and conflict when they intervened in these private matters. The bishop's decree brought into the public domain issues that in practice were regarded as domestic concerns best left to the discretion of honorable men. The higher court's decision to vacate the lower jurisdiction's punishment illustrates the limits of public and religious authorities to impose their moral standards on the domestic sphere. In effect, the audiencia sanctioned Luis's righteous anger and even his unpremeditated homicidal act. Tension persisted over the issue of official intervention into private conflicts.

If two plebeians could fight to the death over a neighbor's surveillance of slaves' sex lives, we might imagine that a nobleman who valued his honor in seventeenth-century Cartagena would react even more decisively to the slightest rumor of insults to his wife's reputation. A case from 1626 features a man who threatened to kill or at least tear off the ears of someone who allegedly insulted his wife.[12] A few days after Christmas in 1625, a young wife called doña Francisca went to mass in the Dominican convent church with several of her female relatives: fifty-year-old Leonarda Baez and three sisters called doña Isabel de Sosa (age twenty-nine), doña María de Sosa (eighteen) and doña Catalina de Sosa (twenty). They sat down on a bench in front of the Rosary altar near Gaspar de los Reyes, another of their relations.[13] Gaspar was a young man employed by a merchant uncle. After a few moments sitting on the bench, doña Francisca's friends saw her blush. Doña Isabel and Leonarda claimed that Gaspar humiliated her publicly because he said these words to his cousin Francisca, "You are a hussy and if you weren't so shameless, you would not let them bring you here." The older woman Leonarda responded by calling Gaspar a *pícaro*. There is some doubt that the insult was actually delivered, because the two younger sisters denied hearing the exchange and a couple of men who were nearby waiting to receive communion also did not hear Gaspar say anything to Leonarda.[14] Although she only heard the insult secondhand from her older friends, doña Francisca went home disconsolate.

Later in the day, doña Francisca sat at dinner with a sad and anxious demeanor, which was observed by the two men also seated at the table, her husband don Diego, and his friend don Jacinto. In their statements, both men described themselves as twenty-six years of age, born in Bogota, and without occupations—though don Diego did have access to an *encomienda* as a source of income.[15] Gaspar's alleged insult caused the men to jump up from the table in righteous indignation. The enraged spouse claimed he went to make a complaint with Governor Diego de Escobar, but he was not admitted because it was the *siesta* hour. Don Diego rounded up a few more men, including Francisca's brother and the majordomo of his rural encomienda, and walked over to Gaspar's rented room to get their revenge. Several men witnessed the resulting scene, aroused from their siesta when they heard a disturbance in the street.

Gaspar, speaking later from prison, presented himself as an innocent victim. He did not acknowledge any interaction with his female relatives at church that day and said that during the siesta hour he was sitting undressed in his room. (Although he described himself as *desnudo*, a friend with him said Gaspar was wearing a doublet and breeches, but no hat.)[16] Gaspar claimed he sat calmly working on arts and crafts projects during the siesta—his statements maintain that he was either cutting out paper letters or piously making a paper cutout of Jesus—when a group of men appeared at his window. He saw several men holding unsheathed swords and daggers and heard don Diego shout, "Get out here, cuckold, because I am going to kill you!" Gaspar remained calm and said, attempting to deescalate the conflict, "That offensive word does not apply to me, since I am not married. I don't want to fight. Go with God." After repeating the insults and again demanding that Gaspar come outside, don Diego threatened to cut off his ears. Gaspar again said, "Go with God," and that he did not want to fight because the governor had forbidden it. Finally, as don Diego and his gang broke down his door and pushed into his room, Gaspar reached for his sword and a small shield. Gaspar and his friend managed to calm their attackers enough to move back into the street, where they fought with their swords until stopped by a passing soldier doing guard duty. The guardsmen incarcerated both men in the public jail.

Don Diego presented the fight differently, saying when he went to his brother-in-law Antonio's house after hearing his wife's complaints, he found doña Francisca's brother enraged because he had heard that Gaspar had ordered a friend of his to beat him up. In don Diego's version of events, it seemed that Gaspar wanted to attack his own relatives on several fronts.[17]

Don Diego walked by Gaspar's room and saw him laughing at the window
with a friend. This was the reason he had called Gaspar a "shameless lout"
(*devergonzado*) and threatened to cut off his ears. After hearing these fighting words, both Gaspar and his friend allegedly ran outside brandishing
their swords and began the fight, which eventually involved several men.

Even if Gaspar did insult the young wife, sixteen-year-old doña Francisca, who was his own cousin, one wonders about the extremely harsh reaction he received from don Diego and from the Cartagena judicial authorities.
Both men sat in jail for months, but Gaspar had to wear two pairs of shackles. Don Diego's punishment was a tiny five peso fine and the humiliating
loss of the right to carry arms, but Gaspar was ordered to leave Cartagena
on the next flota or pay 1,000 pesos. Why such an extreme punishment for
a man described by many witnesses as a quiet, peaceful, good Christian,
a judgment supported by his attempts to pacify his attackers with the pat
phrase "Go with God"?[18] Unfortunately, Gaspar, like many people passing
through colonial Cartagena, became a pawn in greater geopolitical conflicts.
After his imprisonment, the authorities accused him of living illegally in
the Indies as a Portuguese without a royal license to immigrate. Relations
between the two Iberian powers were tense in the 1620s, and soon after, the
entire Portuguese mercantile population of Cartagena was drastically weakened by several Holy Office investigations of rumors of crypto-Jewish practice. In an early sign of these fears, Governor Escobar took the time in 1627
to list all the local foreigners (the vast majority Portuguese) in a report he
sent to the king.[19] From his jail cell, Gaspar insisted that he was born in
Spain to Portuguese parents and that he came legally to help his uncle sell
merchandise. He did not have his royal license on hand due to his confusion
during a severe illness that he suffered upon disembarking in Cartagena.
All this had nothing to do with why Gaspar was arrested, but upon appeal,
the Bogota high court took advantage of the imprisonment and agreed that
Gaspar must leave Cartagena and the rest of the Americas on the next available ship.[20] In this case, a personal dispute changed into an issue of imperial
rivalries, with Gaspar the apparently innocent victim.

Although this conflict started from rumors of a rude comment slighting
a wife's reputation (the case contains no reference to doña Francisca's possible Portuguese heritage), the whole story was probably invented by Francisca's aunt over some family feud and possibly a desire to simply get rid
of Gaspar. Certainly men were permitted to demonstrate extreme sensitivity regarding their wives' sexual reputation. While the authorities did end

the brawl before serious injuries occurred, they seemed to countenance the actions of whoever masterminded the plan to banish Gaspar from Cartagena. Offenses against a man's honor almost invariably provoked real anger and a desire for vengeance or apology, while at the same time individuals and public authorities manipulated violations of the honor code for their own purposes. As we will see again and again, a litigating rhetoric foregrounding sex, honor, and anger achieved goals unrelated to the initial judicial complaint.

Self-protection within bureaucratic hierarchies represented one of the most effective ways to manipulate justice in colonial Spanish America, even when men enacted horrific acts of torture. Of course, as part of maintaining their role as masters, slave owners were allowed to punish, constrain, and, within reason, control the behavior of their slaves. In the case that began this chapter, Luis viewed challenges and even simple questioning of his paternalistic power over his slaves as an affront to his personal and familial honor, an essential element in the glue that held together the race and class hierarchies of colonial life. As a result of an affront of this kind, Luis publicly stabbed the hatter Serpa to death. Luis suffered no repercussions for this act. A slave owner might react with even more extreme acts of violence if the slave carried out the challenge to the master's honor. Since slaves and masters could not duel on the street as equals, violence against slaves took on an even more bloody hue.

When a slave or her defenders called the behavior or veracity of the master into question, the master's honor was immediately at stake, which was especially displeasing when it was paired with allegations that he had also broken the law. However, sometimes the factionalism of competing authorities provided a limited degree of protection for slaves. María Manuel, an enslaved woman living in Cartagena in the early 1600s, suffered horrible physical abuse due to her master's sexual jealousy. Despite her extremely vulnerable status as a nonwhite woman living in bondage, she succeeded in presenting her complaints before the Cartagena governor, who nominally acknowledged the validity of her concerns and the enormous effort required to make her petition. María Manuel interacted with the governor at a moment in the early seventeenth century when the secular representatives of the Spanish crown jockeyed for territory with the new local branch of the Holy Office of the Inquisition. The defense of male honor, derived from elite status and occupational privilege in a volatile combination with sexual jealousy, motivated María Manuel's master to abuse her. María Manuel's ordeals took place because her torturers justified their violence with the rhetoric of honor, which legitimized their sexual dominance over women. María Manuel's master defended himself with a robust certainty that the authorities would show total sympathy for the fact that slaves and social inferiors had affronted his personal and familial honor, and thus his uncontrolled, sadistic anger made perfect sense. He scarcely needed to invoke this challenge to hierarchies, because everyone knew to rhetorically protect the social hierarchy at all costs, despite the governor's personal intervention and paternalism. The master miscalculated only in underestimating how much the governor detested the new inquisitors.

As a descendant of white enslaved women (*esclavas blancas*) and free Spanish men, María Manuel's heritage differed from most African-born slaves living in colonial Cartagena. Born around 1605 in Seville, María Manuel had quite an eye-catching appearance. Her mother described her as "portly, with a white, pockmarked face, with a blue nail branded between her eyebrows and a large brand on her chin."[21] The nail stood for "esclavo" (s-clavo) or slave, since "clavo" is the Spanish world for nail.[22] Her father was a *vizcaíno* from the Spanish Basque territory. Because María Manuel was a light-skinned slave born in Spain, she was usually labeled a *berberisca*, implying non-Christian heritage. To refute this impression, her mother and other Sevillan neighbors asserted that María Manuel was an old Christian, "a descendent of light mulatos, not Jews or Moors or Berbers, but of the black caste." This distinction allowed for María Manuel's legal passage to the Indies. In Seville, María Manuel worked for the pharmacist Pedro Morales and had a son when she was around twenty years old. Her son was named Pedro and was also described as having a white face and blue eyes. A few years later, Juan Ramos Pérez, a *nuncio* for the Cartagena Holy Office, bought María Manuel.

A nuncio, or messenger, held a very low level position in the Tribunal hierarchy. Pérez previously had served as the inquisition court doorman/janitor, but as a nuncio, he exercised the slightly more elevated task of carrying messages, calling on people that the judges needed to question, and serving papers for debts.[23] Before his official appointment as a nuncio in 1617, Pérez worked for the Holy Office without pay at his menial occupations. Why waste his time as a volunteer janitor? Even in a lowly, unpaid position, occupational affiliation with the Holy Office imbued a man with honor. Employment with the Inquisition suggested limpieza de sangre, or pure lineage, deriving from Old Christian ancestry. Pérez also enjoyed the complete judicial protection given to Tribunal employees, a status that helped him avoid Governor Francisco de Murga's wrath after the discovery of his severe abuse of María Manuel. The narrative presented here draws upon the testimony of several witnesses, including María Manuel herself, who spoke before the governor about her terrible experiences in Pérez's service.

For five years, María Manuel served in Pérez's house as his slave and lover, which led to the birth of their daughter.[24] Recognizing this as a sin and choosing a penitential stance in line with her strong personal assertion of her Christianity (despite the assumptions that she was of non-Christian ancestry), María Manuel told the governor that she felt guilty for this sin and wanted to confess it to a priest and receive absolution. She reported that she could not achieve her hopes for reform because Pérez discouraged her, saying that she would never have a respectable sexual reputation because her unmarried status was a public scandal. Pérez also convinced her to give up her hopes for marriage to another man by telling María Manuel that no one would marry her since everyone knew the sin she had committed. María Manuel's version of her attempts at self-reform highlights her desire for reintegration into moral, Christian society, in the face of her master's irrational, unchristian discouragement and denial of the important values of penitence and forgiveness despite his employment by the Holy Office.

María Manuel did find a young Spaniard named Juan de Soto who promised to marry her in front of witnesses, so she had Pérez's majordomo Bonifacio Treviño write to her master to say that she would no longer live in sin with him. María Manuel and her potential husband then went to Cartagena to hurriedly publish their marriage banns. Unfortunately for María, Juan de Soto fled after hearing rumors that Pérez was enraged. It is even possible that Perez bribed him to abandon his fiancée. After Juan de Soto deserted her, María Manuel asked the governor for help in finding her groom. She received no assistance at this time, and so she fell back into Pérez's power. Angered by her attempts to attain respectable, married status and the slight this presented to his dominion over her, Pérez hid María Manuel in various houses in Cartagena and then sent her to live with the family of an inquisition *familiar* near Santa Marta. After several months living with this family, María Manuel's sexual relationship with the familiar's son caused her to again become pregnant, which then prompted a horrific response from her master, who once again could not control his enraged reaction to her sexual activity.

When she was already several months pregnant, Pérez imprisoned María Manuel in stocks at an *estancia* owned by the Holy Office secretary. No one was supposed to talk to her, but people living on the estancia felt sorry for her due to her pregnancy and did not treat her as harshly as Pérez had ordered. When Pérez heard of this, he moved her to another estancia where she would suffer much harsher conditions. María Manuel's torturers were the soldier Francisco de Guerra and the majordomo Bonifacio Treviño, acting on orders sent in letters written by her owner Pérez. These men chained her in stocks, naked except for a small piece of cloth wrapped around her "shameful parts." Her first "martyrdom" took place when they slowly sliced off her left ear, cutting so close to her head that they hacked into some of her cheek. After a few days, Pérez sent them another brutal command, instructing them to cut off her other ear. The cuts left scars around the length of a finger along her jaw line. Only a small piece at the top of her ears remained. When María Manuel appeared in public later, she wore a hood to cover this gruesome mutilation.[25]

While she endured this torture, María Manuel lived in an open hut that did not protect her from swarms of mosquitoes and venomous animals. Pérez dictated more punishments; he wrote that Guerra and Treviño should give María Manuel three hundred lashes over the course of a day. This further abuse left her covered in open wounds, in addition to the sores on her legs from the stocks. María Manuel later told the governor that she began to lose weight and felt "disjointed" from blood loss, little food, and continuous imprisonment. Pérez continued to prescribe more torture, which María Manuel later related she believed would go on until she slowly died or miscarried her baby.[26] Pérez's sadism peaked at the point when he sent his accomplices some iron tools, instructing them to use them to cut out her tongue and burn her by inserting them in her *natura*, or womb. María Manuel said the torturers did not dare continue their cruel abuses until they moved her to a more remote estancia.

Around this time, a young Spaniard named Juan de Cepeda, a relation of María Manuel's former master in Seville, started to worry about her after he missed seeing her in Pérez's house. Cepeda knew María Manuel well because he had helped bring her son to Cartagena from Seville the year before. Hearing gossip about how her ears had been cut off, Cepeda visited the estancia, bringing his friend some raisins, bread, and other food. By this time, she was no longer in irons, due to the orders of a sympathetic passing merchant. Before Cepeda could help her, another slave started to escort María Manuel to a more distant location where the tortures could continue unimpeded by concerned observers. Cepeda went back to Cartagena and ran into the *alcalde de la cárcel* (jailer), who encouraged Cepeda to make a complaint to the governor, which he did fearfully in disguised handwriting.[27] Cepeda's letter, signed, "your slave, María Manuel," pretended to be from the hand of the slave woman herself and blamed Pérez's acts on jealousy due to her pregnancy.[28] Governor Murga, judging this abuse as something a man in his position should help alleviate, reacted by sending out two soldiers to find María Manuel, who intercepted her on the road in a forced march ordered by Pérez.

The governor was willing to help María Manuel and prosecute her abusers, but he was wary of the jealously guarded jurisdiction of the Holy Office. Rightly so, because the inquisitors soon found out that María Manuel was under Governor Murga's protection and that Murga was investigating the case. This provoked a bitter dispute between the governor and the inquisitors over their jurisdictions. The inquisitors were furious that María Manuel or her representative had complained to the governor about her treatment by one of their employees, and they demanded that the governor remand her to the tribunal's custody immediately under threat of excommunication.[29] The tribunal learned important information from their familiar who owned the estancia where María Manuel was being tortured. He had advised Pérez to simply whip his slave since ear slicing was not permitted, but Pérez said that María Manuel's words and deeds so enraged him that he ordered the excessive punishment. The familiar suggested sending her away—out of the region entirely—to avoid further conflicts, a tactic that the inquisitors conceded to be reasonable.[30]

Nonetheless, despite the damning physical evidence, the inquisitors remained fiercely protective of their nuncio and manipulated María Manuel's words and interpretation of her experiences. They even questioned the validity of her claim that Pérez had ordered the beatings, eager to deny or diminish the reprehensible actions done by a man in their employ, regardless of the physical proof scarring María's body. The inquisitors asserted that even if Pérez had ordered the torture, María Manuel and other witnesses could not speculate on his supposed motivations, especially in reference to an intangible, sinful, and shameful emotion such as jealousy. Not viewing this as a case of a master licitly punishing a slave, they wished to downplay the fact that one of their employees might publicly and violently demonstrate such an emotion over an unimportant slave and her sordid illicit affairs. To support this line of argument, once they had María Manuel in their power, the inquisitors asked if she had any previous disputes or enmity with Treviño and Guerra. Their goal was to find other motives for why these men would punish her so excessively. María Manuel admitted that while they were beating her, Guerra reminded her how she had informed her master that Guerra had stolen a silver spoon and an expensive napkin. Treviño also possibly had his own motivations for attacking her, since he told her that he remembered that she had spoken badly about one of his girlfriends. Considering her traumatic experiences, it would not be surprising if the inquisitors found a way to pressure María Manuel into making these statements. The inquisitors also interrogated witnesses about their assumption that Pérez had ordered María Manuel tortured out of jealousy. They wondered how anyone could know the inner workings of Pérez's emotions, although they did concede that the two had been lovers. They concluded that the best solution for ending rumors and scandal was to stow María Manuel away on the next ship leaving for Portobello. Instead of further publicizing the affair, the inquisitors justified María Manuel's banishment with the suggestion that she might be a berberisca or of Islamic descent.[31]

Sneaking María Manuel out of Cartagena by ship was a clear act of defiance against Governor Francisco de Murga. The inquisitors allowed the governor to pursue his case against Treviño and Guerra (certainly a difficult prosecution if their victim had disappeared), but Pérez was untouchable as an employee of their institution. Murga was infuriated at the Holy Office's disregard for his authority and their absurd rationale for banishing María Manuel, who had provided extensive documentation for her Old Christian status, despite her African heritage.[32] Refusing to back down from this test of wills, Murga was so angry that he had her ship stopped on its way out of the harbor and forced María Manuel to disembark. Murga wanted to punish María Manuel's abusers in order to fulfill his role as a royal bureaucrat who intervened in situations where patriarchs or other branches of crown bureaucracy took advantage of their power over the weakest colonial subjects. But in the surviving documentation, the conflicts between two competing imperial institutions submerge María Manuel's individual search for justice. It is possible that the governor found and severely punished Treviño and Guerra, but it is just as likely that they escaped. Despite his blatantly public sins, Pérez enjoyed the full protection of the Holy Office, and his victim María Manuel was effectively banished, even though she had the governor's protection.

Status and competing colonial institutions protected a jealous and vicious instigator of violence, sanctioning righteous rage over insulted honor, even when it escalated into torture of a social and racial inferior. However, the inquisitors who sought to protect their employee Juan Ramos Pérez did not wish to acknowledge the nuncio's sexual jealousy, much less recognize the emotions as justifying his ordering the torture of his slave María Manuel. The sordid envy inspired by a female slave's sexual activity was viewed as an ignoble motivation for violent revenge and was impossible to defend among a group of men who all claimed limpieza de sangre. The inquisitors reacted by denying that Pérez's unacceptable jealousy existed.

Contrary to popular notions, the extreme abuse of slaves motivated by uncontrolled envious wrath did not gain the outright approval of the local judiciary. Although elite Spaniards did not believe that slaves possessed honor derived from lineage, wealth, and status, this case confirms the fact that medieval Spanish legal traditions allowed slaves recourse to courts to complain about mistreatment.[33] A general sense of the reasonable limits for cruel punishments meant that slaves turned to the authorities when they felt their masters' actions had gone beyond a reasonable and acceptable norm. María Manuel went directly to the governor because law codes and traditions in her era did not specify a particular court as the appropriate one for filing these kinds of grievances. When the crown issued a decree in 1789 that intruded more directly into the relationship between slaves and masters, colonial subjects rejected it, and it was retracted within a few years.[34] While late colonial masters feared rebellions might ultimately emerge from a codification of gentler treatment for slaves, it was flexible paternalism that made the Spanish imperial system so effective. Slaves appealed to the authorities not as an act of resistance, but as part of an ongoing negotiation of the precise contours of the master/slave relationship.[35]

Although María Manuel's lack of sexual purity—which she openly acknowledged before the governor—certainly did not work in her favor, her sexual activity did not become an important topic in the documentation. Instead, the inquisitors took advantage of her alleged non-Christianity to justify her summary banishment. However, in the face of institutional rivalries between the governor and the Holy Office, her experiences were little more than a premise to justify the attacks made by each side in a struggle for local bureaucratic preeminence. María Manuel's master, who was unusually sadistic even for this era, wanted her all to himself—what he viewed as normal privileges for a slave owner—and rightly believed that his position in the Holy Office bureaucracy would protect him from secular laws and even the governor's sanctions. The path to misery for María Manuel was her master's perception that an enslaved woman provided him with an inexpensive and convenient outlet for sexual relations outside official ecclesiastical marriage. Their masters viewed these women as offering less of an emotional and material burden than the free women who might willingly take part in the common practice of informal cohabitation. The paternalism of the highest local authority ultimately did nothing to protect María Manuela or punish her abusers, as male rage and litigious posturing in the end overcame judicial sanctions or any kind of organized criminal case.

All three of these cases involve men who demonstrated a sincere investment in the honor code as an effective way to perpetuate social and racial hierarchies and gender roles, specifically illuminating how inferiors figured in the personal conceptions of Spanish male honor. The merchant Francisco Luis killed Serpa in self-defense, but the brawl initially started with a perceived infringement on Luis's authority over his own slaves and their sexuality. Pérez's bloodthirsty rage derived from his fear and need to control María Manuel's sexual agency. Even don Diego probably viewed the Portuguese, unemployed, sometime merchant's assistant Gaspar as an inferior and a very offensive judge of his young wife's sexuality. Slaves and servants were at the core of an honorable man's understanding of his own sphere of authority and control. A slave was a form of personal property that was effectively alienated from her master when an outsider had sexual relations with her, especially within the household itself. But one suspects that many a master was also affronted that his rivals might imagine they had rights to a slave's body when those rights were the owner's alone, whether or not he made use of them. Sexual jealousy was therefore a likely aspect of the sensitivity a man might have felt when his domestic domain was invaded.

The honor code did not necessarily demand that men needed to make a special effort to constrain their sexual impulses, but they did have to exert themselves to preserve their reputations. Men were sometimes obliged to act violently in response to insults and endeavored to prevent their behavior from causing scandal, rumor, and gossip. Elite men possessed both honor and the means to exploit the law in their favor by asserting their honor in court. In theory, honor was a burden to a man, a moral standard to maintain and to protect the reputation of himself and his household, but in practice, men might act immorally as long as they did not attract too much publicity. Honor was not a code that elite men lived by or aspired to but something invoked after the fact to supplement their self-defense if their acts were prosecuted. When it came to self-defense for criminal acts of violence, honor discourse could be used in an apparently cynical way: men often argued that, due to their honorable lineage, it was simply impossible for them to commit immoral acts. This manipulation of honor does not diminish its power to influence behavior or the law; everyone wanted to possess honor but still felt they could break laws and moral tenets and later call on their honor to prove they did not do the crimes.

In this chapter, we have seen the various ways that men responded to affronts to their personal household honor. No one at the time doubted that men should feel affronted, especially men of quality (in Spanish terms, men addressed as don) but also tradesmen such as Francisco Luis and low-ranking bureaucrats like Pérez. Insulted men reacted with violent acts that were often later excused as inevitable, even by judicial authorities. All of the defendants in this chapter escaped justice with minor, if any, punishments for their alleged crimes of passion or violence done for the sake of honor, but their cases would not have been documented at all if some judicial authority had not taken the victim's side, objecting or protesting violence done in the name of honor or sexual jealousy. In each case, the defense cleverly manipulated colonial law or bureaucratic jurisdictions to lessen their clients' personal repercussions. Each perpetrator found a way to argue that his punishment would somehow undermine fundamental societal structures and thus avoided serious castigation. In all of these cases, the judicial authorities ultimately supported acts of private revenge.[36] Colonial authorities therefore also respected honor when necessary, or overlooked it when that better served their purposes. This proves that understandings of honor played out in politically local and socially circumstantial situations. Opportunism in the court room, ironically, did not undermine honor, at least in the short run; honor was always acknowledged and sometimes strengthened, even when it was used to achieve practical or political goals. Critical to these examples of angry men publicly brawling or privately torturing their inferiors over seemingly trivial honor slights is the disputes' international reverberations and connection to internal bureaucratic rivalries. In a colonial crucible like Cartagena, when Portuguese, Spaniards, Britons, Africans, freedmen, and indigenous men bumped into each other in the already sweltering streets, tempers flared; heated imperial rivalries, local factions, and tense institutional competition fanned the flames. Apparently, spontaneous rage and the rapidly ensuing stabbings, beatings, and cuttings indicated perceived slights to honor but also some of the fundamental fears and fault lines in this empire. The next chapter narrates a random murder tied to honor and sexuality that solidifies this link between conceptions of masculinity and the Spanish empire.

CHAPTER FOUR

IRISH HONOR ON THE SPANISH MAIN

Captain Cornelio Cornelius

CARTAGENA MEN UNDOUBTEDLY ANGERED QUICKLY, AND SOMETIMES they even attacked in defense of their wives' sexual reputations or their rights to control their slaves' sexuality. In 1644, an insult directed at a married Irish woman caused a deadly brawl on the streets of Cartagena. As a result, an epic journey that began in Ireland ended with the shameful death of an Irish man named Captain Cornelio Cornelius.[1] Although his compatriots described Captain Cornelio as a man of great honor, disgrace marked his final hours as he died from an apparent random stabbing while fighting dozens of locals in a drunken public fracas. In this particular case and many others that can be found in the judicial records of viceregal Spanish America, the characterization of a man as honorable in the colonial legal system was a rhetorical strategy that sometimes extended far beyond personal identity into the realm of both local and even trans-Atlantic power struggles. Cartagena's position as a gateway into Spain's South American empire meant personal quarrels potentially had international implications. Imperial rivalries fueled the escalation of perceived personal dishonors into serious conflicts resonating across the Atlantic. At the same time, in the case of Captain Cornelio's murder, what appears to be the legal prosecution of a single violent act was actually a manifestation of the endemic rivalries among Cartagena's elite. In this particular case, foreigners became pawns in the hands of bitter local enemies. Again, a dispute over female sexuality barely disguised local political factionalism and the machinations Carthaginians employed to bring down their enemies through slandering their reputations.

Cornelio's widow, known in Cartagena as doña María Nele, hired local prosecutors to represent her in the trial of don Gonzalo Jimenez Coronel, the local Governor Luis Fernandez de Cordoba's lieutenant, whom she accused of murdering her husband. While on the surface this case appears to be a homicide trial, more accurately it was an attempt by an opposing local political faction to bring down don Gonzalo. For some members of the Cartagena elite, doña María Nele and her murdered husband were useful weapons to be used and discarded, common tactics often deployed in the endless feuds among Cartagena's political, religious, and economic authorities. The story told here will highlight the development of a posthumous portrait of Captain Cornelio as a man who possessed status and honor that the prosecution hoped would transcend nationality. Against the odds of deceptions propagated within the archival documents themselves, the following questions remain: Who was Captain Cornelio Cornelius? How did he end up in Cartagena? What were his experiences in Cartagena and how did they lead to his death? Framing his life in terms of the seventeenth-century Irish and Spanish interactions in Europe helps create a hypothesis about how European events affected individual lives in the Caribbean.

A cast of minor characters emerges behind Captain Cornelio and his wife, including several other Irish visitors to Cartagena, various foreign and local ruffians who took part in the brawl, and the numerous observers who witnessed it as they peered out their windows and balconies. This murder trial illustrates how male honor took a central role in legal disputes but was at the same time supremely fragile, especially in the case of unknown non-Spaniards, even those who claimed an elevated heritage. In this case, honor takes its place among several other fictions to disguise an effort to bring down a local leader. While the facts of don Cornelio's claims to honor based on wealth, lineage, and character are open to debate, these documents expose the prevalence of violence on Cartagena's streets.

During the colonial period (and later), violence was common in Cartagena. This violence was not just the implicit, simmering tensions and abuses normal in an extremely hierarchical society situated not far from rebel slave *palenques*.[2] Nor was it simply the port's vulnerability to fearsome pirate attacks and jealous rival world powers. On the contrary, street brawls, torture, and spontaneous brutality were frequent occurrences in this city. Although officially illegal, nobles protected their right to dueling in early modern Spain. This cultural practice explains many of the skirmishes in Cartagena's streets, including the one that killed Captain Cornelio.[3] Many racially-mixed plebeians fought alongside the Irish captain, proving the ineffectiveness of Crown mandates that forbade nonwhites to carry weapons. For example, one evening in early April 1622, two young slaves engaged in a sword fight. One of these men, sixteen-year-old Juan de Salinas, received a sentence of two hundred lashes and a six-year sentence to hard labor for his involvement in the altercation, despite his elderly master's pleas for lenience.[4] A far more shocking act of spontaneous violence took place in 1628. A ten-year-old Spanish boy, working as a servant to a royal accountant, became enraged at twenty-six-year-old Catalina Angola, a slave in a house he was visiting, because she shoved him outside to do an errand. When she grabbed his arm to push him out of her kitchen, he picked up a knife and stabbed Catalina in her right thigh. A short time later, she died of blood loss.[5] Plebeians were not the only violent perpetrators in this city. Cartagena's Spanish elite also quickly drew their ready-at-hand weapons whenever they sensed a slight to their honor. Because deeply engrained concepts of masculinity sanctioned violence between men to resolve issues of status, the authorities struggled to enforce codified judicial punishments for elite Spaniards involved in duels with their peers.

To return to Captain Cornelio, who was this man and how did he come to perish by bleeding to death on Cartagena's streets? The rather confusing answer is a picaresque tale of persecution and shipwreck gleaned from the accounts given by English and Irish witnesses after his murder, as well as documents previously ratified before the Spanish governor in Santo Domingo. We can piece together various witness statements from the murder trial to create a narration of the hours before Captain Cornelio's death. On May 19, 1644, the captain and several of his compatriots passed approximately three hours at various *pulperías*, or general stores, that sold alcohol with an atmosphere more like a *cantina* or saloon. They drank prodigiously and spent the huge sum of six pesos, or a bit under one English pound, on wine in just one stop. In the Spanish viceroyalties, a poor laborer might not earn this amount in a month, although a miner could earn it in a week.[6] One cup of wine cost a half real in 1656 Cartagena, so spending six pesos adds up to ninety-six drinks in one sitting.[7] Listening to the music of a *tamboril*, or small drum, the men called for numerous toasts and more and more wine until they appeared to be very drunk.

When describing the events leading to Captain Cornelio's murder, Spaniards made a point to emphasize the shocking Irish inebriation. The Spaniards disdained the foreigners and expressed a familiar southern European revulsion toward northern European drinking habits. Several residents of the area observed all the activity in their neighborhood pulperías. Although the Irishman Enrico Chames called this outing at the pulpería just a "trago de vino" (one gulp or a quick drink of wine), the excessive drinking evoked the Spaniards' concern.[8] Don Gregorio de Cañizares noted, "It was a miracle of God that more misery did not come to the Irish and Englishmen because they were so drunk that not a one of them was safe." Captain Juan de Uriarte said the men were so "loaded (*cargados de vino*) that nothing good could come out of it." One doña, giving her account of the events she watched from a balcony, said she could not name these men because they were indistinguishable "people of little importance . . . just Englishmen and drunks."

Drunkenness often leads to violence, especially when these two factors combine with Irish/English hatred and direct insults targeting a man's wife's sexual reputation. During the drinking binge, an Indian boy, who served as a page to don Gonzalo Coronel, allegedly insulted Captain Cornelio. In response, the Irish captain beat the servant on the head with his sword (not stabbing him). Witnesses provided varying accounts, but it seems likely that an Englishman living in don Gonzalo's house persuaded the boy to antagonize Captain Cornelio by calling him a drunk and *cornudo* or a *cuerno* (cuckold). The English visitor painstakingly taught the servant the English words to be sure the Irishman would understand this direct affront to his honor. Some witnesses added that the servant might have even called doña Nele a puta, or whore. Whatever was said was so rude that doña Nele was ashamed to repeat it in her statements, other than alluding to the fact that it was "against the honor of married people."[9]

A man with any sense of personal honor in the seventeenth century had no option but to react with violence to an attack on his wife's sexual behavior. Because the boy was a social and racial inferior, he was not an honorable combatant, and Captain Cornelius could not challenge him to a duel, by definition a contest between men of similar noble rank. Not long after this minor altercation (which ended with only the servant suffering a beating), other men gradually joined the fight, inspired by a Spanish cheer to "kill the heretic cuckolds." Within a short time, many of Cartagena's residents woke from their siestas to the clamor of a large brawl that filled up the entire street and involved up to forty men of "different nations and dresses," as well as locals described as negros and mulatos. During the heat of the fray, the Spanish brawlers made comments such as, "It would be easier just to kill these drunks."[10] The combatants "fought furiously" with swords, daggers, stones, and pikes, until Captain Cornelio was mortally wounded.[11]

The Irishmen who spoke during the trial alleged that don Gonzalo Coronel was enraged at the foreigner for beating his servant. They assumed that don Gonzalo ordered another one of his lackeys to "kill that drunk." The prime suspects for the murder were two young brothers, a soldier and a sailor from Andalusia, who accompanied don Gonzalo during the fight. One of them may have attacked don Cornelio on their master's orders. Several locals reported seeing one of don Gonzalo's servants fleeing the brawl with his "espada desnuda."[12] After receiving a wound to his stomach made by a sharp instrument, don Cornelio was carried into the pulpería. He also had wounds in his face, probably caused by unarmed combatants throwing stones. Nicholas Brogan testified that he heard don Cornelio beg for last rites, crying out "Jesus protect my soul, they have killed me." Doña Nele ran in moaning, "My husband is dead!" According to the Scot Diego Hay, Cornelio responded with his final breath, "Goodbye, woman, and may God have mercy on your soul."[13]

In all of their interactions with Spanish bureaucrats, both Captain Cornelio and his wife doña Nele emphasized the Irishman's honor, nobility, service, Catholicism, and status as an innocent victim in hopes of gaining favor amongst the Spanish, drawing on decades of military and diplomatic relations between the two countries. Unfortunately for doña Nele's cause, by 1644, this symbiotic relationship had declined because the Spanish crown faced difficulties in funding Irish regiments and no longer trusted in the willingness of Irish aristocrats such as the O'Neill family and the earl of Tyrconnel to remain loyal, amidst rebellion in Ireland and leanings toward the French.[14] On a more personal level, the Spanish had ambivalent feelings toward the Irish veterans and refugees living in Spain. Some of these typical stereotypes resonated with the events on the night of Captain Cornelio's death and with generalizing negative statements directed at the Irish in Cartagena. Regardless of his heritage and claims to dispossessed wealth, don Cornelio's actions and associates appeared lowly and dishonorable to Cartagena observers. Spaniards had little difficulty respecting and, when possible, aiding aristocratic and clerical Irishmen, in keeping with their highly stratified social structure. However, the perception existed that the Irish boasted too much of their status, and even aristocrats could not assume they would receive Spanish patronage especially if their claims to be Catholic martyrs did not ring true. *Madrileños* viewed Irish vagabonds as a nuisance in their city in the 1610s and 1620s. Commentators such as Quevedo and others went so far as to characterize the poorer Irish residents of Madrid as prostitutes, drunks, and beggars. Despite the local patronage Captain Cornelio received from the former governor of Cartagena and his posthumous claims to the trappings of honor, the Irish travelers' behavior on the day in question mortally offended Cartagena's residents.

Cartagena only had a small Irish community in contrast to Madrid. In Cartagena, Spanish attitudes toward the Irish bordered on the intolerant, despite the high status of some of the foreigners. It is no surprise that these *naufragios* tended to band together. Besides Captain Cornelio and doña María Nele, a former governor's Irish wife named María Roche, and several other Irishmen lived in Cartagena at this time, along with three Englishmen and a handful of Scotsmen, who made up the small local contingent from the British Isles. Among the Scots, only Diego Hay was actually identified by name. As described above, an unnamed Englishman may have stoked the simmering flames of the Anglo/Irish tensions, ultimately causing Captain Cornelio's death. Another resident Englishman was a surgeon known as Juan de Eles, who appears in this case often as the interpreter for the non-Spanish speaking witnesses. The Irishmen involved in the case were Antonio Li, Leonisio Matias, Tadeo O'Brien, Phelipe Reyli (who served as an interpreter for the Englishman Andres Hernriques), Diego Cheli, Baltasar Geraldino, Cornelius Grifa, Terencio de Alin, Guillermo Casis, Nicholas Brogan, and Enrique Chames. These men were either part of Captain Cornelio's shipwrecked escape from St. Christopher or possibly remnants or hangers-on from the recently captured English settlement on Providencia Island. An Irish friar named Diego de la Cruz, active in Nicaragua, personally assisted doña María Nele in translating her judicial interactions. Despite the presence of a numerous Irish Catholic clerics in the Spain and its empire, both in Santo Domingo and Cartagena, Spaniards distrusted the authenticity of Irish and Englishmen's Catholic faith, even when these individuals made the effort to learn the catechism and receive baptism. In the mid-seventeenth century, specific clerics and the Cartagena tribunal of the Holy Office made a special effort to seek out and proselytize to Protestants, even those permitted to reside temporarily in the city as merchants.[15]

But what was Captain Cornelio doing in Cartagena on the day he was murdered? The archival documents present one version of his biography, background, and the events of his life that eventually led to his murder. For reasons that will become clear below, Captain Cornelio and a handful of his compatriots made a statement before the Santo Domingo governor in February 1644. According to notarized documents, Captain Cornelio was a nobleman "born into one of the most illustrious Irish families."[16] He was a good Catholic who served His Majesty "with much approbation" as an infantry captain for several years at Dunkirk; because these statements were composed and written down by Spanish notaries, the inference here is that His Majesty is the king of Spain. During the trial of his murderer, Irish witnesses testified through interpreters that Captain Cornelio's noble surname indicated that he came from the "best blood in Ireland."[17] Several witnesses acknowledged that Captain Cornelio held judicial offices in Ireland. Somewhat complicating the Spanish focus of his military service, the Irish witness Leonisio Matias (a friend of the captain since the early 1620s) claimed that Captain Cornelio served in the "armada de San Martin" under the king of England in the war against France. This statement probably refers to the Duke of Buckingham's unsuccessful 1627 assault on the citadel of St. Martin on the Isle of Rhé.[18]

The biography presented to the authorities continues with Captain Cornelio's immigration to the Indies. At some point in the late 1620s or 1630s, he chose to settle in St. Christopher, where his wife had their son sometime in the mid-1630s. His estate in St. Christopher allegedly added up to 300,000 reales, or several thousand English pounds worth, of land, slaves, silver, and jewelry.[19] Specifically, according to Leonisio Matias and Tadeo O'Brien, Captain Cornelio had sixteen slaves and two priests working as part of his domestic entourage in St. Christopher.[20] Of vital importance for the Spanish was the assertion that Captain Cornelio was a pious and devout Catholic Christian who had priests say mass at his home.[21]

Captain Cornelio enjoyed his prosperity for only a very short time before suffering several tragic events that led up to his untimely end. First, in Captain Cornelio's version of events (as noted, this version was ratified in a document in Santo Domingo before he died), in 1639, the English Parliament decreed that all Irish Catholics must renounce their faith and swear loyalty to the Church of England or suffer banishment from St. Christopher, Barbados, and Montserrat within forty days, along with confiscation of all of their belongings. Captain Cornelio and doña María Nele affirmed that they chose to remain true to their Catholic faith, losing all of their property to flee with one hundred other Irishmen and sixty Irish women. Some of these individuals may have been free people of color. The couple claimed they made the immense sacrifice of leaving their five-year-old son behind, risking that he would become a Protestant, seduced by English proselytizers. They did not explain why they made this choice. But that decision [may have?] ended up saving the boy's life, because, allegedly, nearly three quarters of the fugitives died during the journey. The 160 original refugees left St. Christopher on a ship fortified with artillery, aiming for St. Martin and then Puerto Rico. Tragically, the boat capsized on a place the Irish called *cabo de Tiburon*, or "Sharks' Cape," a rocky and dangerous embarkation point located on what is now the southern coast of Haiti. A total of 117 Irish men and women perished in the shipwreck and the ensuing difficult and mountainous overland trek through territory sparsely populated by French buccaneers. Only forty-three of the refugees managed to cross the island to their destination of Spanish Santo Domingo, where they appealed to King Philip IV of Spain's mercy and protection through the local governor. A group of the surviving men, along with doña María Nele, traveled to Cartagena in order to embark on the next ship leaving for Seville, carrying the official documents narrating this baroque story that they had presented before the governor of Santo Domingo. After a short stay in the port, Captain Cornelio embroiled himself in a public altercation and died by stabbing.

So ends the tragic life of the noble captain. But can we trust this narrative? Before addressing the specifics, this story should be placed in the context of Anglo and Irish persecution/victimization narratives of the 1640s, when a small group of exiled Irish successfully made claims on the Spanish monarch Phillip IV based on a self-presentation of abuse by the English.[22] In line with Captain Cornelio's self-presentation before the Santo Domingo governor, seventeenth-century displaced Irishmen petitioned for patronage from the Spanish king in exchange for their military service in Spain's overextended European theaters of war and even influenced Spanish policies.[23] According to his autobiography as presented to Spanish colonial authorities, Captain Cornelio was precisely the kind of person who could help Spain's military endeavors, and, in fact, he had a record of loyal military service, along with approximately 6,300 other Irishmen who served in Flanders between 1586 and 1621.[24] Continuing his previous service to the Spanish crown even after his tragic shipwreck and Caribbean odyssey, Captain Cornelio officially held the office of a soldier in the Cartagena presidio.

Although Captain Cornelio was not Spanish, he formulated a persona, which his wife maintained after his death, meeting the key requirements for masculine honor according to essential Spanish values. It was necessary to build up don Cornelio's honorable status by speaking of his known wealth, social stature, nobility, service to his crown, and Catholicism. Captain Cornelio, or don Cornelio in the Spanish documentation, did not come from a lineage familiar to Spaniards in Cartagena (although it was perhaps well known in Madrid), but his friends attested to his nobility and Catholic Christianity. In their testimonies, Irishmen living in Cartagena reached back to the captain's past in Europe to prove his status and Catholic faith. It was critical to prove that he was not Protestant, since then the Spaniards would judge him a heretic.[25] Captain Cornelio's narrative follows a familiar model of seeking Spanish patronage by claiming martyr-like status due to Catholic tenacity in the face of English persecution. From the Spanish perspective, was Captain Cornelio as honorable as he claimed to be in all the more trivial particulars of public presentation? Spaniards testified that he was "calm and peaceful" in demeanor and courteously removed his hat when passing their houses. He attended mass at the Santo Domingo church and carried his rosary.[26]

Even with the essential elements of wealth, Catholicism, nobility, and military service in place, Captain Cornelio's foreign status offered a challenge for asserting true honor in a Spanish context. However, the captain and his allies benefited from the special status Irish aristocrats enjoyed from Spaniards dating to the sixteenth century. In this era where lineage and limpieza de sangre bolstered a man's claims to honor, Irish nobles argued for a common racial ancestry between Spain and Ireland, through descent from "the ancient Spanish princely house of Milesius."[27] Backed by this contention, they could take advantage of all the privileges unavailable to any foreigner or other person whose heritage suggested non-Christian origins or a lack of limpieza de sangre. The common Spanish use of the honorific term don before his first name proves that Cornelio had firmly established his honorable status in Cartagena.

Whatever his background, Captain Cornelio and doña María Nele succeeded in entering elite Cartagena society. Coincidentally enough, at this time a representative of an Irish family who had successfully integrated into Spanish courtly life lived in Cartagena. Doña María Roche—the wife of a recent Cartagena governor, Melchor de Aguilera (who held the post from 1638 to 1641)—was Irish-born, so doña Nele and Captain Cornelio lived in her home. Doña María Roche's family, including her brothers, parents, and sons, lived in Madrid or served in the Spanish military or the Catholic Church. Her family actively fulfilled this era's symbiotic relationship of diplomacy and patronage between Irish aristocrats and the king of Spain. Captain Cornelio and doña Nele also hoped to access this network for their own benefit. Doña María Roche traveled with her husband in Europe for administrative posts in Italy and France, eventually settling in Cartagena. Her daughter doña Teresa also married into the high Spanish bureaucracy, in this case a governor of New Mexico.[28]

It is even possible, given that his wife was known as doña María Nele (perhaps a Hispanized pronunciation of O'Neill), that Captain Cornelio and his wife had familial ties with the most prominent Irish noble family affiliated with the king of Spain beginning in the late sixteenth century *and* the leaders of the 1641 Irish rebellion—a connection that would perhaps explain his questionable wanderings in the 1640s. The O'Neill family founded the first specifically Irish regiment in the Spanish Army in 1606. The name "Cornelio Cornelius" is even more mysterious, although the utterly non-Spanish name Cornelius seems to have been rather common among the Irish who affiliated themselves with Spain in the 1600s.[29] "De-Latinizing" this name reduces it to "Cornell Cornell" (or perhaps Connor).[30] Is it feasible that Captain Cornelio was of the aristocratic Tyrconnell family, who represented "the most illustrious Irish émigrés welcomed in seventeenth-century Spain" along with the O'Neills?[31] These conjectures seem less unfounded when we remember that several witnesses claimed Captain Cornelio's name proved that he was related to the best and most noble Irish families. Whatever the case, don Cornelio's life story, as officially documented by the Spanish authorities in Santo Domingo and Cartagena, was full of historical inaccuracies.

Doña Nele's most likely exaggerated claims to property and wealth were another attempt to bolster Captain Cornelio's status and honor after his death in hopes of further patronage from the local representatives of the Spanish crown. Doña Nele and her allies reiterated these embellished claims to honorable status in order to emphasize the seriousness of the captain's murder. Of course, the witnesses for the prosecution told this story to encourage both pity and respect for the tragic but noble victim and his innocent wife. Historical evidence suggests their claims were inaccurate. Even if Captain Cornelio came from a wealthy Irish landowning family, his settlement in the Caribbean suggests dispossession and the unlikelihood of retaining such a large inheritance. It is possible that Captain Cornelio came from a group of noble Irish families who left Waterford county and had to settle in St. Christopher because Virginia rejected them. Irish settlers started farming tobacco in St. Christopher in the mid-1620s, struggling with raiding Caribs and Spaniards, along with poor soil conditions. In 1639, a crown edict attempted unsuccessfully to diversify crops on St. Christopher away from total dependence on tobacco.[32] By 1639, roughly 2,000 Irish settlers lived in St. Christopher.[33] Irish settlers predominated in nearby Montserrat, including Irish governors.[34]

These people were generally poor servants without claim to land. In 1627, a Scottish nobleman named the Earl of Carlisle received from the English King Charles I a "quasi-feudal" patent controlling land ownership in all of the Leeward Islands (St. Kitts, Barbados, Montserrat, and Nevis, among others).[35] This meant that settlers were tenants, not freeholders, on their estates. Even without this issue, given the conditions on these islands in the late 1620s, it is not believable that Captain Cornelio could accumulate or retain so much wealth at this unstable stage of Caribbean history unless he belonged to one of the few families that controlled the land holdings on these islands. However, although a handful of aristocrats like Carlisle, including men with Irish and Scottish connections, made claim to large portions of England's New World Empire in the 1620s to the 1640s, they rarely lived in or even visited their holdings. No aristocrats lived in the English colonies and "even gentlefolk were somewhat thin on the colonial ground." Most settlers sold "all they had" to relocate to the Americas or signed on for terms of indentured servitude.[36]

Because his biographical account contains certain fundamental inaccuracies, it is more likely that Captain Cornelio had to flee St. Christopher for reasons that he chose not to reveal to Spanish officials. The documents do not clearly state this, but his itinerant lifestyle may be more directly related to the Irish rebellion of 1641 than his untrue claims suggest. Irish Catholics living on St. Christopher at this time expressed sympathy with the Spanish, which might have motivated don Cornelio's decision to flee to Santo Domingo instead of Maryland.[37] Rumor had it that some of the Irishmen who ended up in Cartagena "voluntarily spent a great deal of time among rebels and enemies of the (English) crown who infested the waters around St. Kitts."[38] However, despite rebellious tendencies, Irish Catholics in St. Christopher were not evicted shortly after the rebellion but in fact welcomed continuing Catholic clerical missions.[39] In general, Atlantic colonists did not involve themselves in the rebellions of the 1640s, reacting with passivity to appeasing or reforming political gestures from both king and parliament.[40]

The English Parliament did not sit from 1629 to 1640, so Captain Cornelio and his friends certainly did not evince much respect for Spanish knowledge of current events in the British Isles by swearing before the governor of Santo Domingo that a 1639 parliamentary decree evicted them from the English Caribbean. From late 1641 to early 1642, the English Parliament gradually developed a plan for confiscating the estates of Irish rebels and using these new found assets to finance a war against the rebels.[41] It is possible that Captain Cornelio, in an attempt to absolve himself from any implied rebellious activity, based his erroneous claims regarding a 1639 decree on this later occurrence. If don Cornelio was a dispossessed Irish landlord, he may have been affected by 1642 parliamentary orders to arrest certain important Catholics and confiscate their estates.[42]

The testimonies do not explain how Captain Cornelio and the other refugees acquired their armed boat, but they were not the only desperate escapees (and possible boat thieves) who sailed from St. Christopher and other English colonies in the mid-seventeenth century. Given the boasting regarding his assets, it seems unlikely, but not entirely impossible, that Captain Cornelio was one of the many Irish or English debtors who fled St. Christopher in the early 1640s for non-English Caribbean islands.[43] Further dishonorable activity (at least in the Spanish view) took place in St. Christopher and the surrounding seas with the 1642 actions of the pirate William Jackson, who took hundreds of volunteers—including fleeing debtors—on this island and Barbados on raiding and marauding expeditions in Spanish Central America and Jamaica. Admittedly, Jackson would not appeal to an allegedly pious man such as Captain Cornelio, since he purposefully despoiled "Catholic religious objects in settlements he attacked."[44] Captain Cornelio and the other Irish/English and Scotsmen residing in 1640s Cartagena also may have had some affiliation with the nearby Providence Island colony (or Santa Catalina, now Colombian territory). The English attempted a settlement there, but Spanish forces led by an Irish military leader ejected them in 1634. The English returned, along with African slaves, but the Spanish permanently dispersed them in 1641, possibly imprisoning some of them in Cartagena jails. The Spanish confiscated all English property and forced the Anglo settlers to leave within ten days, terms oddly similar to Captain Cornelio's claims.[45] The discontented Irish, possibly including Captain Cornelio, living on St. Christopher in the 1630s and 1640s also appealed to the monarchs of Spain and Portugal for permission to settle outside English territory.[46] Captain Cornelio and doña Nele chose not to mention peaceful petitions or criminal suspicions, instead playing on Spanish anti-English sentiments with a story of abuse at the hands of the English.[47]

Every one of dozens of witnesses offered a different perspective on the events leading to Captain Cornelio's death, but the best support doña Nele had for her accusation were the vague statements made by fellow English speakers. The prosecution's case took the angle, partially influenced by doña Nele's need to reinforce her own vulnerable position, of emphasizing the seriousness of killing a man with Captain Cornelio's degree of honor and noble blood. This was a difficult task, since how could locals judge an impoverished foreigner's status? The Spanish prosecutor himself understood the value placed on honor in his own society and certainly was familiar with using the rhetoric of the honor code to advance a client's case. It is harder to ascertain if the prosecutor actually believed in Cornelio's status, especially given the corruption that saturated this particular trial. The witnesses for the prosecution attempted to create and document a highly reputable, wealthy, upper class background for a man whose actions and experiences suggested he was actually a very marginal individual both in Ireland and the circum-Caribbean.

But the defense employed its own tactics to undermine this heart-stirring biography by exposing the story as coming from highly untrustworthy sources and emphasizing the good character of the defendant. It is not surprising that the accused don Gonzalo Coronel, age thirty, presented his side of the events very differently than the non-Spaniards. In his statements, don Gonzalo showed very little respect for doña Nele, referring to her simply as "the foreigner who claims to have been married to don Cornelio." He repeatedly pointed out that none of the untrustworthy, foreign witnesses could identify don Gonzalo as the murderer by name. Instead, each witness simply repeated again and again that a man wearing black was fighting close to the Irish captain shortly before his death. The Spanish-speaking witnesses also made this observation. Local Spaniards did not slander the victim but in fact praised Irish loyalty and military service to the Spanish crown. Don Gonzalo's testimony and the witnesses who spoke on the part of the don stressed his peaceful, respectable, and honorable actions and status. The accused did admit that he had an Englishmen living in his house for the alleged purpose of instructing him in Catholicism, but don Gonzalo said he would never have such a rude servant, and if someone hit his servant over an insult, it was beneath his dignity to pay any attention to such a "boyish thing."[48]

On the day of the fight, don Gonzalo claimed he was sitting at home unoccupied, a peaceful, honorable man untouched by plebeian street activities. He sent a message to a friend (who happened to be a knight of Calatrava), asking if they might meet to play a game of chess. Don Gonzalo left his house without his sword, since he claimed to never walk around carrying weapons, given his non-military career and training. He noticed a small fight of four or five men and thought, "it was of little importance," since it was only one of four violent mêlées that took place in Cartagena's streets between noon and 3:30 p.m. that day. Anyone walking outside in the blazing tropical noon sun undoubtedly was either drunk or irrational and volatile enough to easily start a fight. He and his small entourage tried to separate some of the men, but as they did, more and more men began fighting, including the Irishmen who were savagely attacking the Spaniards. Since don Gonzalo had no weapon, he persistently tried to stop the fight just using his hands. All of his witnesses said that he was at least several paces away from don Cornelio during the entire scuffle. Despite this strong defense, the governor sentenced don Gonzalo to two years' banishment and a fine of 2,000 pesos. Around this time, don Gonzalo also faced censure for his marriage to a local woman, so it is likely that the whole case simply served to hasten his political disgrace.[49]

Don Gonzalo advanced his case for appeal (which he brought before the Bogota audiencia high court) significantly by exposing a bribery scheme among some of the English-speaking witnesses. Allegedly, the English surgeon Juan de Eles had offered various other English and Irish speakers sums up to 150 pesos to testify against don Gonzalo. Eles often served as a Spanish-English translator for the witnesses, which also seemed very suspicious to the defense. Don Gonzalo called on other prisoners to speak as witnesses to the bribery—but since they did not speak English, they testified that they learned what was going on by reading signs and gestures. One Englishman supposedly said he refused to lie, even if it meant decapitation, because he was a Christian.[50] Doña Nele had to undergo handwriting and oral examinations to prove if she actually signed and/or understood any of the statements made on her behalf in Spanish. Ultimately, she admitted that she encouraged the witness collusion, claiming she was a victim of local backstabbing and political maneuvering common among her elite patrons, in an effort to disgrace don Gonzalo.

This summary only scratches the surface of the complex maneuverings of doña Nele's advocate and the local authorities as they took advantage of a possibly random killing to bring down don Gonzalo, with the help of don Gonzalo Coronel's enemy the local official Diego de Mesa. In the end, as part of his appeal before the Bogota audiencia, don Gonzalo convinced doña Nele to admit that her side had framed him. As a socially and politically weak foreign woman, doña Nele had to confront the fictitious web she and her local and foreign allies had spun in hopes of avenging her husband's death. While it seems clear that witnesses' vague claims that don Gonzalo had assaulted don Cornelio were outright lies, no one involved openly questioned the narrative device of framing the unknown Irish captain's biography as a story of tragically insulted honor. This is a testament to the usefulness of the rhetoric of honor in a judicial context, as well as the strong diplomatic relationship between Spain and Ireland in the 1600s. The ultimate lack of success in winning doña Nele's case against don Gonzalo testifies to the sharp decline in this relationship by the 1640s. Male jockeying for position in a competitive society and its implications for transatlantic empires overshadow the initial motivation to violence here: the insult to doña Nele's sexual reputation. The next chapter presents another case of the tempestuous combination of honor, sex, violence, and politics in mid-seventeenth century Cartagena.

CHAPTER FIVE

MARRIAGE, SEX, LOVE, AND POLITICS

IN COLONIAL CARTAGENA, PRIVATE LIVES AND THE COLONIAL COURTS intersected via the rhetoric of honor and the hazy, disputed boundaries between licit and illicit sex. Court records show that colonial women were at least exposed to, and sometimes able to enjoy, a less limited range of sexual behavior than might first be assumed by studying the moralizing literature of the day. While some decisions regarding sex went terribly wrong and led to murder, imprisonment, or inquisition trials, others ended less badly. Married and unmarried women did conduct affairs or intimate friendships with eligible men in the privacy of their own homes. This chapter will explore two linked litigations that tie together themes of female negotiation of marriage, sex, love, and politics, and the conflicts these created when they ran up against men's sense of personal honor. In these intertwined examples, both taken from 1642, a patriarch followed a judicial path to retribution and did not resort to violence as he defended his right to control the intimate lives of both his niece and his female slave. The first case suggests the possibility of a loving marriage with an elite woman freely choosing her spouse, challenging historical generalizations about the potential for marital love in this era. In the second case, which took place in the same household, this elite woman's slave and her sexuality became pawns in a male game of political posturing and disputes over honor.

Was a loving marriage possible in colonial Cartagena? The available documentation suggests that Cartagena men and women sought passionate love in different contexts than the romantic ideal of loving spouses that we cherish today. This also holds true for other regions, as historians of Latin America have not found traces of the idea of affectionate love within marriage until the nineteenth century. A study of marital love in colonial Latin America shows that:

> Individuals sometimes used words such as love, affection, and esteem when commenting on spousal responsibilities and family structure.... Women demonstrated their love by undertaking household chores and respecting a man's right to make final decisions, whereas men demonstrated their love by providing economically for the family and administering household authority.... In short, marital love demanded that spouses assume gendered obligations.[1]

Although these statements present a bleak or banal picture of colonial marital affection (perhaps because the documentation comes from records of violent crime), the authors of this study found expressions of love in around 20 percent of the trials they researched. Sadly, these expressions are not linked to happy marriages: for example, a man who murdered his wife in a drunken rage confessed that he "'loved her dearly.'"[2] Apparently, only after independence and the birth of romanticism did individuals express "a more abstract concept that included emotional satisfaction and an enlightened sense of fairness."[3] Divorce cases in the late colonial and early national periods of Mexico also contain expressions of romantic love in the nineteenth century.[4] However, Spanish ecclesiastical court cases involving male impotence in the seventeenth and eighteenth centuries indicate that "the marriages that early modern Spaniards idealized were to be affectionate and sexual." Guido Ruggiero comes to a similar conclusion in his study of late medieval Venice.[5]

In New Spanish archival cases documenting prenuptial disputes, litigants often expressed their desire to marry a certain individual without reference to the word *amor*. In the medieval Spanish tradition, love meant a loss of will and self-control—indeed a kind of madness—while in the early modern era, marrying for love came eventually to be thought of as an expression of free will. Still, couples continued to express their desire to marry an otherwise unsuitable partner by invoking the need to protect female virtue and honor. Patricia Seed believes that in the eighteenth century, ideas about love and marriage changed again, reverting back to the vision of love as an insane and impracticable passion.[6] This chronology is difficult to trace for Cartagena since some women and men desired love or sex outside or within the bounds of marriage in all eras. Other historians emphasize marital love as either an eighteenth- or nineteenth-century occurrence, implying it was less common in previous eras.[7]

Spanish siglo de oro literature provides a great deal of information relating to sex and love; although, as in the case of honor killings, fiction may represent unrealizable ideals more than documented practice. Early modern poetry offers countless examples of masculine expressions of love, but literary scholars working on earlier eras have struggled to find manifestations of female subjectivity, love, and desire in literature until the sixteenth-century writings of Teresa of Avila, the work of the great seventeenth-century Mexican poet Sor Juana Inéz de la Cruz, and in María de Zayas y Sotomayor's seventeenth-century "Exemplary tales of love."[8] Literary scholars describe Zayas' poetic strategies toward love as "acceptance, adaptation, or subversion of the established masculine discourses . . . by repeatedly emphasizing feminine constancy and masculine fickleness." In some of her work, we can find reflections of the experiences related in this book because Zayas emphasizes fulfillment of love and "sexual satisfaction" as "fantasies that must be lived through in some form, but she represents marriage more often as a way station or a literal dead end, not a happy ending for her female protagonists."[9] Despite this uninspiring prognosis for marriage, love and desire remain fundamental to her work. In contrast, citing Lope de Vega and Cervantes among others, Seed notes that an ideal of marriage for love did exist in early modern Spain, although it is certainly debatable if this fictional ideal for the wellborn carried through into daily life in colonial Latin America.[10] Confessional manuals from this era also spoke of love as an ideal for married couples.

One young woman in colonial Cartagena believed in an ideal, loving marital relationship. In 1642, Ana de Bolívar's mother, the widow of a royal accountant, and Ana's uncle don Pedro, a military captain and knight of the prestigious Order of Santiago, made a criminal complaint accusing don Diego Ortiz de la Maza of breaking into their house to seduce the young woman under their care.[11] Under the gaze of several slaves, the two lovers allegedly contrived to marry without telling Ana's mother or uncle. Although doña Ana's guardians had not given their approval, the matrimony took place on March 9 in the cathedral, with two priests acting as witnesses, but without the customary three announcements or marriage bans. Instead of challenging don Diego to a duel, doña Ana's male protector don Pedro chose to use the courts as a way of defending personal honor and strengthening his patriarchal control over the domestic realm. A man of honor took a risk in resorting to legal action against his transgressor, rather than erupting in "spontaneous" violence, suggesting a certain lack of authenticity to his outrage. But, of course, even in a world regulated by honor and acceptance of anger and outrage as sparks for violence, men felt different degrees of personal affront and might respond immediately at the scene or later in court. Each method helped solidify the fact that his personal honor extended from the sexual behavior of his dependents.

As don Diego's legitimate wife, doña Ana protested the prosecution of her husband. However, her guardians insisted that don Diego had committed a crime by sneaking into the house and persuading doña Ana to marry him with his "gallantries" (*galanteos*). The complainants stressed the usual rhetoric of male offended honor and, ignoring doña Ana's decisive behavior, female sexual passivity. They did not wish to portray her as a sexual actor within the context of this judicial process, despite the fact that she arranged her own marriage in line with her emotions and desires. Doña Ana's mother and uncle instead argued that it was illegal to enter a house "with the goal of marriage against the will of her owners, parents, and brothers because this is an atrocious crime . . . and an obvious offence to procure by such illicit and reprobate methods to subdue the will of prominent and secluded *doncellas*." Again stressing her position as a secluded virgin, they pointed out that doña Ana was a minor younger than twenty-five years old and still under the "dominion of her parents and the enclosure of her secure house." Calling on both canon law and social hierarchies, the guardians complained that don Diego's deceptions went against the decrees of the Council of Trent and were harmful to the family's reputation. They were especially criminal due to her "noble quality . . . known throughout the city."[12] In support of the inequality and status discrepancy between the two, a witness mentioned that others in doña Ana's social circle were dismayed that the couple "went about as lovers . . . considering the reputation and relatives that [doña Ana] has."[13] The guardians' dissatisfaction came from doña Ana organizing her own marriage based on personal affections, even if they presented don Diego as the aggressor. In her petitions, doña Ana tried to counter these reproaches by repeatedly stressing that no crime had been committed, since now she was a "legitimate wife." She cited "a newer royal law that favors marriage, especially because I am older than twenty." She believed, with good reason given the backstabbing and competitive political climate in colonial Cartagena, that her husband's enemies (including her own uncle don Pedro) masterminded the dispute.

As this case involved a private seduction, domestic slaves represented the best possible witnesses. Since we know that doña Ana and don Diego did marry, the accounts of their developing affair as witnessed by household slaves ring true. Obviously, the couple did have to discuss their elopement, and other than using messengers, the best place for making these arrangements was doña Ana's house. Several slave women owned by either don Pedro or doña Ana's mother testified to observing the couple interacting inside the uncle's house, where Ana was visiting her sister (who was married to don Pedro, following the incestuous example of seventeenth-century Spanish monarchs). Several female slaves reported that one afternoon, doña Ana and don Diego spoke together in the sala. Doña Ana sat on the window seat and her *novio* occupied a chair close to her. A few days later, fifty-year-old María Arara, eighteen-year-old Isabelica Bioho, sixteen-year-old Ana Criolla, and twenty-year-old Agustina Criolla (María Arara's daughter), saw don Diego wearing a red cape and carrying his unsheathed sword, as he climbed the stairs to the second floor of the house and later sat, resting on the stairs. María Arara confronted don Diego, asking him what he was doing in "a house full of girls at this hour of the night because this would go very badly for him." Don Diego said doña Ana sent for him and they were planning to marry.[14] Clearly, doña Ana was a willing partner in this plan, regardless of the image of innocence her guardians chose to create for the purposes of litigation.

Doña Ana's guardians called on other witnesses outside their home to prove that unacceptable acts of seduction had taken place. But what emerges instead is that the young couple courted each other and organized their own personal lives, acting against familial pressures by choosing to marry for love, sexual attraction, or simply because they desired it. Their love affair was common knowledge: witnesses testified that doña Ana came up in a conversation between two lieutenants who were chatting about "women and bachelors [*mancebos*] in this city." In the course of the conversation, one of the soldiers wondered why don Diego, who was "so diligent, had not married." The other replied, "He has not married because he is very ambitious." When the lieutenant revealed that don Diego targeted doña Ana, his companion said, "How can he do this, since she is such a secluded [recogida] girl?"[15] Despite this conventional assessment of doña Ana's character and way of life, the soldiers went on to discuss the notes that were passed between the two with the help of a slave. A soldier who served with don Diego said that he saw doña Ana gesticulating to don Diego at a window. Witnesses also noted that doña Ana, in a loving gesture, sent don Diego a green belt in which she had embroidered their names in pink silk thread. Don Diego wore this thoughtful handmade gift out to fiestas, publicly admitting that they were in love with the display of his intimate and romantic keepsake.

Shortly after these statements were made, the governor organized a group of armed men to go to don Diego's house, arrest him, and put him in prison. But don Diego had already taken refuge with the friars of San Agustin. In this situation, all the secular authorities could do was confiscate his possessions and offer a 500 peso reward for anyone who apprehended him when he went outside the church. The town crier publicized the reward offer in the major streets and plazas of the city.[16] The fact that doña Ana's uncle made another complaint about the defloration of his slave Agustina on the exact same day that he started the case involving his niece suggests that all of this was part of a larger conspiracy to bring down certain elements in Cartagena's military and local government, a theory in fact proposed by doña Ana herself. Once again, female sexuality played a central role in political machinations.

Doña Ana and don Diego's experiences illustrate the challenges of marrying for love in this era. Married people did not necessarily associate love and sexual fulfillment with their spouses in the seventeenth century, and these attitudes continued to the eighteenth century. However, this example proves that, although they faced challenges from the older adults in their life, some elite young men and women did choose their own spouses inspired by feelings of affection. Even young women publicly known as recogida found opportunities to court their novios through romantic, loving gestures, such as a personally embroidered belt.

Almost simultaneous to his niece's elopement, don Pedro also claimed that the *alcalde ordinario* don Juan Cabrillo Albornoz invaded his house and seduced his young slave Agustina.[17] Don Pedro alleged that don Juan then continued to enter his house regularly to engage in a long-term relationship with Agustina.[18] Agustina certainly had a very different experience than doña Ana of sexual agency and the potential for marriage. At first glance, the defloration case brought forward by don Pedro suggests a master paternalistically protecting his slave and her sexuality. In fact, the case revolved around the master's desire to use the judiciary to reassert his authority over his household. Unfortunately, we can learn very little about Agustina's legal self-presentation and negotiation of her own sexuality in this case, because the court scribes recorded only her barest testimony. Only two witnesses briefly mentioned her doncella status in passing, although the virginity of the complainant was usually a subject of extensive debate from numerous angles and witnesses in most estupro cases.

Instead, we learn a great deal about how her master don Pedro considered protecting Agustina's presumed virginity and the inviolability of his house as fundamental weapons for aggressively asserting his own personal honor, his local factional affiliation, and political alliances. Along with his dispute with doña Ana and don Diego, this case contributes to don Pedro's strategy to promote and defend his reputation and forms part of a larger disagreement between various elite men. Sex was at the center of their public rivalries, a common way to do political business in colonial Cartagena. As we know, don Pedro also claimed that his niece had been seduced out from under his control by another man in his own home, although the evidence suggests that doña Ana and her lover don Diego eloped as a result of an actual love affair and romantic courtship. In initiating judicial actions accusing two different men of deflowering two women under his protection, don Pedro publicized female sexuality and the tensions that came as a result of a woman choosing her own spouse. However, both alleged male seducers claimed that don Pedro made these complaints only out of political enmity arising from support for the election campaigns of opposing alcaldes.

In contrast to doña Ana's ability to arrange her own marriage, Agustina's case indicates no hope for love or marriage. Instead, it supports the argument that women's sex lives were eminently political. Far from being secluded or jealously guarded, female sex and sexual reputation were popular tools to publicly manipulate status, including in the political realm. This should come as no surprise, given the centrality of sexuality in asserting the Spanish monarch's domination, dating back at least to the infamous, so-called Enrique el Impotente. Sex scandals were common, not exceptional, tools in factional disputes. Working within the legal traditions and values of their era, Spanish elite men affirmed their masculinity through this judicial context, with more finesse and effectiveness than the cruder, dishonorable methods of brute sexual domination. Clearly, two simultaneous seductions of two different young virgins under his authority or living in his house

represented a serious affront to don Pedro's honor. Surprisingly, sexual reputation and the policing of household sexual activity—on the surface, the
central issues at stake here—actually mattered little to the two Spanish dons
involved in this affair, who expended their efforts instead on other aspects
within honor's broad spectrum. The documents in don Pedro's litigation
emphasize not sexual activity, but the inviolability of the domestic domain
and the rules of etiquette for interactions with the justice system expected
by a man claiming noble status.

It is impossible to know the precise intimate dynamics of Agustina's
relationship to her alleged seducer, the appropriately named don Juan.
Cartagena's history provides several examples of other women of African
descent who complicate stereotypes of persistent sexual victimization to
say the least—the next chapter will present one of the most compelling
examples. One piece of evidence arguing against portraying Agustina as
the familiar vulnerable nonwhite victim is the fact that her fifty-year-old
mother María Arara also lived in this household. This mother emerges
as quite strong and outspoken as a protector of household female sexual
purity in the two separate estupro cases. As mentioned above, when María
encountered don Diego creeping up the stairs to seduce doña Ana, María
claimed she confronted him and assertively asked him what he was doing
and warned him to get out of this house full of young girls.

Much of the evidence suggests that Agustina was bribed with gifts and
galanteos and not forced to have sex with don Juan (although it should be
stressed that the accused in fact denied all of the allegations and may have
been framed by don Pedro). Agustina's dictated statement said that don Juan
"courted" (*requebró de amores*) the young slave, passing her notes through
his page while she attended mass with her mistress at the San Agustín convent. As in many cases of this kind, the documentation suggests that slaves
witnessed and often were complicit in the gradual process of seduction. With
the continued help of his black page Dominguillo, don Juan allegedly used
a gift of a petticoat lined in green taffeta and a letter containing ten pesos to
persuade Agustina to submit to his desires. María Folupa said that she saw
don Juan's young black page asking for Agustina and that don Juan gave
Agustina a cloak lined in green Chinese silk that she claimed was a gift from
the niece doña Ana.[19] Some witnesses said that he loitered suspiciously and
scandalously on the street corner near her house at night with his friend
don Diego, who later eloped with doña Ana. In fact, don Pedro accused
don Juan of seducing Agustina simply so his friend and coconspirator don

Diego could more easily enter the house to make engagement arrangements with doña Ana. The two men were both friends and political allies, and allegedly both of them succeeded in seducing don Pedro's dependents, repeatedly raiding his house, and undermining his authority, status, and, by extension, his political repute and authority. Don Pedro viewed these crimes as severe enough to deserve capital punishment.

After his aforementioned courtship through notes and gifts, don Juan supposedly either bribed or forced Agustina to have sex with him. This led to several months of *amancebamiento*, all taking place at her master's house, often while he was out on guard duty. Several members of the household gave evidence testifying to the fact that don Juan entered don Pedro's home without his consent in order to have sex with Agustina. Don Pedro described the relationship between Agustina and don Juan as "cohabitation" or "concubinage" and claimed that it had lasted over a year. On the nights when don Pedro was on guard duty, don Juan sometimes even spent the entire night in Agustina's company.[20] Agustina said don Juan visited her at night (wearing a cape and carrying an unsheathed sword) until she "conceded to his desire." Don Juan allegedly deflowered her in a small room near a stairwell in her master's house, the same place where Agustina's mother observed don Pedro's niece's lover loitering about. After their initial encounter, don Juan continued to visit Agustina regularly.

Five domestic slaves testified to seeing don Juan in the house. In their statements, they implicated themselves in the affair. For example, the thirty-year-old Domingo Bañón, a slave blinded by small pox, had the duty of locking don Pedro's main door in the evening. One night he "sensed" a stranger in the *zaguan*, discovering shortly thereafter that it was don Juan with Agustina. On this occasion, the alleged seducer bribed Domingo with two reales to use to buy tobacco. Despite the bribe, Domingo claimed he tried to discourage the notes and gifts passed via don Juan's page. He also claimed he heard Agustina resist don Juan. According to Domingo Bañon's quite explicit account, don Juan

> wanted to sleep with Agustina, but she resisted, saying that she was not a *bozal* black woman that one could sleep with right there with him. He was forceful with her, judging from the noise made by the sheath of his sword when it hit the floor.[21]

This testimony highlights several different assertions of slave agency and methods of manipulating and self-presenting in court. Domingo was the only witness who spoke of force in the encounter, force not being an essential component of a successful estupro claim. In this statement, Domingo gave his own take on the classic need to assert Agustina's passivity and victimhood by presenting her as protesting in her own way against having sex with don Juan. After making this statement, Domingo assured the court that he was also not a victim in that his master had not coerced or threatened in him any way to force him to make these damning accusations against don Juan.

This case does not follow the normal patterns for a defloration accusation in other ways as well, because no investigation was made to confirm in any way that Agustina did not have any previous sexual partners. The specifics of her first sexual experience with don Juan were not deeply explored, but the fact that she accepted money and gifts from him would almost automatically negate any sympathy from the court adjudicating an estupro case. Perhaps because she was enslaved and not Spanish, the prosecution did not think to establish her reputation and her eligibility to pursue a defloration accusation, although don Pedro did use all the classic terms familiar from other estupro cases. He asserted that Agustina was a doncella and that don Juan had "enjoyed her" and "violated her virginity."[22]

However, the documents in this case focus not on these generally essential aspects of litigating estupro but almost entirely on two issues relating to male posturing: first, the accused don Juan's claims to honor and nobility; and second, whether the household slaves who accused don Juan were trustworthy witnesses. Despite their status as lacking honor and gravitas as witnesses, court cases in colonial Latin America often depended on insider information known only to domestic slaves or servants. When masters faced judicial sanctions, domestics did have a say in their owners' fates. In this case, one of the legal advisors to the prosecution specified that slaves were the best possible witnesses for cases that were "secret and difficult to prove," given their access to private matters.[23]

The accused don Juan subjected the Cartagena judiciary to persistent declarations and proofs of his noble status to argue against or mitigate what he considered to be his unjust imprisonment. To disprove that he would ever violate an honorable man's slave or, more important, his household, don Juan submitted piles of documents, tapping into networks in the new and old world to back up his claims to the highest status. Witnesses who spoke for him said don Juan respected nobility and would never violate a noble house for such a disgraceful motivation. They backed up these claims by referring to don Juan's documented heritage and service to the crown. Don Juan defended himself by asserting his honor and claiming his enemy don Pedro manufactured the whole case to defame him, although he also said that he had too much respect for don Pedro to ever violate his household. He summarily dismissed the specific accusation that he had deflowered Agustina and focused on affirming his honor at every possible opportunity during the judicial process, expending far more energy on negotiating his incarceration than he did in defending himself against the charge of illicit sexual activity. These niceties of treatment by the authorities mattered more to him than his alleged affair with Agustina.

Upon his arrest on March 14, don Juan was imprisoned in the hall where the town council met. The prisoner said this arrangement offered "complete security, where it is customary to hold persons with my endowments and quality [*personas de mis partes y calidad*]." But to don Juan's chagrin, he was moved shortly afterward to a heavily guarded dungeon in the public jail. In response, he demanded incarceration that was "more decent according to the quality of my blood and the offices that I have had, such as infantry captain, *alcalde ordinario*, and many others." At this time he held the office of Protector of the Natives in the region of Cartagena. Since his first petition did not succeed, don Juan tried several more appeals to the local judiciary, complaining that the prison was "so severe and indecent" especially considering his "known nobility." He continued his petitions with a more theoretical stance, arguing that "each imprisonment conforms to the individual and their quality and that which I have is indecent and prohibits communication with my relatives and friends." As he pursued his complaints, don Juan gave more specific reasons why he required an immediate transfer:

> with great indecency to the quality of my blood and that office of
> *alcalde ordinario*, that I held until very recently, I am imprisoned
> among black prisoners and many common and ordinary people.
> ... This is unjust for a person of my quality.[24]

However, even don Juan's dismay at his lowly fellow inmates did not convince the judicial authorities to move him, since they feared he was a flight risk.

The jailer disagreed with don Juan's complaints, observing that his cell opened out to the jailhouse patio and also that he was shackled to a long chain, so he was able to walk around the entire jail. The town council's meeting room was unsuitable because it had windows without locks and a low balcony where any prisoner could escape if he was not fettered. Also, this room was never locked because people constantly passed through it in order to bring food into the jail itself.[25] If don Juan jumped from the balcony, he could easily run across the plaza into a church, where he would receive immunity from justice, a common tactic in colonial Cartagena. Even the presence of two guards was not enough to prevent easy escape.

The prisoner found this response even more insulting and replied with more petitions asserting his dependability. He succeeded in wearing down his captors and improving his situation, eventually returning to the more pleasant *sala de cabildo*. Persistence and the funds to pay for a prolonged case often were the simple keys to a successful trial outcome in this system. Through constant petitions and by calling on his high-ranking connections and their ready cash, after a few weeks the jailers detached don Juan from his chain, under bond of one hundred pesos. Not long after, he was able to negotiate the removal of the shackles themselves, and within a few weeks, don Juan demanded furlough during Holy Week. Prisoners had to maintain and fight for their honor if they wanted privileged treatment, including paying for the scribes to write and submit all of their numerous petitions. Don Juan succeeded in forcing a more lenient incarceration through these tactics. However, because don Juan's demands specifically undermined the authority of certain local officials, the terms of his imprisonment were appealed to the Bogota high court.[26]

Throughout the case, don Juan persistently returned to the issue of personal honor. To explain why he would never enter don Pedro's house uninvited, he said:

> I would not enter his house [without invitation] for anything in the world, because I have always had the proper respect and courtesy for such a renowned gentlemen's house. Having been his friend, I always treat him with great honor [le ha hecho siempre dos mil honras], and knowing the great honor and *clausura* maintained in his house, where they always protect the decorum of their obligations . . . as is public and notorious, and credible coming from an honorable and important resident such as this testifier.[27]

Don Juan also provided certifications confirming his honorable lineage and the achievements and royal service done by his male ancestors, who resided on the Canary Islands. Not only did these efforts represent an attempt to improve his incarceration, but they were also meant to prove that an honorable man such as don Juan could not have acted in such a dishonorable way by violating a peer's slave and household domain. In his view, honorable status equated to good behavior and respect for peers.

While don Juan subjected the Cartagena judiciary to persistent assertions of his besmirched status and unjust imprisonment, the domestic slaves affected by the case suffered far more severely. Their anguish occurred because the two dons, in their competing claims to violated honor, argued over the validity of testimonies made by the slaves. Don Juan asserted that don Pedro forced his slaves to speak against him, his personal enemy, for sinister reasons. Witnesses for don Juan claimed that the slaves spoke in fear of their master's punishment and deserved pity. Don Pedro stressed that don Juan had broken into his house (a crime he said was punishable by death), which moved the focus of the inquiry away from Agustina. For don Pedro, sexual violation intersected with housebreaking because while don Juan was in the house, he also allegedly helped another man seduce doña Ana, don Pedro's niece.[28] Since his domestics were not considered trustworthy witnesses, don Pedro found several Spanish men willing to say that they had seen don Diego and don Juan conspiring outside his house to seduce both Agustina and doña Ana.[29]

On the defensive, don Juan asserted that don Pedro forced his slaves to speak against him, his personal and political enemy, for sinister reasons. Witnesses for don Juan claimed that the slaves spoke in fear of their master's punishment and deserved pity. The defense witnesses said don Pedro was known to beat his slaves. One claimed that

> he heard from many people, whom he could not remember, that the slaves that testified in this case were rigorously lashed so that they would give their statements. And this witness also heard that one of the female slaves was close to death to a terrible punishment she received.[30]

Others argued that slaves did not understand the meaning of swearing on their oath and only testified out of fear. On the opposing side, several hostile witnesses assured the court that don Pedro was a Christian who would never beat or threaten his slaves to testify in his favor. Both men argued that Christian virtue prevented them from abusing slaves. While this may have been typical empty rhetoric, on the other hand, it may reflect the influence, however superficial, of two famous local Cartagena contemporaries, Alonso de Sandoval and Peter Claver. But, as part of the ratification of their statements, the enslaved witnesses were tortured because their testimony would have more credence if they did not deny their previous statements under torture.[31] Obviously, violence remained institutionalized in the judicial system. Five enslaved witnesses, including Agustina herself, were caught in a no win situation. They possibly lied for their master to avoid a domestic punishment and to frame don Juan, but all five still endured turns on the *mancuerda* to prove they had *not* falsely testified for their masters.

However, the slaves stood by their original claims and the Bogota audiencia gave them credence.[32] Despite don Juan's argument that defloration in the case of a slave of doubtful virginity was an "unpunishable" crime (in his words, "it is not punishable by nature because the victim is a slave-woman and there was no evidence if she was a *doncella*"),[33] the Bogota audiencia decided to banish don Juan from Cartagena for two years and fine him 200 Castillian ducats. Don Juan was in fact correct in these assertions, even if we naturally sympathize with Agustina and her trapped position as a victim of don Juan, don Pedro, and the judicial system. The point of an estupro case was to judicially compel a man to either marry a deflowered woman or give her money for her dowry. These cases rested on proving previous virginity and a record of resisting even the most persistent seducers. In this case, marriage was impossible, and apparently Agustina did not merit a dowry to help her find another man to marry her in the perceptions of the audiencia. In fact, Agustina's master must have known the case would not unfold like other estupro cases and simply made his petition to publicly destroy his enemy don Juan. Don Juan reacted appropriately, with dozens of pages of self-aggrandizing testimonies to his nobility, but he did not bother to demean Agustina's virtue and reputation, which would have been the usual technique if a Spanish woman had made the accusation. Because it was so risky for a woman to assert her violated virginity, unless she had the purest possible reputation and a great deal of communal support, local Spanish judges often decided in the woman's favor in estupro cases. Usually a woman and her family or protectors would avoid going before a court unless they already knew the judge would be kind to them. Once again, sex scandal was (and is) a successful tactic to bring down a political rival.

Don Juan's scrupulous defense of his honor in the matter of his imprisonment did not ultimately distract the court from ruling on his guilt in the primary offense against the sanctity of don Pedro's home. Although don Pedro resorted to legal action and not violence, he also included his household slaves' sexuality within the sphere of his household dominion and thus, as an extension of his own personal honor. In don Juan's case, it was to improve his prison conditions, but by drawing attention to his honorable credentials, he also hoped to cast doubt on suggestions he would violate another honorable man's domestic space for sexual purposes.

While two male friends may have simultaneously seduced doña Ana and Agustina in the same house, each woman experienced a very different outcome to the decision to have sex or seek love and affection due to their different race and status. Declarations of love, longing, and passion appear more often in cases involving elite women in this book, such as doña Lorenzana's determination to be with her lover don Francisco or doña Ana's success in choosing her own husband. Although their expressions of love for particular men were not so directly expressed, plebeian women also sought affection and sexual pleasure from men they desired and loved. The use of the word amor in the cases discussed here implies seduction, or the disruptive act of men enticing women.[34] Witnesses in the trial over doña Ana's elopement said that the two "went about as lovers" and that don Diego "was in love with doña Ana."[35] The word love also came up often in cases of seduction. For example, recall that the father of doña María, the doncella desenfada, claimed in 1598 that another don Juan came to his daughter's window and spoke "words of love and flirtatious remarks [*requiebros*] . . . gentle and loving words."[36] In Agustina's estupro case, the alleged victim said that don Pedro "requebró de amores" or "courted her" constantly. Witnesses were also asked how long don Pedro "solicited and courted [enamoró]" her.[37] Of course, as in our usage of the term "make love," the word amor could simply refer to sex, as noted in chapter 3 when María Manuel said her lover Francisco "la recuesto de amores" (slept with her). María Manuel admitted she had sex or "amor torpe y deshonesta" (illicit and dishonest love) with her master.[38]

Case studies from Cartagena support an observation made for early modern Europe, that "romantic love was once seen as dangerous and irrational, a threat to the stability of both family and individual."[39] In the early modern era, love was a "dangerous and disorienting emotion . . . not particularly suitable for marriage."[40] Don Diego and doña Ana's rebellious matrimony most clearly brings this point to life, as does the use of the word amor in Cartagena cases generally in the context of sexual seduction. Although doña Ana and don Diego ended up marrying, other Cartagena men and women usually experienced their passionate, romantic love outside of marriage. Elite marriages often joined individuals of widely differing ages, such as doña Lorenzana and her husband Andrés. Their lack of personal connection and Andres's extensive sexual history, when paired with the adolescent Lorenzana's relative naïveté, drove the couple apart and into the arms of their various lovers. Although we may be hopeful about the match made between doña Ana and don Diego, certainly most of the marriages described in this book do not exemplify the modern ideal of loving spouses, nor is the word amor ever used in the context of marriage.

This is not to say that a loving marriage was impossible in the early modern era. Nor was this just an entirely unattainable ideal, as the historians cited earlier in the chapter imply. A set of early seventeenth-century letters composed by an enslaved woman of African descent to her husband shows the affection and longing that could exist between a non-elite married couple.[41] In 1603, at around the age of forty-five, an Afro-Sevillan man named Antonio Sigarra and described as "heavily bearded and of good stature" was manumitted in his deceased owner's last will and testament. He left his enslaved wife Felipa de la Cruz and their son Cristobal to start a new life in Veracruz, New Spain.[42] Antonio achieved some modest prosperity in Mexico but neglected his correspondence with his wife in Spain. At his death in 1612, an official found two of her letters dated 1604 and 1608 among Antonio's possessions. The first letter began with these words, "my brother . . . and the one my soul craves. I received your letter with great happiness to know that you are healthy and that you had a good voyage."[43] Felipa continued by passing on news about births, deaths, and petty disputes among their friends in Seville. She ended the letter affectionately, repeating the phrase, "I kiss your hands," several times. However, her last letter from 1608 had a much sadder tone:

> To my husband Anton Segarra, whom our lord protects in the Santo Domingo convent in San Juan de Ulua.
>
> My brother, at this time we are fine and healthy. I and your children crave to know how you are. God knows how I much I wish this, because I am very sad because of your lack of care in not writing me in such a long time. I do not know what to blame for your

forgetfulness, but it must be the very small amount of love you have for me and your children. Your love is not as steadfast as mine is, because every hour and every moment I think of you. I never go to mass without asking God to protect you and do the same when I am at home. I always have you in my mind's eye, as do your children . . . because we have such a great longing to see you.

Again, Felipa turned to the local news in Seville, ending her letter with a sad conclusion:

This letter is very long but the messenger is trustworthy; he is señor Juan García. And with this I have nothing more to say other than God protect your health—this I want for you—and [God] bring you all the good that you desire. Signed in Seville, 15 March 1608. Your wife, Felipa de la Cruz.

Their simplicity and informality suggest that Felipa actually either wrote or dictated these letters.[44] Still, she had to entrust her missive to a messenger traveling to the Indies, so she probably wrote or composed the letters with some sense that they were not entirely private.[45]

Although it is only an ephemeral trace, this one document suggests that the hopes for affection, even within marriage, of seventeenth-century plebeian women were not so different as to assume an unbridgeable gulf between their emotional lives and ours today. We have seen that anger was a staged emotion that men deployed in a court setting to defend their prized male honor, and love was usually a disruptive, confusing sensation that legal authorities tried to ignore or disguise with conventional rhetoric, especially when women felt it and acted on their emotions, as doña Ana did. This letter exposes the sadness, loneliness, and longing familiar to anyone who has suffered, distant from the one they love and utterly powerless to reunite with them. Fortunately for doña Ana, her social position allowed her to marry for love. Once the deed was done, she confidently fought her guardians' objections to her decisiveness. Agustina was less fortunate, and her sexuality became a pawn in the political machinations of elite men. The degree of sexual agency she exerted in choosing don Juan as her long term lover remains a mystery given her scanty testimony in her own defloration case. However this affair unfolded, surely Agustina did not embark on it anticipating she and her peers would suffer torture in its official investigation. The next three chapters return to the files of the Cartagena Holy Office of the Spanish Inquisition Tribunal to further explore far more extreme and dangerous paths that women took to fulfill their desires to find a mate who could function as both a sexual partner and a provider. While it is more difficult to discern than in the records of doña Ana's elopement, these trials hint at the love and sexual desire felt by plebeian women toward men of their choosing.

CHAPTER SIX

CARTAGENA'S MOST NOTORIOUS SORCERESS

Paula de Eguiluz

AS A HISTORIAN PORES THROUGH DOCUMENTS HUNDREDS OF YEARS old, sometimes an almost invisible dust swirls above the surface of paper covered in hastily written notarial scrawls and whips itself into a tiny imaginary tornado, and a fully embodied human takes shape. The written records that outline Paula de Eguiluz's life reveal her to be an astoundingly opportunistic, canny woman. Her decades of interactions with the Cartagena Holy Office over the course of three separate trials for sorcery and witchcraft have intrigued historians since the nineteenth century.[1] Paula thoroughly exploited every available advantage, striving to survive and prosper against the odds of birth into slavery and the machinations of her lovers, friends, foes, adversaries, and highly suspicious Spanish inquisitors. In the 1620s and 1630s, her nemesis was Diego López, a mulato freedman and her competitor in the local healing trade marketplace.[2] The documentary traces of Paula's life center on the bitter rivalry between these two healers, exposing the vibrancy and tensions of the Cartagena market for love potions, medical remedies, and even fatal poisons. Aggressive competition for clients was common practice among colonial Latin American women, and Paula drew on her businesswoman's wit in the even more stressful setting of an inquisition trial. While

female sexuality often became political in a judicial setting, this perception is muted for free nonwhite women, due to their greater need to focus
on economic goals and basic day-to-day survival.

As noted in chapter 2, the early seventeenth-century market for love
magic revolved around social ties among white and black women and the
occasional man. The exchange of knowledge of spells and healing flourished
in the Circum-Caribbean among men (especially with ties to the church)
and women of African, Iberian, and indigenous heritage. Inquisitors encouraged these possessors of special knowledge to self-confess their tres-
passes. After her second arrest by the Holy Office, Paula pointed her finger
at dozens of women (and one man) involved in sorcery and possibly orgiastic, Satanic gatherings.[3] The lone male figure of Diego López mirrors Juan
Lorenzo and his ties to doña Lorenzana and her clique two decades before.
This chapter draws on statements voiced by Paula's dissatisfied clients and
rivals, including Diego, as well as Paula's ruthless efforts to defend herself.
The focus here is Paula: her love life, her dramatic manipulations of the
inquisitors, her clientele, and her bitter enemies and competitors in the
healing trade. Despite her low status as a black freedwoman and a *peniteni-
cada*, Paula won these battles, even overcoming Diego López's inflammatory attempts to turn the inquisitors against her. What we know of Paula's
biography shows how seventeenth-century inquisitors increasingly linked
women's illicit and disruptive sexual desires to an unchristian world of
demons, despite the belief in using spells and potions to aid love affairs
among all social classes. Love magic's popularity proves women attempted
sexual agency against the momentous odds of the honor code, gender hierarchies, and a paternalistic society.

Born in the 1590s and the daughter of Africans enslaved in Santo Domingo, Paula passed the most important years of her young adulthood in
Cuba as the slave and lover of Joan de Eguiluz, an important administrator
in the Spanish mines.[4] Eguiluz freed her and provided her with material
wealth, but his patronage did not protect her from accusations of sorcery
and dealings with the devil.[5] Paula first came to Cartagena in 1624, where she
suffered inquisitorial interrogations, a march in an auto de fe, reconciliation,
and penance. By the time of her second arrest, she had lived in Cartagena
for eight years, first as a prisoner in the Tribunal secret prison, and then as
a menial servant at the Hospital of the San Juan de Dios friars. While serving her penance washing filthy linens for hospital charity cases, Paula again
started to arouse the inquisitors' suspicions. Paula's high profile, even as a

penitent *reconciliada*, inspired the Cartagena Holy Office to attempt another crackdown on love magic. The inquisitors arrested her for the second time in September of 1632. They did not immediately reveal the charges against her, but Paula quickly assessed her vulnerable position. At this time, she described her occupation as a curandera; she was a popular healer in the city of Cartagena and its surrounding regions. She worked and socialized with a number of other Afro-Caribbean women who sold love potions and taught incantations and conjurations to a large clientele of women, rich and poor, white and black.

Throughout her three trials, Paula de Eguiluz developed strategies for dealing with the inquisitors. Her responses to interrogation did not necessarily lead to lighter punishments, but they do reveal a sense of self and even what might be called personal integrity or a code of honesty, however strange this may seem in the context of a small witch craze in which she was the primary accuser. Paula de Eguiluz's stories were remarkably consistent over the course of four years. When the inquisitors presented her with a set of accusations taken from other people's confessions, as was normal practice, Paula unfailingly confirmed the details she had originally stated, sometimes years before, and she modified other people's statements according to her chosen version of events. This is an impressive feat, given that her second trial in 1632 and 1633 had generated seventy-one different accusations. She faced twenty-five new accusations in her third trial shortly afterward, and her memory never failed her. She always stuck to her original stories, regardless of slanderous statements made by her enemies in the healing trade. As we will see, even after years of imprisonment and interrogation, Paula challenged interpretations of her behavior that violated her personal code of moral and sexual behavior. With her astounding powers of memory when it came to creating a persona for the inquisitors, Paula strictly controlled the oral history of her dealings with fellow healers and sorceresses, as well as her version of her relationship with a demon called Mantelillos.[6] From her cell in the secret prisons of the Holy Office, Paula also dominated other imprisoned women, overcoming Diego López's attempts to destroy her defense tactics, and she continued to manipulate the inquisitors themselves.

Paula's second and third trials began with a typical scenario: in 1630, two years before her second arrest, a thirteen-year-old girl was the first to testify to the healer's reinvolvement in magic.[7] This child spent time at the San Juan de Dios hospital visiting her grandmother, where she slept near

Paula de Eguiluz's bed. She saw the penitenciada, known by the bizarre nickname "Aleluya," dressed in a habit as part of her punishment, with yellow and red crosses on her front and back. The only suspicious acts the girl could report had to do with the beaker of unguent and the herbs that Paula kept under her bed. The girl claimed that she saw Paula putting this unguent on her arms and "nether regions," an action commonly associated with witches preparing to fly. One night, Paula's face seemed strangely shiny to the girl, due to the unguent.

Gradually new evidence against Paula de Eguiluz emerged out of voluntary confessions made by young Spanish doñas. These confessions highlighted Paula's amazing powers of sexual attraction, which were the envy of various Cartagena women. The first doña to speak against her was Magdalena de Estrada, age twenty-three, who came to the inquisitors in 1631 in response to an Edict of Faith.[8] Doña Magdalena provided information about Paula's ability to control men's affections, confessing that one night she had discussed the penitenciada with one of Paula's lovers, a Spanish soldier named Diego Núñez. Núñez admitted that, "he loved and desired Paula so much that he could not stop thinking about her, day or night, even when he was with another woman." These feelings were so extreme that he feared she "had given him something" to provoke his intense desire and longing. In his view, love and powerful sexual desire were wild and dangerous emotions, very likely fueled by magic.[9] After the soldier left, doña Magdalena, out of "womanly curiosity," questioned Paula, who lived at her house working as a servant and washerwoman at the time. Paula laughed heartily at doña Magdalena's curiosity. As the two women stood on the balcony, the doña reported that the sorceress pointed to the clear, starry sky and invoked the brightest star in a conjuration mentioning demons, reciting an invocation that compelled a man to love and desire a woman. Paula lived with doña Magdalena as her servant for six months and otherwise appeared to be a good Christian, according to her mistress. Their conversation about Paula's knowledge of sexual magic brings to life the way elite women might turn to nonwhite women with reputations as skilled and experienced lovers when they were themselves interested in sexual exploration.[10]

After hearing the testimonies given by doña Magdalena and the young girl, the inquisitors did not arrest Paula. They did not have enough damning evidence against her at this stage. However, when another doña, Ana de Fuentes, confessed more serious evidence of Paula's involvement in love magic in 1632, her statements led to Paula's arrest, igniting what turned into a witch craze lasting several years.[11] These investigations differed greatly from the handful of trials that had taken place two decades before, revolving around doña Lorenzana and her circle. This time, no Cartagena doña were required to do penance.[12] This change apparently occurred because in her confessions (which fueled nearly all of the Holy Office's arrests in this set of witch trials) Paula de Eguiluz generally accused a circle of women comprised of her peers, including free and enslaved Afro-Caribbean women. As will be seen in the next chapter, this group of women did meet socially and formed a competitive community of love magic practitioners. In the 1630s, Cartagena inquisitors were attempting to control local society by weakening the groups they perceived as threatening and these women must have stood out as a likely target. Paula's finger-pointing led the campaign to weaken these successful healers. After this witch hunt began to taper off, the Holy Office turned its attention to local Portuguese converts from Judaism and proceeded to drastically reduce the influence of these men on the local slave trade.[13]

Paula de Eguiluz was one of the city's most skillful incarcerated negotiators, a talent she picked up as a successful free businesswoman and during her long stints as a captive in the Holy Office secret prisons. She learned a great deal from her first arrest in 1624 and applied this knowledge to her second incarceration and trial. Paula's primary defensive tactics were to accuse other women among her peer group of sorcery and pacts with the devil. After the women were arrested, Paula attempted to control their relationships with the inquisitors from her cell. For the first three days after her second arrest and imprisonment in September of 1632, Paula stayed in her cell, planning her next move. After this interlude, she asked for an audience with the inquisitors and confessed that she had made a new pact with her demonic familiar Mantelillos, her companion dating back to her days in Cuba. She also immediately began naming many other alleged witches.

Negotiating personal conditions was a common tactic in Cartagena secular holding cells and the Holy Office secret prison, but Paula de Eguiluz took a more creative approach than many other convicts. She did not follow the common path of claiming illness or offended honor (especially popular with Spanish men) to influence the inquisitors to improve her incarceration. As a nonwhite woman, these methods would not have convinced the inquisitors to improve her conditions. She instead appealed to their emotions and used her storytelling skills to exploit their fears, manipulating her known affiliations with the supernatural. Shortly after her arrest, Paula recounted an incident that compelled the inquisitors to move her from jail cell number twelve to number eight. Paula said that two nights before, after midnight, the sound of footsteps in her cell woke her up and terrified her. The next night at the same time she woke up with a sensation of heaviness and heard a high voice saying, "Ay dios" (Oh God). In response, a quiet voice, seeming to come from a "dead thing," said, "Hang yourself here like I hanged myself here." Paula was petrified with fear and swore this story was the truth, begging for God's help (with the inquisitors as her intermediaries). The next day, in her second audience, she retracted all that she had confessed about witches' gatherings and those she had accused of attending, saying she had lied because of her dread of the phantasm that visited her in the night. A few days later, she retracted the retraction, claiming that Mantelillos and another devil spoke to her through the tiny window in her cell, telling her not to accuse the other witches. But now she wanted to confess all and rejoin the Church. She again listed several names and went into the details of various women's sexual encounters with the devil.[14] The Holy Office's dependence on finger-pointing and self-motivated confessions left them vulnerable to the schemes of a conscious negotiator such as Paula.

With her confusing and dilatory confessions and extensive accusations, Paula de Eguiluz controlled her case and the inquisitors to the best of her ability. After a week in cell number eight, Paula de Eguiluz again demanded changes and succeeded in receiving them by once again describing a fearful supernatural experience. A few nights before, she had awakened around midnight and claimed that for the length of time it would take to say a "Hail Mary," she had felt ghostly hands from the "other life" touching her left thigh and torso. The entire area was chilled and Paula felt scared almost to death. She appealed to the inquisitors, saying she could not survive another experience of this kind. She feared entering her cell and begged for companionship.[15] Again the inquisitors took her complaints seriously and suggested that she move for a second time, this time to a cell shared with other women. The inquisitors knew that Francisco Angola, a slave from Habana on trial for witchcraft, had hanged himself in cell number eight a year earlier in the summer of 1631. Francisco was buried in the garden behind the secret prison.[16] Undoubtedly, Paula had heard this tragic story and counted on the fact that the Holy Office would not want another suicide in its cells. The inquisitors justified putting three other women in the same cell with Paula de Eguiluz by recording in writing that they were running out of space and all four women were involved in the same circle of witches. The cell had a window into the patio, so the inquisitors asked for a good guard and that the door be locked with a key, which suggests this was not always the case. This entire incident shows how Paula used her knowledge of prison gossip about the suicide to arrange a living situation where she could attempt to influence other women's confessions.

To return to Paula de Eguiluz's main accuser and her narration of doing business with the sorceress, doña Ana de Fuentes was born in 1610, married young, and, like doña Lorenzana, after a few years living as an unhappy wife, began to have serious fights with her husband. At around age twenty-one, doña Ana had sought help from her slave, a black woman from Lisbon named Barbara Gómez, for persistent and worsening fights with her husband don Francisco. Barbara was an experienced diviner, who later confessed to having her own demonic familiar and to having learned prognostication techniques (such as the famous suerte de habas) from a gypsy in Cádiz in an attempt to reignite her own relationship with a Spanish friar.[17] When doña Ana complained that Barbara's remedies had no effect on don Francisco and that their relationship was growing worse every day, the slave suggested that her mistress call on Paula de Eguiluz.[18]

At first Paula distanced herself from the request for help, but doña Ana insisted, so Paula began a long and increasingly more intense relationship with the young doña, who confessed her version of their exchanges to the Holy Office. It was these confessions that prompted Paula's second arrest. First, doña Ana said that Paula requested the couple's nightshirts that they wore when they were together and don Francisco's stockings and shoes, along with more intimate items including hairs from his head and beard, as well as his urine. Doña Ana said the sorceress told her that boiling all of the items together and then putting them under their bed would make her husband love her very much. After two months and various payments adding up to fifty pesos, doña Ana saw no improvement in her marriage, so she accused Paula of fraud. In response, doña Ana said Paula tried more drastic methods, such as mixing chicken talons with herbs and placing this paste on doña Ana's doorstep. Paula also gave doña Ana a small scarlet purse full of strange herbs. Nothing had any effect, so Paula suggested that doña Ana put her menstrual blood in her husband's drinking water. This spell did not reach fruition because her husband spilled the pitcher. Paula then asked for a drawstring from don Francisco's undergarments, which she made into a rope full of knots. This was supposed to "bind" him to doña Ana, not allowing him to have affairs with other women. After a few months, doña Ana undid all of the knots because she decided that this method also had no effect. One of Paula's last efforts involved her asking for don Francisco's right-hand glove so Mantelillos would take it to hell to subjugate doña Ana's husband. It is probably because none of these nostrums appeared to have any effect that Ana ultimately went to the Holy Office.

Paula de Eguiluz also suggested several techniques to doña Ana that were similar to the erotic magic used by doña Lorenzana's circle. She told doña Ana to gather some of her husband's semen in a rag and fry it in some oil. Doña Ana did not do this, fearing it would harm her husband. Paula then recommended anointing the inside of don Francisco's shoe and her own slipper with some semen, which doña Ana did twice to no effect. Paula's next piece of advice was to mix water used to wash doña Ana's genitals into an egg cooked for her husband. Doña Ana, who could not sign her own name, confused the directions of another love spell, confessing to the inquisitors that she recollected that Paula had told her to rub some pork on the length of her husband's "genital member," fry this meat, and feed it to him, which she did. Paula later clarified that the pork was supposed to make contact with doña Ana's genitals, not her husband's, before he ate it. Paula's version follows the standard love magic logic, whereby women's effluences could control men if they were ingested.[19] Rubbing greasy meat on her husband's genitals certainly implies that the couple maintained a degree of intimacy and trust, despite all of their problems. It also makes clear that women used seduction techniques or erotic methods, with varying degrees of sophistication, for improving the actual experience of sex.

Beyond this correction and in her defense, Paula de Eguiluz painted her relationship with doña Ana quite a bit differently, with the Spanish woman as an enthusiastic instigator of witchcraft, rather than the innocent victim of fraud. This defense is reminiscent of Juan Lorenzo's version of his relationship with doña Lorenzana. As in the earlier case, Paula placed herself within a broader community of magic practitioners. Her defensive tactics both marketed her reputation as an effective curandera (despite doña Ana's disappointment in her services) and attempted to decrease her culpability before the inquisitors.

Paula first brought up doña Ana in her fifth audiencia after her imprisonment, in the context of reporting the younger woman's repeated insistence on meeting the demon Mantelillos. Even beyond this sinful craving for a demonic experience, in Paula's version, doña Ana appeared far less devoted to her husband and the improvement of her marriage.[20] Paula confessed that doña Ana's slave Anita *la bañona* asked her to go to Ana's house along with other witches including a mulata from Santo Domingo named Barbola de Albornoz. Paula said doña Ana wanted the women to "stupefy" don Francisco, scaring him so he would become too "simple" to see anything doña Ana did.[21] According to Paula, doña Ana did not seek spells and potions to improve her marriage but to harm her husband and seduce her lover, along with every other man she encountered. This time Paula spun a predictable narrative web linking illicit female sexuality with magic, an effort to divert the inquisitors' attention away from her own activities and toward doña Ana's immorality. Paula claimed that she only asked for various items belonging to don Francisco to dissuade or distract doña Ana from harming her husband, though she did not deny helping the Spanish woman pursue her sexual goals. In regard to the "binding" spells, Paula said doña Ana wanted to "bind" her lover, not her husband, in order to prevent him from talking to or having relationships with other women. Paula said her demon companion Mantelillos gave her a root that would inspire love and desire in "all the men who saw or embraced her."[22] Doña Ana wore the root tied to her arm with cotton twine. Ana also wanted potions that would make "everyone that entered her house" love her, so Mantelillos told Paula about the concoction made of chicken talons and herbs. Paula said that doña Ana seemed very satisfied with a small magical pouch made with Mantelillo's guidance that was meant to cause great desire in "every man who saw her." In her defense, Paula purposefully emphasized doña Ana's urgent sexual desires in order to exculpate herself.

Over the course of her testimony, Mantelillos becomes such a real presence that it is sometimes difficult to believe that Paula was consciously inventing him.[23] Was Mantelillos modeled on a man she knew, her ideal man, or her general experience with men? Or did he represent "the container or cipher for the witch's own desires and anger" or other emotions?[24] His most salient characteristic was his dependability as a mentor and helper: he always advised Paula on how to cure her patients or in her efforts to help them satisfy their sexual needs. Beginning with her first audiencia only a few days after her second imprisonment by the Holy Office, Paula de Eguiluz did not waver in presenting Mantelillos as a helpful advisor. Of course, it was convenient for Paula to blame Mantelillos for her transgressions. She stated that he started to tempt her back to evil only three weeks after the Tribunal sentenced her for the first time in 1624.[25] He appeared when she was working in the hospital washing clothes for her penance. Mantelillos had quite a different temperament from the demons described by the other alleged Cartagena witches, discussed in the next chapter. Paula said that he always appeared to her as a *galán*, or an attractive man, which more closely resembles the stories told by contemporary women involved in European witch crazes.[26] To persuade Paula to give him her soul and once again be "his" following her reconciliation with the Catholic Church, Mantelillos offered her wealth and slaves, but he also tried to make her feel guilty for deserting him, complaining that he had been severely punished in hell for losing her "friendship." After three visits in the mid-1620s, Paula said she submitted to Mantelillos' entreaties and again renounced the Christian god and religion in a witches' *junta*.

In Paula's world, witchcraft and sex were inseparably linked. For example, in her testimony, she recounted a story about a friend named Juliana, a *zamba libre*, who bragged to her about how one night she had sex with one young don in Tolú, left him asleep in bed, and sought another man for sex at an estancia three leagues (roughly ten miles) away. Juliana then returned to the first man as the cocks crowed and found him still sleeping. In response to this story, Paula said, "If you did this, you are a witch."[27] Paula used countless *hechizos* to help women attract men and attributed many of these remedies to Mantelillos. But she adamantly denied having sex with Mantelillos when she described her participation in devilish orgies. The inquisitors specifically asked her to explain the course of events in these gatherings or juntas with this question, "If, after you had supper and put out the candles, did the demon know you carnally and where?"[28] Paula responded, "Many times I was stimulated because of the fervor and fire in these juntas in Cartagena, but I never let the demon know me carnally, nor did he request it of me." A few days later, Paula repeated that several women had sex with demons at juntas, but that this had never happened between her and Mantelillos.[29] The inquisitors briskly imprisoned the victims of Paula's accusations. Despite the fact that she made confessions that strain credibility and snitched on her comadres, Paula worked hard during her several months of interrogations to maintain her personal sense of integrity. She admitted that she practiced love magic, cured people, and had a demonic familiar, but her self-conception did not allow her to admit to sex with a demon, in the European understanding of this kind of entity who worked in Satan's thrall. She may have envisioned Mantelillos very differently than the inquisitors understood her references to a personal familiar. She admitted that the juntas were sexually charged and erotic, but she and Mantelillos had moved beyond sex. Instead, he manifested her fantasy of an ideal, if slightly intimidating, partner and friend.

Although it is difficult to understand what Mantelillos really meant to Paula de Eguiluz—whether or not he was a conscious invention or a living being who dominated her mental and spiritual world—she knew how to use her demon to manipulate the inquisitors. She claimed Mantelillos whispered instructions to her through the window in her cell in the Holy Office jail.[30] In her third trial, which began in 1634 (Paula was not let out of jail between her second and third trials), she revealed that Mantelillos scared her into going back to the juntas. She elaborated on her earlier story, saying that one day she entered the garden of the Espíritu Santo hospital, thinking this would lift her spirits. Mantelillos appeared to her from a hiding place behind a vat, poorly dressed and assuming the form of a *dominguillo*, or moveable mannequin, similar to those used in bullfights to enrage the bulls.[31] He frightened Paula with the fire that emanated from his entire body and threatened that he would kill her if she did not give him her soul. In this audiencia, Paula clarified that she did not have sex with Mantelillos, because, as she confessed in her first trial, this act wounded her nether regions when she did it many years before in Cuba.[32]

Although in her final trial Paula repeated that she witnessed and took part in the standard feasting and dancing typical of a witches' gathering according to the European understanding of such juntas, she qualified her description of the orgiastic element of the proceedings. She said that since it was dark after the candles were put out, she could not see anything, but she *presumed* that each witch coupled with their devil, because "it was the custom for male and female witches to *juntarse unos con otras*" (for some people to have sex with others).[33] This language confirms Paula de Eguiluz's desire to present witches' behavior according to the accepted template without compromising the presentation of her sexual restraint and her special relationship with Mantelillos. She also may have drawn this picture from real events, actual sexually-charged drumming and dancing that so disturbed Cartagena's authority figures throughout the seventeenth century.

Paula de Eguiluz was not the only person familiar with Mantelillos: Paula's clients doña Ana de Fuentes and Juana Zamba, among others, knew of this demon. Paula insisted that doña Ana in particular obsessively desired to see Mantelillos, seeking some kind of evil or illicit sexual contact, but Paula restricted her demon's appearances jealously, almost as if he were her lover. After hearing so much about him, doña Ana no longer wanted Paula as an intermediary, but she craved to speak to Mantelillos personally, as long as he did not appear in a frightening form.[34] Paula lied to doña Ana, telling her that the demon always revealed himself with a terrifying appearance that would horrify the Spanish woman. When Paula finally tired of doña Ana's constant begging, she called on Mantelillos to appear. He fulfilled her request, but this time he looked quite strange, as a *mestizo* with rooster's talons.[35] Doña Ana also said the demon could appear as a goat or a black man and reported that Paula told her his typical appearance (as her ideal lover?) was a good looking, racially-mixed (*de color quebrado*) man.

The inquisitors were interested to learn that members of the Catholic Church and other authority figures were heavily implicated in Paula's affairs. She had a baby with a friar while she was serving her inquisition penance working in the San Sebastian hospital. Rumor had it that when she was in the inquisition jail, another lover, this time a Spanish seminary student, visited her and she reassured him by saying, "*hijo*, don't worry, they cannot touch us."[36] The inquisitors made a point of highlighting this clerical infraction with a marginal note in the trial documentation. But most of Paula's efforts were directed toward a lover called Diego de Avedillo (also spelled Badillo), described only as the "nephew of the chandler." She denied all accusations of maleficio in her own love life, always presenting herself as curandera, but she confessed that after hearing that Badillo was having an affair with her mestiza neighbor, she would have murdered the woman with no concern for the consequences. In response to Paula's "dishonoring" of himself and his new lover, Badillo attacked Paula de Eguiluz with a knife ("le dio una cuchillada a esta [testigo] en la cabeza.").

Some historians believe that in early modern Castile, "the sorceresses themselves did not believe in the efficacy of spells and in the necessity of sorcery; but these things helped them relieve their misery by earning a bit of money."[37] To the contrary, Paula admitted that she used magic to help her own complex love life. She confessed to using the traditional incantations on her own lovers, trying to influence Badillo's affections with the "Prayer to the Star," well-known in Iberia, not the more explicit and erotic potions she suggested to Ana.[38] Paula probably chose to hide her true secrets—her most personal and possibly dangerous rituals—from the inquisitors.

In dozens of pages of testimonies, Paula consistently presented herself not as a local leader in magical knowledge and practice, but as a student and client of other, more expert, sorceresses, who were always free women of color. She consulted these women to help her after her lover Badillo's attack. Paula's sorceress peers spread knowledge of seemingly harmless techniques such as using powders from plants to improve their hair and eyelashes, but they blended their cosmetic routines into magical seduction practices. They exchanged recipes and incantations almost always related to finding love, keeping men's affections, or harming their rivals. For example, Paula said she depended on another penitenciada, a free mulata named Bernarda Álvarez, for powders brought from Santo Domingo, hoping they would make Badillo reunite with her.[39] Paula also made a wax doll and said the famous prayer to Santa Marta and the "Conjuration of Souls" so that he would "love her well." Paula learned the following version of the "Conjuration of Souls" from Bernarda:

> Sister souls in Purgatory,
> I need nine of you.
> Three that died by hanging,
> Three that died by beheading,
> Three that were dragged [*arrastradas*].
> All nine of you come together
> In Diego de Badillo's heart.
> Gather in the cross at his house
> And trouble him night and day.
> [Directed to Badillo] You will not rest,
> You will not stop on the corner,
> You will not speak with a friend.
> Souls, my souls,
> On the life that you live,
> On the death that you die,
> On your judgment day,
> On the pains that you suffer,
> On the glory you await,
> You will bring [Paula de Eguiluz] to your house.[40]

Paula de Eguiluz said Bernarda taught her another spell that invoked several devils:

> I conjure Baltazar, Mateo, and Juan of the twisted legs.
> Arise, fear, and close those doors.
> I conjure all [three] of you so that
> You will all come together in Diego Badillo's heart
> And take five ounces of blood from him.

Bring me three for Paula de Eguiluz,
Fried, very well fried,
Burning in bright flames of love.
Don't leave me, don't stop, do not rest,
Until he comes to see and speak to Paula de Eguiluz.[41]

Paula had the ability to recite several of these incantations from memory. All of them sentenced Badillo to great physical pain if he did not return to her. Paula also said she often heard women say another incantation, which bears some resemblance to a spell cited in María Ramirez's trial two decades earlier:

You will not see me,
I will not see you.
I sent three messengers for you,
So that they will bring you here now.
I sent you Barabas.
I sent you Satan . . .
They will bring you here now.
Caught by your lung,
And by your testicles,
And by your heart,
And by all the members of your body.
They are slaughterhouse devils.
Bring me it now today, oven devils . . .
Bring me it now, plaza devils.
Bring it now to my house, fishing devils.
Lame devil, since you are the greatest devil, bring it now.[42]

Paula said this incantation was intoned while a woman tapped castanets with her fingers. All of these spells were part of a cross-Atlantic, cross-Caribbean traditional love magic, a kind of popular poetry passed along mainly by women but also priests and a few other men. Sorceresses in early modern Castile recited virtually the same chant, mentioning the "diablos del horno" (oven) and the "diablos de la plaza" and the "carniceria" (slaughterhouse or butcher's shop) before the Toledo and Cuenca tribunals. The threat of "you will not rest" and invoking various parts of a man's body were also common in Spanish spells.[43]

Paula de Eguiluz tried these three spells, as well as several other rituals, in her efforts to reunite with her lover Diego de Avedillo. Her trial clearly reveals that many other freedwomen and Spanish women also attempted the same kind of love and erotic magic. Paula's confessions suggest that she in fact believed in the efficacy of love magic and did not sell her skills purely for economic gain. Her own belief and participation refutes the idea that women like her practiced magic as an assertion of resistance to Spanish power that inverted racial hierarchies, as does the fact that most of the women involved were not Spanish. These plebeian women dealt in conjurations that would affect poor, nonwhite women like themselves who were their rivals for men's affections. Instead, this practice highlights women's use of sex and sexuality to influence their own fate. Paula emphasized her occupation as a healer, not as a local leader in the field of love magic or as the most successful seller of spells, although her enemies like Diego López portrayed her far more maliciously.[44] Stories of poisonings and efforts to control Spanish men were the stuff of inquisitorial fears and have little relation to women's day-to-day attempts to influence passion, devotion, and attain the economic security that a stable lover might provide.

Paula repeatedly alluded to a large circle of nonwhite women who tried a variety of methods to influence their lovers, sometimes inspired by her advice. Other than doña Ana, all of the women Paula mentioned as her clients or sister healers were free or enslaved women of African descent. The snippets of information provided in Paula's and other women's confessions suggest a vibrant world of love magic practice in Cartagena set in motion by the frantic search for devoted men. These women's search for lovers who would support them financially do not sound all that different from the feeling of need expressed by the women in the next chapter who explained that they succumbed to the temptation of sex with a demon for material gain.

Along with doña Ana, two women described as mulatas testified to calling on Paula to help them inspire love in certain men. They voluntarily confessed to the Holy Office and the inquisitors did not punish or imprison them, which supports the idea that the inquisitors were not attempting to eliminate this entire class of women from Cartagena, but instead seeking to control a few high profile leaders.[45] Both mulatas framed their confessions with Paula as the instigator, deemphasizing their own efforts to use these remedies. The first was a twenty-three-year-old free woman named Marta de San Antonio, or San Anton, who confessed that in September 1632, Paula found her crying because her lover, a shoemaker named Pedro, had left her for another woman.[46] Paula reassured Marta that Pedro would come back within a few days. After repeated questioning, Paula explained to Marta that she had said the "Prayer to Santa Marta" for her. Marta claimed that she did not want to know anything more about the prayer but told inquisitors that Pedro had returned. She wanted to unburden herself to them because she heard Paula had been arrested. Two months later, Marta admitted that she gave Paula a jar of Pedro's urine that they buried under Marta's bed. Paula gave Marta some powders, instructing her to wash with them and then give the water to Pedro, which Marta said she did not do.

Another free mulata, the twenty-six-year-old Francisca Garcia, also voluntarily came before the Tribunal to confess shortly after Paula's imprisonment.[47] Francisca said that Paula came to her house and asked Francisca why she was so sad. Francisca told her that her lover of four years, a treasury official named Antonio, had recently left her. Paula reassured her and asked for pieces of the couple's clothing and six pesos. Paula also taught Francisca a few spells similar to the ones cited previously. One commanded that Antonio, "would not have peace, would not feel pleasure, would not sleep in a bed, would not fornicate with a woman or speak with a friend, until he returns to my door." Francisca tried the incantations but claimed that Antonio returned to her simply because she sought him out.

Paula did not mention these interactions in her first several interrogations, possibly because she thought the inquisitors did not know about them or that they were not serious infractions. But she did volunteer information regarding her attempts to help other free women of color. In response to her request, Paula said she gave herbs and powders to a María de Herrera, a mulata who lived in Getsemani, so that men would "love her well." She also gave María a bag of herbs to put under her bed so that the man who slept there would always want to be her lover.[48] Paula was hesitant to help Tomasa de Clavijo, another mulata, because she knew that Tomasa talked too much.[49] She finally decided to give Tomasa *tostón*, a plant frequently used in love magic in seventeenth-century Cartagena, in exchange for information about other effective ways to make "men love one well." Tomasa allegedly taught Paula how "inland" women rubbed their genitals with pork and then cooked it and fed it to the men they desired. This was the technique Paula had, of course, passed on to doña Ana and another clear example of the exchange of erotic magic techniques between indigenous, Afro-Caribbean, and Spanish women. Tomasa and Paula exchanged information about other spells and Paula asserted that Tomasa was very knowledgeable in love magic, but the

Holy Office did not arrest her, possibly because Paula did not mention her in her accounts of witches' juntas.

Paula reacted strongly to the accusations made by Marta de San Anton, arguing that Marta was well versed in conjurations, even more so than Paula herself. According to Paula, Marta performed numerous love spells in order to regain the affections of a cobbler named Pedro de Cazorla, who had deserted her for a white woman.[50] Paula said Marta had other advisors, such as Bernarda and Barbola de Albornoz, who suggested she bury Pedro's urine and mix a complex paste of lime taken from a variety of houses to further influence him. Paula accused Marta of poisoning Pedro's chocolate in a fit of anger and jealousy over his affair. When Pedro asked Marta for a cure, she responded with the dismissive, "Go with God," causing the injured lover to ask Paula for help, complaining that he felt like his stomach contained a dancing creature. Despite Marta's insistence on leaving Pedro to die, Paula cured him with rosemary oil mixed in wine and an unguent of sweet wormwood. Although Marta was not arrested, Paula tried her best to contradict Marta's statement, emphasizing her own positive, healing role and the other woman's desire to control her lover and wreak her personal vengeance on him.

As I have suggested, Paula's strategy was to accuse other women and then attempt to influence their confessions by communicating with them during their incarceration in the secret prisons of the Holy Office. The fly in the ointment of Paula's maneuvers was the free mulato surgeon Diego López, born to an enslaved mother in 1593 in Cartagena. Paula had mentioned López in passing in one of her numerous confessions, leading to the surgeon's arrest and interrogation. In casually listing him with many other alleged coconspirators, Paula underestimated Lopez's rage and desire for revenge, which were later manifested in calumnious accusations against her. In his audiences with inquisitors after his arrest and imprisonment, López formulated his entire defense around the notion that, "Paula was the dogmatizer and master of all . . . the maleficio that led to crimes and irreparable damages notorious all over this city harming important people of this republic," thus directly contradicting Paula's defense tactics and carefully-worded confessions.[51] To back up his claims, when the inquisitors asked López to inform them of specific examples of maleficio, he passed on several rumors that Paula had poisoned people with powders.

Paula and López were both healers who sometimes met when called to help the same person. They competed over clients and they negotiated various requests by magical practitioners to *not* cure certain individuals, such as the victims of their spells and poisons. Most likely, they had very different healing techniques, as López was trained in a hospital and Paula first gained her expertise in social gatherings in kitchens, undoubtedly from other women, including those of African descent. López's accusations were deathly serious: he claimed Paula poisoned a treasury official (hired by his rival's lover), taking away his reason or stupefying him so he had to give up his profession. In a related incident, López alleged that some of her poisonous powders were confused with a marzipan, thus leading to the death of a young girl, despite Lopez's efforts to cure her. López claimed that Paula bragged about several people she had killed or harmed. He framed these cases as situations where jealous women asked Paula to poison their husbands or lovers. For example, López alleged that Paula killed a doctor at the request of a doña out of jealousy for the doctor's lover. López mentioned several other examples where women "stupefied" their husbands, often with Paula's help, to achieve certain goals. López even alleged that Paula was involved in a 1628 fatal poisoning of the Governor Diego de Escobar via a cup of wine given to him by his assistant. He also mentioned a large number of people of different races and social levels who had Paula as their "godmother," or guide, for entering into the practice of witchcraft.[52] López did his best to manipulate the inquisitors with captivating stories of a powerful and malevolent sorceress who fit all their preconceptions of a terrifying and uncontrollable woman; this was especially horrifying when the person was a sexually aggressive freed black woman. However, even if he had won them over with his prolific confessions, he did not stand a chance against Paula, who was smarter, infinitely more subtle in her manipulative confessions, and a far more popular prison leader—an extension of her role as a successful businesswoman in the local love magic marketplace.

In 1634, the inquisitors read Paula a summary of Lopez's statements against her, which was presented as a list of twenty-five new accusations.[53] Although his name was not mentioned, Paula recognized the source of the new "evidence." As she heard the new list of charges, her rage grew against this man who was thwarting her jailhouse strategies and her carefully-constructed character. Paula admitted to relatively harmless love magic and binding spells, but she would never admit to harmful acts such as poisoning. To the first few accusations, she responded to the inquisitors that she had already confessed the specified acts. As the list continued, Paula reacted by saying that she did not commit this or that particular maleficio or that she did not know anything about what was described in the accusation. The next day, as the reading of accusations continued, her responses became more definite, including the phrases, "I deny that, there is no such thing," "this is false and untruthful," "I deny that and I know no such thing," "I did not do that evil act," and "I neither said nor did what is accused." When given the opportunity to respond in more detail, Paula directly attacked López after each statement was read, saying phrases including:

> I say that I know nothing about this because this witness is my enemy Diego López. I take him as a man with a bad conscience and I challenge his statements. . . . This witness does not say the truth because he is Diego López and a liar and an imposter. He lies and does not say the truth and gives false testimony.[54]

Paula then asked the inquisitors to investigate why López would make this "false and worthless deposition," adding that he was a mulato *cabra* (female goat) and her capital enemy.

Although López made his best effort to bring down Paula de Eguiluz and though she certainly did not escape punishment (a long stay in jail and two hundred lashes), in the aftermath of this particular conflict of wills, Paula retained her authority over the other prisoners and even her captors. In 1635, the inquisitors questioned a handful of female inmates about the relationship between López and Paula to explore the idea that the surgeon made up his accusations because he hated her. The first witness, Isabel Márquez, said she heard López shouting from his cell beneath hers, "You bitch Aleluya [Paula's nickname], you've been whipped and *encorozada* [made to wear a humiliating cap in an auto de fe]. *Yo te haré el caldillo con tus especias* [I am going to make a stew out of your spices]." In other words, he threatened to beat her to a pulp or give her a taste of her own medicine. Sixty-year-old Elena de Viloria claimed to hear an even ruder string of insults emanating from Lopez's cell: "You whore, witch, and sorceress, whipped and encorozada, I am going to make you dance the *gatatumba*" (I will make you die *or* I will shame you) and "I am already making you pay for this" (*Ya yo os voy haciendo el caldillo con sus especias*).[55] Paula maintained her faithful following among the female prisoners, and Diego López, with his bitter, uncontrolled rage, did not stand a chance.

In response to these statements, the inquisitors moved López to another cell so he would have less communication with the women. His new cell also presented problems because it had a hole in the roof, possibly made by mice, that was useful for communicating with other prisoners.[56] The result of this cellblock bickering was that López retracted all 147 of his accusations and confessions, including those he made against Paula de Eguiluz. Unfortunately for López, retractions usually led the Cartagena inquisitors to order torture. They tied López to the rack and stretched his legs and arms until he confessed the truth. He continued to deny all of his involvement in witchcraft and juntas, but the inquisitors decided to punish him just as harshly as they did Paula, with a public march in an auto de fe and two hundred lashes.[57]

Prisoners in the theoretically terrifying Holy Office dungeon managed to move cells, communicate with the other inmates, and otherwise improve their incarceration. Certain inmates, most notably Paula, became de facto prison leaders. They bribed and manipulated the jailers, sometimes with sex, until the guards let prisoners escape temporarily. Diego López claimed that the jailer's slave Juanillo helped and encouraged women to escape temporarily.[58] López also said that another slave working in the prison, named Isabel, helped Paula by passing on chocolate and soap from her friends on the outside. In another case from the 1630s, an inquisition prisoner accused of practicing Judaism arranged to have his personal slave, Sebastian Bran (husband of the prison slave Isabel), feed and assist him during his imprisonment.[59] Sebastian suffered an inquisition trial himself for *fautoria*, or "aiding and abetting," because he helped his master by undertaking tasks such as bringing in a hidden chicken stew. Through the machinations of skilled manipulators, the Holy Office "secret" prisons were certainly more porous than their fearful reputation suggests.

López was an untrustworthy witness, but he sensed what the inquisitors wanted to hear and whom they would target next. Given the significant number of free, relatively prosperous, and unattached women of African descent in Cartagena, López rode the tide of disapproval of these women by accusing them of the most damning acts of poison and all of the other classic behaviors for witches. Paula was certainly vulnerable on account of her ties to white women, suspicious healing practices, and her record as a convicted witch. She definitely took part in "cures" that had nothing to do with the official European understanding of physical disease. Even when dealing with physical ailments, she undoubtedly used herbs and methods contrary to those López learned in a Spanish hospital.[60] Paula may have learned curing from her mother or other Africans, working within a broadly Atlantic school that drew on African, indigenous American, and traditional Iberian healing techniques. All of these strains came together in the Caribbean and were practiced by women like her, who competed for business as curanderas and experts in love magic.

It is very likely that Diego López considered women healers such as Paula as his rivals. In his confessions and in various ways, he disassociated himself from the mulata women who had been his intimate companions or otherwise members of his close social circle. López also started an anti-Jewish frenzy in Cartagena through his lurid and extensive accounts of the behavior of local Portuguese, including a fellow surgeon named Blas de Paz Pinto. He attacked another surgeon named Martín Sánchez, accusing him of Protestant words and acts even though the two men were previously close friends. Ill-disguised in the dozens of pages of testimony recording López's efforts to bring down Paula, Sánchez, and the local Portuguese population, are López's professional rivalries and the desire to eliminate some of his competitors. Paula's confessions employed emotions and fear to manipulate her treatment at the hands of the inquisitors, as well as to place herself as only one individual amongst numerous other local healers, claiming some were far more skilled and knowledgeable than she was. In contrast, López had more cowardice and less backbone as he bitterly and petulantly denounced his competitors with the most damning accusations possible, hoping that these extreme and patently absurd allegations would divert the inquisitors' attentions away from himself.

Despite all this, both Diego López and Paula de Eguiluz continued practicing their trades after surviving their public and painful autos de fe.[61] López moved away for a time, then regained his practice in Cartagena. Paula remained in prison but allegedly enjoyed furlough to travel in a sedan chair, luxuriously dressed and well paid, to advise bishops and inquisitors on their medical care.[62] Unfortunately, this is the only extant information about Paula's later life, but given her powers as a leader, a negotiator, a curandera, and an expert in love and sexual magic, her success most likely continued as she passed from middle age into her final years. López took advantage of Inquisitional fears of Protestantism, Judaism, and the Portuguese to bring down two of his male rivals, but Paula (on the surface, a vulnerable freedwoman), remained a prosperous Cartagena healer, according to some reports. The two of them had to learn to coexist in the packed and competitive local curing market, where erotic magic blended with attempts to heal the physical body. Typical for Latin America, this market blended European, Indian, and African traditions, both in the use

of certain plants and herbs, as well as in its general overarching philoso-
phies.[63] The next chapter will continue the story of Diego López and Paula
de Eguiluz, as well as further examine the several dozen women affected
by Paula's accusations, how sexuality and economic needs and survival
emerged in their confessions, and the actual social gatherings that were the
basis for their outrageous tales.

CHAPTER SEVEN

SORCERY, SEX, AND SOCIETY IN SEVENTEENTH-CENTURY CARTAGENA

IN 1627, ALONSO DE SANDOVAL, A TWENTY-YEAR VETERAN OF Cartagena's Jesuit mission, condemned the materialism that he believed saturated the Spanish and Portuguese empires.[1] Love magic, of course, concentrated on sexual attraction and eroticism, but for many Cartagena women—especially women of African descent with no chance of inherited family wealth or parental support—retaining a man's devotion also meant a chance at some degree of economic stability. In a gruesome way, the women who confessed to submitting to sex with the devil out of greed in the 1630s highlight this society's association of sex with even more destructive and avaricious desires. Nearly all of the witches (*brujas*) arrested in the 1630s (almost all due to Paula de Eguiluz's finger pointing) confessed to having sex with the devil as a consummation of their rejection of Christianity and their pact with the devil, but they highlighted that they did these horrific acts in the hopes of improving their economic situation. Almost every detail of these Cartagena confessions adhered to an established witchcraft confessional model in place from the late fifteenth century to the late seventeenth century in Europe.[2] However, "nearly every witch made the story her [or his] own, conveying complex emotions or providing idiosyncratic detail."[3] In these details lurk insights into accused witches' personal experiences or understandings of sex and relationships with men and their need to connect sex with material gain.

It should come as no great surprise that nonwhite women accused of witchcraft in seventeenth-century Cartagena associated sex with pain and suffering or, at best, a way to escape poverty. This chapter will explore the confessions made by women arrested and questioned by the Holy Office as a result of Paula de Eguiluz's defense tactics, described in the previous chapter. In most cases, these were the same women that Paula competed with in the buying and selling of love magic remedies. Diego López, her most bitter opponent and the only man arrested as a participant in the juntas, presented the inquisitors with an especially revealing confession, one that offers a rare glimpse into the sexual desires, extramarital affairs, regrets, and fantasies of a non-elite, nonwhite man in colonial Spanish America. For him as a man with a gainful occupation, sex did not directly link to economics, although we have seen how he feared for his competitiveness as a healer and thus attacked other local surgeons and Paula herself. In their confessional narratives, all of the accused witches spoke of incredible supernatural events, but they saturated their stories with the lingering psychological residue of sad and painful life experiences. While indulging the inquisitors' predetermined vision of satanic orgies, the alleged witches hinted at tangible occurrences and some of their own understandings of sex. The confessions also alluded to real life social gatherings, including the parties and wakes that the local authorities feared but found impossible to suppress. Because of all these complex elements at work, this chapter will attempt to explore the sexual mindsets of the accused witches, their real world social lives, and their deep concerns regarding their economic survival.

The literature of European demonology demanded that those who confessed to a pact with the devil consummated their evil rejection of the Church with an act of illicit sex with a demon. In effect, brujas, to fit the template for this kind of inquisition interrogation, had to admit that they rejected all that was good in the world, especially what was right morally, spiritually, and sexually. In her testimony, Justa, a mulata freedwoman, voiced the most basic elements essential to early modern visions of a satanic orgy. Justa admitted that "she received and recognized Lucifer as her god and lord, kissing his backside, dancing around him holding candles in her hands, eating a witches' supper, and that a devil given to her as a companion, called Nassao, knew her by the front [vaginal] opening."[4] Almost every Cartagena woman interrogated by the Holy Office in late 1632 and early 1633 repeated this story. However, in nearly every case, unique details surfaced. The free mulata Rufina, who served the widow of Amador Pérez, told a similar story, but she linked it to her desire for a man who would love her and generously give her presents.[5] In Rufina's story, a demon named Chochuelo marked her as his slave on her left ankle and "knew her carnally by the front vessel, spilling something hot." The slave Lucía Biafara said her devil Tongo "knew her through the back opening, spilling something as hot as candle wax."[6] Juana de Ortensio, a black freedwoman also known as "*la colorada*" (the scarlet one), said that her devil Ñagá "put her on hands and knees and knew her through the natural opening, spilling cold semen."[7] The black freedwoman María Méndez also spoke of the spilling of "very cold semen" from her devil Zampapalo, as did the free mulata Ana María de Robles.[8] While the descriptions of hot semen sound more like an experience with a mortal man, the bizarrely cold ejaculations (also common in witches' testimonies in Europe) suggest a "vision . . . of a congress which was cold, joyless, and had no fruit."[9]

A black freedwoman named Catalina de Otavio told a similar story but gave more details about what happened to her after the junta. After her denial of the Christian god and religion, Catalina's *madrina* introduced her to her demon companion, who marked her left arm to show she was "his."[10] The demon then commanded her to make a cross on the ground and erase it with her backside, which she did. Afterward, he ordered her to dance around a male goat and kiss his posterior. At this moment, the goat released a fetid gas reeking of sulfur. After she ate a meal of meat cooked without salt, the candles were blown out and her demon "knew her from the front and from the back in the natural opening, spilling out something very cold. When these abominations ended, she went back to her house. This horror sent her to bed sick for three months, given holy oil [for last rites]." Participation in this perverse sex act, according to her story, led to misery. It was a repentant account that probably pleased the listening inquisitors.

It is hard to believe that Catalina had a supper with demons, but it is not difficult to imagine that a violent sexual experience led her to a severe sickness or even simply an unendurable pregnancy. She may have made up some of her testimony to satisfy the inquisitors and prove she regretted her actions, but she probably did not make up a long illness. Catalina was not the only woman who confessed to pain or sickness resulting from intercourse. Why would a black slave named Gerónima embellish the standard story by saying "she had sex with a demon called Gallo, who knew her through the posterior opening twice, wounding her so that she bled?"[11] In saying these words, Gerónima admitted that either a wound of this kind had happened to her or she had heard other women discuss bleeding from sex. Why did she choose to give these details to the inquisitors? Perhaps it was to shock them or to try for their sympathy, or maybe it was because Gerónima thought this is what they wanted to hear. These stories probably owed something to coaching (most likely by Paula de Eguiluz herself) that took place in the cells before the witch opened up to inquisitors. Each of these stories also demonstrates remorse, because no woman among those confessing to the inquisitors said they enjoyed themselves and benefited greatly from their alliance with Satan. They presented their submission to temptation in their confessions, exposing their feelings of sexual shame, regret, or guilt to the inquisitors. As in Europe, these physically painful and humiliating deals with the devil sadly never resulted in long-lasting, real wealth or improvements in daily life.[12]

All of the above statements come from the tribunal's description of their 1633 auto de fe. They are summaries of trials conducted in late 1632 and 1633. The complete documentation for each woman's trial no longer exists or is irrevocably lost; the unabridged version of each trial could have extended to at least forty hand-written pages. These summaries do not illuminate the back and forth of interrogation sessions, so they do not reveal the process by which the inquisitors reached this level of confession. On the other hand, there is no record that these women were tortured into making these statements or even that the inquisitors asked leading questions. In Paula de Eguiluz's confessions—which made up the only existing complete case—Paula voluntarily described sex with the devil in explicit and unpleasant detail, although, as explained in chapter 6, in her second and third trials, she did not admit that she experienced it herself.

In September and October of 1632, Paula testified that several women allegedly took part in witches' juntas or gatherings involving painful and violent sexual encounters with demons.[13] One of the first women Paula named as a sister witch was Teodora de Salcedo, or Saucedo, a black freedwoman born in Havana and residing in Cartagena. According to Paula, five years before, "carnal acts" with a demon wounded Teodora.[14] Paula cured her with the help of her demonic familiar Mantelillos, who instructed the healer to use dust made from cat feces to remedy the "burn on [Teodora's] nether regions." When speaking for herself, at first Teodora did not deny she was a witch, that she had rejected God and religion, nor that she had sex with a demon; but she corrected Paula and said that her burns came from purging herself.[15] In her account, Paula took advantage of her knowledge of Teodora's genital burns, giving them a supernatural and gruesome context that would have pleased inquisitors' ideas about women tempted by Satan. Paula's accounts show her to be eager to expose shameful details about a friend to lessen her own guilt, even hinting at abortion attempts causing the injuries which Paula skillfully healed.

Paula's occupation as a healer kept her informed of the state of health of various individuals and whether they were suffering from sicknesses derived from natural, unnatural, or even supernatural causes. Another one of her patients was the twenty-six-year-old black freedwoman Luisa Domínguez, who was born in Santo Domingo. Domínguez resided in Getsemaní in the 1630s, earning her living making buns and empanadas, along with washing and starching clothes.[16] Luisa Domínguez testified that she was tempted to become a witch because she believed it would make her rich. She probably deeply regretted her avariciousness because, according to Paula, she came away with a very nasty reaction to sex with a demon.[17] Luisa reported that at a witches' junta, "after eating some cakes made of who knows what, they put out the candles that the devil gave them, and each of the witches had sex with their devils, and her own devil had carnal relations with her from behind."[18] After this encounter, Luisa supposedly told Paula of her horrific reaction to physical contact with the demon. According to Paula, Luisa said that while the demon was having sex with her, she remembered her *amigo* (boyfriend), or as Paula also called him, her galán, Juan Enrique. Suddenly the demon, perceiving that Luisa's mind wandered to fantasies of another lover, angrily separated himself from her and "the semen that he had to ejaculate spilled all over her body, leaving her covered in leprosy [*lepra*] . . . for a long time."[19] Either Paula or Luisa herself (if she did in fact tell this story) focused on pain and punishment as the moral of a story of a sexual encounter.

As in the case of Catalina de Otalvo, who said sex with the devil scared her so much that she almost died and was bedridden for three months, and Teodora's logical explanation of her scalded genitals, Luisa's story contained truth about her vision of sex. Paula did not say Luisa's skin condition was permanent, so it is unlikely that she actually had leprosy. Paula may have used the term lepra as a catchall description of skin lesions or as a way to shock the inquisitors into listening more closely to her stories.[20] It is likely that Luisa contracted a sexually transmitted disease from a mortal sex partner, perhaps even an actual man who took part in parties that transformed into Satanic juntas in the inquisitorial setting. Even if sex with a demon was a fantasy or a lie told to fit the inquisitors' expectations, these women, not unlike their contemporaries accused of witchcraft in Europe, drew from their own experiences when they associated sex with pain and disease.[21] While these testimonies certainly do not call up an image of sexual agency, they do continue to show how seventeenth-century women, like men, used sex and stories about sex to achieve certain practical goals and to create a specific persona for themselves. Sexual activities and sexual reputation were readily available negotiating tools in a variety of contexts.

Early modern European women described their demonic lovers as attractive and flashy but believable and realistic characters, who tempted them with appealing promises of marriage or economic support because this is what the women expected in exchange for having sex with a man. Even the extremely repetitive template set for witches' confessions could reveal a woman's sense of self-worth by her own admission of what was offered in exchange for her sexual surrender. What women expected in exchange for sex equaled the price they set for their own sexual value, heavily influenced by their historical context. In early modern Europe, women assumed that premarital sex would lead to a more permanent alliance.[22] Their disillusionment and abandonment after sex with the devil may offer a veiled commentary (given directly to powerful men while confessing to witchcraft) on female opinions of stricter enforcement of sacramental marriage after the Council of Trent. In contrast, none of the witches in the Cartagena witch craze confessed that they had sex with a demon because he was disguised as a man who wished to marry them. Their expectations of the results of sexual activity differed from their contemporaries in Europe; they carried no illusions that sex led to marriage, but they did pin some economic hopes on their sexual partners. For example, Teodora de Saucedo said that someone persuaded her to become a witch because "it would bring her a great deal of money and rest."[23] Juana de Mora, a widow of an African man, had a friend who persuaded her to become a witch so she would have "a man who would give her presents and many possessions in this life."[24] Catalina de Otavio said she received the same promise, possibly before her marriage to the free black man Pedro Angico.[25] The free mulata Rufina also heard this promise, with the added temptation that this fantasy man "would love her," while Dorotea de Palma hoped she would be "*estimada*" by this generous lover.[26]

Typically, these promises tempted the women when they felt particularly hopeless about their lives and their futures and were vulnerable to Satan's offers of an easier life.[27] Almost all the alleged witches in Cartagena stated they were weak and greedy, rhetoric that perfectly fit the inquisitors' understanding of women. The free black woman Bárbola de Albornóz made a more personal appeal to their pity. She claimed that a year before, a friend of hers had found her working hard, even though she was sick at that time.[28] Bárbola's friend persuaded her to go to a junta so she would not have to work so much because she would find a man "who would love her and give her many presents." Bárbola, "seeing herself so afflicted and understanding that she could fulfill her needs by taking this path," agreed to go to the gathering. María Méndez resisted the temptation at first, but then she "greedily" fell for the promise of "a great deal of wealth to free her from her misery."[29] Luisa Domínguez succumbed to the temptation of freedom from slavery and access to wealth.[30] Some of the women did seem simply greedy: "persuasions" could not "defeat" Ana María de Robles's will to refuse the offer of becoming a witch, until her tempter, another free mulata, gave her forty pesos and a gold necklace.[31]

All of these testimonies came from the accused witch's experience, imagination, a sense of what her judges wished to hear, or coaching from another inmate, so it was only natural for these women to present a version of their fantasy lovers, a disguised version of someone they knew, or a composite character who contained elements of several different men of their acquaintance. The Cartagena witches—including Paula de Eguiluz, in her frequent references to her demon familiar Mantelillos—did not state that the devil or his demons appeared to them disguised as specific human individuals, but that does not mean they did not have a certain man in mind when they described their experiences. Their association of sex, especially unpleasant sex, with monetary gain or even permanent financial stability reveals a great deal about their experiences and self and societal identity. It is possible that some of these women tended toward occasional prostitution to find an economically supportive lover. To more fully comprehend female sexuality, it is imperative that we view colonial women's economic dependence on men shading toward sex-for-sale as a gray area, moving away from the pervasive virgin/whore dichotomy we have inherited from moralizing tracts produced in Iberian and other patriarchal societies. These women simply needed financial support from their lovers in one way or another, as was the case for many of the Iberian women who dabbled in or more seriously practiced love magic.

Many of the names of demonic familiars were also heard in Spanish cases, most notably Chochuelo, named in Rufina de Amador Perez's testimony.[32] Chochuelo was a misspelling of Cojuelo, meaning "one-legged" or

crippled, the name of a famous demon from the Basque cases. This particular satanic envoy was so well known that he was the subject of a picaresque
novel written by Luis Velez Guevara, published in 1641. Taravira, Gallo, and
Zampapalo were names for demons known in both Spain and Cartagena.
However, Tongo and Ñagá, more African-sounding names that came up
in the testimonies of Lucía Biafara and Juana de Ortensio, were not mentioned in the Basque trials. This mix of Spanish and African worldviews
and traditions reflects the fact that these women were Creoles living in the
Caribbean and were in frequent contact with both Spaniards and Africans,
as well as others born in the New World. The entities that the inquisitors
designated as familiars, including Paula's Mantelillos, might have had a
very different character in the mental and spiritual understanding of the
women. As the only man involved in this set of trials, Diego López's confessions offer an especially eye-opening perspective on demonic familiars,
both in terms of his own sexual experiences with one of them and in his
descriptions of other women's relationships with their demon lovers.

Similar to the small number of men involved in large European witch
crazes, López was implicated because in the 1620s and 1630s, he was sexually
involved with women accused of witchcraft. López's lovers included Juana
de Ortensio and another enslaved woman named Rufina de Rafael Gómez,
who happened to be a cousin of the accused witch Teodora de Salcedo.[33] He
took part in activities on the edges of this large group of individuals that,
in the world outside satanic fantasies, actually were connected by social ties
and their participation in Cartagena's lively nightlife. In late 1632, toward the
end of her second trial, Paula mentioned in passing that she saw Diego López
in the vicinity of a wake held for Juan Bran, a "great witch." She later insisted
that she never saw López actually take part in a junta.[34] Regardless, the tribunal imprisoned López on January 8, 1633. Diego López's statements reveal
a man full of guilt for his marital infidelity, who was willing to implicate
friends, lovers, acquaintances, and strangers to turn the inquisitors' focus
away from himself.[35] While there is no doubt whatsoever that López lied
during his confessions, both his lies and his more believable stories reveal a
great deal about his inner life, fantasies, and the guilt he felt about his extramarital affairs. As noted in the last chapter, López did what he could to soften
the inquisitors' suspicions, but he fell far short of Paula's clever, emotional,
and manipulative storytelling. This makes him a more transparent confes-
sor from the twenty-first century point of view. The inquisitors probably
also found him less mentally and emotionally complex and challenging.

From start to finish, López's testimonies show that he associated his imprisonment with his sex life, although unlike most of the individuals encountered in this book, he did not really know how to use this information effectively to improve his case. He felt guilty for actions that he feared the inquisitors considered sins, as well as a deeper personal remorse for things he had done that he knew were wrong. He regretted his lack of control over his sexuality, but he did nothing to alter his behavior, and his testimonies reveal a spiteful person willing to bring down anyone if there were any chance that this might help his own case. After spending just over two weeks in the Holy Office jail, López asked for his first hearing in order to take a stab at guessing the cause of his arrest. Hoping for the best, he confessed that "he had carnally known several women, whom he named, by putting them facedown, although he had sex with them through the front opening." Other than that, he did not think he committed any crime of interest to the Holy Office, nor had he been a bad Christian.[36] For three months, López refused to acknowledge that he was a witch.

Finally, and perhaps simply worn down by his time in prison, López confessed, linking his affairs and parties he had attended to the group of female witches.[37] His accounts of the gatherings clarify the social connections suggested in Paula's and the other women's confessions. López said that five years before, he was having an affair with Juana de Ortensio (also known as "the scarlet one"), who at that time was twenty-one years of age and still enslaved to her master Juan de Ortensio. One night in 1628, López went to look for Juana and found her dancing with "many black women" at Elena de Viloria's house. He asked Juana about the dance, and she simply replied that they were having a good time. Later, Juana confessed that everyone who went to dances at Elena's house was a witch. Diego claimed he was shocked and the two lovers fought over this. But a few days later, he was curious about their gatherings and asked Juana to tell him when they assembled again for their *brujerías*, because he wanted to watch them. Juana said they met at Elena's house or at the Manzanillo swamp on Friday nights. Then, López went to Elena's house on his own and asked about the next meeting, which was set for 9 p.m. in the swamp. Later he called on Elena and she took him by the hand to meet Lucifer, who sat on a sumptuous black throne looking "ugly and abominable." With Elena as his godmother, Diego denied the Christian god and religion.[38] At what point did Diego's account move from the real world to the world of fantasy? Whether or not Diego knew the template for a witches' *junta* before his arrest, he could have easily learned what the inquisitors expected him to confess while in his cell in the tribunal's prison. There is no doubt that the prisoners of the Cartagena Holy Office communicated amongst themselves and could hear each other's voices even if they were not in the same cells.

Seemingly unprompted by the inquisitors, after describing these social encounters, López then proceeded to narrate a unique account of anal sex with a demon. Why would Diego choose to bring up this highly taboo subject? Perhaps the other prisoners accused of witchcraft, all women, told him the inquisitors wanted a sexually explicit confession. Even if they knew generally what the inquisitors wanted to hear, the female prisoners could not be sure of how a man should frame his involvement in sex with demons. The classic seduction narrative did not seem to fit in this case. For the most famous and trusted European demonologists and in the accounts given in European witch trials, only heterosexual acts took place at witches' Sabbaths. In the early modern mind, witchcraft and sodomy were similar perverted, inverted acts against nature, but they did not occur simultaneously. As presented in books such as the *Malleus Maleficarum*, generally Satan acted like a run of the mill human being because the authors of these tomes hoped this convinced readers that the devil was real, not imaginary.[39] A sodomite devil may have been too much for the average early modern European to grasp, even though some historians argue that there was a "widespread existence of a male culture of homoeroticism" in early modern Spain.[40] Even the idea of a man seduced by a demon appearing as a woman was not common in witness accounts.[41] Demonologists, as clergyman, wanted to spread knowledge and fears of Satan, but not necessarily information about sodomy. López did not know this demonological tradition; most likely, he said what came out of his imagination and what he learned after three months communicating with other prisoners. The fact that part of his story fits the standard account and part of it does not proves that fantasy, personal experience, and gossip fueled these confessions.

López said the devil gave him a companion named Taravira (also spelled Taracita), who looked like a male dwarf dressed in clothes typical of a Native American man. In contrast, the scant number of European men who admitted to pacts with the devil in the seventeenth century said that their demon lovers looked like attractive women.[42] Taravira commanded Diego to make a cross on the floor with his foot and then erase it with his rear end. Then Taravira gave Diego a candle and they danced, circling around a male goat and eventually kissing him on the "trasero." Later they ate some tasteless rice without salt. Continuing the set account told by hundreds of accused witches, they then put out the candles. But in this darkness, Diego "had sex with his devil and took him through the back opening." López confessed that when "he copulated from behind with his devil Taravira, it was very pleasurable, more than if he were with a woman."[43] Diego's words do not clearly indicate if he was the passive or active participant in this act, a detail that historians now realize was not vital to colonial understanding or condemnation of sodomy.[44] In the written account, after López admits his enjoyment (in great contrast to the horrific stories told by the women cited above), the inquisitors quickly deflected this line of confession, asking him where the gatherings took place and then moving on to asking Diego to list more witches that were present. This attitude was in line with the contemporary vision of sodomy as the "pecado nefando," or the abominable, nefarious sin that should remain nameless and hidden. Despite the harsh persecution of some convicted same sex lovers and the fact that sodomy was theoretically punishable by death, historians conclude that in many cases, the Catholic Church chose to hide or downplay evidence of sodomitical practice.[45] Obviously, López believed the inquisitors would appreciate hearing his confession to enjoying anal sex or he felt the need to reveal his own fantasies in this confessional setting.

Other than his initiation sparked by his dealings with Juana de Ortensio, Diego attributed most of the information in his confessions to his former amiga (girlfriend) Rufina.[46] In the late 1620s and early 1630s, López spent many nights with his sometime lover Rufina de Rafael Gómez, but by the time of his trial, he considered her his enemy and suspected that his former amiga Rufina, along with Paula, accused him of being a brujo (male witch), leading to his imprisonment and trial.[47]

Among all the dozens of witness testimonies, only López accused Rufina de Rafael Gómez of interaction with demons and practicing magic. Although Rufina (or López's version of Rufina) bragged about being a close confidant of Paula de Eguiluz, Paula never mentioned her. Paula implicated many other women other than Rufina, and the inquisitors trusted her enough to arrest nearly all of them. Diego started mentioning "his" Rufina in his confessions on April 24, 1634, eventually saying that back in 1627, when she was supposedly only fourteen years old, Rufina bragged to him about her knowledge of the numerous male and female witches in Cartagena, along with the maleficios they had committed. Within a few days she was arrested.[48] Because she said she claimed that she was only twenty-one years old in 1634, the inquisitors provided her with a *curador*, a legal advocate for minors on trial. Rufina spent under two months in the inquisition jail, far less than most of the women involved in this set of investigations. The inquisitors interrogated her in eight audiencias, but she persistently denied all of López's accusations. In early June, the inquisitors released her and suspended her case. Their lack of interest in Rufina suggests that the Holy Office put little stock in López's accusations and viewed the young-looking Rufina as a weak and unthreatening woman, even if she did dabble in magic and was allegedly a close friend of Paula de Eguiluz. Rufina effectively played the role of a helpful informer, a method Paula and Diego also tried. Whether or not she literally used magic, Rufina undoubtedly had a certain degree of power over Diego López and their relationship.

The fact that only López's words attest to Rufina's actions highlights the fantastical nature of the majority of his confessions, especially those involving a group of Cartagena residents whom he accused of practicing Judaism, a topic outside of the scope of this book.[49] In fact, Diego's descriptions of Rufina's words and deeds often reveal nothing more than his own daydreams and concocted visions of his relationship with Rufina; these were offered according to what he believed the inquisitors wanted to hear, given that he thought Rufina's accusations brought him to their attention. López probably thought that they would prefer to blame a woman for crimes connected to witchcraft and sex, just as he hoped to redirect their interest from himself to the bizarre and shocking Jewish conspiracies he concocted. In fact, the Holy Office would have ignored Rufina if López had not mentioned the "many maleficios she had done and [that she was a] vile person."[50] In only a handful of cases, López presented information that rings true to conversations or experiences he had with Rufina, although not necessarily "real" events.

Time and time again Diego presented himself as a voyeur, passively observing countless scandalous occurrences. López usually framed his confessions by setting the scene, explaining that he witnessed unchristian behavior during the time he spent with Rufina (or occasionally another lover). Starting in around 1630, Diego and Rufina slept together in a house behind her owners' house, often in the room of an Indian woman named Mother Catarina, who lived next to a staircase that climbed to the roof of the house.[51] From this vantage point, López claimed he witnessed all sorts of illicit, heretical, and even supernatural activity. On one occasion, Diego went to an estancia owned by Rufina's master in order to sleep with her. This farm happened to connect to a beach known as Manzanillo, a popular location for witches' gatherings. Rufina, fully understanding his weaknesses, allegedly tempted Diego's voyeuristic tendencies, asking him "if he wanted to see the white witches that went there, because she would show them to him that night."[52] Diego agreed, and at midnight, they went down to the beach where he allegedly saw several doñas led by Paula de Eguiluz enacting all of the rituals associated with witches: dancing around a male goat and kissing its posterior, denying god, and eating a feast. Each woman arrived flying through the air with their devils, wearing their skirts wrapped around their legs like breeches. López claimed he could see everything because everyone held candles. A large devil was in attendance and the devoted were either kissing Paula or putting food in her mouth. Afterward they flew home, and Diego went back to the estancia with Rufina.[53]

López paints a picture of Rufina as a boastful, jealous, and troublemaking young woman. She was wary of her lover spending too much time with his female patients and seemed to assert her connections to witches as an aspect of her attractiveness. Certainly this technique worked with López. When he was helping the other Rufina (de Amador Pérez) in his role as a surgeon after she gave birth, the recovering Rufina said, "Here comes my namesake," as López's girlfriend happened to pass by.[54] The younger Rufina started chatting about white witches and how they were all Paula's disciples and that Paula did not want any black or mulata women at her gatherings, so Rufina de Amador Pérez (probably knowing it was all nonsense) asked, "How do you go then?" The other Rufina responded, "All of them are happy that I am there." Later, she offered her two listeners the opportunity to witness another gathering of white witches. López and Rufina de Amador Pérez traveled to a turret located near the Santa Catalina port and watched, hiding behind a large pile of odiferous plants, as a group of doñas flew in after 10 p.m. It was a clear night illuminated by moonlight, so López saw that they were led by his amiga and Paula and they did not come accompanied by their demons. He observed that they appeared to fly in a normal human bodily form. Most of the witches were in dresses, but shockingly a few of them wore men's hats, pants, and doublets. The transvestism only made this a more sexually charged, illicit scene, and López apparently relished that Rufina provided him with these opportunities for voyeurism. Or he felt it was to his advantage to illustrate the numerous sinful temptations she offered him.

López also perceived Rufina as a vengeful, terrifying lover, a perception that highlights his own guilty conscience. For a time in 1627, he did not visit his amiga for several days, because he was at home caring for his wife and newborn daughter.[55] One night at 10 p.m., everyone in the house awoke from the clatter of three stones landing on the roof. One can imagine the distress of López's wife as her infant woke up suddenly from the racket. López ran outside with a priest who was also in the house. Both men carried swords (contrary to colonial regulations regarding non-Spaniards bearing arms, as well as norms for the clergy) and López also had a small wooden shield. Each man ran in a different direction down the street, looking for the culprit. López saw a woman on the wall and recognized Rufina. He asked her what she was doing there, and she replied, "That's a good question since you haven't seen me in so long." López replied that he was in charge of his wife after she gave birth and that he had to attend to her. Rufina retorted, "Your grace should be very content to have a daughter because before long she will be gone." López begged Rufina, "On your life, do not touch her." She said nothing could be done because her demonic familiar, called Rompesantos (saint-breaker), was the one who had thrown the stones that disturbed the household. Rufina then took to her heels and ran. López chased after her and caught her in his embrace, but he said she then literally flew from his arms into the air. Two days later his infant died. Rompesantos probably did not kill the baby, as this story implies, but certainly López felt he deserved this cruel punishment for his sexual transgressions with Rufina. In this account, a remorseful López presented the inquisitors with an eloquent and even tragic example of how he had already been punished for his sexual transgressions.

Rufina's fantasies also emerged out of López's stories. His version of their affair effectively intertwined illicit sex and submission to demonic temptations to commit evil acts. Although often López used the "Rufina told me" rhetorical ploy in an attempt to disguise his own culpability, in certain cases, his accounts of Rufina's experiences rang true to her own self-presentation, an ongoing sexually-charged drama. Rufina's demonic allies took an active role in her complicated love life or at least allowed her to maintain an illusion of control. To aid these machinations, Paula de Eguiluz put her in contact with a demon called Huevo, who could assume Rufina's appearance. Huevo then did Rufina's housework and "attended to" her master when he sought her out for his *torpezas*, or crude lusts.[56] Meanwhile, she went out all night on her own business. However, Rufina only received these benefits due to a harsh pact or bargain she made with Huevo. In return for her freedom,

Rufina had to inexplicably eat lime (*cal*) and "allow the demon to carnally know her through the rear opening."

López benefited from Rufina's arrangement because his amiga came to see him on the nights that her master went to look for her for sex. Because Rufina was with López, her master unknowingly had sex with the demon instead of her. On one of these occasions, the next morning the slave owner called on Rufina again. He said to her, "Come here, so I can see if you got rid of the *mal de madre* [menstruation] that you told me you had last night." He claimed that after they had sex, he was nauseous and smelled of sulfur. She replied, "Yes, sir," but when he sniffed her body he observed that she no longer reeked of sulfur. Her excuse was that she had put on clean clothes. López believed this story because once when Rufina and he were chatting in Madre Catalina's room, he noticed another woman of a similar figure leaving the kitchen in Rufina's clothes, moving around the house and talking to Rufina's master.[57] In this story, López passed the blame: Rufina seduced him with the help of her demon, but Rufina's master had begun the corruption by lusting after Rufina.

Rufina was not alone in fantasizing about escaping the duties imposed by men, especially sex. She told López that the *doñas blancas* who were witches also took advantage of demonic doppelgangers. Apparently, the doñas befriended two devils: one to take them to the juntas and another to stay in bed at home with their husbands.[58] Presumably, the ladies had sex with one demon, while the other pretended to carry out their wifely obligations at home. This particular anecdote piqued the attention of the listening inquisitors, who often took a special interest in investigating situations where it appeared that nonwhite women were corrupting Spanish women. In this case, they perceived an opening for digging into López's conscience, which was, after all, crucial to their role of helping sinners return to the Christian faith. After hearing this story, again put into Rufina's mouth, an inquisitor said to López, "You have confessed you are a witch and that you are married, tell us if you have two devils for your companions, and if you have used this remedy of leaving one devil as a representation of your person while you are absent, so your wife does not miss you."[59] López responded, with a note of regret, that he only had one devil, the aforementioned Taracita, or Taravira. He had no need for these precautions because his wife knew of his *entretenimientos*, or diversions, and she bore them with patience. With this admission, the day's hearing ended.

Several years into his relationship with Rufina in 1631, López fell in love and began an affair with one of his patients, a mulata born in Jamaica.[60] Of course, Rufina found out and in a jealous rage sought vengeance. López heard that Paula de Eguiluz and Rufina were working together, arming themselves with two bludgeons to give the new lover a severe pummeling. López followed the two women to a bridge and he watched them sit down where they could keep an eye on everyone passing by, presumably looking to trap his girlfriend. Before any violence occurred, he claimed that Rufina and Paula folded up their headscarves and tied their skirts around their legs to make them into breeches, and then flew away into the air.

Drawing from their own experiences, accused witches told these confessions of satanic sex in a desperate effort to free themselves from the tribunal prisons. The stories open a tiny window into their perspectives on sex, even through the powerful filter of inquisitorial interrogation and the complex ways they transferred the blame to others. Inquisitors wanted to hear about sex, and the imprisoned witches fulfilled their desires. However, the religious authorities also had a more social and tangible goal for their attempts to weaken Paula and her circle of friends, love magic clients, and practitioners. Many Spanish clerical and secular bureaucrats deeply feared the sexually-charged illicit dances and feasts that frequently took place in and around Cartagena. The alleged witches may have been thinking of some of their sexual and erotic experiences during real parties and dances when they confessed to witches' juntas.[61] The Catholic Church forbade these gatherings because the festivities seemed to draw African and Afro-descended participants back to their non-Christian roots and, by extension, put them under demonic influence. However, even the local saint Peter Claver was not able to put a stop to them, despite his best efforts. It is likely that the Holy Office also hoped to end these celebrations, often called lloros or wakes, by imprisoning some of the attendees in the 1630s witch craze, a reaction to the increasing influence of Creole women of African descent over the town's population. It should be stressed that all of these efforts failed and these officially frowned-upon festivities continued throughout the colonial era. The sexualized sociability found at these parties offered an insurmountable challenge.

The confessions provide glimpses into seventeenth-century Cartagena's lively and racially-diverse nightlife. Both Diego López and Paula de Eguiluz mentioned a famous lloro for the gran brujo Juan Bran.[62] This gathering went down in local history because, reportedly, after leaving the wake, some of the participants ran through the darkened streets and shape-shifted into a herd of pigs. Although the name of the deceased indicates he was African-born, this was not a strictly African event. López described the partygoers as Creole black women and friends of Juan Bran's daughter. He also said that Spanish and mestizo men came to the party as amigos of some of the women, and an elderly African man named Bartolomé Arara, who lived nearby, wanted to disassociate himself from the festivities. He told inquisitors that he woke up on the night of the wake to loud noises in the street and thought it was a passing *guagua* (cart). He fearfully put a cross on his door, in hopes of discouraging witches from harming him.[63]

According to a Cartagena ecclesiastical magistrate, baptized African men and women held lloros even decades later, coming together in great numbers to dance all night to the beat of drums in honor of a deceased member of their ethnic group or *nación*.[64] The participants called these events *amanecimientos*, literally "daybreakers" or "sunrisers." Despite the Church's concern that these were occasions for enacting "gentile and superstitious rites and committing great offenses against Our Lord God," they continued at least into the 1650s and probably were never entirely suppressed. Church officials went so far as to confiscate the drums, food, and drink prepared for the lloros, threatening lashes and imprisonment without effect. Saint Peter Claver personally charged into the dancers gathered in the city streets and plazas "like an enraged bull," scattering the dancers, who dropped their large, heavy drums and fled from the saint, who was wielding both a whip and bronze crucifix.[65] Saint Peter might have even seen the "malignant spirits who incited these blacks in these dances." The descriptions included in Claver's beatification process depict parties that took place roughly twenty years after the witch hunt that implicated Diego López, Paula de Eguiluz, and all of their associates, proving that the harsh imprisonment and penances inflicted by the Cartagena Holy Office had little long term effect on the local nightlife. No wonder, as in the seventeenth century, Cartagena's Catholic authorities sent a mixed message by officially permitting African drums and dances, as well as parades including transvestite African brotherhoods, during Carnival.[66] The cutthroat competition between the Holy Office, the bishop, the Jesuits (not to mention the factions that existed within the Company of Jesus), and every other religious institution in the city prevented a unified suppression of African-influenced festivities.

The Church viewed lloros as African gatherings, but witnesses including Diego López claimed to see doñas blancas also taking part in orgiastic revelries. An especially notorious case came from nearby Tolú, a smaller coastal town with close ties to Cartagena, particularly among the accused witches. In 1632, several Tolú slaves reported witnessing bizarre events on the beach late at night.[67] When a young Creole black man on an errand for his mistress happened upon a scene of human forms dancing with torches in hand around midnight, he fainted away in fear and awoke crying out for Jesus and making the sign of the cross with his fingers. One of the central participants was doña Elena de la Cruz, age forty, a wealthy Spanish woman. Along with the standard details of dancing with a male goat and kissing his posterior, the witnesses said they saw doña Elena and the others walking around wearing a garment similar to a loincloth, naked from the waist up, playing a Moorish-style drum, and singing in a way that sounded like a bleating sheep. The participants also wore white clothes on their heads and were locally reputed to be witches. Apparently, these *recocijos*, or jubilees, even took place in a plaza within the town itself. During the course of many interrogations with the inquisitors, doña Elena denied a few details relating to other stories told about her, but she fully accepted her guilt in taking part in these scandalous juntas. Although the Holy Office persecuted doña Elena, around the same time, doña Ana de Fuentes advised Paula de Eguiluz to go to Tolú "because there one can do many more things than in Cartagena because there is more freedom and no one dares to discover or discuss anything like in this city."[68] At least to doña Ana, the tribunal's fearsome range extended less than a few days' journey from the Cartagena headquarters. Allegedly as close as Tolú, even doñas danced publicly, semi-nude, scoffing at strictures regarding female sexual seclusion and modesty.

The fact that Africans and their descendants danced and celebrated alongside Europeans and white Creoles might seem surprising, but it was not all that unusual in Cartagena. Throughout the seventeenth and eighteenth centuries, Cartagena bishops ineffectively prohibited *fandangos*, which they viewed as sinful, although perhaps not quite as demonic as the lloros. However, in the 1680s, a bishop described with evident moral outrage the "'scandalous abuse of holy celebrations through the excessive rowdiness of drinking and fandangoing in the streets, disturbing solemn religious processions, creating a carnival atmosphere, and seductively enticing good citizens, even priests and nuns, into committing violations of the most sinful nature.'"[69]

Cartagena descended into a witch craze of sorts in the 1630s, although a very mild one in comparison to other seventeenth-century hunts in Central Europe or the English-speaking world. Some of the accused were tortured because they denied their previous confessions, but no one was executed. Diego López's malicious testimonies helped transfer the inquisitors' focus to the local Portuguese Jewish population, leading to a far more destructive persecution and even executions. Clearly, suspected Portuguese *judaizantes* provoked more fear and inquisitorial retributions than Creole witches did.

Nearly all of the alleged witches were Afro-descended women brought to the inquisitors' attention in the 1630s by Paula de Eguiluz, as comadres in a large, socially-connected community of Creole healers and practitioners of love magic. As Paula observed, "There were so many brujos and brujas that they seemed like an ocean and it was impossible to count them or know who they were."[70] Paula succeeded in channeling the inquisitors' fears of social disruption, represented by the very real and large gatherings in the city itself, complete with drumming, dancing, and most likely sex, toward fantastical sex with demons and the scarred, but penitent bodies of her comadres. Their boisterous parties, flashy attire, and jewelry also drew the attention of the inquisitors, especially when it was clear that Spaniards, both men and women, were very attracted to women like Paula. Her public, even proud, assertion of sexuality played a role in the attraction, as both black and white women hoped to manipulate men by taking advantage of their lusts and affections; this despite the inquisitors' attempts to link illicit sex to Satanic rituals and lurid group sex and the pain and disease sex might bring to women. Fantasies such as those López told support the argument for an active, yet risky, sexuality in Cartagena women. López's musings on his own sexuality prove that colonial men felt a strong sense of remorse and guilt when they strayed outside of the marital bed, even if they did nothing to mend their ways. López clearly regretted his dalliances. If he behaved like an aggressive macho, he did not assume the inquisitors would approve of this persona.

The next chapter turns away from psychologically probing, painful confessions, highlighting instead how women boldly asserted their sexuality in the course of their daily lives. We have seen that they spun stories of pacts with the devil motivated by guilty feelings toward their own greed and how this may have led to sexual compromises. But if these women did have ill-gotten gains, how did they spend their money once they secured food and shelter for themselves and their dependents? Simply by expending a great deal of effort into their dress and physical appearance, these women flaunted social and racial hierarchies wherever they went.

CHAPTER EIGHT

SEX, DRESS, AND THE INQUISITION

AS OBSERVED IN THE LAST CHAPTER, WOMEN OF AFRICAN DESCENT AND their social lives infuriated the colonial authorities for centuries in Cartagena. But it was not just their loud parties, drumming, and dancing that disturbed the inquisitors and the rest of the city. These women's brash and disruptive public presentation made them stand out on the city streets even as they went about their mundane daily tasks as washerwomen, servants, cooks, and seamstresses. Their dress styles fueled a perception of confused social hierarchies. Prominent leaders in the local church felt especially concerned about policing women's dress in this era, and this concern extended to Spain and other areas of the Spanish empire. Clothing styles and women's physical appearance also played a critical role the manipulation of sexuality that took place in the Holy Office secret prisons during witchcraft trials. This book began with an incident of an inquisitor succumbing to sexual temptation, offering an accused woman a lighter penance in return for sex. The women's choice of outfits during the seduction and interrogation process played an important role in the internal investigation of this secret and shameful inquisitorial scandal. Continuing the story of Paula de Eguiluz and her comadres from the previous two chapters, this chapter intersperses inventories and descriptions of clothing and jewelry with men's perspectives, as voiced in moralizing literary, religious, and judicial observations, exploring the tension caused by clothing choices made in this hierarchical society.

Women who wished to attract sexual partners in Cartagena faced stiff competition.[1] Eligible women resorted to love magic in some cases to get the upper hand on their rivals. Seventeenth-century Cartagena doctors recommended that women care for their teeth and breath by eating healthy foods, cutting back on their tobacco habit, using toothpicks, and rinsing their mouths out with vinegar. Women in Cartagena could use cosmetic masks to whiten their hands, breasts, and faces.[2] Elegant dress represented another weapon in this arsenal. A woman who sought financial support from a man did well to highlight her sexual desirability through her stylish clothing, demonstrating that she was not in an economically precarious situation. Despite their race, illegitimacy, and unmarried circumstances, some of the women accused of witchcraft in the 1630s were well off and had a certain degree of authority, so they dressed the part. They defied standard racial and social hierarchies by constructing their public external selves with personal display as a form of self-assertion.[3]

In Cartagena, elite status usually equated to European descent, often from the early settlers of the region. The local ruling class flaunted their slave ownership, access to rural land holdings, ties to or involvement in mercantile or government activities, and conspicuous consumption in the form of lavish dress, horses, carriages, jewelry, and entourages. The elite left evidence of their material possessions and demonstrated their piety in their last wills and testaments. Often piety and wealth were intertwined through donations to churches and convents, images and portraits of saints decorating houses, and wearing jewelry such as crosses. These various material marks of conspicuous consumption proved that the pious wealthy did not suffer hunger or endure manual labor. Slaves carried women in covered litters and men could ride horses so they did not have to exert themselves in the tropical heat. Others made their food and cleaned for them. The elite confirmed their status through the public display of their wealth, especially in their clothing.

In Cartagena, slaves and free people of color filled the ranks of the poorer residents. Women in this situation might only own a few articles of clothing and collections of rags.[4] In theory, they had no honor to protect and thus had no right to surround themselves with the accoutrements of a status and leisure that they could not claim as their own. From the colonial perspective, an African or Afro-descended woman who appeared before the Holy Office lacked honor due to her origins in Africa, connections to slavery (even if freed) or manual labor, and her doubtful Christianity. She might even be judged to be less physically attractive because she did not meet European ideals of beauty. To the Spanish colonial elite, if this woman were wealthy, her possessions confused and even mocked the accepted symbols of social status, honor, and even the race hierarchy itself. However, inventories made by Cartagena's inquisition court demonstrate that some women of African descent did possess a decent amount of wealth, owning land, rental properties, jewelry, and numerous slaves, pointing to a diversity in Afro-Colombian women's experience. This complicates the link between social class distinctions based on wealth and colonial hierarchies based on race or place of origin. The inventories show the range of wealth possessed by Afro-Colombian women and document both sparse and extravagant consumption of material goods, including objects related to religious practice, despite the fact that the women had been tried by the Holy Office and some were accused of denouncing the Christian religion.

Historians who study clothing do not underestimate the importance of enforcing new styles of dress, and by extension new identities, in the wake of imperial expansion. As Jean Comaroff writes:

> Clothes were at once commodities and accoutrement of a civilized self. They were to prove a privileged means for constructing new forms of value, personhood, and history ... [and] forge new self-sustaining orders of desire, transaction, and value.[5]

Clothing played this kind of critical role in early modern European interactions with Africa. The Jesuit and Cartagena resident Alonso de Sandoval described in great detail the ostentatious European-style clothing adopted by central African elites who traded with Spaniards and Portuguese in coastal cities.[6] For a much later period, Comaroff observes a playful and imaginative use of the European clothing imposed on Africans living in Protestant missions. While Christian missionaries regulated clothing and outfitted Africans in European castoffs, individuals modified the new imposed dress styles according to personal taste and local styles. A similar process took place in colonial Latin America. From first contact, Spaniards pondered what they perceived as native nakedness and called for a modification of dress to conform to assumptions about modesty and shame. As decades passed and colonial society grew more complex, the introduction of Spanish ways of dress and bodily adornment fostered consumption of mineral wealth, expensive European cloth, and countless other products that helped support the ventures of international merchants and the Spanish crown. Meanwhile, non-elite women began to embrace an elegant, flashy style of dress that caused a great deal of frustration for the imperial authorities. While the Cartagena region produced inexpensive cotton cloth, those consumers who wished to follow the dictates of fashion eagerly bought millions of pesos worth of imported contraband material.[7] Merchants must have been pleased to have enthusiastic consumers of imported ribbons, petticoats, and shoes, but moralizers struggled with public displays of wealth that confounded social and racial hierarchies.

Early modern Spaniards imagined that only the honorable elite could wear the luxurious fabrics, expensive jewelry, frills, laces, and ornaments that signified wealth, nobility, prestige, and pure lineage in their society. For them, clothing was an extension of social and racial hierarchies: clothing marked status.[8] But in the Americas, everyone dressed as extravagantly as they possibly could, confusing observers and provoking the continuation of sumptuary laws into the eighteenth century. Modestly well-off nonwhite women who could not claim the honorable status of wealthy españolas still dressed as if they were rich and lived in luxury. In 1698, Agustín de Vetancurt observed that in viceregal Mexico City, even "the poorest woman has her pearls and jewels, and considers herself unhappy if she does not have her gold jewelry to wear on holidays."[9] Sumptuary laws were in no way effective, but instead demonstrate a strong belief in the importance of clothing "employed only in cultures which consider it possible to disguise one's status via clothing."[10]

Europeans traveling in colonial Latin America noticed that residents dressed in a European style but always with more jewelry, ribbons, frippery, and embellishment. This public display and strategic self-presentation suggests the assertion of a particular identity, defying hierarchies, or perhaps demonstrating their flexibility.[11] As Comaroff states, "in a commodity culture, identity is something owned apart from one's self, something that must continuously be 'put on' and displayed."[12] The outward show of expensive apparel and accessories fits well with colonial Spanish American ideas of honor as equivalent to public reputation. But even those who did not possess the inborn qualities required for elite Spanish honor chose to dress as if they did. In some of the examples given below, the fashionable and sumptuous clothing paraded by poor, single women of African descent paraded on the theater of Cartagena streets belied the rudimentary housing in which they lived. But given the climate, Cartagena residents only needed a hammock in a room that had a slight breeze to get through the hottest hours of the day. They could afford to channel their resources into their clothing.

In contrast to his presentation of African nobles as well dressed and eager to wear European fabrics, Sandoval, writing in the 1620s, often referred to the pitiful dress (or lack of) endured by humble African slaves in Cartagena.[13] Sandoval's point was to chastise slave owners for treating their chattel as subhuman because the purpose of his book was to promote Jesuit efforts to catechize and baptize Africans. He stressed the Jesuit charity of clothing the naked slaves whenever possible:

> The slaves cannot provide clothes for themselves, so we beg their masters to at least cover them decently. But often we have to bring them some rags to wear, and they are so grateful that we might have given them the most elegant brocades. This gratefulness proves that they feel ashamed of their nudity, but they cannot do anything about it.[14]

In his view, owners who did not help clothe their slaves even stood in the way of their slaves' progress toward becoming good Christians. Sandoval valued clothing a great deal, insisting that slaves at least wear a scrap of fabric during their baptisms. He understood that in his world, beauty came from bodily adornment in the form of clothing and jewelry and not naked physicality, which he considered gross, barbaric, and crude. Although he recognized that Jesuits might struggle to maintain nonsexual thoughts when working with naked slaves, he argued that well-dressed Europeans, skilled in their own culture's flirtation and seduction techniques, represented a much more serious temptation to a priest's chastity. On the other hand, Sandoval admired the exotic and intricate tattooing and scarification that frequently marked African bodies. However, Sandoval's descriptions of *bozal* nudity should not be confused with the elegant fashions worn by Creole freedwomen and even many slaves.

Sandoval's companion, the local saint Peter Claver, campaigned against immodest dress, proving that church authorities associated certain outfits with sexual immorality. However, most clerics, despite the actions of this controversial saint, did not want to challenge noble women and their fashions. Although his fellow Jesuits chastised Claver with the admonition that a priest could not reform dress, the saint tried to prevent women from entering the church wearing the *guardainfante*, or farthingale, and other ornaments. In 1644, he publicly shamed a Spanish doña (in the presence of others, including African slaves) by turning her away from the entrance of the church because she was wearing this scandalous style of skirt. The attack caused the woman to argue loudly, drawing the attention of Claver's superior, who calmed her within one of the Jesuit church's side chapels. Claver was then scolded and told that he could only advise women about their dress in the privacy of the confessional. After his death, witnesses testifying in Claver's beatification process claimed that he ordered women to burn their farthingales and quoted him as saying, "the confessional does not have space for a farthingale, only poor black women."[15] Oddly enough, this dichotomy does not apply well to his own milieu, since some of the nonwhite women actually dressed rather sumptuously in Claver's Cartagena, although there is no record of them owning the scandalous guardainfantes. Farthingales, the pinnacle of expensive Spanish dress in this era, may have been one clothing item out of reach for all but the wealthiest españolas.

Another church authority in Cartagena took a different perspective, commenting on a royal decree meant to enforce dress styles that coincided with social status. In 1683, bishop Miguel Antonio de Benavides wrote to King Charles II to report that he was working on encouraging elite women to dress appropriately by preaching sermons about this topic.[16] The bishop observed that "black men and women, mulatos and mulatas, and freedmen appear ostentatious, dressed in costly clothes, [with] silver swords and a great deal of finery. [The women] wear short cloaks and skirts of wool, camlet and silk." Returning to Sandoval's concerns from several decades earlier (although Sandoval argued that slave nudity was not sexually attractive), Benavides added that masters still did not dress their slaves properly, allowing them to "go about very indecently, nude, and very provocative." Due to the hot climate, slave owners did not believe it was money well spent to clothe their slaves.

Imperial authorities often made ineffective rulings or pronouncements targeting fashion when faced with more serious problems. A devastating eighteenth-century earthquake in Lima led to an ultimately unsuccessful morality campaign against women's behavior and dress. After this natural disaster, residents believed that women had to dress and behave more modestly or the city would face more destruction. Immodest dress was sinful, and if reformers did not effect change, the city risked more of God's ferocious wrath. Friars even judged women who wore revealing clothing as more sinful than prostitutes and the root of all immorality in the Viceroyalty. The links between race, sexual freedom, and immodest dress hint at the far more fearsome problem of social disruption and the disintegration of colonial hierarchies. Travelers to Lima felt compelled to view mulata women as especially sexual in their public appearance.[17] Some French and English travelers in the eighteenth century viewed Lima's night streets as a year-round masquerade, where both men and women hid their identities (especially through the use of the seductive *tapada*, a head shawl that hid all but one alluring eye) as they roamed on foot or in carriages with their lovers.[18]

In terms of clothing and social rank, the street scene in seventeenth-century Latin American cities, especially Mexico City and Lima, differed from contemporary Paris, where even new arrivals to the metropolis conservatively adhered to conventions regarding dress.[19] Cartagena, according to Juan and Ulloa, was only the size of a European city "of the third rank," but in its more limited way it still maintained public promenades as opportunities for physical display.[20] Elite Cartagena residents believed everyone had an appropriate attire suiting their status, race, and occupation, but in practice, everyone tried to decorate their bodies according to conventional demonstrations of wealth. In the Spanish viceroyalties, this meant wearing several pieces of jewelry and at least two layers of expensive imported fabrics. People had a "desire to wear something recognizable in order to be someone on the street,"[21] and for women in Cartagena and other Spanish American cities, this "someone" was wealthy enough to own jewelry. But the question remains: how did stylish woman afford their luxuries? The answer must come from their occupations and possibly inherited wealth. Lacking wealthy relatives or lucrative employment, the only other option for women was patronage, a position as a favorite of an elite man or woman. If a woman chose to put on a "costume" or something that disguised her status, she presumed that others would recognize the costume and treat her as the character she wanted to play—i.e., an honorable, wealthy lady.[22] Or did the combination of nonwhite skin and splendid attire send the message of a woman supported by or hoping to attract a wealthy lover?

The wardrobes owned by women of elite European descent in Cartagena offer a contrast to nonwhite women's attire.[23] One surviving testament documents doña Catalina Vásquez's large quantity of plain but functional clothing. Doña Catalina was a Spanish woman born in Pinto, just south of Madrid, who died in Cartagena in 1679.[24] Two times widowed with two children and two stepchildren, while she passed through Cartagena on her way from Peru back to Spain, doña Catalina lived in a house near the Santo Domingo convent. In Cartagena, Catalina became fatally ill, so she arranged to bequeath religious items in her possession to various friends and relatives.

She made many pious bequests directed to various religious institutions in Spain as well as asked for a full baroque funeral mass and two thousand masses for her soul in Cartagena, which contributed 416 pesos to the local clergy. Like many Spaniards, Catalina placed great importance on the clothing she wore in her coffin; she was buried in a Franciscan habit at a cost of twenty pesos and posthumously bought eight pesos' worth of black taffeta to line her coffin. Highlighting the importance of clothes as marking the difference in social rank, doña Catalina bequeathed a blue skirt to a free *parda* who attended to her in Cartagena and added that if this woman did not want the skirt, she could have cash or a piece of wool instead (presumably to use to make another article of clothing). She added a codicil to her will requesting that her linen clothing go to her daughter. Catalina's wardrobe included twenty-three shirts, eight petticoats, and six embroidered bodices, including two made of silk. As was usually the case, her skirts were the most impressive items—two were made of colorful silk, with one of these lined in red taffeta with gold decorations. Two other skirts were of *felpa*, a kind of silk, and the last was of yellow baize. These items proved that wearing colorful outfits did not necessarily suggest sexual availability. She did not own a great deal of jewelry besides a ring with tiny diamonds, two pearl bracelets, and of course, rosaries. She also had several hundred pesos in cash on hand. Despite her ready cash flow, the officials making this inventory judged about hé of Catalina's clothing as "old" or "used." Doña Catalina, with her status as a respectable, honorable, pious widow, presented quite a different public appearance than Paula's circle of accused witches. Although she was far richer than these non-elite women, her clothing and jewelry were not necessarily more expensive, though her clothing was far more plentiful. However, she valued her personal appearance and chose to emphasize clothing and decoration even in the ceremonies connected to her death.

Ideally, this doña and her social and racial inferiors dressed in a way that clearly indicated their status. Early modern sumptuary laws often targeted sexually suspect woman in an effort to identify such women easily by their dress. In places where prostitution was legal, lawmakers wanted to make sure that sex workers did not dress in exactly the same fashions as honorable wives and virgins. These women "should not pass themselves off as better than they were"—i.e., "reputable ladies." By forbidding expensive attire, the authorities tried to make wealthy or just flashy prostitutes look like poor women on the street. Men also feared that their wives and daughters would seek to imitate the glamorous styles worn by unrespectable women because

Clothes and jewels were the most obvious markers of social, professional, moral and gender distinctions in a deeply hierarchical society and since prostitutes transgressed many of these boundaries, their attire was a particularly sensitive issue.[25]

For prostitutes, gifts had a history.[26] Cartagena women received jewelry and clothing from men, signifying that these men had at least temporary access to their sexuality, which was highlighted by the perceived beauty and value of expensive metals and gems. But for a working woman, jewelry functioned as a savings plan or retirement fund, often pawned or sold, perhaps more readily than if the jewels were owned by a respectable matron. Prostitutes' jewelry and clothes had a more storied past and future than those items owned by less sexually active women. Some of their possessions were bought used, and in the cases explored in this book, some were auctioned off publicly if a woman came before the Holy Office or was murdered. Various local residents, including priests, the town crier who called the auction, and the inquisitors themselves, made purchases at these public auctions. One can only imagine which woman later received them as gifts and in what context.

While laws targeting prostitutes' dress did not exist in colonial Cartagena because prostitution was officially illegal by the 1620s, the attitudes behind this kind of regulation certainly did. Suspicious women did raise eyebrows due to their dress styles. For example, from the early 1620s to the late 1630s, Paula de Eguiluz walked on a razor's edge between fragile prosperity and utter defeat at the hands of the Cartagena inquisitors. Paula seemed unable to maintain a low profile and avoid envious and malicious attacks, going all the way back to her younger days in Cuba through to her middle years and beyond in Cartagena. It is very likely that her flamboyant appearance fueled envious feelings that contributed to some of the original accusations made against her in Cuba. As an enslaved woman of African descent, Paula's privileged access to luxurious clothing, due to her sexual relationship with her master, disrupted accepted social and racial hierarchies. She seemed to benefit and prosper from her immorality, and her wardrobe mocked the costume of proud Spanish doñas obligated to keep their affairs slightly more private or risk public shame and dishonor. When Holy Office familiars inventoried the contents of her room in Cuba in 1624, they found the following pieces of clothing: nine skirts, seven bodices, six shirts, and four headscarves.[27] This represents an immense wardrobe for a slave, especially since this clothing was not old and worn (terms commonly used to describe inventoried clothing, even articles owned by wealthy Spanish women). For the purpose of the Inquisition's financial records, notarized inventories provided detailed descriptions of Paula's wardrobe: her skirts were generally made of a heavy wool fabric called *perpetuán* dyed either blue, scarlet, brown, dark green, or a dark gold called *leonado*. Two of her skirts were even more sumptuous, made of blue damask or a heavy yellow satin fabric called *raso*, in one case decorated in fine silver. Paula's bodices were also made of satin and damask, colored blue with gold braid, green and scarlet with silver buttons, or yellow and white with silver braid. In any of these ensembles, how could Paula fail to catch an observer's eye? Other gowns were simpler, but still of imported fustian or *ruán*, a linen from Rouen, France. Her shirts were also made of embroidered ruán or *holanda*, fine Dutch linen, as were her headscarves, including one with silk embroidery. In this attire, Paula was clearly a woman with an overpowering and striking appearance. She inspired jealousy in women and obsessive love in men around the Caribbean, even after having several children and into her forties. When she entered the Holy Office prison in Cartagena after her voyage from Cuba in 1624, Paula wore jewelry made of gold and coral, which she had to surrender to the jailer.[28]

Paula could not regain her Cuban high standard of living as a free penitenciada serving as a washerwoman in the Cartagena charity hospital for eight years, although it's possible her work as a healer, her love magic practice, and her several lovers helped her avoid abject poverty. Some observers claimed she maintained a high standard of living while in the Holy Office prison, but no historian has found an extant inventory of her possessions for her second imprisonment and trial. When Paula entered the Holy Office prison again in 1632, the inquisitors cattily ordered the arresting officers to bring her in without "silks, or gold, or other precious things." Like the other individuals put in the secret prisons, Paula brought with her only a few basic changes of clothing and her own bedding. She had to surrender the one gold real she had in her skirt pocket.[29]

Although Paula manipulated the personalities of her fellow prisoners and even the inquisitors' emotions and fears, no reports suggest that she overtly called on sex to influence her 1630s trial. Of course, her sexually-charged confessions and her denials of her own participation in the standard orgies reveal a complex sexual persona that certainly intrigued her listeners. This behavior contrasts with the explicit strategies of other women imprisoned by the Holy Office in this era, such as doña Rufina (mentioned in the Introduction), who used sex to negotiate the outcome of their inquisition trials. Even if it is harder to document, sex and sexuality played a role in the experiences of most of the other women involved in the 1630s witch trials. Cartagena women in the 1630s justified their pacts and fantastical stories of sex with the devil by presenting themselves as financially desperate for male patronage. This kind of explanation reflected inquisitors' fantasies about morally weak women, but given their involvement in love and sex magic, it is also possible that some of these women dabbled in some form of prostitution, whether formally with an exchange of cash or gifts or informally through liaisons with wealthier men. Many of these women probably sought financial support from long-term lovers. Their stories of greed tempting them to have sex with the devil closely resemble Renaissance literary accounts of prostitutes tempted to sin by the promise of beautiful clothes and costly jewels.[30]

Detailed inventories of their confiscated clothing prove that the alleged witches liked to "dress up" (*vestir de gala*), a phrase often used in colonial documentation to imply an immodest public appearance. Like most other non-elite subjects, women of African descent in Cartagena asserted the most elegant public persona possible, which made a statement about their economic status. The English Dominican friar Thomas Gage believed nonwhite women dressed in jewels, ribbons, and lace to attract Spanish men and that "women's domestic demesne centered on the display of adornments that would signal the status of their male providers."[31] Inquisition records show Cartagena women's willingness to use magic to attract men or harm their female rivals. If nothing else, their wardrobe inventories demonstrate that some of the alleged witches maintained an elegant style of dress and this, along with their social ties to Paula and their participation in raucous dances and parties, helped bring them to the attention of the inquisitors, who were very happy to confiscate and auction off their valuable jewelry and clothes, in addition to sentencing many of them to the publicly humiliating and painful punishments of walking in autos de fe and one hundred lashes.

Working off the lists provided by official inventories, it is difficult to visualize the complete outfits worn by women of African descent in seventeenth-century Cartagena, but fortunately, Gage visited Mexico City in this era. His lengthy description of local women of African descent emphasizes their attractiveness and elegant, expensive dress:

Their clothing is a petticoat of silk or cloth, with many golden or silver laces, with a very broad double ribbon of some light color with long silver or golden tags hanging down before, the whole length of their petticoat to the ground, and the like behind: their waistcoats made like bodices, with skirts, laced likewise with gold or silver, without sleeves, and a girdle about their body of great price stuck with pearls and knots of gold (if they be any ways well esteemed of), their sleeves are broad and open at the end, of Holland or fine China linen, wrought with some colored silks, some with silk and gold, some with silk and silver, hanging down almost unto the ground; the locks of their heads are covered with some wrought coif, and over it another network of silk bound with a fair silk, or silver, or golden ribbon which crosseth the upper part of their forehead, and hath commonly worked out in letters some light and foolish love posy; their bare, black, and tawny breasts are covered with bobs hanging from their chains of pearls. And when they go abroad, they use a white mantle of lawn or cambric rounded with a broad lace, which some put over their heads, the breadth only reaching to the middle behind, that their girdle and ribbons may be seen, and the two ends reaching to the ground almost; others cast their mantles only upon their shoulders, and swaggerers-like, cast the one end over the left shoulder that they may better jog the right arm, and shew their broad sleeve as they walk along; others instead of this mantle use some rich silk petticoat to hang upon their left shoulder, while with their right arm they support the lower part of it, more like roaring boys than honest civil maids.[32]

Gage's purpose for including this extensive description of clothing worn by Afro-Mexican women was to prove how Spanish lust and wealth had corrupted New Spain. He emphasized how these women, with their seductive clothing and body language, lured even "Spaniards of the better sort" away from their wives. A well-adorned body equaled sexual temptation. Gage, who converted to Protestantism after his return to Europe, would not have appreciated the comparison, but Cartagena inquisitors shared his fears and associated local women of African descent with sex, sin, and the devil. Moralizing narratives from the Italian Renaissance also highlighted the elegance and wealth prostitutes might enjoy but warned of a future of disease and death.[33]

To turn to inventories of the clothing owned by Paula's comadres, in one of her first audiencias with inquisitors, Paula accused Juana de Gramajo, a twenty-eight-year-old free black washerwoman born in Cartagena, of participating in juntas and having sex with the devil. In September 1632, the Holy Office confiscated and inventoried Juana's possessions. One might assume a washerwoman lived on the edge of poverty, but Juana in fact owned jewelry including two gold necklaces, one of which had thirty-one gold beads and a pearl pendant worth twenty pesos, gold and pearl earrings, and a garnet bracelet. Juana's clothing was not extensive, but what she had was ornate and expensive. For example, she owned a new lined taffeta outer skirt, as well as another made of yellow Chinese-style silk. She also had plainer clothes, such as a brown serge skirt and a cotton corset. All of her shirts and cloaks were embroidered and she could appear in public in a vicuna hat, wearing one of a few pairs of good new slippers or mules. Attired in a dress of Chinese silk, a hat, and slippers, Juana dressed like an elite, wealthy woman. Juana's room was furnished decently for the time period with a mattress, sheets, damask-covered pillows, dishware, and religious images.[34]

Far wealthier than Juana was Teodora de Saucedo (or Salcedo), a free black woman born in Havana and residing in Cartagena with no clear occupation. Paula accused Teodora of involvement in all of the juntas, as well as several maleficios. Teodora herself admitted that her demonic familiar gave her a powder to throw into another woman's eyes (the victim was Teodora's sexual rival), causing permanent blindness.[35] When the Holy Office auctioned off her possessions in 1632, Teodora owned a house and five slaves, worth in total over 2,000 pesos. Outside of her comfortable home (which was well stocked with extensive linens, four paintings, silverware, and furniture), Teodora adorned herself with a white head kerchief (she had eight), a vicuna hat, one of several pairs of gold and pearl earrings, a gold necklace (choosing between two that she owned) or a pearl necklace, a colorful silk corset, a black or a gold embroidered bodice, a new, embroidered silk cloak, a green and gold taffeta skirt or another colored black and yellow, and two large coral and gold bracelets. She might carry a small gold purse and her rosary. Among her many possessions, Teodora had items imported from Japan, France, Spain, and even cloth from Africa. Her wardrobe encompassed the broad reach of early modern Iberian imperial expansion. In terms of quantity, the specific garments she owned closely resemble the outfits of seventeenth-century Roman prostitutes—only two or three expensive and brightly colored ensembles, with numerous accessories such as headgear, scarves, linens, and jewelry to add variety.[36] This is not to suggest Teodora explicitly sold sex, but she was certainly single and sexually active, as were all the women in Paula's circle.

Paula accused another wealthy free black woman, thirty-five-year-old Ana Suárez, known as Ana de Zaragoza, of participating in juntas and making a pact with the devil. Like Juana de Gramajo, Ana was quite wealthy considering her stated occupation was washerwoman and cook. Ana owned two Angolan women as slaves. The Holy Office sold them at auction for a total of almost 700 pesos, a price that included María Angola's young daughter.[37] Ana also owned a modest property auctioned off for one hundred pesos, but her jewelry and clothing (worth 230 pesos at auction—and undoubtedly these sales offered some incredible bargains, especially considering that many of the bidders worked for the Holy Office) were her most impressive possessions. Ana's jewelry included two strings of coral; two necklaces of several dozen gold beads, one with a gold pendant; a pearl necklace; a gold chain with a weight of thirty-nine pesos; two emerald rings; and several pairs of earrings (two made of gold, pearl, and emeralds and another with pearls). Like some of the other accused witches, Ana owned popular religious items, including a scapular of blue taffeta inlaid in silver and an image of the Virgin decorated in pearls. Taking into account this ostentatious jewelry, Ana's wardrobe was small if elegant. One of her outfits was a black skirt and bodice of some kind of ornate, embossed fabric. Of course, black clothing equated with respectability and modesty; supposedly Roman prostitutes in the Renaissance always owned a black dress in order to pass as widows.[38] Her second outfit was a taffeta skirt with gold ornamentation and a silver colored bodice made of *tabí* (or tabby), a heavy silk with a woven wave pattern, a fabric often listed in these inventories, and silk tassels. She even owned one of the classic early modern shirts adorned with a large ruff and massive sleeves (*camisa alta con balona de pita y mangas barahundazas*). If nothing else, this shirt proved she did not pass all of her time washing clothes and cooking.

One of Paula's closest confidants, Barbola de Albornoz, a twenty-eight-year-old freed slave from Barquisimiento (Venezuela), owned almost nothing besides her jewelry and clothing.[39] She lived in a single room furnished with a mattress, bedding, and a few odds and ends, such as a tortoiseshell snuffbox, a container for chocolate from New Spain, and a chamber pot. But for such a poor woman who said she "lived by the work of her own hands,"

Barbola's public presentation was more than respectable.[40] She outfitted herself with several headscarves and two good quality outfits (other than what she wore when she was arrested): two pairs of cotton stockings, two decent skirts, and two taffeta bodices, including one with bronze buttons. She also owned older cotton clothing. Her jewelry included gold and silver rings, two gold bracelets, and a gold necklace with twenty-four beads and a pendant made of gold and pearls. Barbola's physical ornamentation extended to a taffeta scapular of the Virgin of Mt. Carmel decorated in pearls and gold, along with a corset (*apretina*) with silver hooks.

Angelina de Nava, a twenty-seven-year-old seamstress and washerwoman often mentioned in these trials as a participant in witches' juntas and a practitioner of maleficios, owned land and houses worth 1,300 pesos at auction, as well as a slave she rented out as a day laborer.[41] Angelina did not admit that she was a witch until her fourth session with the inquisitors, but in her second audiencia she did confess that she had sought an abortion.[42] Despite this and her eventual confession to the typical rituals of the satanic pact, Angelina was sentenced to only a year in prison, an auto de fe, and afterward, three years' banishment from the diocese. After confiscating her possessions, the Holy Office scribe noted down a small but eye-catching wardrobe, which consisted of only one outfit and a few linens. Although she owned a farm and some rudimentary houses, Angelina dressed in nothing more than a skirt of floral camlet (a fabric made of goat or camel hair and silk) decorated in gold tipped tassels; a green and black doublet with silver braiding; a black taffeta neck ruff (a *golilla*); a pearl choker; a blue taffeta scapular with a small silver insignia; an embroidered blue petticoat; two pairs of silk stockings, including one buff-colored; and the less glamorous wool underwear and an old, torn cotton cloak. Angelina also had some basic furniture and bedding, along with items related to her occupation, including a skein of blue Guinean thread.

A few of the women arrested in the 1632 witch hunt appeared to care more for their private living conditions as opposed to their physical appearance. This seems to be the case for the free mulata Ana María de Robles, age thirty, who worked as a washerwoman and seamstress and came to Cartagena from Santo Domingo.[43] Perhaps expressing frustration with her hardworking but unrewarding life, Ana María claimed she made a pact with the devil after being offered forty pesos and a gold necklace. Besides her alleged participation in juntas, she also knew love magic and herbal lore.[44] Ana María was the only woman among those whose goods were confiscated who did not own a *saya* or skirt worth a mention in the Holy Office inventory. Sayas were probably the most expensive basic item of clothing—a possession consisting of at least two layers of pricey imported fabric covered in decoration such as ribbons, tassels, and braiding, or gold, silver, and jewels. In Ana María's house, the scribe listed a handful of shirts, stockings, and bodices without specifying their fabric, so one presumes it was just the most inexpensive, common material, probably locally produced cotton.[45] However, despite her unprepossessing appearance, Ana María owned two simple wooden houses and a plot of land (measured at about 18 meters by 25 meters) in Getsemaní auctioned off for 500 pesos.[46] Her furniture included a wooden bed, a rare possession for a poor woman in this climate where hammocks were more popular. Many other Spanish Americans just slept on floor mats. Ana María also had bedding, chairs, and cane mats, so clearly she spent some of her income on her personal comfort, not flamboyant clothing. Ana María was one of a handful of women involved in these trials who had a known occupation and appeared to dress in a manner consistent with this line of work and her humble social and racial position.

In her fourteenth audiencia with the inquisitors on November 6, 1632, Paula de Eguiluz first accused two sisters, free mulatas named Justa and Rufina, of witchcraft.[47] Other than Paula herself, this Rufina (one of at least three women with this name targeted by the Holy Office in the mid-seventeenth century) was the boldest and most successful freedwoman involved in these trials. Paula's accusations prompted inquisitors to arrest and imprison the sisters in their "secret" cells in 1633. Further allegations came in 1634 when Diego López claimed that he saw the two sisters fly to a gathering of witches.[48] Justa, born in Cartagena around 1603, had the last name Perez, and Rufina, who was born around 1606, occasionally used the last name Ortiz.[49] Both admitted that they had sex with demons after succumbing to temptations of material wealth. Although other alleged witches took time to break down or needed a few weeks in the prison before they developed the story they wished to present to the inquisitors, both Justa and Rufina confessed to a satanic pact during their first audience. Justa said that her "godmother" (or the woman who led her to the devil's sect) took her to meet Lucifer one Friday night after 11 p.m. In very similar descriptions of the junta, both Justa and Rufina said that they could not see Lucifer's face because it gave off a brilliant light. Rufina added that the devil wore a miter in the manner of a bishop. Both Rufina and Justa said they had sex with a demon and received marks on their left ankles.[50]

In March of 1633, Justa and Rufina received a sentence of reconciliation in an auto de fe, short prison sentences (six months for Justa and one year for Rufina), and confiscation of all of their belongings.[51] By August 1633, the two sisters were implicated as among the leaders of an extensive plot that spilled out of the secret prison involving some of Cartagena's most important civil officials, as well as the forty or more witches imprisoned in the Holy Office jail.[52] Diego López and many of the women retracted their confessions of witchcraft and satanic pacts, with some of the retractors claiming that other prisoners advised them to confess because this would help them avoid torture. During the inquisitors' investigation of the plot, they heard that Rufina bribed another woman to retract by offering her a gold chain. Unfortunately, the retractions led inquisitors to torture the accused witches (they were not tortured during their previous confession sessions), who then withdrew their denials before enduring too much physical pain. All of those involved in the retraction plot were resentenced, sometimes with harsher punishments. For Rufina, and possibly also her sister Justa, involvement in the retraction plot was tied to a sexual relationship with the local lieutenant general, don Francisco Llano de Velasco.

Due to the overcrowded conditions in the secret jails of the Holy Office, Justa and Rufina shared a cell with several other alleged witches while they served their short prison sentence. The communal cells meant cellmates could nurse each other during illnesses. These cells were located on the first floor of the Holy Office building and had windows facing a public plaza. While Rufina was in this cell, she heard Lieutenant General Velasco call her name and ask after her wellbeing. Rufina could not see the man, but she recognized his voice. Shortly after, he sent Rufina's slave to the prison to give her mistress gifts of cake and chocolate. Rufina said she heard him call out to her (addressing her with a word that suggested sexual promiscuity), "*loca, loca*, how are you?"[53] On three occasions, a slave working in the jail opened the shared cell during the night to release Justa and Rufina, allowing them to speak with the lieutenant general. Diego López claimed he did not hear their cell doors open again until just before dawn. Rufina also said that "an important man from the Armada" spoke to her in her cell, promising that he would help her get out and take her to Spain.

Rufina denied that she received gifts from Velasco and that she left the jail on two or three occasions. Working with her advocate, she said the witnesses who made these accusations about her prison escapes were untrustworthy because they were her enemies, and she had fought with them while

they were in prison together. One of these untrustworthy women allegedly warned her, "don't think that you will be released by putting on amber
pumps to go sleep with the lieutenant," implying that seducing Velasco with
elegant clothing would not help Rufina's case. In Rufina's version of events,
late one night Velasco entered her cell, after bribing the prison slave. In her
cell, the lieutenant general kissed and embraced her, "intent on knowing her
carnally, but she did not desire it, and seeing that she resisted," Velasco spoke
with her for forty-five minutes about her case and how he could help her. He
kissed her and "groped her legs and shameful parts until he left." He tried
the same techniques a few weeks later, again with the help of the prison slave,
and again Rufina said she resisted his "dishonest and obscene desire."[54] Like
Paula and many of the other women mentioned in this book, Rufina created a sexual identity that she hoped would make her appear favorable to
the inquisitors. In her story, she virtuously resisted the sexually aggressive
Velasco. Again like Paula, Rufina could only present this resistance as a single example of sexual propriety, not proof of a chaste reputation or the honor
that a married Spanish woman could claim, since both women had illegitimate children.[55]

Rufina made the mistake of opposing Paula de Eguiluz, claiming that
the healer told her to accuse other women and admit to being a witch. Inquisitor Argos decided Rufina should be tortured in order to investigate her accusations that Paula masterminded this witch craze. So at 9:45 a.m. on July 24,
1635, Rufina went into the torture chamber, undressed, and was threatened
with the rack. Rufina called on the help of the Virgin of the Rosary and refused
to deny her accusations against Paula, so she was strapped into the rack with
belts around her waist and arms, as she continued to beg for the Virgin's help
and pity from the inquisitors. Just as the first knot was tied and tightened,
Rufina admitted that all of her original confessions were true, so the ropes
were loosened and she was covered with her shirt. The inquisitors continued
to question her, eventually untying her completely and letting her sit on a stool.
In explaining why she retracted her confessions of witchcraft, she brought up
the local living saint Peter Claver, who did not believe she was a witch.[56] As a
result of her misguided retraction, Rufina received a harsher punishment than
her original sentence: two hundred lashes and ten years' banishment from
the diocese of Cartagena and Santa Marta, as well as the archdiocese of Santa
Fe de Bogota. Justa also suffered the threat of torture and actually endured
one "turn," or tightening of the ropes around her body, until she admitted that
she retracted her statements under advisement of Lieutenant Velasco.[57]

Rufina Ortiz may come across as a humble mulata servant manipulated by both Paula de Eguiluz and one of the most powerful secular officials in Cartagena. However, knowledge of Rufina's material wealth changes these initial perceptions of her low status based on her precarious social position as a single woman of African descent with at least one child. Rufina in fact owned two houses, one made of stone and the other described as "larger than average" and made of cedar.[58] Rufina rented her stone house out to a couple (the woman was a doña) for twelve pesos a month. At auction, Rufina's real estate holdings were sold for just less than 3,000 pesos. Rufina also owned three female Angolan slaves and another woman named Mariquilla Biafara. Rufina earned of the labor of one of these women, who worked for a chocolate maker. Another was trained as a cook and a dressmaker. At auction, two of the women were sold for 500 pesos, a third for 420 pesos, and the last for only 100 pesos because she was suffering from diarrhea and tuberculosis.

The rest of Rufina's possessions, some of which were sold at auction for a total of about 300 pesos, suggest that she made some income through preparing food at home, with the help of her slaves. Her luxurious clothing evokes an image of a woman who also wore quite a bit of jewelry, but unlike the other inventories mentioned here, jewelry was not listed. With her very high connections in Cartagena society, it is possible that Rufina was able to hide it before her arrest. Rufina had a large amount of linens, including seventeen shirts, five wool embroidered petticoats, eight sheets, ten pillows, a bedspread, hand cloths, and a cotton bed canopy—a symbol of wealth in colonial Cartagena.[59] She furnished her home with a wooden bed, four stools, three chairs, and a hammock. Rufina had four silk bodices, a green and black tabí (heavy, watered silk) skirt lined in blue taffeta, a brown wool skirt lined in pink taffeta, another skirt made of silver Mexican taffeta lined in heavy silk, a petticoat made of crimson taffeta, several shirts and petticoats made of linen from Rouen, France, and slippers with silver decoration. Along with most of the other outfits here, bright and flashy colors made these items stand out in a crowd. Rufina's hats were made of vicuna wool, lined in pink or brown taffeta. Rufina's large inventory of storage or food related items suggests more than personal use: forty-two empty jugs, a grinding stone, nine trays (possibly for serving) including one with eight red cups, six glass bottles, a large jar with two cups (perhaps to serve drinks), brass, earthenware, iron casserole dishes, and two plates from Lisbon.

Why Rufina owned these items and how she achieved such wealth remains a mystery. She certainly could have lived well by simply renting out one of her houses and a few of her slaves and running a home business. Other Carthaginians maintained elite Spanish households by doing these things on a slightly more lavish scale. But how did Rufina first purchase her homes and slaves? Was she just a good businesswoman? Did she run some kind of tavern or restaurant or did she entertain many people in her home? She certainly had the wardrobe of a sophisticated hostess. Of course, taverns were viewed as the haunts of loose women in this era. Since she had at least one child, she was sexually active and perhaps received some patronage from a lover such as Velasco himself. Since she was labeled a free mulata and was associated with one of Cartagena's elite families, Rufina may have had a Spanish father who helped her establish herself financially. With her expensive home, elegant clothing, and retinue of slaves, she undoubtedly had a voluntary social or sexual relationship with Velasco before her trial, since she said she recognized his voice when he called through her cell window. Instead of being imprisoned and victimized by aggressive visitors who appeared unwelcome and uninvited in their cell, other prisoners reported that both Rufina and Justa left the prison willingly to spend three nights with a powerful local official. The implication was that Rufina organized a campaign of seduction to help her case. Unfortunately, as a result of this plot, Rufina suffered the threat of torture and the physical punishment of whipping.

In contrast, Rufina's sister Justa Perez owned nothing more than a box of clothing and linens worth forty-five pesos at auction.[60] Her possessions were in line with her occupation as a servant to doña Mariana de Armas, an elite Cartagena widow. Justa dressed very well but was not quite as ostentatious as some of her peers. Over the course of a week, she was well off enough to not have to wash clothes and could cycle through eight shirts of Rouen linen, three petticoats, three white bodices and two made of black taffeta, an old cloak, and some bedding. She owned four good quality skirts, one of black wool, another violet in color, made of the heavy woolen fabric called perpetuán. One of her outfits was made entirely of white tabí, which must have given her a very striking appearance. Justa's clothing was plentiful enough so that she would always appear tidy and clean as a decent representative of doña Mariana but not embarrassingly gaudy.

In general, Paula and many of her comadres defied social and racial hierarchies with their wealth and ostentatious dress style, which made it hard for Cartagena residents to ignore them, which in turn contributed to their conflicts with the Holy Office. However they behaved and regardless of how many possessions they accumulated, these women were born lacking honor as local Spaniards defined it. Non-elite women sometimes called on their status as married women to prove their respectability in the context of judicial proceedings, but this was impossible for Paula and her friends. Even if they were not prostitutes, they did not enjoy the overt, openly acknowledged male protection and the possibility of seclusion experienced by women of Spanish descent. This made them especially vulnerable to the tribunal, which made money off their confiscated property. In 1648, Justa Perez, living banished from Cartagena in Porto Bello, made the mistake of stating this fact publicly and faced another arrest by the Holy Office fifteen years after her first trial. Justa reportedly said she was not a witch and that the 1630s accusations against her were made out of envy and a desire to impoverish her sister and herself, hinting at an attempt to bring down their patrons as well. This was in line with the normal sex scandals and exposés so typical of colonial Cartagena. When her confidant argued that the inquisitors were very honorable, Justa said, "Silence, your grace, they are very, very partial to money."[61] As they did a few years later with local Portuguese merchants suspected of practicing Judaism, in the 1630s, Cartagena inquisitors confiscated the wealth owned by individuals who did not fit into colonial hierarchies, channeling it back to Spanish institutions and, ultimately, certain individual clerics/bureaucrats.

Seventeenth century wardrobe inventories support travelers' observations that non-elite women chose to put forward an elegant persona when they appeared in public. Though the generous material wealth owned by some of these women contradicts assumptions about the extreme poverty suffered by non-Spaniards in colonial Latin America, their audacious disregard of social hierarchies as expressed in dress attracted the jealousy of their neighbors and, eventually, the condemnation of fearful authority figures. Similar to the wealthy Portuguese merchants harshly punished for allegedly practicing Judaism, these well off African and Creole women represented an entire social niche that did not fit contemporary elite social ideals, flaunting wealth that did not match their dishonorable status.

Because Paula de Eguiluz and the other Creole freedwomen and slaves on trial for witchcraft in the 1630s could not claim honor (in the conventional sense, based on possessing a good sexual reputation, social status, wealth, and Spanish ancestry), no one commented on their clothing as pointing to an immoral or criminal persona during their Holy Office interrogations. Public physical appearance was not explicitly discussed in any of the seventeenth-century Cartagena witch trials—it was assumed that these nonwhite, sexually active, single women lived outside the realm of moral and honest women, so their dress would neither help nor hinder their ultimate judgment. For elite women allegedly involved in sexual activity that betrayed their social rank, the authorities sought information on their dress as a way to prove their immorality. The fearful reign of the Holy Office of the Spanish Inquisition endured in Cartagena for only a few decades, and even at its harshest, clever manipulators might skillfully negotiate their treatment while imprisoned in the so-called secret cells. Although it was a standard tactic for men, many of the women mentioned in this book could not call on the rhetoric of the honor code to assert their personal status and, by extension, argue for their rightful access to judicial privileges not granted to plebeians. Women such as Rufina, lacking Paula de Eguiluz's wit and ruthless resourcefulness, resorted instead to sex to achieve their goals.

By creating their own interpretation of honor and reputation, the women interrogated by the Holy Office in 1630s Cartagena put forward a public persona that defied their apparently marginal social status, knowing that in public they would be judged by their physical presentation. Although clearly one's skin tone, hair, facial, and bodily features were critical in the assertion of status in Spanish America, clothing was another obvious and far more malleable way to manipulate identity. In a purposeful detour from the viceregal obsession with racial categorization, the exploration of the complexity of clothing styles in this chapter hints at plebeian women's contribution to the constant negotiation of reputation and self-definition done on the streets of colonial Cartagena.[62] After all, race and/or caste were categories favored by the Spanish administrators, not necessarily the key markers of social boundaries for women. Physical presentation and dress, as well as a more subtle understanding of sexuality and sexual agency, may have been even more important for women than the male-defined honor-based assertions of masculine status. The next chapter will put forward another woman who defied masculine definitions of self-worth based on the honor code, as it considers the tragic demise of doña Manuela de Andrade, a woman permanently marked by her status as a public prostitute.

CHAPTER NINE

VIOLENCE, HONOR, AND SEX FOR SALE

Doña Manuela de Andrade

AS THE SUN ROSE AT 6 A.M. ON NOVEMBER 7, 1655, IT ILLUMINATED A woman's body that had been abandoned the night before in a deserted Chambacú lot in the desolate outskirts of Cartagena.[1] The body was of a female around thirty years old, of average build, apparently of Spanish ancestry, and dressed in a blood-soaked green skirt and a striped cotton bodice. She lay in a pool of congealing blood that had gushed from a deep slash in her throat from the previous night. Local residents immediately informed Cartagena's lieutenant general, who viewed the body and identified it as that of doña Manuela de Andrade.[2]

Surviving evidence about doña Manuela's life comes from the investigation of those involved in her murder. Witnesses testifying in her case quickly began to spin fantasies about the most lurid causes of her murder, even bringing up hints of cross-generational, incestuous, unrequited love. However, doña Manuela's biography, as presented in criminal court documents, reveals how temporary and permanent residents of a major Spanish American port city thought about and discussed an elite Spanish prostitute and her brutal end. Witnesses' statements recreate the mental and physical world that surrounded doña Manuela, a world where ideas about sexuality remained constantly visible. Given her occupation and her fate, all discussions of doña Manuela and her life foreground her sexuality and the looming violence inherent in its public display. By making her sexuality a public commodity, doña Manuela disregarded all of her society's official expectations for a married Spanish woman. In doing so, she took an enormous risk of igniting the violent flames of masculine retribution. As we have seen in previous chapters, traditional honor codes based on controlling female sexuality sanctioned anger, enraged reactions to perceived insults, and the brutality that almost inevitably followed. Strict adherence to the honor code did not govern all sexual relationships in colonial Cartagena and not all cases of adultery or cheating on lovers led to violent attacks on either a woman or her lover. However, when some men became jealous of a woman's sexual activity and sought to control her sexuality, they might act with vindictive cruelty. Concepts of honor and the violence needed to protect it varied regionally in Spanish America; but in all contexts, some men justified the rage provoked by spousal infidelity as a technique to defend themselves in court and in order to excuse murdering their wives to legal authorities, even if the technique ultimately proved ineffective.[3]

Honor killings, despite their rarity among Spaniards in the Americas, were a key literary theme in Spanish siglo de oro dramas and continue to support a vision of Spain as "a uniquely violent, honor-obsessed country quite different from the rest of early modern Europe," despite the fact that reality utterly disproves the theatrical depiction.[4] The crimes of passion enacted by noblemen that were depicted so frequently in siglo de oro dramas provided the theatrical model for the righteous anger of a dishonored man whose rage was itself a testimony to his personal nobility and sensitivity on the point of honor.[5] Lope de Vega observed that playwrights would do well to write plays about honor killings because the vulgar masses were very willing to pay to view this spectacle.[6] Early modern male theatergoers perhaps fed into their own revenge fantasies as they watched wives who entertained even the slightest adulterous thought murdered on stage. Although some historians apply these literary conventions to day-to-day understandings of gender roles, others warn against using literature to explain daily life.[7]

Since race, gender, and sex for sale remain controversial and confusing subjects to this day, perhaps it is not surprising that historians of colonial Spanish America usually downplay the existence of prostitution. However, this occupation was usually legal and/or tolerated in Spain and its dominions, as it has been in many other empires in world history:

Although our own modern prejudices may keep us from taking it seriously, prostitution should not be dismissed as marginal in Iberian society, considering the cultural, economic, political, and social import it reached in medieval and early modern Spain.[8]

Historians of Spanish America tend to view prostitution from the side of institutional regulation, as well as cultural and social control, including an emphasis on the idea of *recogimiento*, or withdrawal from the secular world.[9] But it was not until the late eighteenth century, over 250 years after Cartagena's foundation, that local authorities made tentative steps toward controlling local prostitutes. This does not mean that sex workers did not exist until the late eighteenth century; until 1622, prostitution was legal in Spain and its colonies. In fact, in the fifteenth and sixteenth centuries, the Spanish monarchs, including Ferdinand and Isabel (the so-called Catholic monarchs), regulated and farmed out prostitution monopolies in Spain to enterprising businessmen. A 1538 royal decree authorized the foundation of a legal brothel in Mexico City, although it seems that prostitution usually took place in smaller, more intimate establishments throughout the Spanish American viceroyalties. Spanish legal traditions going back to the *Siete partidas* targeted *alcahuetes*, or procurers, as deserving legal sanctions, but prostitutes themselves, while socially marginal, were tolerated due to the clerical view that they fulfilled a useful function by satisfying lustful men who would otherwise target women with virtuous, honorable reputations.[10]

Late in his reign, Philip II began to regulate prostitution, but official brothels remained open legally until the guilt-wracked Philip IV shut them in 1623. After decades of royal sexual scandals, the desperate king ordered all prostitutes arrested in 1661. Lacking the discipline to control his own proclivities despite the patient and wise ministrations of his spiritual confidant, the learned mystic Sor María de Agreda, Philip IV hoped that a nationwide moral reform would strengthen Spain in desperate times, including helping with his own fertility. These decrees may have had little effect even within Spain, not to mention its imperial outposts, where prostitution and other "public sins" were viewed with toleration for centuries. Certainly, the new regulations did not help in engendering a healthy heir to the throne.[11] Although the authorities did not seek to publicize this constant in viceregal life, prostitutes were far from invisible, as they remain in English-language historiography of colonial Spanish America.

To counter this prolonged erasure, this chapter aims to bring the professional Spanish American prostitute out of the shadows by presenting four separate perspectives on the murdered prostitute doña Manuela. Some of these stated attitudes follow the expected parameters for a male-dominated, hierarchical society, while others are a little more surprising. The speakers in the case can be divided as follows: the judicial authorities seeking to investigate and punish the murderer(s); doña Manuela's female friends, including both white and nonwhite women; younger local men (her stepsons and their friends are among this group); and her husband and those sympathetic to his side. Each person who spoke about doña Manuela told a story, or as Zemon Davis would term it, a fiction (fact mixed with opinion and the narrative devices of the era), about her life as a prostitute.[12] Of course, everyone testifying designed their version of her life with a conscious understanding of how it ended and thus tended to formulate stories where doña Manuela did or did not get what she deserved. Those on the defensive, as we will see, saturated their stories with gendered language emphasizing shame, sin, honor, violence, and retribution. One of her young stepsons added a touch of forbidden romance to his testimony. Doña Manuela's female friends and the other women she interacted with provided the simplest, most realistic stories of her life. This chapter gathers all of these stories and weaves them together to narrate the course of a criminal investigation; in this particular example, it is one that had a very unsatisfying conclusion: a narrative that starts with a death and then simply trails off. The question remains: was justice (even in the seventeenth-century Spanish understanding of justice) served? The chapter will conclude with a few details of the continuing history of prostitution and the feeble attempts to suppress it in colonial Cartagena.

After identifying her body, *teniente* don Miguel Pérez de Villena immediately began an investigation into doña Manuela's murder. He started by questioning Ana María, a fifty-year-old woman who ran a tavern on a corner near the Media Luna gate, where the city of Cartagena connected to the mainland and not far from the scene of the crime. This *pulpera* was probably the last person to see doña Manuela alive. She told a straightforward account that focused on the practical concerns of a woman who runs a bar, including her memories of her patrons, the drinks they purchased, and the money they spent. Ana María stated that at 7:30 p.m. on the night of November 6, she saw a white woman of average build wearing a silk cloak leave the city with two white men whom she did not recognize. Ana María observed the woman sit on the corner of the street near her tavern, while one of her companions approached the publican as she stood in her door-way. The man purchased a half real of wine, which he gave to the woman. Then the group left and Ana María could provide no more information.

A day or two later, the teniente continued his investigations. He heard a variety of statements rife with rumor and gossip pointing to the obvious suspect for the murder. The next stop in the investigation was the house of a Granada-born widow, doña María de la Cerda, age thirty. Doña María lived near the San Agustin convent and said that doña Manuela had just moved into her house a few days before. Doña María had last seen her housemate on the morning of November 6, when doña Manuela said she was going to mass. She never returned to the house. Another roommate, a young doña Ana Altamirano, repeated this story. Both women also mentioned that they had already heard rumors about the murder. Doña María said that gossips whispered that two men were hiding from the law in the San Francisco convent. Doña Ana repeated the rumor that don Felipe, a knight of the elite Spanish order of Santiago, had come to Cartagena to kill his wife.

While at doña Manuela's last place of official residence, the teniente inventoried the luxurious possessions remaining in doña Manuela's room (in fact, expensive jewelry had already disappeared before the inventory was made), including seventeen letters and poems from her husband and a let-ter from another man giving her advice about her husband, later revealed to be a warning regarding the impending plot to kill her.[13] Doña Manuela's personal effects were more than sufficient to allow her a decent burial in the cathedral, as befitted a doña; it was officiated by a priest and a sacristan and lit by three candles. Given the tropical climate, doña Manuela was buried almost immediately after the discovery of her corpse.[14]

Since he suspected his prime suspects had taken refuge in a religious institution, a very common strategy in colonial Cartagena, teniente Villena had to probe tangential witnesses for a bit more hearsay before he could move forward with his case. Villena discovered that two figures had approached a Sergeant Mateo Gómez after dark when he was walking back to his guard post following supper at home. They turned out to be two Franciscan friars who asked the soldier if he knew that doña Manuela was married to a knight of Santiago. He replied that he did not know anything about doña Manuela other than rumors that said she was separated from her husband. The ser-geant also heard gossip that two men, including a knight of Santiago, were hiding in the Franciscan convent. The teniente learned that doña Manuela may have been spending time at the house of a mulata named Rufina Tocorotoco (a nickname that might refer to a Cuban bird). Villena's next step was a visit to the house of doña Luisa de la Cueva (alias *Merendona,* or "picnic," a nickname that suggests doña Luisa was also a prostitute),[15] where her estranged husband don Felipe had lived for two months with his two sons until he fled to the convent. When asked if she had seen anyone else with don Felipe, doña Luisa replied that a don Andrés Escalante (age thirty-nine) frequently visited, including for a meal just a few days before. Doña Luisa knew that don Andrés was a retainer for the *fiscal* of Mexico, and she added that often saw him in the company of mulatas (perhaps implying that he associated with prostitutes—this detail might even suggest that she knew the plan for the murder).[16] A twenty-four-year-old vizcaíno named Gabriel de Buitrón Moxica was another frequent visitor at don Felipe's rooms. With this information, the teniente moved forward on plans for arresting his suspects.

However, don Felipe and his accomplices planned the timing of the uxoricide well: the ships of the Spanish flota were about to leave for Porto Belo, Panama. Even though Governor Pedro Zapata de Mendoza ordered that don Felipe should be arrested and sent to prison with all of his belongings confiscated, the authorities feared that their prime suspect would sneak onboard a ship and flee the city. The accomplice Escalante was found without difficulty, as he showed no fear of the law. Escalante was arrested while playing cards with some guardsmen. Moxica, don Felipe, and his fifteen-year-old son, having left the convent, embarked on a ship about to leave the port less than three days after doña Manuela's death. Governor Mendoza himself thoroughly searched the ship, arrested the three men, and transported them in a boat back to the city, where they were locked up in different cells in the municipal jail.[17] These efforts were, in fact, a frustrating waste of time and resources; the authorities should have focused on arresting doña Manuela's eldest stepson, the actual murderer, who successfully fled the city.

Shortly after his arrest, doña Manuela's estranged husband don Felipe gave a long, rambling narration of his personal history, emphasizing his honorable status as a knight of Santiago and ending in his admission that he encouraged his son, referred to as don Felipe *el mozo* (the younger), to kill his stepmother doña Manuela to satisfy his father's offended honor.[18] Obviously, the purpose of every word he spoke was to present doña Manuela as a woman who deserved to die a horrible death, and at the same time, to prove that he was justified in killing her. The odd twist was that he did not actually commit the crime but instead only created a conspiracy to make it happen. The twists and turns of his defense attempt to justify the conspiracy.

While attempting to present his inborn nobility, the murderous husband let a few unsavory details slip in the course of his narration. Don Felipe *el grande* said he was born in Durango in the Vizcaya region of northern Spain in 1611. At the age of eighteen, he traveled to New Granada in the *armada* of general don Fadrique de Toledo with a relative, another knight of Santiago. While residing for twenty years in Santa Fe de Bogota, he married twice: first to doña Francisca de Bocanegra and then in 1645 to doña Manuela. Don Felipe had two sons with his first wife, the youngest called don Agustín, who was born in 1640. He apparently had no children with doña Manuela. Don Felipe traveled to Peru in 1649 to seek funds that he was supposed to receive from his deceased first wife's dowry. Around that time he received his knighthood, although, inconveniently enough, he could not produce the paperwork before the Cartagena officials because he claimed it had sunk to the bottom of the sea in a shipwreck in 1654.[19] He moved to Cartagena during Lent of 1655, in order to leave with the next armada.

In response to the question of why he had retreated with his younger son to the Franciscan convent along with two trunks, his clothing, and a hammock, don Felipe replied that he had been innocently eating a dinner of fried fish at home with don Andrés when two friars arrived and said that his older son was hiding in the convent for having killed someone.[20] Upon learning this information, the elder don Felipe decided to hide as well. When asked why he secretly boarded the ship without putting his name on the official passenger list, don Felipe said (with great logic) that he did not want to offend the officers of the law because he knew they were looking for him.

Finally, don Felipe was asked point blank if he knew that his wife doña Manuela had died from having her throat slit and had her body abandoned in a deserted Chambacú wasteland. He replied that he was separated from his wife at the time of her residence in Cartagena because she lacked the "proper decorum and spousal loyalty, committing adultery with many men, day and night."[21] This was all public knowledge and an offense to her husband, "a noble and important person, and a knight of the Order of Santiago." He wanted to satisfy the offenses to his honor, but he could not find the right opportunity because of an illness (possibly a stroke) that prevented him from walking and made it difficult for him to speak. His said that his son don Felipe pitied him and wanted to take part in the revenge, so the younger don Felipe carefully followed his stepmother doña Manuela's movements over several days. Recently don Felipe el mozo discovered that she was in Getsemaní, where she had left her young son for a year with some mulatas. The two don Felipes developed a plan involving their two confidants. One accomplice would act as a sentinel and another man would lure the estranged wife and stepmother out to an abandoned guard tower in Chambacú to have sex with her. These accomplices, identified as Escalante and Moxica, were the two companions seen by the publican. Meanwhile, don Felipe el mozo hid near the empty watchtower, carrying a sword and a dagger. When he emerged, according to this secondhand account, his stepmother allegedly said, "It cannot be you, my son, what do you want to do to me?" Don Felipe el mozo said, "This," and slit doña Manuela's throat his knife. Then he fled to the convent. This was the story told by don Felipe's father, who was, of course, not present during the actual murder of his wife.

Because Moxica denied any involvement, the authorities questioned the fifteen-year-old don Agustín, who repeated his father's account by specifying that Gabriel Buitrón de Moxica acted as doña Manuela's potential lover/client.[22] In young don Agustín's version of the events, his brother don Felipe gave the Biscayan a *real de plata* because Moxica said that he would not leave the house if he did not see some silver first. Teniente Villena interpreted this payment as contributing to the expenses of "going courting [*galantear*] at the mulatas' house." Once Moxica lured doña Manuela to Chambacú for their tryst, he said he wanted to go ask for a light for his cigarette in the closest house, a short walk away. In the young don Agustin's version, tinged with incestuous thoughts and sympathy for his stepmother, doña Manuela said, "Don't leave me alone here." To which Moxica replied, "I will be back soon." Don Agustín believed that just before her murder, upon seeing her elder stepson, doña Manuela said, "It cannot be you, my son, what do you want with me?" because (in don Agustin's opinion) she thought her stepson don Felipe el mozo wanted to have sex with her. Don Agustin, continuing the more emotional tone of his narrative, reported that his brother responded by saying, "I love you."[23] The teenager had obviously heard the murderers' report after the fact and had also witnessed his father planning the act with the three other men. His understanding of their motivation was that "doña Manuela went around taking away his father's honor as man of substance."[24]

Lucrecia de Reyes, a twenty-five-year-old unmarried mulata, provided a female perspective on these events, but gave an account that made the crime seem even more sad and sordid. Like all of the women who testified in this investigation, Lucrecia deliberately chose not to frame her story in terms of men's honor and women's shameful sexual acts. Instead, she emphasized specific details of clothing, appearance, domestic setting, and mysteriously threatening men. Lucrecia lived in Getsemaní with another mulata called Ana de Arenas. Doña Manuela visited them on Saturday, November 6, presumably to see her young son who lived in the care of these two single women. At 7:30 p.m., Lucrecia said that a thin, young man with stooped shoulders entered the house and went into the room where doña Manuela sat. Later, the Spanish woman called him *paisano*, and they whispered together as they sat on the edge of a well. After a while the man went outside and doña Manuela told the two *pardas* that he offered her two pesos to go with him to his house for the night.[25] Lucrecia noticed that the man tried to hide his face. When she left, doña Manuela said, "Adios, see you tomorrow." The fifty-year-old free parda Ana de Arenas added that when the man entered, doña Manuela was stripped down for bed to her shirt, so she had to change her clothes to go out. In a macabre twist, before they left, doña Manuela asked her *galan* to cut some thread off her clothing with his dagger.[26] Ana begged her not to go because the next day was Sunday (the only indication in this case that the female witnesses put stock in the behavior codes of the Catholic Church), but doña Manuela said she wanted the two pesos. After her testimony, Lucrecia picked Moxica out of a lineup of twelve other men.[27]

Doña Manuela's sometime roommate doña María de la Cerda, who actually found herself in quite a bit of trouble because she hid doña Manuela's jewels, later revealed some ominous details regarding the days leading up to the murder. Like Lucrecia, she focused on appearance, clothes, and vaguely threatening occurrences. Perhaps both these women wished to convey to the teniente that they had feared for doña Manuela and the risks she took by unabashedly commodifying her sexuality, and that they had communicated their fears to her before her murder. They stressed their understanding of society's moral codes and knew that doña Manuela risked death by her husband's (or his accomplices') vengeful violence when she flaunted her sexual availability. On the Friday night before the murder, doña Maria reported that five burly men wrapped in cloaks and wearing gloves loitered near her window from 9 p.m. to 3 a.m. They wandered around nearby, sitting on benches or on the ground. One came to the window asking for doña

Manuela, so the widow assumed the men were looking to have sex with her boarder. Doña María woke up her other roommate, doña Ana, and they both saw doña Manuela approaching the house "shoulder to shoulder, talking" with one of the men, who turned out to be don Felipe el mozo. Perhaps don Felipe did love his stepmother and killed her out of jealousy, because these women said don Felipe had warned her of the murder plans in a letter. Doña María also warned doña Manuela that she took a great risk sleeping around (in their words, *dormir afuera*) because her husband was looking to kill her. The women feared that the men came to their house to carry out the murder.[28]

Given the convincing evidence of Lucrecia's identification of doña Manuela's seducer in the seventeenth-century version of a police lineup and the revealing testimonies provided by don Felipe and his young son, one might assume this was an open-and-shut case. Instead, readers of the trial records are more likely to throw up their hands in frustration at the evasiveness of the three key perpetrators. The actual murderer don Felipe el mozo escaped successfully and could not be found, despite an intense manhunt. In his absence, he was sentenced to death by hanging, but no evidence records that this sentence was carried out. Escalante and Moxica, the sentinel and the man posing as a john, adopted the tactic of deny, deny, deny. Both gave elaborate reasons for why they recently had spent a great deal of time at don Felipe's house. Moxica claimed he had legitimate reasons for sneaking on a ship about to leave the port. Escalante made many petitions imploring that, as a gentleman, he deserved better treatment in jail but received no sympathy when he complained bitterly of the pain that made his imprisonment unendurable. The local constable shackled and threw don Andrés into a calabozo, or a dark, dank, underground dungeon, shortly after his arrest. After sixteen days incarceration, don Andrés begged for a bit a fresh air and permission to move around outside of his filthy cell. He even claimed that his jailers did not open the door to feed him.[29] When another month had gone by without any improvements, don Andrés resorted to claiming illness to justify more lenient treatment.

Complaining that his life was at risk and that he was enduring purgatory, don Andrés demanded a doctors' exam. The *protomedicato*, or the leading local doctor and appointed crown official, visited the convict and said don Andrés had long term liver problems that did not present a great risk.[30] Two other doctors examined him and reported that he moved sluggishly and appeared dejected and melancholic. From a prone position on a mat, don Andrés described a terrible burning ache in his left side that reached all the way up to his ear. He claimed that the pain was driving him mad, he could not sleep, and sometimes he could not speak and vomited bitter bile and blood. The doctors were skeptical because don Andrés had an even pulse and no fever or inflammations. Later they noticed that when the patient was enraged, he suddenly possessed a firmer, more energetic voice and his movements became much more agile. With this changed demeanor, they doubted very much that he was suffering intense bodily pain, especially in his ear. In response, don Andrés admitted that the pain came on in sudden attacks and was not continuous. The authorities were not impressed with this report, which concluded with the observation that the inmate's only problems were "passions of the spirit." Asserting that his "sickness was false and feigned in order to defraud all administration of justice," the governor ordered the jailer to take care that don Andrés remained confined in his damp, dark dungeon with "a pair of riveted shackles." Clearly Andrés was both a bad actor and an unsympathetic character, especially given his likely involvement in a gruesome murder.

As the mastermind behind the murder, don Felipe el grande believed planning his wife's death was perfectly legal as a crime of passion in defense of his insulted honor. His defense strategy consisted of reiterating the specifics of how his wife had dishonored him. Each time he made a statement to the authorities, he emphasized his own personal honor and painted a worsening picture of doña Manuela's character. To justify deputizing his son to commit the brutal slaughter of his stepmother, don Felipe presented himself as severely handicapped, trapped in bed or propped up in a chair. He rarely spoke and when he did it was almost incomprehensible.[31] Don Felipe tied his notion of honor and his desire for revenge to his Christian virtue. He claimed that on discovering that he and his wife happened to be living in the same city, he hoped doña Manuela would "repent and emend what had happened, asking his pardon and reconciling with him so they could return to married life." She rejected his pious Christian intentions, however forgiving and merciful they may have been. Instead, doña Manuela

> lived publicly and scandalously, having sex [*mezclandose carnalmente*] with any man that approached her with this in mind, and this depravity was her occupation because she was paid for it. Every kind of man asked her for it because she was known as a lewd

common prostitute [*mujer mundana y deshonesta*] and she interacted with other women of the same way of life, all of which was
publicly known in this city.[32]

Don Felipe also knew doña Manuela had a son "engendered in adultery."
The existence of a child "did not allow for moderation because this denied
the passion of offended honor inclined to vengeance." The offense was more
serious because of his noble status, which don Felipe proved by claiming
that his father, who held a government position in Vizcaya, was a knight of
another prestigious military order (Alcántara). He asserted that his maternal grandfather was also a knight of Santiago, as were two of his brothers.
Although don Felipe did not use the term limpieza de sangre, he implied it
when he said that doña Manuela "stained his noble rank [*calidad*] publicly
and daily."[33] Since, in his opinion, father and son were essentially the same
person when it came to honor, a son's action was no different from a husband
killing his wife in a crime of passion, and, in fact, a son had an obligation to
revenge an offense done to his father.

Even after almost a month in jail, don Felipe was still confident that
"current opinion and practice" dictated no judicial punishment for a husband who killed an adulterous wife and that the same lack of reaction also
applied to any relative concerned. As he continued his technique of flesh-
ing out doña Manuela's sordid past, one begins to wonder why such an allegedly aristocratic man would marry a woman so lacking in honor.[34] The
parallel life stories of the man and wife, in his version, diverge farther
and farther apart, as he became unimpeachably noble and she descended
ever more deeply into the mire of lust and sin. In his mind, each degree of
moral polarity provided more justification for murder. In his most complete account of doña Manuela's biography, don Felipe roughly sketched his
vision of his wife's life as follows: her mother, a "licentious woman" based in
Bogota, never married. At a very young age, doña Manuela married in San
Luis Potosí, but due to her customary vicious habits, she compelled her first
husband to kill two men, one in San Luis Potosí and one in Lima. This anecdote set the pattern of a woman whose sexuality provoked men to commit
violence. Doña Manuela lived as a "free woman" for seven years, until she
returned to Bogota in 1644, her first husband apparently now deceased. At
this time, don Felipe was in jail in this city, for reasons unknown. Perhaps
due to the "pain he endured in his body and soul," he fell for the *engaño*
(deceit) planned by doña Manuela and her mother, who, by exaggerating

their calidad and other wiles (he refers to their *tan ardilosas manos*, or very crafty hands), trapped him into marriage. Very quickly he discovered doña Manuela's "inborn evil" and how she was a "public adulterer and fugitive bandit." He claimed that they never spent more than a month together and by 1648 she had fled to Cartagena. At first she lived in a respectable house, but she was kicked out because men came to her door at night looking for her. Don Felipe characterized her activities there as those of a "public adulterer and prostitute [*ramera*], [having sex] for a small or large price with any person, even those of lowly status [*vil condición*]."[35] In justifying his plan to kill doña Manuela, don Felipe argued that she repeatedly and continually violated his honor. Although the customary crime of passion took place when an unsuspecting man caught his wife *in flagrante delicto*, don Felipe claimed that this kind of unpremeditated sudden act was difficult when adultery was his wife's profession. In other words, given her continuous acts of adultery, it was impossible for him not to premeditate the murder, and, as a bedridden man, he could not actually carry out the act.

In view of the fact that he had already confessed to his role in planning the killing, Don Felipe was so confident in this approach that he planned his defense strategy around providing witnesses who would do nothing more to defend him than confirm his noble status and his marriage to doña Manuela and testify to her bad reputation. Don Felipe's defense presented seven witnesses, interrogating them with the following leading questions, which he hoped would prompt them to fit their stories to his version of events:

Was doña Manuela married to don Felipe in 1645?

In Santa Fe [de Bogota] did doña Manuela live separately from don Felipe, scandalously and dishonestly committing adultery, which led to his imprisonment [these details are never clarified] and allowed her to live with even more freedom and boldness, her mala vida being publicly known?

Did doña Manuela come to Cartagena, where she continued her public and scandalous mala vida, as a female prostitute [the term used here was ramera, or whore], having sex for little or no pay with men that came to her for this, since she was so corrupt that she did not distinguish amongst even persons of the most vile state and condition?

Did doña Manuela live and associate with well-known lewd and lascivious women and was she known as such in this city?

When doña Manuela fled her husband did she give birth to a son conceived and engendered in adultery that is being raised and fed in this city in the house of some mulatas?[36]

The last few questions asked witnesses to confirm numerous details about don Felipe's handicapped condition and also the illustrious status of don Felipe's father, mother, and brothers.

All the witnesses simply had to answer these questions in the affirmative in order to support don Felipe's case. The range of persons willing to testify for don Felipe reveals his rather limited status and reputation in the city, and his self-declared poverty meant he probably could not bribe any of the witnesses. Therefore, the responses he received were perhaps a bit more uneven than he might have wished. Oddly, given that one might assume this was the typical gendered understanding of illicit female sexuality in this era, don Felipe only found one witness willing to provide a narrative that closely matched his own. Two Spanish dons simply testified that they knew don Felipe was of noble heritage. They did not engage with the questions that discussed his wife. The only witness that apparently bought into this line of questioning was a forty-four-year-old knight of the Order of Calatrava who had known don Felipe for nineteen years. There is no way to confirm if this man made his statements to support his friend or if they were accurate, but in giving his version of doña Manuela's character, he did provide some revealing details for understanding the life of a Cartagena prostitute:

I have known doña Manuela by sight for around three years, since I came to this city from Santa Fe. I saw that she lived in a house on the corner of the Santo Domingo convent in front of Pedro de Segovia's tavern. I passed this street every day in order to go to my house and night and day I saw entering and leaving men of little quality and with a depraved and dishonest way of life, both foreigners and locals, all of whom came to see doña Manuela and she received them. I heard it said publicly that said men went there to have carnal acts with her. She was very well known in this city as a dishonest woman, with whom it was very easy to commit sin.[37]

Don Juan confirmed that doña Manuela lived with other mujeres de mal vivir, or prostitutes.

Another witness, Juan de Uribe Salazar, actually the son of don Felipe's cousin, fleshed out this vision of local prostitution, in this case associating the question about doña Manuela's "lewd" female companions with the "single women" she lived with in Getsemaní.[38] Since this part of town was known for its slave barracks, boarding houses run by women, and African residents, this witness mentally connected prostitution with doña Manuela's parda associates. Even more interesting, this witness, despite his conventional views on gender and race, went on to sharply disagree with don Felipe's account. Juan gave a different perspective on the troubled marriage when he said that doña Manuela fled Bogota because don Felipe spent all her money and treated her badly. Since don Felipe also sought out his first wife's dowry, it seems he was a man who tried to live off women. It is possible that he benefited financially from doña Manuela's affairs in Bogota and was behaving more like a jilted pimp then a dishonored husband when he carried out his Cartagena revenge.

Two very different women made statements for the defense that also complicated this narrative of justifiable violence resulting from dishonor. These women's stories demonstrate that elite women were not all that concerned about associating with a reputedly "fallen woman," even a confirmed prostitute. Their testimonies show empathy for doña Manuela, but withhold the moralizing judgment so common to men's stories. A doña María Suarez, age twenty-five, said she was a close friend of doña Manuela and spent many hours with her. She refused to answer the leading questions about don Felipe's illustrious relatives, as well as those that demeaned her friend. She only admitted that doña Manuela would leave her house day and night, saying, "I am going to find my men," which doña María took to mean that she had sex with different men.[39] A less elite Spanish woman, thirty-year-old María Becerra, possibly a prostitute herself because she was described as a *mujer soltera* (or "adult single woman," a label that, in contrast to doncella, implied sexual activity), also chose simple honesty over degrading doña Manuela's reputation. María summarily dismissed any knowledge of don Felipe's nobility and said that she knew only that he was doña Manuela's legitimate husband. To her knowledge, doña Manuela came to Cartagena as a stop before going back to Spain. In terms of doña Manuela's occupation, María said that "sometimes she found herself at the same house with doña Manuela and when doña Manuela left she said that she was going to see her men and [María] understood this meant she was going to sleep [*iba a echase*] with them."[40] These Spanish women, one superficially respectable and the other less so, saw no reason to present themselves as pious and moral in front of their interrogators as they testified to their deceased friend's sexual activity.

More information about doña Manuela's experiences as a mujer de mala vida emerge from the inventories of her possessions. While Paula and freedwomen friends negotiated their precarious social status every time they walked down the street (as discussed in chapters 6, 7, and 8), doña Manuela constantly confirmed her well-established sexual identity through a specific style of dress. The Spanish prostitute/doña did not dress as lavishly as the free mulata Rufina, who also bargained with her sexuality, but doña Manuela's collection of gems rivaled the jewelry worn by the wealthiest women involved in the 1630s witch hunt. Unpacking the trunks left in her rented room after her murder in 1655 hints at how she publicly and privately presented herself in the contradictory role of a sexually available, elite española.

Doña Manuela's surviving clothing was ostentatious although her wardrobe was smaller than that of some of the non-elite women of African descent described in chapter 6. Her clothes were also older and more worn out than theirs; actually buying new clothing, instead of receiving it as a gift or a hand-me-down, was a rare and special experience for the typical seventeenth-century unmarried woman. And who ended up wearing all the clothes that the Cartagena Holy Office or the secular judiciary auctioned off?[41] Although doña Manuela had not lived for a long period of time in Cartagena before her murder, it is possible that some of her associates wore the remnants of the supposed witches' glamorous outfits auctioned off in the 1630s. Perhaps, despite her higher social rank as a white woman, doña Manuela could not buy new clothes as often as Rufina, Teodora, and their peers could. This suggests that their more subtle approach to monetarily beneficial sexual liaisons was more profitable than the doña's style of street solicitation. Possibly before her death Manuela was suffering through a period of declining income. When her body was found, doña Manuela was wearing a silk cloak, a green skirt, and a striped bodice. She had been carrying a purse containing nine reales.[42] In her room, judicial officials found a matching crimson skirt and bodice made of the fabric called *chamelote*, or camlet, decorated in gold; it was certainly an eye catching ensemble, with the flamboyant color obviously underscoring her profession. Doña Manuela had another complete outfit made of lined black silk, also decorated in gold, sold at auction for the bargain price of twelve pesos. One of her several shirts was made of linen from Vizcaya and had a blue *tirilla*, used to hold up a high collar or neck ruff, in the classic style seen in many early modern European paintings. Her plainer clothing included a brown wool skirt decorated in black (auctioned off for five pesos), four old linen shirts, and one shirt made of wool. Her outer garments consisted of another cloak, this one in blue baize or flannel, an old silk cloak, as well as a buff-colored silk brocade jacket and an old doublet made of two layers of taffeta.[43] The numerous cloaks suggest the possessions of Roman prostitutes, known as *zimarinne*, a reference to their cloaks or *zimarra*.[44]

Other than her jewelry, some of the more expensive items owned by doña Manuela were her undergarments and stockings, not entirely surprising considering her occupation. She owned petticoats that, although old and used, were made of Chinese silk, along with plainer ones made of wool. One pair of stockings was made of scarlet silk, embroidered in silver, and sold for four pesos at a used clothing auction. Doña Manuela's undergarments also included orange taffeta garters. Her room also contained men's stockings. In terms of bodily decoration, doña Manuela sometimes wore old black silk gloves and carried a small fan and one of various rosaries she owned. Like many of her clothes, her shoes were also old and worn.

Despite her frequent changes in accommodation, Doña Manuela's rented room contained a bed frame, a comfortable amount of bed linens, and several religious items. In furnishing her place of work with Catholic signs of religious piety, she resembled Renaissance European prostitutes, who might have had small statues of the Virgin holding the Christ child at their bedside.[45] Doña Manuela decorated her room with gilt paintings of Christ of the Expiration, Saint Roque, and the Virgin Mary. She had three sets of cotton sheets and a handful of decorated pillows, along with two trunks with green taffeta cushions. Although it is not mentioned in her killers' trials, doña Manuela must have been at least a part time seamstress, because her room contained several pieces of fabric and other items used in sewing.[46]

Two women were arrested and questioned regarding possessions that might have been stolen from doña Manuela's rooms before the official inventories were made. The items allegedly stolen included clothing, underclothing, two silver cups adding up in weight to a pound of silver, eight silver spoons weighing five ounces each, silver thimbles, gold brooches and earrings, seven gold rings (one had nine emeralds in the shape of a rose, another a small diamond, a third with an amethyst stone, and lastly a fourth ring displayed a garnet), three pearl chokers, a chain of thirty gold beads looped to hang on the forehead, a silver plate, bracelets made of pearls, jet beads and silver, and a box of doubloons.[47] Clearly, doña Manuela was not financially desperate or she would have sold these items. On the other hand, they probably represented her life savings or perhaps possessions she believed were essential to her survival. The fact that, in contrast to the nonwhite women's clothing, most of what doña Manuela wore was old and ragged, if ostentatious, suggests that the some of the unmarried Afro-descended women were far wealthier than this publicly recognized Spanish prostitute, who did not own slaves or real estate.

To return to the prosecution of doña Manuela's murderers, despite don Felipe's claims that he planned to kill his wife for acceptable and even moral reasons, the local judicial authorities took this case seriously and did not condone honor killings. Despite the popularity of revenge wife killings in siglo de oro dramas, this was in line with contemporary Spanish moralizers, who disapproved of the unforgiving, unmerciful, jealous spouse who killed his wife in an act of private revenge instead of seeking the help of the authorities.[48] Despite popular and literary presentations of husbands' right to kill their adulterous wives, Spanish legal traditions going back to the *Siete partidas* forbade uxoricide. Francisco Gutiérrez, the government's prosecutor, opined that this "atrocious and terrible crime . . . [a] premeditated and treacherous homicide" was done "with little fear of God and their consciences and disdainful of the royal justice administered by Your Grace [the governor]."[49] The prosecution did not buy into don Felipe's argument regarding crimes of passion and especially a legal transference of a father's honor to his son. The fiscal argued that, despite a customary belief allowing that a husband might kill his wife if he caught her in the act or about to commit adultery, this did not mean that murderers would avoid punishment for a premeditated killing of their wives. And obviously the accomplices Escalante and Moxica did not fit under the umbrella of committing a crime of passion.[50]

This case survives because it was appealed to the Bogota high court for several reasons, first among them because don Felipe el mozo had fled, most likely out of the governor of Cartagena's jurisdiction. Another reason for an appeal was that local authorities disagreed over sentencing the three men. The teniente sentenced the father don Felipe to four years' banishment and wanted Escalante to be "rigorously" tortured, presumably because this accomplice was so persistent in his denials. On February 22, 1656, teniente Villena decreed a death sentence on Moxica, doña Manuela's seducer:

> He should be taken from the public jail riding a packhorse with his hands and feet bound, and taken by the public and customary streets with a town crier announcing his crimes to the watchtower in Chambacú where he committed the murder and where a gallows will be erected. There he will be hung until he dies a natural death and the noose cannot be removed until I give the command.[51]

Clearly, despite the honor code and this society's known misogyny, at least some justices harshly condoned spousal murder even as an alleged crime of passion.[52] Moxica's defense appealed his death sentence. The public prosecutor disagreed with the light sentence given to don Felipe, who freely confessed to the murder and thus also deserved the death penalty. He viewed banishment as virtually no punishment at all, since none of the men were permanent residents of Cartagena.[53]

The *abogado de la ciudad* Francisco Reje disagreed with all three of the teniente's sentences, insisting that all three men should only receive six years' banishment.[54] His justifications for this lenient stance reflect all of the traditional colonial conceptions of race, gender, status, and honor, which he implies would be violated if the men were harshly punished.[55] First off, he dismissed don Felipe's confession for legal reasons relating to the fact that he was an accomplice to the crime. Next, he said don Agustín at age fifteen was too young to testify. As don Agustín had given voice to the most damning testimony, this completely undermined most of the evidence for the involvement of the two accomplices. Thirdly, the lawyer argued that the two pardas Lucrecia de los Reyes and Ana de Arenas were women, so they could not be trusted in their descriptions and identification of the accomplices. In Reje's opinion, the only women who could give trustworthy testimony were those who were honest and secluded (*recogidas*), and these two did not fit that description.[56] For crimes punished by the death penalty, Reje argued that prosecutors had to provide the best possible witnesses to avoid any room for doubt, especially "in this city where most of the residents were blacks and mulatos."

Lastly, Reje provided a dissertation on the topic of honor killing, citing numerous laws and authorities that supported not severely punishing men for murdering their adulterous wives.[57] For an honorable man, Reje stated that banishment was an appropriate and traditional punishment, while a plebeian might receive a sentence of hard labor. Reje argued that because defending one's honor equated to defending one's life, a man could kill to protect his honor. He wrote that although killing another human being went against natural law, it was not intrinsically and absolutely evil, but was justified in certain cases. However, in Reje's opinion, adultery with a married woman was never licit and could justify murder. Unfortunately, the audiencia's decision left some questions open regarding the fate of don Felipe el grande, Escalante, and Moxica. The judges in Bogota simply stated that they agreed to uphold the local decision, but the documents written in Bogota include no reference to executions, so it seems likely that ultimately all three men were banished from Cartagena for six years, a nonexistent punishment since all of them wanted to leave anyway.[58]

Despite the unforgiving tone heard in some of the statements, the testimonies in the case reveal many aspects of the hidden world of colonial prostitution, as perceived by judicial authorities, Spanish men of various ages, and a diverse handful of women. Nowhere in these documents do the authorities describe doña Manuela's alleged profession as illegal, nor do they speak of any local houses for penitent fallen women or a need for this kind of institution. They do not use the more modern term "prostitution," speaking instead of the mala vida, rameras, and illicit sex in more general terms. All of the judges and lawyers involved placed some value on her life in the sense that they believed her murderers should be punished, and some asked for a severe punishment. Despite her occupation and her illegitimate birth, Manuela was always given the honorific doña. In Cartagena, men did not have to find sex for sale in the poor, predominantly nonwhite barrios including Getsemaní: they could just cross the street from the Dominican church in the center of the walled city and enquire at a known house of prostitution. The occasional Spanish woman, in fact, made a living off more direct, straightforward transactions of money for sex. Perhaps most shocking, some elite Spanish married women were potential and willing lovers, so having illicit sex did not always mean taking advantage of nonwhite servants and slaves, a fact that few historians of Latin America seem willing to consider, as it challenges our familiar ideas about race, gender, and, most important, female sexual agency. When denouncing their own society's ills, contemporary observers such as Alonso de Sandoval emphasized how the Indies centered on greed for material wealth. The idea of even elite women selling sex fits squarely into this critique.

It is also worth emphasizing that none of the female witnesses were overly concerned about doña Manuela's many partners, except when her vengeful husband loomed nearby. The women who spoke feared men who would enact the dictates of the honor code, but they did not indicate that they had internalized the idea of male honor based on female chastity, nor did their words demonstrate that they inherently rejected sexual promiscuity as immoral. Several women, both Spanish and racially-mixed of African descent, willingly shared their houses with doña Manuela, even when men came knocking at the door in the middle of the night looking to purchase sexual favors. In Cartagena, it is very likely that many Spanish and nonwhite women did run informal brothels out of their houses. Before her husband came to town, doña Manuela must have worried about taking care of her young illegitimate son and, like any prostitute in history, continuing this life as she grew older (she was around thirty at the time of her death). But she had saved up quite a large inventory of jewelry and that might have eased some of her concerns. Doña Manuela died a horrible death, but as an elite Spanish prostitute, she had more personal choice and freedom in her sexual partners than did María Manuel, the victim of another jealous man in colonial Cartagena.

The only evidence available points to weak and ineffectual efforts to legally control or suppress prostitution in Cartagena. Instead of a desire to suppress the sex trade, it implies a generally tolerant, or even apathetic, attitude. These disinterested attitudes suggest that jurisdictional competition and concerns about the larger empire distracted local authorities from harshly punishing women's criminal behavior or sexually illicit acts. The first documented attempt to enclose nonreligious Cartagena women comes from a last will and testament made in 1682 by Maria Cabana de Vaca, a childless widow. Doña María attempted to bequeath her own funds, real estate holdings, rental incomes, and all of her personal furniture and kitchenware to support the foundation of an infirmary for women. Due to a raging conflict between different branches of the church and state in 1680s Cartagena, the bishop did not examine her bequests until 1691.[59] In her will, after arranging several other pious bequests (including funding her niece's seclusion in a convent), María explained that she had often discussed with her husband and mother-in-law the desperate situation experienced by poor local women who became sick. She said it would give her great pleasure to help them in their need for medicines and medical treatment, so she wanted to found an infirmary in the houses she owned on the Calle de Media Luna.

Doña María wanted to donate almost all of the income earned by her various estates to this charitable venture. But this infirmary would have strict rules as to who could be treated. It would serve poor women, but "they had to be Spanish, without Indian blood to the fourth degree nor mulato [blood] to the second degree." Slaves, servants, and women with contagious diseases such as leprosy were also not permitted to use the proposed infirmary. Doña María hoped that the acceptable women would be entirely cured before leaving treatment, but she encouraged "virtuous white women" to live in the infirmary after returning to health. These acceptable candidates would receive food, clothing, and a respectable burial when the time came. The residents would be served as if they were elite women, attended by several servants or slaves assigned to the tasks of cooking, washing clothes, and making the beds. The administration of the infirmary should be done by a "virtuous, secluded [recogida], woman" over forty years of age, with the title of matron or rector. Although María clarified that this was not a religious institution, the patients had to be "poor, honest, and virtuous." The matron should strictly control visitors, forbidding "dances, parties, theatricals, gambling, or loud conversations with non-residents."[60] The only official religious element should be an ornate chapel with a chaplain appointed by the bishop and paid out of the income of a few of María's urban properties. The chaplain would be paid 150 pesos a year to say one hundred masses.

Despite its limitations, this infirmary might have been a welcome refuge for some poor local Spanish women. Unfortunately, under the corrupt and combative bishop Antonio Benavides y Piedrola (1681–1691), doña María's funds disappeared.[61] The conditions she set for suitable patients reflect local attitudes toward race, gender, and honor. While doña María dismissed women with a small fraction of Indian ancestry as inadmissible, she was more lenient toward women descended from mulatos, who made up probably at least 30 percent of Cartagena's population. Women could have some African blood and still be considered honorable and virtuous enough to enter María's infirmary. While doña María viewed the virtue of Spanish woman, due to their honorable status, limpieza de sangre, or less diluted European Christian heritage, as more trustworthy than that of women with non-European ancestry, she did not assume that all Spanish women were "honest." Doña María implicitly acknowledged that dishonorable Spanish women lived in Cartagena. Most likely, María did not want to extend her charity to women recognized as prostitutes, or at the very least, women who had open and publicly acknowledged sexual relationships with men who were not their husbands, regardless of their racial designation.

Given that local archives do not survive in Cartagena, it is difficult to document the continuing colonial history of prostitution in this port city, although selling sex was a widespread practice over the centuries. In 1790, after two hundred fifty years of Spanish rule, Cartagena's religious bureaucracy and town government finally tried to come together to address local prostitution. The bishop proposed donating money and a building to found a "house of reclusion for courtesans and married women undergoing difficulties [*casadas mal avenidas*] in their marriages."[62] Bishop José Fernández Díaz de la Madrid (1778–1792) planned an institution for "licentious women" resembling a prison but with a strong religious emphasis. He viewed offering "certain fallen women whose passions cause scandal" the option of "voluntary reclusion" as an act of charity and a chance to improve the city:

> The bishop of this diocese, continuing the exercise of his zeal for serving God and the king, and for the wellbeing and peace of this city, arranged to buy a suitable house to enclose the scandalous women who, with so much debauchery, live in disregard of the holy fear of God and the judiciary so that, within the limits of reason, the fatal consequences that these women bring about with their wanton and licentious lives, will be avoided.[63]

In his proposal, the bishop set down his expectations and ideas for maintaining order in this new institution, but unlike the plan offered a century before by María Cabeza de Vaca, he did not place any racial or moral restrictions on the inmates. The (presumably) penitent women should be strictly guarded, especially at night. They would live under the spiritual care of a chaplain who would make sure they had access to the Holy Sacrament, as well as "attend to and console their spiritual afflictions."

The town council approved the plan, so it was forwarded on to the viceroy, who added more details regarding guards and financing the venture, suggesting that this new institution follow the regulations of the royal jail. The viceroy demanded that two soldiers stand on guard at night to avoid any contact with outsiders and that the main door or patio was always brightly illuminated.[64] The guards and the warden should forbid the entrance of any guests at all times. Although constant guards and lighting ran up expenses, the viceroy would not allow any new taxes, writing that this venture had to fund itself entirely through charitable donations. Women with some property should pay their own way, at half the rate of prisoners in the royal jail. Those who had no funds had to work at unraveling ship's rope or washing the regiment's dirty clothing. The viceroy also saw the value in outfitting a chapel with all of the appropriate ornaments and ensuring that the chaplain said mass regularly.

In the end, this plan failed because the financial arrangements displeased the higher secular authorities. They also viewed this as a "temporal" prison that went beyond ecclesiastical jurisdiction and objected because bishops were only allowed to impose "spiritual penalties."[65] The authorities expressed discomfort with the idea of imprisoning poor women driven to "profit from their bodies." These women were so accustomed to "exercising their sensuality, [that it was] harsh and inhumane to enclose them." Some of the prostitutes were described as so "arrogant, capricious, or delicate," that it would be very challenging to "subject them to the work . . . of washing soldiers' clothes or something similar." As a result of these objections, a more useful and pious charity was put forward: taking care of abandoned children. This charity seemed much more appropriate for a bishop, since, in line with a 1787 royal *cédula* forbidding ecclesiastical judges from imposing temporal punishments, imprisoning women for "the sin of incontinence . . . [was] absolutely outside the jurisdiction and understanding of the bishop."[66] Cartagena authorities had a certain reticence in reining in prostitutes and a clear desire to avoid disrupting the undoubtedly tolerant, paternalistic attitudes toward women who sold sex.

Less than a century after she died, women such as doña Manuela already had disappeared from superficial understandings of colonial street life, as they also seem to have slipped through the net of surviving judicial records. According to Jorge Juan and Antonio Ulloa, Spanish naval officers that traveled through Cartagena in the 1730s:

> It is not normal in these countries to have public prostitutes, as there are in all of the great European cities. However, the women do not maintain their honesty as married women should; so that despite the lack of prostitutes in those cities, their dissolution is almost beyond imagination, because the essence of honor there consists in not profanely revealing the wide range of individuals that the women solicit, and doing it with one or another [man] is not a disgrace nor something considered unfavorable.[67]

In this quote, the writers define honor through women's behavior but argue that in Spanish America, honor had become not sexual control, but sexual discretion. While this observation fits well with eighteenth-century evidence presented in the final two chapters of this book, Juan and Uloa's point regarding prostitutes being replaced by widespread female moral laxity actually conceals the fact that prostitution did exist in cities like Cartagena. Despite the presumed sexual willingness of the women in Juan and Uloa's self-righteous fantasy, well-known and publicly recognized prostitutes did work in Cartagena throughout the colonial era.[68] By accepting Juan and Ulloa's confusing and even contradictory morality without deeper analysis into the often hidden world of Spanish American prostitution, historians erase prostitutes from colonial history. But neither eighteenth-century reforms nor moral prejudices could put a stop to local prostitution. Surviving archival records suggest that institutionalizing restraints on prostitution was not a priority at any time in the history of this city. Only one criminal case exists investigating prostitution in Cartagena. In 1805, town authorities investigated the home of the mother and daughter Magdalena and Micaela Mangones because of claims that they ran a brothel staffed by servants and slaves. The case was dismissed summarily due to lack of evidence; we can only imagine the real reasons for burying the scandal.[69]

Juan and Ulloa's observations support don Felipe el grande's seventeenth-century understanding that women's behavior was critical to male honor, but the travelers went even further, observing that honor was corrupted by Cartagena women's illicit sexual activity so that the entire code had become debased. Before accepting their generalizations about the invisibility of public prostitutes Spanish America, we should take caution and remember what don Felipe did to remove his wife doña Manuela from Cartagena's streets, more carefully considering why open colonial prostitution and the willing sale of sex has such a neglected history. This erasure may also rest on the stories that women (motivated by economic need, political maneuverings, or the desire to protect their reputations) told to judges. Their tales of sexual victimization by aggressive men, despite all evidence to the contrary, created such compelling sexually passive self-portrayals that we continue to believe them two, three, and four centuries later.

CHAPTER TEN

Sex, Love, and Marriage in the Eighteenth Century

IN THE EIGHTEENTH CENTURY, CARTAGENA AND EVERY OTHER CITY in Spanish America experienced shifts in the tone of Spanish rule as the crown put into effect the new policies known as the Bourbon reforms. Carthaginians may have perceived an increase in Spanish bureaucrats, new taxes and regulations, and a much larger military presence.[1] Fortifications grew and with them came more convict labor, drawn from a wide swathe of the new viceroyalty of New Granada.[2] Some specific kinds of archival documents, most notably divorce documentation, suggest a greater judicial involvement in personal life and even more female access to the courts, although the scarce evidence prevents perceptions of a dramatic shift in understandings of female sexuality. With honor enduring as the keystone of personal identity, women continued to modify their rhetoric and self-presentation in court to work with contemporary expectations and conventions regarding their ability to exercise sexual agency. This chapter explores the tension between emotions and societal expectations as mediated through the eighteenth-century colonial courts, specifically divorce petitions and complaints related to sex before marriage. The handful of surviving cases show that some eighteenth-century nonwhite women claimed honorable doncella status, while in other examples it becomes very clear that this society retained and even strengthened its association of women of African descent with illicit, dishonorable sexuality. Contradicting this stereotype that only nonwhite women had nonmarital sex, this chapter and the next (which has a focus on military social milieu and its negotiation of honor) will introduce two married women of Spanish ancestry who enjoyed sexually-charged relationships with single men, seemingly under the approving or tolerant eyes of their husbands. All of these cases demonstrate how eighteenth-century women continued to negotiate with colonial courts in an effort to perpetuate the institution of marriage (when they wanted it), expressing themselves in the language of passive female sexuality, even when their acts flagrantly flaunted this socially accepted self-characterization.

In Cartagena, divorce petitions or other complaints relating to unfulfilled marriage promises came before two different local authorities: the bishop and the governor. Married women dealt with the local bishop if they faced insurmountable challenges to continuing cohabitation with their husbands. Men also petitioned for divorce, especially if they suspected their wives had committed adultery. In the case of sex before marriage that did not result in official matrimony, the surviving cases for Cartagena derive from complaints made to the local governor, the highest regional military and political representative of the Spanish crown. If litigants disagreed with local decisions, they appealed the judgment higher up the bureaucratic and judicial hierarchy to the viceroy and audiencia judges in Bogota. More divorce cases have survived from eighteenth-century Cartagena than earlier eras, suggesting that men and women involved these court systems more readily in their private lives.[3] Again, it is not clear that sexual attitudes changed dramatically between the seventeenth and eighteenth centuries. One noticeable change is the different kinds of sources available for a study of intimate life and sexuality. For the seventeenth century, Holy Office sorcery investigations and one trial for murder prove that both married and unmarried women took lovers. The evidence below from divorce procedures or child support petitions suggests this practice continued in the final century of Spanish rule but with a fresh new vocabulary.

Because different legal structures produced the records for the two eras, different kinds of evidence have survived. In the earlier inquisition cases, defendants probed their memories and guilty consciences for material to weave narratives that would appease the inquisitors, sometimes exposing their own fantasies. Their confessions reveal an interplay between cultural creations such as the witches' Sabbath and the dark corners of their own minds. Criminal case litigants, on the other hand, used tightly controlled witness statements to push their own side of the story forward. These statements tried to build on strong public reputations for honor, status, and nobility. In contrast, seduction and divorce cases preserve the material, but ephemeral details of daily life that would otherwise be forgotten: love letters, courting practices (such as how couples arranged rendezvous and where and when they met), and the tokens and signs of affection exchanged by lovers. Almost any gift, even a mouthful of food or drink, exchanged between members of the opposite sex might be interpreted in court as a tacit commitment to marry.[4] Although gifts and love letters breathe life into the tender feelings and loving actions of colonial Carthaginians, in the context of the courts, they represented evidence of unacceptable behavior—either a man's seduction techniques or proof that a married woman was having an affair.

Historians have turned to the documentation produced by parental objections to marriage as a source for understanding legal and individual interpretations of matrimony, love, and family.[5] When a couple found love, lust, and/or companionship and hoped to marry against their parents' or guardians' wishes, they could turn to the Catholic Church, which always defended marriage as a sacrament entered into freely, regardless of parental, social, political, or economic pressures. In 1778, the reforming Spanish crown extended what is known as the *real pragmática* to the Americas. This meant parents/guardians could use secular courts to block marriages between couples they considered to be of incommensurate social or racial backgrounds. This was supposed to achieve two goals: to weaken church jurisdiction over family life (which extended deeply into local or regional economies and politics) and to prevent further racially mixed officially recognized sexual unions.[6] Unfortunately, since I have found only one existing marriage objection for colonial Cartagena resulting from doña Ana de Bolivar's elopement in 1642 (as seen in chapter 5), Cartagena does not offer any insights into the effect of the real pragmática. Instead, the surviving evidence suggests that the authorities did their best to maintain the peace whenever possible, without disturbing the race, gender, and political hierarchies already firmly in place. At times, this might mean agreeing that a marriage was not meant to be.

Divorce in this era was only possible via ecclesiastical channels. A church divorce meant nothing more than what we would view as legal separation or "a separation of bed and board," and divorced individuals were viewed as married but separated and not forced to cohabitate, as opposed to single and permitted to remarry. Historians have investigated divorce cases in detail for other areas of Spanish America. For example, in late colonial Mexico City, women filed most of the requests for divorces despite the threat of enduring a terrible limbo in *depósito*, a living arrangement for women ordered by the court during the proceedings.[7] Those who filed for divorce had to have serious complaints, such as spousal impotence, adultery, abuse, abandonment, insanity, incorrigible drunkenness, or attempting to force a spouse into criminal activity, including prostitution. Women frequently used the term la mala vida, or a bad life, to explain a lack of spousal cohabitation, nonexistent financial support of wife or children, rampant unfaithfulness, or excessive physical punishments.[8] Although this society did not frown on controlled castigatory violence in the home, Cartagena women had standards for their husbands and did not tolerate everything when it came to marital sex, abuse, or treatment within the marriage in general. Communities protected vulnerable women and neighbors watched out for each other and stopped or reported excessive domestic violence.[9] More rarely, men sought divorces due to their wives' extramarital affairs. The difficulty and expense of divorce may have motivated the majority of plebeian couples to simply avoid marriage in favor of committed cohabitation.

Despite the risk of possible public humiliation by exposing their sexual activity, eighteenth-century Cartagena women prosecuted men who did not carry out their promises of matrimony. In three cases from this era, women presented themselves as victims in an effort to guarantee official judicial or ecclesiastical protection. Unfortunately, in these three cases, certain aspects of the petitioners' circumstances prevented the authorities from giving the women their full sympathy and support for their claims. Although the nonwhite status of one of the petitioners may have stood in the way of a successful petition, the other two women had higher social status but took an extreme risk in exposing their lover's or husband's sexual frailties.

By this time, some nonwhite women also expected that their sexual partnerships would be sanctified by the church in the sacrament of holy matrimony.[10] Eighteenth-century plebeians had formulated their own personal understanding of honor, despite the fact that they could not claim the elite status or limpieza de sangre that was supposed to ensure enclosed and protected female sexuality. For example, in May of 1751, Martina Francisca Morales complained to Cartagena's bishop that she had sex with twenty-five-year-old Felipe Santiago de Soto (both were described as *sambos libres*) because he promised to marry her, even going so far as to publish the marriage banns. In effect they were married, although they had not celebrated the culminating sacrament in the church. But Felipe did not fulfill his promise to marry, and as a result, he had "prostituted" Martina and "left [her] pregnant with a son."[11] In using these words, Martina seems to mean that Felipe used her for sex, not that she actually became a prostitute, because she described her lifestyle as "secluded and honest." Note that her parents did not present the case for her, which argues for her independent status and sexual agency. Martina demanded his arrest and imprisonment. In response, Felipe acknowledged that they were in a sense married and that he had "copulated with her under this condition." However, he noted that Martina and her sister had discovered he was having an affair with his sister-in-law, so they attacked him, stabbing him three times. The assault put him off the marriage, despite the promises he had made. Implying that marriage required affection, Felipe declared that he no longer "felt any love" for Martina, although he understood that a father should support his children. He said he would name his son as his legal heir.[12]

Martina rejected Felipe's excuses, arguing that the marriage promise superseded any of their petty squabbles. She claimed that she had given Felipe some very minor wounds while he tried to take a knife out of her hand. While Martina asserted that the grazes healed quickly, Felipe said they made him "gravely ill." He claimed Martina stabbed him near his lung and this wound regularly throbbed. The other cut was in his arm and a final cut could have cost him his life because Martina stabbed him in his belly. Felipe offered more evidence against Martina: he tried to find witnesses that would testify to her affair with a man called Basilio Segundo and he even claimed that she had a son with her uncle, "committing incest." Clearly, she was "a corrupt woman, hardly secluded [*de poco recogimiento*] nor a maiden that he had deflowered."[13]

The Cartagena bishop saw that these two could never succeed as a married couple, given the rage and discord that they had already displayed to him. He allowed Felipe to forfeit his promise and demanded that each individual pay his or her own court costs. Felipe had to support his son with the sum of four reales per week. But Martina refused to accept the decision, apparently still hoping to marry Felipe, and she sent her advocate to continue the case with the archbishop in Bogota.[14] Almost two and a half years after Martina made her initial complaint, the archbishop agreed with the original decision. Despite Felipe's insulting tactics that degraded Martina's sexual reputation and the common occurrence of unmarried mothers in local society, Martina stood by her conviction that she was officially married. Martina wanted Felipe to carry out his vow, even if high authorities in the Catholic Church undermined their own sacrament by allowing a man to break his promise due to obvious incompatibility. Women of African ancestry like Martina, despite living in a society that did not categorize them as honorable and generally viewed them as symbols of illicit sexuality, placed a great deal of value on their sexual reputation and marital status, not unlike elite women of European descent, but Martina's admitted violent acts lost her sympathy from both the bishop and archbishop.

Fifty years later, a similar case came before Cartagena's governor, but this time the woman, María Josefa del Carmen del Oro, claimed that don José Joaquín Ampuria seduced her simply with flattery and "sweet nothings."[15] Employing the classic rhetoric of corrupted innocence, she claimed she was just a

> girl who was tricked by his enchanting words, promising me that
> . . . we would be bound by the church and we would rest in the sweet
> bridal chamber. . . . I surrendered, tricked by his deceptive words,
> and he violated the promised flower granted to me by nature.[16]

Sadly for this poetic girl, don José already had a wife in Bogota, so she could ask for nothing more than a dowry in return for her virginity. María Josefa was not satisfied with the 454 pesos that don José supposedly gave her in the form of paying for her housing, furniture, clothing, and food, so she appealed the case to the audiencia. In the face of her tenacity, don José demanded secrecy, saying he could not engage in litigation that would disturb his "marital peace and tranquility." The Cartagena governor agreed that it would be best if she dropped the case, observing that María Josefa should have known that don José was married and that she had not proven her virginal state.[17] It seems that María Josefa did give up her case, perhaps due to her poverty or just because it was clear that the authorities would not support her claims that might disturb the life of a respectable married man. Unlike her seventeenth-century predecessors, such as doña Maria Montemayor (as seen in chapter 1), María Josefa unwisely did not make her claims in the context of a political rivalry that might have caused the governor to seek to publicly humiliate her lover.

In 1768, doña Marcelina Martínez bravely requested that the Catholic Church annul her marriage to don Nicolás de la Parra on the grounds of impotence.[18] The exposure of sexual shortcomings should have humiliated don Nicolás more than his wife, but unfortunately, this case had the opposite result and doña Marcelina in the end suffered an even more shameful stay in the women's jail. In a petition that must have drawn on doctor's reports, Marcelina described the "irregularities in the matrimonial usage," or sex act, because he ejaculated out of a "perforation underneath the gland," which prevented insemination.[19] After leaving her husband and moving into another house or casa de *depósito*, she explained this to the cleric who dealt with local marriage conflicts and he had four medical men examine don Nicolás. Unfortunately for doña Marcelina, two of them declared her husband impotent and two of them did not, so the ecclesiastical judge (provisor) sent her back to her husband's home. Doña Marcelina appealed the case to the archbishop, who rejected it and imprisoned her in the "jail for adulterers and women lacking honesty or good lives." With the help of her mother, doña Marcelina appealed to the audiencia in Bogota, complaining that, instead of seclusion in an "honest" depósito (such as an approved, respectable house), Marcelina was imprisoned in stocks in a dark cell. Doña Marcelina's advocate before the high court argued that this young woman (around eighteen years old) was poor, honest, and of "distinguished quality" and should not be imprisoned alongside "vile black women" with only two reales daily spent on her food and other needs. For Marcelina, this represented "extremely violent oppression," but even the "lowliest black woman" could not live on that little food. The advocate demanded that don Nicolás contribute at least one peso per day for her upkeep in confinement. Unlike the allegedly immoral and criminal women in this jail, obviously doña Marcelina and her supporters believed she had done nothing wrong.[20] The assessment of the medical practitioners continued the tone of racial mockery: the examiners were described as "a man-midwife [*comadron o partero*], a pharmacist, and a *mulatillo* that entertains himself with popping abscesses."[21] Doña Marcelina's advocate recommended appointing two doctors certified by the protomedicato to reexamine don Nicolás. Doña Marcelina's fate is unknown, but it seems likely that she returned to live with her husband, having no other satisfactory options. The comments made in this case prove that the attitudes toward nonwhite morality and especially sexuality on display were common in this era. People still equated sexual immorality with African ancestry, despite ample evidence that Spanish women were also sexually active with men other than their husbands.

Among the handful of divorce proceedings that survive for eighteenth-century Cartagena, one offers fascinating insights into how elite women negotiated their sexuality both publicly and privately and the material details that document an affair's trajectory.[22] In 1778, an offended husband petitioned for divorce from his wife, a woman named doña Estefana Calderón. The husband, don Francisco Ignacio de Lavayen, used handwriting analysis to prove that doña Estefana was having an affair with don Juan José de Sagastuy. This dispute moved from the ecclesiastical court (which decided to punish don Juan with banishment) to the viceroy in Bogota, because don Juan was a royal bureaucrat sent to Cartagena to run the tobacco monopoly, one of the crown's more successful eighteenth-century reforms.[23] Ultimately, the higher court upheld the local church court's decision. Political rivalries may have sparked this dispute, but they are muted here, unlike nearly every other case of adjudicated sexuality explored in this book.

Don Francisco documented his accusations with several letters that proved an intimate friendship existed between doña Estefana and don Juan.[24] These notes take the form of small pieces of paper containing only a few informal lines. The writing style varies from extremely familiar to hostile, both suggesting a very emotional, private relationship. Because the love letters were unsigned, don Francisco also included examples of a friendly correspondence between himself and don Juan to serve as handwriting comparisons. Several witnesses also admitted observing suspicious behavior on the part of don Juan and doña Estefana. While love triangles have come up before in this book, in this case (unlike the examples of seventeenth-century adulteresses who practiced love magic) husbands tolerated men interacting with their wives through the acceptance of a new cultural practice. Doña Estefana and don Juan's relationship exemplifies the eighteenth-century practice (documented in Spain and New Spain) of elite married women enjoying relationships with *cortejo*, intimate single male companions, with the full knowledge of their husbands.[25] Cortejos were supposed to be courteous paramours or consorts, not sexual partners, but as time passed, moralizing observers tended to equate this practice more and more with adultery. Starting from the 1760s, Spanish high society saw less ambiguity in the courteous escort, starting to censure the practice as open adultery. This ethical dilemma fits doña Estefana's case well: what was worse for a husband and society as a whole, hidden adultery or a publicly known and acknowledged ambiguous flirtation?[26]

The letters reproduced in this case file include various proofs of excessive intimacy between the adulterous couple, clearly documenting their sexual liaison. The lovers often discussed Estefana's unwanted pregnancy, and don Juan wrote affectionately about her son, calling him Pepito. One letter dated August 21 (probably in 1777) was especially warm. Don Juan wrote:

> Estefana: you will always be a girl, even when you are a hundred years old. Last night, you should not have done with me what you did, but I must endure that, and much more, considering what you are and knowing that when you are pregnant [illegible] . . . I am amazed that you have not written me in so long, but on the other hand I am not, because in all this time that we have loved each other, I hardly deserve you. Give Pepito a kiss, and accept many kisses from me. By God, my beloved darling, I really want to see you. Your greatest slave until death, do not ignore me.[27]

The lover's entirely informal salutation shows his close and personal relationship with doña Estefana. His style is simple and generally unpremeditated, using some of the timeless emotional wording also seen in the early seventeenth-century letters discussed in chapter 5.

Don Juan's letters to the husband don Francisco were also very intimate and full of domestic informal discussions, such as Pepe's health and how much doña Estefana missed her husband when he was away. Don Juan even went so far as to ask the husband to think fondly of his beloved Estefana. For example, on March 24, 1777, don Juan wrote don Francisco:

> I went to your house and . . . found Pepe very happy and he ate very well today, but he made very few evacuations. If he does not have a relapse tomorrow he is not very sick. Yesterday they called [Dr.] Gaviria and he recommended a poultice and told them to give him a drink made of cinnamon, sugar, and other ingredients that he drank very well. They miss you very much at home. . . . I heard many expressions [of affection] from everyone in your house. Accept my affections as you wish without forgetting your beloved wife, in the meantime, I pray that God protects you for many years. . . . I kiss your hand, [signed] your most affectionate compatriot of the heart, Juan Josef de Sagastuy.[28]

Despite the fact that they were presented in the context of a marriage dispute, these letters bring to life the relationships between married couples and the eligible men that might enter their lives. Don Juan seems to even take the role of a kind stepfather to Pepe. His comments regarding the child's health convey that the family included him in their private domestic sphere to the point of a full knowledge of Pepe's every bodily function. This sexually-suggestive friendship and the fact that men such as don Juan freely entered other men's houses to interact privately with their wives illustrates the complex social life (with potential for illicit sex) experienced by married women in Cartagena. An eighteenth-century husband such as don Francisco who approved of his wife's male friend risked opening the door to full blown adultery and public scandal.

One of don Juan's letters took a more formal tone, presumably in response to doña Estefana expressing concern about where she could find him and her assertions about the father of her child. In response to her apparently jealous investigations and questions, he wrote in a much more formal tone:

> Señora doña Estefana. My dear lady: I received your letter and I found what you said to be very informative, but all of this is an obvious lie because if I went outside my house to sleep, they would not have found me, and even less likely would I be found in my house when they went to find me to give me some message from Your Grace. This is clear, that they would always find me at home or in my office; therefore all that Your Grace tells me is an enormous lie. Moving on to the rest, it is very certain that it is very much mine and I cannot deny that it is engendered with my very blood, nothing can take away the fact that it is mine and the day will come that [the child] will know his father, and with this I will not discuss this matter further.[29]

Don Juan continued this letter in a similar injured tone, suggesting that perhaps it was too difficult for Estefana to see him often due to conflicts with her husband or even that she now decided that she "loathed" him. He sounded aggrieved about returning gifts of clothing that they had sent each other. They must have made up after this fight, because don Juan wrote this long letter before the one cited above, when he sent her kisses and said he was "her greatest slave."

Several other confusing fragmentary notes are included in this file, all labeled as written by don Juan. They were probably sent to don Francisco, although there is no salutation; this is a far cry from the formal, polished, respectful, structured letters typical of this era.[30] These fragments trace the decline of what had once been a civil triangle of friends. One dated June 2, 1777, says, "Although you want to keep watch as in the past, now it is hopeless, because she is pregnant and it is not yours." This letter sounds like a rude and contemptuous dismissal of doña Estefana's husband as both the protector of his wife and a potent lover. Another odd note written a few days later says, "Today my legs behaved in a very strange fashion, but I didn't say that you don't have the balls, as you thought. The man who is afraid is a real coward, but I am brave, so I am hitting the road, but not out of fear."[31] These two brusque notes most likely represent macho posturing on the part of don Juan in reaction to threats made by don Francisco after he caught the lovers in conversation in his home. The aggrieved husband said that after he told don Juan to never step into his house again, he found his wife's lover on their staircase, talking to Estefana at dawn. Meeting face to face, the two men exchanged threats: don Juan challenged the husband to "come down to the patio because [don Francisco] told him [he] would cut off his legs." Don Juan may have even threatened that "he would drink [don Francisco's] blood!" This incident may explain why don Juan wrote the note asserting his own courage, although he did run away from the fight.[32] Despite this, don Juan continued to communicate with doña Estefana.

Although the men threatened each other with bodily harm, the rhetoric of the honor code did not come up often in the short documentation connected to this case. Instead of the violent revenge we sometimes saw in the seventeenth century, don Francisco sought the help of the Catholic Church after the aforementioned violent incidents. In his official petitions, the husband mentioned the "offense to conjugal honor" because don Juan "maintained illicit carnal correspondence with my wife," and he asked for a sentence that "corresponded to my honor."[33] This demonstrates a milder, more adjudicated approach to honor than we have seen in examples from the seventeenth century where some men chose to maim or even kill for their wives' honor. Eighteenth-century men used very carefully choreographed displays of violence that resulted in no actual physical harm to assert their sexual control over their wives before quickly turning to the authorities, taking a different approach than the bold public acts of actual mutilation or death that men carried out or explicitly threatened in the seventeenth century.[34] Although honor of course continued to function as a central focus of Spanish men's self-representation, in the eighteenth century men seemed slightly less likely to publicly display their honor through street violence. It is possible that the increased presence of Spanish authorities, especially in the form of a larger population of soldiers, during the era of the Bourbon reforms provided the stage for a modification in public violent expressions of honor.

Following the standard procedures seen elsewhere in this book, don Francisco interrogated several witnesses with a series of very leading questions that reveal his own understandings of his wife's behavior. Don Francisco's questions targeted the accepted signs of adultery: gift-giving, secret communications, suspicious loitering in a woman's neighborhood, and public fights between the husband and the lover.[35] Don Francisco asserted that don Juan gave doña Estefana gifts, such as discounted tobacco, gold bracelets, a filigree gold rosary, another rosary for Pepita, superior cloth from Holland, fine Flanders lace, and a gold belt. Several witnesses confirmed don Francisco's claims by replying in the affirmative to his leading questions. A doña María del Pilar Gómez knew about the gifts and told doña Estefana several times to consider what a good husband she had, but the adulteress replied, "These words show that she did not know him [her husband] and that she would die a thousand times for don Juan." Although doña María maintained that she virtuously avoided involving herself in the affair, doña Estefana did trust her enough to ask if she would help the lovers buy a house where they could meet privately. Doña María said she would not do this because "being a married woman with maiden daughters, I was not in a state to get mixed up this kind of business." Doña Estefana also repeatedly told her friend that she was pregnant with don Juan's child.[36] Even if doña María tried to present herself as morally opposed to the affair, the fact that she continued to associate with doña Estefana, listening to her confidences, suggest that Cartagena doñas had tolerant attitudes toward illicit sex. Doña María pretended to be quite concerned about her reputation, but not enough to cut ties with a known adulteress.

Witnesses who lived near don Francisco's house observed the erotic scheming done by the two lovers, even when they were exposed to the entire neighborhood. Fabián Gago often saw don Juan passing through the plaza surrounded by the Santo Domingo convent and don Francisco's house while doña Estefana stood on her balcony. At night, don Juan approached the house with his saber unsheathed in the classic stance of an aggressive man ready to meet his lover. Another witness, Jerónima Barragán, confirmed this detail, adding that the lovers gestured to each other while Estefana was on her balcony and that the married couple was constantly fighting. Domingo Villegas also saw don Juan pass the balcony two to three times each day and heard the "quarrels and disagreements between man and wife, and the entire family's trouble and grief, because they could not live harmoniously." Don Luis del Prado said doña Estefana often went to visit her uncle because from his balcony she could make signs to don Juan while he stood in the doorway of the tobacco warehouse.[37] Clearly, this affair was publicly known and even tolerated. None of the witnesses mentioned that it was a public scandal, and before testifying before the ecclesiastical court, they had to swear they would not repeat any information revealed during the inquiry, despite the fact that everyone in the neighborhood already knew about the affair. This attempt to maintain secrecy illustrates the delicate balance between publicly known illicit sex and officially acknowledged immorality: scandals considered detrimental to the public good ignited when institutions such as the Church or the military (as discussed in the next chapter) recognized ongoing extramarital affairs among the elite.

Don Francisco produced even more evidence of the audacious behavior of his wife and her lover. In February of 1777, Estefana traveled to visit her family. She sent an affectionate letter to her husband, concluding with the lines, "your wife with heartfelt regards," and adding, "Pepe thinks of you often, he will not stop saying *tayta* all day long and gives you a little kiss." The warmth of the letter cools quite a bit when we discover that it was written by don Juan, not a loving wife! Don Francisco asked four notaries to compare the handwriting in doña Estefana's letter to that seen in two signed notes from don Juan to don Francisco, including one with a very friendly tone, sent several months later. The scribes also looked at the previously cited missives that bore witness to the affair and judged all them as written by the same hand. While committing adultery with his wife, don Juan signed his letters to don Francisco, "your most affectionate and heartfelt compatriot." It should be no surprise that don Francisco, who had lost faith in a friend and in his wife, disagreed with the mild sentence given to don Juan, especially considering that don Juan was only living in Cartagena for his royal appointment. Both the governor and the viceroy confirmed that banishment was the appropriate action to take and that don Juan should be allowed plenty of time to organize his accounts.[38]

Doña Estefana's affair exposes a new kind of social, flirtatious interaction enjoyed specifically by eighteenth-century elite women. Known as the *chichisveo* or cortejo, this male escort served as conversation partner and potential lover, approved by husbands and tolerated by family and friends, for wealthy Spanish women. In a scenario very similar to doña Estefana's interaction with don Juan, the cortejo and a married woman took part in "an ambiguous code of companionship and escorting. . . . [of] noblemen allowing their wives to become friends with a member of the opposite sex." The goal was a platonic friendship, but it is no surprise that the relationships might go beyond conversation. Although this tradition had roots in an earlier century (as did married women having lovers in Cartagena), eighteenth-century moralists and commentators perceived it as a corrupt and scandalous French or Italian import. Others viewed the cortejo as a highly civil practice and rated jealous violent husbands as antiquated and obsolete, a commentary on changing attitudes toward the supposedly eternal belief in an honor code based on female sexual behavior. To some who looked to a new, perhaps French-influenced (given the pedigree of the new dynasty holding the throne in Spain) model of gentility in the eighteenth century, a truly civil husband turned a blind eye to his wife's cortejo, preferring a steady, and even prearranged, companion to a range of admirers or, in the worst case scenario, a variety of lovers. This institution only worked for experienced married women—a young, naïve, single girl should have a novio, or fiancée, not a cortejo—and also served to offer single men an intimate female friend (and flirtation partner) of a similar social class without marriage.[39]

While doña Estefana enjoyed what seems to be a quite civil relationship between her husband and lover, at least until the divorce proceedings began, other women had less fortunate domestic arrangements. Some women bravely (with family and community support) sought official help to escape from domestic violence.[40] In 1806, Lorenza Leal complained that her husband Juan de Castro, a soldier and occasional blacksmith, was habitually drunk and so violent that she feared for her life. She was pursuing a divorce but dreaded her husband's presence anywhere around Cartagena, so she filed a criminal case against him with Governor Antonio Zejudo (who served from 1796 to 1808).[41] Castro had attacked her brother-in-law with a machete and almost killed her by stabbing her three times with a dagger (*navaja*) while shouting blasphemies against the Virgin Mary and the saints in front of several witnesses. Castro made life unbearable because, when he was drunk on *aguardiente*, he became enraged and acted like "a wild beast [*fiera*]."[42] His behavior was widely known in the city and on the harbor island of Tierrabomba. The couple lived in Caño de Loro on this island, the location of the local leper colony, apparently in connection to Castro's military duties or possibly where he worked at his trade. Lorenza Leal received help and protection from the San Lázaro chaplain and the military captain in residence, who hid her in the Lazaretto buildings when she fled her husband. These officials, along with other residents including several of Lorenza's relatives, testified to Castro's abuse. Lorenza begged the governor not to sentence her husband to serve in the military by working on the local presidio, because his proximity posed a continuing threat of violent revenge to herself and her family. The governor and the audiencia were sympathetic and agreed on a sentence of five years of unpaid labor working on the Morro fortifications in Habana, a judicial penalty only given to the worst criminals in New Granada.[43] Lorenza's case proves that Spanish judicial systems, combined with wholehearted and enthusiastic community support, did function as effective protection for vulnerable individuals, especially women victimized by men's abuse.

Every woman mentioned in this chapter actively maneuvered their sexuality to achieve specific goals leading to marriage or within the context of marriage itself. In all cases, as a result of sexual activity, the women either started court cases or became involved in them due to the actions of their official male protectors. The intervention of the authorities usually concentrated on diffusing the conflict, in hopes of avoiding further violence or scandal. The pregnant *sambo libre* Martina demanded marriage even though she seemed drastically incompatible with her chosen mate. Instead, she received monetary compensation. Another pregnant woman, María Josefa, called on the rhetoric of abused innocence in hopes of receiving child support from a married man, but the court decided she had been sufficiently compensated through more informal gifts. A doña Marcelina took active steps to remedy both her marriage to an incurably impotent man and her imprisonment in the women's jail. In doña Ana de Bolivar's and doña Estefana's choice of husbands/lovers, we can observe women striving against familial opposition toward agency and control over their romantic and sexual partners. Lorenza Leal successfully called on her neighbors and the courts to escape her abusive drunk husband. These women reacted against male treatment, appealing to colonial institutions for protection from men who did not fulfill their duties as husbands or fathers.

Of all the women discussed so far in this book, going back to the love magic practitioners doña Lorenzana (in chapter 2) and Paula de Eguiluz (in chapter 6), only doña Ana (in chapter 5) succeeded in achieving her aspiration to marry the man of her choice. More often than not, the search for sexual and emotional satisfaction pushed women to look beyond the matrimonial bed. We have seen that women sought out and achieved nonmarital sexual fulfillment in the seventeenth century, but from the mid-eighteenth century forward, some fortunate elite married women may have enjoyed a more sophisticated, cosmopolitan toleration of their male companions due to the recognized custom of the cortejo. The cortejo simply provided another social structure or cultural interpretation for the timeless practice of a sexually-charged love triangle involving a married woman. It was an especially effective frame for the conditions of the Bourbon reforms, which introduced many more socially active, successful, bored Spanish bachelors into Cartagena's population. As will be seen in the next chapter, in the eighteenth century, men and women gathered more readily in different kinds of parties, carrying out a more acceptable (to most) social interaction between the sexes than we have seen in the seventeenth century. Men still worried about their honor as defined by their wife's sexual virtue, but according to new social and more cosmopolitan practices, they learned to calm their violent impulses as they observed their wives interacting with their cortejos. However, if adultery was proven and acknowledged by unanimous public confirmation, as in doña Estefana's case, it seems that eighteenth-century men turned to the courts for retribution. The next chapter will present the complicated case of another woman with a cortejo and the risk she took in flaunting military honor codes.

CHAPTER ELEVEN

SEX, SCANDAL, AND THE MILITARY

Doña Luisa Llerena

WHEN PRIVATE SEXUAL MATTERS BECAME PUBLIC, ESPECIALLY AFFAIRS that rejected the sacredness of the sacrament of marriage, Spanish authorities in Cartagena attempted to stop the spread of scandal. But the involvement of any court, except perhaps the officially secret Holy Office of the Inquisition, often served to spread scandal-mongering gossip. This chapter explores how one couple's interpretation of socializing, marriage, sexuality, and even personal appearance and dress clashed with entrenched Hispanic military ideas of honor and reputation. Public outrage reached the point of explosion in late 1756 when Captain Francisco Piñero's fellow officers in the *batallón de pie fijo* (a "permanent" Spanish army battalion, stationed in Cartagena from 1737 to 1768) decided that he could no longer alternate with them in their guard duties because he was allegedly complicit in *lenocinio*, or prostituting his own wife, doña Luisa Llerena, for personal gain.[1] This case ends this book with a final example of how colonial sexuality was essentially political and public, and how race, sex, and gender roles were tied to global changes in the Spanish empire.

As previous chapters have shown, in colonial Cartagena, local rivals often used criminal complaints involving sex and honor to bring down their enemies. Although the rhetoric of the honor code demanded that secrecy should shroud elite sexuality, the apparent willingness to provoke popular scandal proves the hollowness of this prudish stance. Claims that sexual

scandals should be tamped down coincided with a perverse joy in exposing them. Then as now, enemies could manipulate rumors and gossip (and
the truth) relating to sexual activity to achieve political goals or further
ambitions.

Judiciously choosing from the paperwork generated by the captains, the
audiencia, the Cartagena governor, the viceroy, and, of course, the clergy (it
is easier to measure this stack of documents in square feet than numbers
of pages), this analysis will explore the following themes: how honor and
sexuality were constructed at the household or family level; how the larger
community interacted with honor and sex to create a scandal; and especially how doña Luisa forged her own honorable identity despite her reputedly unconventional and spirited behavior. Those involved in this case voiced
their opinions in all of these matters at great length, so this chapter will
probe their eighteenth-century understandings of sex within marriage and
what this meant for private life and public reputation. Despite disapproval
on some fronts, this case shows that elite colonial women did have intimate
relationships with men who were not their husbands, disregarding official
pronouncements on female sexuality.

Through the statements of numerous character witnesses, doña Luisa
gains solidity as a comprehensible and vibrant individual, even though these
testimonies were made over 250 years ago. Doña Luisa's self-presentation
and occupations add further complexity to the history of Cartagena women.
Like Paula de Eguiluz and the prostitute doña Manuela, doña Luisa was a
well-known, high-profile local woman. Like other women encountered thus
far, doña Luisa earned an independent income through her home candy-
making business. Obviously, Paula was far more vulnerable to inquisitorial
interrogation, imprisonment, and punishment due to her marginal position
as a freed slave and *penitenciada*. But it appears that, at least to many military
officers, doña Luisa's reputation was as bad as that of doña Manuela, a common prostitute. However, even though doña Manuela was a Creole of Spanish
ancestry married to a man who claimed noble blood, she did not have strong
family links to Cartagena high society, and no one, not even her sympathetic
friends, denied that she sought out her male clientele. In contrast, doña
Luisa's elite status and strong Cartagena family ties afforded her the familial protection that both of these seventeenth-century women lacked. Unlike
Paula, doña Manuela, and the other seventeenth-century women discussed
in previous chapters, doña Luisa's several ways of making an income generally adhered to the occupations considered appropriate for an elite woman.

Doña Luisa also enjoyed the support of many women in her elevated social circle who ardently defended her reputation. Whatever doña Luisa did—and it remains debatable if she did commit adultery—the local ladies could not defame her honor, because in insulting doña Luisa, they admitted that dishonorable acts occurred and were even tolerated within their own ranks. They protected themselves by remaining loyal to their friend, because, as in seventeenth-century Lima,

> Women's notions about honor differed from what the dominant rhetoric said about relations between men and women. . . . A sense of female dignity, different from the one defined by men, was expressed by women from upper and lower groups of the city.[2]

The Llerena case proves that women's opinions had an important stake in determining public reputation. Admission into a social circle of elite women was perhaps the most important way women protected their honor, even in the face of strong rumors of nonconforming sexuality. Cartagena's doñas had their own set of standards for whom they would include among their ranks. Doña Luisa created and maintained her own honor not just through her status as a wife and mother, but through her personal connections, personality, and even her achievements.

In 1750s Cartagena, doña Luisa's reputation and sexuality drew intense scrutiny, starting at the level of the local military, clergy, and government and then escalating to a debate before the Council of the Indies in Spain. A local Dominican friar, Dr. Ignacio de Barragán y Messa, highlighted the shameful widespread knowledge of sexual impropriety that started the local scandal. Fray Ignacio testified in 1756 that the "city in general spoke badly" of the interaction between doña Luisa and her lover don Juan de Arechederreta for a long period of time. This was a "well-known scandal" for the "city's eyes and ears." The friar advised the governor of Cartagena, Diego Tabares, to deal with this scandal immediately and to ignore other more minor issues. Since the governor and the church could not reform the presumed culprits, Fray Ignacio suggested that the governor call on the viceroy himself in Bogota to have the most exalted authority in America apply "his powerful hand . . . for the spiritual edification of the Christian republic."[3] Other testifiers emphasized how everyone in Cartagena knew of the love triangle, and the simple existence of the gossip disrupted natural social and racial hierarchies by allowing inferiors to speak disrespectfully of their superiors. A letter from a local Jesuit to Governor Taberes stressed that everyone knew the rumors "without distinction of states, quality or condition," the standard all-inclusive colonial terminology for anything that encompassed the entire society. Witnesses mentioned various lower class people discussing doña Luisa, including maids. Even a tavern keeper (*pulpero*) publicly chatted about doña Luisa's illicit affairs. One witness summed up the dire situation, using some of the words commonly spoken in other testimonies: "what I have said and declared is so public and notorious, publicly spoken and known, that every inhabitant of this city, from the smallest to the grandest, knows of it. Everyone you ask has heard about it because everyone speaks of it."

How could the love triangle, comprised of the husband don Francisco, the lover don Juan, and doña Luisa, possibly counter these rumors when the rumors themselves proved they were guilty of causing scandal? The three lovers under attack defended themselves by calling on dozens of supporters who stated that they viewed the gossip as slander and calumny. Thus, the case divided the city in two. On one side were Luisa's friends, acquaintances, and family representing the local elite, especially women. The other side included certain members of the clergy, a significant faction of the military officer class, outsiders (albeit powerful, high status outsiders), the governor, and his wife. Over eighty people gave statements, with nearly all of them admitting knowledge of the scandal. But some witnesses denied the rumors, hinting to an understanding of honor as linked to less conventional views of morals and private behavior, not just hints of a negative public reputation.

Doña Luisa Llerena Polo de Aguilar was born in Cartagena in the late 1710s into a family firmly ensconced among the South American elite. Her father, don Joseph de Llerena (born in 1693), held the position of *capitán de armas* and jealously guarded his privileged access to residence in a house known as the *casa de armas*, one of Cartagena's finest private homes. Doña Luisa's mother, doña Josepha Polo, was a close relation and heiress to the fortune of Juan Nieto Polo de Aguilar, who was bishop of Quito from 1750 to 1759.[4] Doña Luisa enjoyed a privileged upbringing and married the Spanish soldier don Francisco Piñero in 1735, probably when she was still in her teens. Shortly afterward, the Spanish crown created Cartagena's *batallón fijo* to defend the Caribbean coast of South America from foreign invasions and contraband trade. Don Francisco joined the battalion with the rank of *ayudante mayor*.[5] In 1737, the governor of Cartagena rewarded Piñero's excellent service in helping organize the battalion by promoting him through the ranks from sergeant to *alférez* to captain. Eventually Piñero had command of over fifty artillerymen. He worked directly with the first viceroy of New Granada, Sebastian de Eslava, who was appointed by King Phillip V in 1739.[6] In 1741, the batallón fijo helped the city successfully withstand an attack by 186 English ships led by Admiral Edward Vernon (an important battle in the 1739 to 1748 conflict between England and Spain known as the War of Jenkins' Ear).[7] In the 1730s, 1740s, and 1750s, Captain Piñero's family grew and he prospered financially, especially via inheritances he received through doña Luisa and her skillfulness in earning money from rental properties, collecting the wages of ten slaves, and her home business.

This was the couple's official biography, but their enemies presented a less rosy version of doña Luisa's and don Francisco's story. One Fray Braulio de Herrera, a Dominican friar whose wagging tongue and personal interventions provided immense fuel for the scandal, claimed that before she married, rumor had it that doña Luisa "was very lively, so that it was feared that disgrace might come of it, because she went out every night with two mulatas, who quickly became pregnant."[8] Again and again, hostile witnesses referred to associations with nonwhite women to denounce doña Luisa. As a result of these unsavory social ties, Fray Braulio believed fears of a scandal prompted doña Luisa's early marriage to the socially and economically inferior don Francisco.

Don Francisco's fellow captains gathered evidence in an attempt to demonstrate a long history of dishonorable behavior, not worthy of an officer in their ranks and an insult to the battalion's corporate honor. Three different sets of interrogations investigated the two opposing sides in the battle over doña Luisa and don Francisco's reputations. To justify excluding Captain Piñero from the battalion guard duty *alternativa*, a group of officers gathered together twenty-three witnesses and asked them ten leading questions. The captains presented their answers, along with supporting letters from Fray Braulio and others, to Governor Diego Taberes, who sent the information to the viceroy and the audiencia. The questions probed issues such as:

Have you seen doña Luisa out at odd hours of the night, enjoying herself, and with whom?

Have you seen doña Luisa at fandangos with scandalous women, and there has she shown signs of a licentious and disorderly life that causes great scandal to everyone in the city?

Has doña Luisa had evil and abominable friendships with residents of this city and was her husband don Francisco Piñero aware of this?[9]

The remaining questions asked witnesses if they knew about the efforts made by the bishop, three different governors, other clerics, and the captains themselves to chastise and warn the couple.

Using statements made by these witnesses for the prosecution, it is possible to piece together doña Luisa's alleged extramarital affairs. According to several soldiers, officers, and other witnesses, in the early 1740s, after about five years of marriage, supposedly doña Luisa had an illicit relationship with a man called don Francisco de Bobadilla.[10] One witness claimed that he had seen the couple sitting together on a bed. An *alcalde mayor* maintained that he saw the two lovers out near the wall after midnight during the fiesta of the Archangel Michael. Shockingly, he first thought he was observing two men, because doña Luisa wore a man's cape over "clothing appropriate to her sex."[11] Fray Braulio added that Luisa and Bobadilla rode together in a *volante* (a horse-drawn carriage with two large wheels and a single bench seat) around the beaches and narrow streets. The friar also retold some gossip he heard from another doña, again reiterating the scandalous socializing with nonwhites: supposedly some slaves were sitting outside talking about how doña Luisa was waiting for Bobadilla and one of the mulata women said, "Ask doña Luisa if I am a cheap whore like she is."[12]

Several other witnesses who testified before the officers reported a notorious incident that took place in the presence of doña Luisa's mother and don Francisco in the family home. One soldier claimed that when her husband had his back turned, Bobadilla grabbed doña Luisa by the shoulders "or on the breast or at least in some less than decent way." Fray Braulio added that the two might have been kissing. When don Francisco turned around and saw this activity, whatever it was, he grabbed his sword and stabbed Bobadilla's seat. Bobadilla jumped up, questioning the cause of the attack. Don Francisco then responded by pounding the tables with his sword, yelling about his wife being treated as a whore and his mother-in-law as a procuress, until a crowd gathered. This incident led to a brief imprisonment for Captain Piñero, ordered by his military superiors. What most shocked the public was the fact that don Francisco quickly forgave both his wife and her alleged lover, resuming a friendly relationship with both of them.[13] In fact, his violent reaction was not typical of don Francisco's behavior or his methods of protecting his own honor through controlling his wife's sexual activity. Taking into account the magnitude of the accusations against her, it would not have been surprising if doña Luisa's husband resorted to violence on numerous occasions, but don Francisco almost always defended himself and his wife through official, written channels. This is unlike the seventeenth-century insulted men described earlier, especially doña Manuela's husband, who organized her murder, and María Manuel's sadistic owner. Don Francisco's attitude contradicts the popular vision, mainly based on literary sources, of violent men willing to kill straying wives and perhaps reflects a code of behavior viewed as "civil" in Spain during this era, which embraced toleration of one's wife's admirers or cortejos.[14]

If Bobadilla were Luisa's only rumored lover, this scandal would have died down, especially since don Francisco reacted with mild violence (not actually striking Bobadilla). Of course, this was the traditionally correct rejoinder for a husband in his position, according to the conventions of the honor code. However, witnesses testified that "the common understanding and the general voice of the people has it that this woman has had various illicit friendships." The general consensus among the hostile witnesses was that Luisa had a total of four or five publicly known affairs. Even doña Luisa's cousin (on the maternal side, his father was one of the officers attacking her husband) said, "he heard publicly that doña Luisa has had abominable friendships with various men." A local merchant mentioned hearing of two lovers. Allegedly, he saw doña Luisa lounging in *traje de mulata* (the typical clothing worn by a mulata, discussed in detail below) in the bedroom of a man called don Cristobal de Barragán (alias el Barbón, a manly nickname highlighting his possibly substantial beard). Supposedly el Barbón had to leave town due to the scandalous affair. Luisa also allegedly had a well-known liaison with a merchant named don Diego de la Corte. Another officer in the battalion mentioned a lover named don Jerónimo Corte. A chatty surgeon also affiliated with the battalion confirmed the names of three of these lovers, adding that he saw Luisa and Bobadilla whispering together on secluded staircases in her house. A town magistrate repeated the rumor that doña Luisa and el Barbón took his small boat to secluded spots for meetings.[15]

It appears that these affairs were tolerated until certain elements in Cartagena society began to denounce doña Luisa's ongoing intimate friendship with a wealthy merchant and slave trader named don Juan de Arechederreta.[16] By 1756, their two year relationship had generated an uncontrollable public scandal, so that many of the witnesses simply reiterated the existence of the scandal (not that they actually had seen anything suspicious) in their statements. This was in itself damning evidence against Luisa. Actual eyewitness accounts of illicit activity between don Juan and doña Luisa were scanty and often given by the officers intent on bringing down don Francisco. The avid gossip Fray Braulio also provided a large portion of the evidence of adulterous sexual activity. Most of the testimonies took the form of repeating slanderous rumors. For example, doña Luisa's aforementioned cousin (the son of Francisco's most adamant opponent) repeated servant gossip that Luisa often spent nights with don Juan. The talkative merchant mentioned above reported that everyone in town knew that Luisa had her *negrito* care for don Juan when he was ill, although the merchant admitted he visited don Juan's sickbed and never saw Luisa. This seems perfectly innocent, but tending a sick friend (even indirectly through one's slave) was viewed as a clear sign of an intimate relationship, along the lines of sharing a plate at meals.[17] Some believed that don Juan became ill because he was caught in a tropical storm while en route to doña Luisa's country estate for supper. The voluble army surgeon added that one day he entered doña Luisa's bedroom and found her alone with don Juan. She was nude under the sheets while he wore a *chupa*, or jacket. Don Juan frequently took all of his meals at Luisa's house and had his siesta on a cot in the living room. Other witnesses mentioned that the two were seen at night in a volante or walking in the same general vicinity (of course, Luisa also had a female companion). These observations represent nearly all of the hard, eyewitness evidence against the allegedly adulterous couple.[18]

All of these supposedly eyewitness accounts suggest that don Juan fit the eighteenth-century Spanish custom of the cortejo, an accepted intimate companion for a married woman, with very ambiguous sexual overtones. Obviously, many factions in Cartagena disapproved of this practice. The overheard words and public actions of doña Luisa's parents, especially her father don Joseph, supplied more proof of don Francisco's dishonor. According to the Hispanic honor code, a woman's father guarded her virginity until marriage and then turned the responsibility of maintaining her sexual propriety over to her husband. Several soldiers and officers recounted a public argument between don Joseph and his son-in-law where the sixty-three-year-old apparently excoriated don Francisco. In their tussle, don Francisco grabbed the older man's shirt and shoved him into a chair, while holding his rapier in his other hand. Meanwhile, don Joseph called Francisco a "cuckolded panderer [*alcahuete consentido*]." The sergeant on guard who separated the men said Piñero asked him to "step back, your grace, there is nothing for you here." One of most forthcoming officers claimed he heard don Joseph say, "you are a vile pimp [*pícaro cabronazo*] and it is notorious that you sell your wife's flesh for money." Another witness said he heard don Joseph say, "you cuckold, you would sell your wife for a piece of butter or cheese." An eighty-three-year-old man in charge of the Holy Office secret prison testified that don Joseph said his son-in-law had no honor or shame, and out of greed, he encouraged doña Luisa's iniquity.[19] All of these statements suggest that the witnesses wanted to communicate that don Joseph both knew of his son-in-law's dishonor and, most important, chose to publicly air don Francisco's shame and disgrace, even at the cost of his daughter's dignity.

No witness surpassed the garrulous Dominican provincial Fray Braulio's enthusiasm for fomenting scandal, all done while posing as a chastising spiritual advisor to the lovers don Juan and doña Luisa. Braulio wrote a twenty-five page letter presenting his views on the affair, repeating the most lurid gossip, especially the slurs that came from the mouth of Luisa's archenemy, the governor's wife.[20] While he undoubtedly exaggerated his anecdotes, some truths about attitudes toward what Cartagena society considered unsuitable behavior for a married woman emerge, as well as some possible hints about the couples' actual relationship, suggesting the two might have interacted as a cortejo and paramour, according to the current fashion in Spain. Some of the friar's stories simply reiterate the most familiar misogynistic understandings of women's sexuality and emotions as the instinctual reactions of bitter and voracious harpies. For example, one of Braulio's first anecdotes describes doña Luisa's rumored reaction to hearing that don Juan was trying to arrange a marriage with the daughter of the president of Panama. Supposedly, "with fury enraging her blood," doña Luisa told don Juan that if he married, "she would stab him to death and when his wife arrived, she would go to the *contaduría* [the counting house, perhaps where the potential wife would disembark], slit her throat . . . and drink her blood." Don Juan allegedly reacted to this threat by reversing his plans, and these new arrangements were rumored to have cost him over 8,000 pesos (presumably to undo his marriage contract). However, at this time don Juan did not marry, whether or not doña Luisa's fury caused him to avoid matrimony. In contemporary Spain, the cortejo might also view his attendance on a married woman as a way to avoid marriage.[21] Confirmed bachelors did exist in eighteenth-century Spanish America.[22]

According to the friar, because don Juan ate every meal at doña Luisa's house, he stored his silver flatware, clothing, and other belongings there, implying the couple cohabitated. He also underwrote doña Luisa's parties, including an "extremely costly gala after a bullfight, with a dance and a very sumptuous banquet." As a result, her home had the reputation of being a "house of scandal or devil's house." The friar said that when doña Luisa nursed don Juan during his illness she behaved like a "public concubine" (*manceba*). Clothing and bodily adornment come up frequently in these rumors of scandals. It was said that when she visited don Juan's house, Luisa did not wear a shawl, as if she were his "*manceba publica*." Fray Braulio claimed he actually saw don Juan dressing and putting on his stockings in Luisa's bedroom, as if he were her husband. Supposedly he gave her expensive emerald jewelry and cash, a common custom of the Spanish cortejo, whose role included spoiling his married lover with gifts of luxurious finery, a practice husbands supposedly liked because it saved them money.

Perhaps what most enraged Cartagena clerics such as Fray Braulio was the fact that no member of this love triangle seemed concerned about the alleged public outrage and official censure of their behavior enough to drastically amend themselves. Either public censure did not concern them or Francisco, Juan, and Luisa did not believe they were doing anything wrong. The honor code seemed of no concern to them. The Viceroy of New Granada José de Solis,[23] Governor Diego Tavares, members of the Company of Jesus, and of course Fray Braulio (as well as other clerics) and the military captains all reprimanded the three lovers but to no effect. These authority figures chastised Francisco, Juan, and Luisa publicly and privately, in sermons, face-to-face encounters, and personal letters, as well as other missives that were read and publicized throughout the city. Members of the audiencia in Bogota and eventually even the Council of the Indies also weighed in on how to suppress the scandal. This overblown reaction demonstrates the typical superficial appearance of pious attempts at suppression, while clearly publicizing the scandal better served don Francisco's enemies, as all of this attention only increased public knowledge of the alleged adultery and infuriated those involved. Don Juan reportedly went so far as to declare, "he was so annoyed with this life, that he would go to England to live in liberty."[24]

For their own personal and political reasons, don Francisco's fellow officers, supported by the governor and some members of the clergy, fomented this scandal to destroy the public reputations of the three alleged participants in the love triangle. In effect, important authority figures publicly declared Juan, Luisa, and Francisco dishonorable and provided evidence to prove it. Others, even witnesses hesitant to criticize the accused, proved their dishonor by simply repeating that they heard rumors of scandal. These three had lost their honor, perhaps permanently, because it was publicly and officially besmirched. However, dozens of witnesses speaking in support of don Francisco and doña Luisa disregarded official pronouncements and openly supported their friends. They denied the scandal and reaffirmed the couple's reputation and honor.

Despite the officers' obvious intent to bring down don Francisco by recording the opinions of hostile informants, eight of the witnesses questioned by the presidio captains refused to repeat the scandalous gossip. They justified their lack of interest in gossip by distancing themselves from the kind of social events that promoted this kind of exchange of information. The sargento mayor, Antonio de Mola, said he could not discuss fandangos and the like because he "did not attend such events, especially not at night, because this was not in line with the honor of his occupation and reputation." Along with nearly everyone in town, he had heard about the efforts made by clerics and the letters and communications involving the governors, including the widespread rumor that the Lenten sermon preached by a Jesuit at the cathedral specifically targeted the couple when the speaker denounced local scandals. A second lieutenant in the artillery company admitted to hearing vague rumors about doña Luisa and don Juan, but this witness described himself as a "secluded man, who dedicated himself to carrying out his obligations" instead of gossip. Two other lieutenants replied in a similar way, one explaining that he was too busy with his occupation to spend much time at home or visiting doña Luisa. The local Dominican prior also denied knowing anything about the scandal (hard to believe, since Fray Braulio was the Dominican provincial), as did three others questioned by the captains.[25]

Governor Taberes, in league with the captains, obstructed doña Luisa and don Francisco's self-defense by trying to prevent them from reading the statements made in response to the officers' questions and refusing to sign off on or otherwise acknowledge paperwork from the defense. The governor argued that the case was closed and don Francisco's reputation was ruined, so there was no need to investigate further.[26] But don Francisco was relentless, gathering statements from thirty-three individuals, men and women, including some who had testified before the hostile captains. Even his father-in-law, don Joseph, made a new statement in favor of don Francisco. For her part, doña Luisa gathered statements from sixteen elite women and seven men, all of whom spoke favorably of her character. Taken as a whole, these fifty-nine informants prove that in eighteenth-century Cartagena, an honorable reputation was both fluid and debatable, even in the wake of an outrageous sex scandal promoted and spread by the highest authorities in their pretense of denouncing it.

All three of the accused made numerous lengthy statements describing their honor and attempting to poke factual and logical holes in the rumors. For example, don Juan said it was impossible that he and doña Luisa were seen late at night in the volante, because the city had a strict 9 p.m. curfew. Captain Piñero expressed shock at the gossip. In his statement, he referred to his noble ancestors and "hidalga honrosidad" and presented his thoughts on honor as follows:

> Among all the natural assets possessed by man, the most sacred and inviolable is his reputation. . . . In all times [I] have zealously protected [my] reputation, which is so spotless and healthy, with such care that no one in the world would dare to say anything about it, having always lived with Christian modesty and with the dignity corresponding to [my] noble birth and military profession, in which [I] was raised and I continue to the present. . . . Until 1756, [I] was calm and tranquil, when suddenly [I] became aware of vague and confused talk all over this city.[27]

He blamed the governor and his wife, as well as his enemies among the military officers, for spreading the rumors that besmirched his reputation. Despite some examples of modern behavior toward his wife's male friends, don Francisco's rhetoric asserts his adherence to traditional Spanish values and ideas about honor.

Don Francisco asked his witnesses a set of questions that forced them to present him in a positive light. The questions emphasized certain issues in order to downplay what don Francisco viewed as his weak points. In a set of ten questions, the thirty-three witnesses were asked to discuss the captain's years of royal service; if he was known to "tolerate the tiniest atom of an offense against his honor, in regards to himself personally, his wife, or his servants"; if doña Luisa comported herself with decency throughout the marriage; if she purchased adornments, jewelry, or spent any money whatsoever without his knowledge; and if don Juan, her alleged lover, maintained a decent "spiritual relationship" with both doña Luisa and himself, including supporting Luisa's home business. The captain also phrased one of his questions to clarify that he had overreacted to the "polite greeting" made by Bobadilla to Luisa and later asked Bobadilla's pardon and welcomed him back as a frequent visitor to the Llerena/Piñero household.[28] This version of events painted the notorious fight as a minor disagreement between gentlemen, ending courteously and hospitably, as opposed to promoting that he was a husband who tolerated visits from his wife's lover, possibly even for financial gain. After all, everyone knew that the incident took place in the middle of the day in the presence of doña Luisa's mother. Don Francisco's violent reaction to Bobadilla's possible physical advances only proved the husband's desire to maintain his honor. Certainly, witnesses could not censure this acceptable reaction.

The questions also stressed doña Luisa's "studious economy" in managing four rental properties, ten slaves, and her other ventures that helped the couple maintain their establishment despite Francisco's modest salary of only sixty pesos a month.[29] In his efforts to deny that he made money by selling his wife's sexual favors, don Francisco prodded witnesses to provide contradictory evidence; they had to agree that the captain both controlled all of the household finances and simultaneously benefited from his wife's excellent financial management. The question regarding doña Luisa's appearance was critical to proving her decency as displayed in her physical appearance, and at the same time, it guided witnesses into confirming that don Francisco retained his paternal domination over his household. Piñero simply had too many different issues to dispute to maintain a logical integrity within his set of questions.

Doña Luisa's clothing and jewelry were an important concern in attempts to prove or disprove her honor. Hostile witnesses intertwined immorality with a certain style of dress in their testimonies, demonstrating that to them illicit sexuality was associated with nonwhite women and their fashion sense. From the perspective of some witnesses, doña Luisa's dress, behavior, and the company she kept linked her with local mulatas, which undermined her reputation and represented a threat to Spanish honor in general and a disruption of race hierarchies. Although it was normal for doña Luisa to be surrounded by nonwhite servants, witnesses loaded her interactions with non-Spanish women with less acceptable sexual implications. Her behavior disrupted social hierarchies based on the assumption that Spaniards were more honorable, due to their moral reputations as proven at least in some small way by their privileged access to expensive clothing. Witnesses could only frame doña Luisa's impropriety by connecting her actions to their understanding of how nonwhite women behaved. To them, she could not be Spanish if she disregarded her modesty. Instead, she seemed closer to their understanding of African-descended women's supposedly highly sexualized behavior. For example, a Spanish merchant testified that he heard doña Luisa had been seen in a man's bedroom, wearing "traje de mulata," or the typical dress of a mulata woman. A local surgeon, Juan Bornell, saw doña Luisa in "traje de mulata" in the street at 9 or 10 p.m. or even later, in the company of a mulata slave.[30]

Fray Braulio as usual repeated the most scandalous gossip, often referring to clothing in his testimonies as pointing to Luisa's questionable honor. The loquacious friar told a story about how doña Luisa and her lover Bobadilla rode together in a volante through Cartagena's narrow alleyways and nearby beaches, even entering the main plaza near the contaduría and the palace where the viceroy happened to be staying and where don Francisco served him. Fray Braulio claimed, "she put Bobadilla under her skirts [polleras] and approached the palace and spoke with her husband." On another occasion, one of the friar's informants overheard a conversation from a balcony: some Portuguese men asked doña Luisa which color stockings she preferred, because he wanted to give some to a woman. Luisa gave her preference but later saw a mulata wearing the stockings, so supposedly doña Luisa called the mulata a puta. The recipient of the stockings replied, "No, you are the whore" and hid in the Portuguese man's house. When don Francisco heard about the fight, he complained to his mother-in-law, who allegedly responded by cleverly reversing connections between clothing and gender by associating don Francisco's dress with his wife's shameful behavior: "Listen, don't you enjoy going about well dressed and well fed? So put up with it and shut up." Fray Braulio went on to report that doña Luisa visited the house of her most recent lover don Juan "without wearing a shawl [rebozo], as if she were his public concubine."[31] The idea is that Luisa would only discard her public signs of honor (modest clothing) in her own home, where she was free to dress as she pleased (although the presence of frequent male and female guests in Luisa's home complicates this situation). If she visited don Juan en déshabille, one presumed they were lovers.

Descriptions of the typical clothing worn by Spanish women in Cartagena survive in the writings of Jorge Juan and Antonio Ulloa. In 1735, the year doña Luisa married don Francisco, the two naval officers passed through her hometown. They observed that men and women in Cartagena dressed similar to Spaniards, and the clothes they mention, especially the pollera and the pañito, fit with gossip about doña Luisa's attire:

The Spanish women wear a kind of petticoat, which they call a pollera, made of thin silk, without any lining; and on their body, a very
thin waistcoat; but even this is only worn in what they call win-
ter, it being insupportable in summer. They however always lace in
such a manner as to conceal their breasts. When they go abroad,
they wear a mantelet. . . . Women wear over their pollera a taffet[a]
petticoat, of any color they please, except black; this is pinked all
over, to show the other they wear under it. On the head is a cap of
fine white linen, covered with lace, in the shape of a miter, and,
being well starched, terminates forward in a point. This they call
pañito, and never appear abroad without it, and a mantelet on their
shoulders. . . . It greatly becomes them; for having been used to it
from their infancy, they wear it with a better air. Instead of shoes,
they only wear, both within and without doors, a kind of slippers,
large enough to only contain the tip of their feet.[32]

To outside observers such as Juan and Ulloa who may have met a young
doña Luisa at social gatherings she attended with her father or husband,
Cartagena women dressed rather lightly (sensible in the local climate) but
with elegant flair. But even these foreign men noted that the women had certain rules, such as not appearing without at least wearing a short cape. Juan
and Ulloa do not illuminate what was considered "traje de mulata," instead
noting that the *castas* "all affect the Spanish dress, but wear very light stuffs
on account of the heat of the climate."[33]

Although Juan and Ulloa wrote several pages on the intriguing, deca-
dent, and even scandalous clothing styles worn by women in Lima, they did
not carefully distinguish the dress of eighteenth-century Afro-Peruvians in
this account. John Adams, their early nineteenth-century translator and edi-
tor, added a footnote to the effect that, "the lower class of women, whose
whole stock of apparel seldom consists of more than two *camisas* [shifts] and
a *saya* [petticoat], wear bracelets, rosaries, and small golden images about
their necks and arms. . . ."[34] Limeña dress seems to be quite different from
what travelers described for Cartagena, not surprising considering the two
cities' differing climates, population, and economies. To give one example,
the notorious tapada is not mentioned as popular in Cartagena—Juan and
Ulloa instead directed their genteel pious shock toward Cartagena's famed
fandangos.

What hostile witnesses meant when they accused doña Luisa of wearing traje de mulata makes more sense when put into the Caribbean as opposed to the Peruvian context. In the nineteenth century, the term traje de mulata was used to refer to an outfit consisting of a cotton or silk skirt and a batiste blouse that revealed the woman's shoulders. The skirt was hitched up to show off a cambric petticoat and the women wore little jewelry, emphasizing the beauty of their own physicality instead of material adornment.[35] This classic Caribbean style of dress remains popular to the present. If doña Luisa adopted any aspects of this form of dress, it is no wonder that observers expressed shock, considering the importance placed on finery and at least some degree of formal structure in dress. Despite the very Caribbean context of this style, doña Luisa also may have had a more metropolitan influence for her fashion choices. In the same era, elite men and women in Spain took up a trend of imitating the dress and conversation styles of the poor, young *majas* of Madrid, most famously represented by Goya's 1803 painting of the Duchess of Alba as *la maja vestida*.[36]

Fray Juan de Santa Gertrudis Serra also passed through Cartagena in the mid-eighteenth century and noted down his observations on typical women's attire, including the ostentatious jewelry worn by slaves doing errands for their mistresses. After describing some of the beautiful local birds, Fray Juan detailed "the ladies' dress" as follows:

> A shirt embroidered in silk as well as gold and silver thread, with a collar the width of three fingers, which falls to one side and is square on the other, which they call *pechitos* [little breasts]. Their skirts have lace for the width of four fingers. Over the shirt, that has broad sleeves without cuffs and lace inlays, they dress in Breton cotton over a hoop, one joined to the other. They do not wear a bodice, but only a batiste or Breton cotton shawl with lace edges. When they leave the house, they wear a taffeta cloak and skirt with silk stockings. . . . Instead of shoes, they wear a kind of small slipper . . . heavily embroidered in silk, bordered in silk ribbon. All around the sole of the slipper on the upper part is silver or gold braid.[37]

When these señoras sent their slaves out to deliver messages or gifts, they "decked them out" (*engalanan*) in "gold chokers, earrings, and chains, pearl bracelets." It is interesting to note that Fray Juan described outfits roughly similar to those seen by Juan and Ulloa, but the cleric provided much more information about the finer details. It is clear that an eighteenth-century

Cartagena lady such as doña Luisa had to budget for a certain amount of finery above and beyond her basic clothing to adorn herself in the expected costume of ribbons, lace, shawls, and elegant slippers.

In his attempts to defend his honor, don Francisco prodded his witnesses to discuss doña Luisa's appearance by asking them "if in her finery, adornment of jewels, and management of funds, doña Luisa could do anything without my knowledge."[38] Many of his witnesses took the bait, providing flattering details that supported don Francisco's assertions of his wife's good morals and his control over her sexuality, implying that she did not receive gifts or money to buy ornaments from don Juan de Arechederreta. A young cadet observed that doña Luisa wore her "jewelry and finery . . . with her husband's approval, as he played a role in its acquisition." Another young man reported that his mother told him doña Luisa possessed the same amount of jewels and luxuries as at the time of her marriage. Another cadet had witnessed doña Luisa discussing the purchase of "jewels and other things conducive to her adornment" with don Francisco. Doña Luisa's father proudly admitted that he and his wife maintained their daughter's fine and decent appearance. Another of Luisa's relatives said that she was always "decently adorned" but her husband intervened in any decision involving her purchases. A doctor testified that doña Luisa "depended on don Francisco's will in regards to her jewelry, finery, and the management of money." Witnesses described this relationship as "harmonious" and that doña Luisa discussed financial matters with her husband "out of love."[39] Overall, the witnesses created a narrative of Luisa's honorable appearance and dress throughout her life: first her parents supplied her with the correct luxuries and then her husband took over this role. According to this version of her life, Luisa never independently purchased her clothes or jewels, nor did she receive gifts from men besides her husband or father. In these statements, we hear the acceptable story of where one woman's clothing came from and are reassured that it is correct for a man to claim control over his wife's appearance, even if in actual fact the woman provided all of the money to buy the clothes and ornaments. In contrast, for the seventeenth-century women described earlier in this book, we only know the gifts, not the givers or the situations that resulted in the gifts. In both cases, public appearance and clothing defined the individual, even if the public persona did not adhere to a person's actual status. In both the seventeenth and eighteenth centuries, colonial bureaucrats and clerics connected dress to immorality and social or racial disruption. Travelers to Lima, continuing Thomas Gage's perspective from over a century earlier, felt compelled to view mulata women as especially sexual in their public appearance.[40]

Fray Braulio reiterated the importance of race, sex, and clothing in a final anecdote meant to show the lovers' utter disgrace. During Holy Week, the couple went to a corner to watch the processions, with don Juan wearing a *capote* (cloak or cape) and doña Luisa with a pañito (small kerchief). As they stood among the crowd, a mulata scandalized everyone because she "could not contain herself, and said don Juan was a pícaro, wicked, a bad man, and a cuckold." Shockingly, don Juan remained silent, as if nothing had been said. In other words, he did not defend his honor.

On the contrary, don Francisco's witnesses buttressed his honorable reputation by first confirming that the captain had served the king in positions of great trust and honor, earning a decent income throughout his marriage, which implied he had enough to support his wife and her luxuries. Even before his union with doña Luisa, locals averred that Piñero was a man of means, contributing six slaves to the couple's shared household at their marriage. In an implicit response to the *lenoncinio* accusation, witnesses agreed that sixty pesos a month, plus all of their other legitimate sources of income, would allow don Francisco to maintain his household and even set aside money. They agreed that don Francisco was moderate in his spending and maintained a respectful and harmonious relationship with his wife. He did not fit common Spanish fears and perceptions of an increase in materialism, impiety, and frivolity in this era.[41] It was said that he attended mass on a daily basis either at the Jesuit church or the cathedral and did charitable work. Many witnesses declared that Francisco was absolutely intolerant of the slightest insult to his honor and reputation. If such a thing did occur, the captain would demand "vindication" or respond violently according to the honor code. A few witnesses argued that their understanding of Captain Piñero's "fiery and jealous disposition" proved to them that the accusations were false and calumnious. They stated that no man could more zealously protect his house and that he probably had more honor than many of the other officers. Even don Joseph, doña Luisa's father, humbled himself by admitting that he had insulted don Francisco in a fit of rage. It is interesting to note that the testimonies suggest that the captain's way of life, including his career and his finances, not his lineage, created his personal honor. None of these witnesses mentioned Piñero's family background or anything about his past in Spain before he arrived in Cartagena in the 1730s.[42] This differs from the seventeenth-century model seen in other cases in this book, whereby Spanish men on the defensive always resorted to narratives of their noble lineage.

The above descriptions provide a template for a traditional honorable man's behavior, at least according to the Cartagena elite. But even in the statements made by don Francisco's witnesses, doña Luisa stands out, emerging as a more vibrant and vital personality than her husband. To support the argument that don Francisco did not sell his wife's sexual favors to maintain his upscale lifestyle, witnesses reported that the "industrious" doña Luisa profited considerably from the candy-making business she ran out of their household—described as her "trabajo" (work) or "granjerías que doña Luisa hace en su casa" (the handmade sweets doña Luisa made in her house)—with the help of her slaves. Due to his "spiritual relationship," don Juan contributed the cacao, sugar, and cinnamon that Luisa and her slaves used to make the candies. Nearly every witness observed that doña Luisa always had many elite señoras visiting her house because she had a "festive and generous disposition," but they said that all of her socializing never prevented either Luisa or her husband from fulfilling their duties.[43]

This is a much more subdued version of the sinful parties sponsored by don Juan mentioned in Fray Braulio's inflammatory letter. As noted in chapter 5, Cartagena's fandangos were famous, even going back to the 1600s. When doña Luisa was a young woman, the Spanish naval officers Jorge Juan and Antonio Ulloa passed through Cartagena and described the local social customs, perhaps even drawing from events attended by doña Luisa:

> One of the most favorite amusements of the natives here, is a ball, or Fandango. These are the distinguished rejoicings on festivals and remarkable days. . . . These diversions, in houses of distinction, are conducted in a very regular manner; they open with Spanish dances, and are succeeded by those of the country, which are not without spirit and gracefulness. These are accompanied with singing, and the parties rarely break up before daylight.[44]

Unlike Fray Braulio, the visiting Spanish naval officers found nothing disgraceful, and certainly not satanic, in these gatherings. Perhaps the friar believed doña Luisa's parties were more like those Juan and Ulloa described for the general populace, where the main activity was supposedly "drinking brandy and wine, intermixed with indecent and scandalous motions and gestures; and these continual rounds of drinking soon give rife to quarrels, which often bring on misfortunes." Juan and Ulloa found that the hosts of both types of parties shared doña Luisa's generous and hospitable character, warmly welcoming sailors and visitors into their homes and social gatherings.

Socializing in the home was perceived as a new trend in the Hispanic world of this era; perhaps in Cartagena it offered an alternative to congregating at gambling dens or outdoor dances with largely nonwhite attendance. Parties held in homes also meant more money spent on decor and furnishings, possibly an expense funded by a cortejo, especially given the perception that doña Luisa and don Juan served as cohosts for devilishly sinful gatherings held in her house.[45] Doña Luisa fully participated in this newer kind of socializing, demonstrating what might be viewed as a "modern" personality in the mid-eighteenth century.[46] Her bold style of dress, extroversion, and her businesswoman personality contributed to military and clerical disapproval, but her friends appreciated her vibrancy.

Doña Luisa's witnesses, among them sixteen of Cartagena's elite women, confirmed the picture of doña Luisa's sociable but respectable character as presented by those testifying for don Francisco; but Luisa's questions focused more on proving the existence of a plot against her, originating from the enmity of the governor's wife and her friend, doña Isabel, the wife of an artillery captain. According to doña Luisa, when this captain came to Cartagena, he wanted to occupy her father's residence in the Casa de Armas, but the viceroy decided in favor of don Joseph, influenced by doña Luisa's protests. Doña Isabel and her best friend *la gobernadora* were enraged and began a campaign to destroy doña Luisa. The two women orchestrated two public humiliations. The first one took place during mass at the San Juan de Dios church, when doña Isabel apparently tread over or stepped on doña Luisa's foot.[47] This rude act drew much attention from others attending mass. The interrogation questions doña Luisa put forward also clarified the notorious Lenten sermon, when, according to hostile witnesses, a Jesuit mentioned her personally as involved in scandals. According to doña Luisa, the Jesuit preacher was generally discussing local scandals and la gobernadora rose and walked out of the church. As she left, she loudly declared that the sermon referred to doña Luisa's "dishonest impudence and the ugly adultery that [doña Luisa] committed with [her] compadre don Juan." Therefore, she began the rumors and suppositions that the preacher purposefully shamed Luisa publicly. Doña Luisa asked her witnesses to testify if they knew that the governor and his wife and their allies openly called her a "ramera" (prostitute) and made statements such as that they could not count "the number of my lovers" (mancebos). Doña Luisa also asked her witnesses to describe her relationship with don Juan. All of them depicted it as a perfectly acceptable "spiritual relationship" between two people of quality.[48]

Beyond presenting her understanding of the scandal that led to her dishonor, doña Luisa formulated questions that established her own personal sense of honor based on her heritage, character, and ties to the elite. The twenty-three witnesses speaking in doña Luisa's favor corroborated her noble heritage and said that she would "never allow insolence from [her] inferiors, nor disrespect from [her] equals, nor rebuffs from [her] superiors, whom [she] respects without adulation." Before this "*cizaña*" (discord), doña Luisa asked her witnesses to confirm that she socialized with all of the most important local women at both religious and private events, and that "none of the señoras ever scorned her, nor did they have any reason to."[49] Of course, all of the witnesses agreed to the statements (hence the defense selected them to testify), and their answers often repeated the wording of the questions. The women were questioned in their homes and ranged in age from approximately thirty to more than sixty, representing a significant slice of Cartagena's elite female population. Many of them could sign their own names, and one even held the title of countess of Santa Cruz de la Torre. Nearly all of them substantiated the story that the conflict over the Casa de Armas started the scandal. The one elderly woman who did not hearkened back to older more traditional female socializing models by claiming she lived a *recojida*, or reclusive life, and she was unaware of any local events or gossip.[50]

Doña Luisa constructed her honor around two key attributes: her character and the company she kept. If she associated with women of honor, by extension she had honor herself. The reverse was also true; if doña Luisa was dishonorable, she brought dishonor on all of her social connections, unless they refused to associate with her. Doña Luisa's social ties with the elite were strong, but misbehavior could easily sever them, because her friends also had to protect their honorable reputations. The forty-three-year-old wife of the Cartagena sergeant major made this issue very clear when she observed that Luisa's relationship with don Juan fit within what was "honest, decent and permissible among the friendships of distinguished ladies, but if on the contrary she had observed the slightest demonstration of less decency from that moment forward she would stop visiting and communicating with [Luisa]."[51] This point highlights the importance of social ties as proof of honor and, by extension, protection against accusations of immorality. All of the witnesses confirmed that all of the señoras, even Luisa's enemy the governor's wife, welcomed Luisa at public and private functions. No one rebuffed her while dining or dancing at elite soirees. She was treated equably and women willingly sat next to her, showing no disdain.

The doñas questioned admitted to knowing about the officers' attempts to exclude don Francisco and some acknowledged that doña Luisa was implicated in a scandal. The interrogation questions themselves exposed the women to insults that could be viewed as shocking, which is perhaps why one woman denied knowing anything about any of the gossip, describing herself as recogida. Others took a less naïve stance and were not afraid to repeat the slander directed at Luisa, probably to prove that she only had certain enemies trying to bring her down. The witnesses did not believe the gossip about their friend's adultery even though a handful reported hearing certain captains say Luisa was an "enormous whore" (grandisma puta) and "that her husband was a cuckold."[52] Doña Luisa's male witnesses were more forthcoming in repeating the rumors, one even quoting one of her enemies who said, "That one? More than a hen (alluding to doña Luisa's alleged lewdness)."[53] These elite women clearly took part in frank male conversations and were not socially recogida.

Did the rumors of doña Luisa's adultery affect her social life? A doña Rosa, more than fifty years of age, said that despite gossip about Luisa's honor, the other doñas still esteemed her and admitted her in their functions. One of the handful of favorable male witnesses said the "gossip" (murmuración) had not limited doña Luisa's social connections. Other statements suggest that attempts to defame her character at the moment prevented doña Luisa from socializing, although the witnesses imply Luisa made a choice to "withdraw" and "deny all types of visits" while she "vindicated herself" for the defamation.[54] Perhaps relationships with other women were more important than official decrees:

> Many women would not shun a friend or neighbor simply because a constable or magistrate stigmatized her. . . . For more respectable women, the importance of neighborliness, friendship, sociability, compassion or kinship outweighed the taint of unchastity in determining their relationships with 'fallen' women.[55]

Despite the slander and public humiliations, doña Luisa continued to fit securely into the elite female networks, and Cartagena's doñas judged her behavior leniently. They did not disassociate themselves with her. Many of them also distanced themselves from repeating "unladylike" gossip. They were not innocents, nor were they sexually or socially naïve; they knew about the scandal, but they chose to reject its validity in rating their friend's character.

Several of the witnesses described doña Luisa's proud character in their own words, with an emphasis on her strong sense of personal honor and her active defense of her own reputation. Taken as a whole, along with previously cited descriptions of her lively, sociable, and generous nature, these statements further demonstrate that modest seclusion was certainly not the only acceptable behavior for an elite woman in eighteenth-century Cartagena. Two sisters, age thirty-five and thirty-eight, who testified together, portrayed doña Luisa as of "distinguished quality with a magnanimous heart, very pious and serious at the same time." Doña Rosa said Luisa had a "passionate disposition" (*genio ardiente*) and she would not "permit anyone to offend her" regardless of their status. The countess of Santa Cruz de la Torre (age forty-six) agreed that doña Luisa "rejected the snubs or slights" (*desaires*) made by her social superiors, including the rude incident that took place during mass in the San Juan de Dios church. The sergeant major's wife said doña Luisa "does not permit a lack of respect or courtesy from any class of person, as is her due." A doña María Josefa de la Torre, who had known doña Luisa her entire life, said, "in line with her noble birth, she has a stubborn [*rispiada*] heart, but she is not arrogant nor haughty and she will never permit insolence nor disrespect." Doña María Josefa believed that doña Luisa came off better in her public altercations with la gobernadora, observing that she "quedó satisfecho y con el mayor aire." Another witness said that doña Luisa repulsed the public insults decorously, and one of the male testifiers agreed that she "graciously ignored a public rebuff." A male witness said that doña Luisa had a "valiant spirit . . . that did not allow anyone to abuse or scorn her."[56] She did not wait for a male guardian to step to her defense. This final characterization fits especially well with a new understanding in this era of certain "modern" Spanish women who did not succumb to traditional ideas of a demure, modest, reserved demeanor, eyes always downward. Doña Luisa seems to have had the "pertness" (*despejo*) noted as a popular but new female personality type among her Spanish contemporaries. She knew how to interact vivaciously and openly in social settings, and she sounded like the kind of woman who looked everyone straight in the eye.[57] All of these witnesses also had no doubts that doña Luisa was capable of protecting her own honor while maintaining a friendly and affectionate relationship with her husband.

Despite the fact that some of the most powerful men (along with la gobernadora) schemed to bring down doña Luisa and don Francisco through spreading gossip about outrageous sexual sins, at the highest levels of the viceroy, the audiencia, and the Council of the Indies, this case ultimately was not serious enough to bring down Captain Piñero or threaten his status and effectiveness as a military commander. However, his actions may have indirectly led to the precipitous decline of Cartagena's *batallón fixo*. The battalion dissolved in around 1768, partially due to Piñero's 1764 flight (along with his men) to Portobello, Panama, at the orders of the new governor, the Marquis don Jose de Sobremonte, in order to diffuse the scandal. The marquis de Sobremonte also had several other serious disagreements with the commander of the local permanent battalion, who wanted more control over the soldiers and their discipline.[58] Piñero's company was only allowed to return to Cartagena, where most of the men's families lived, when don Francisco died in 1765. Meanwhile, doña Luisa remained in Cartagena, where she eventually asked to receive the pension due to a captain's widow.[59] In 1773, doña Luisa testified in her daughter María Merced's divorce from a local official. Although the marriage was not a success, her mother's reputation did not prevent María Merced's alliance with an elite man.[60] In 1798, doña María Josefa Piñero, either the same person involved in the 1773 divorce or another daughter, still depended on don Francisco's pension, but she begged the viceroy of New Granada for more money, claiming she lived in misery and not at the standard appropriate to her class.[61] In her petition, doña María spoke only of her father's record of forty years' distinguished service (thirty years is a more accurate account of don Francisco's time in the military). Although her request for an increased pension was denied, the reason given was a general Bourbon policy of reducing pensions. Despite the tens of thousands of words expended on this case a generation before, apparently her parents' scandal was long forgotten.

Doña Luisa's case shows that what at first glance might seem to be a quibble over precedence and honor actually had broader importance, even touching on issues affecting an international empire. Though it may seem that Cartagena's touchy young men, military officers, government, and clergy focused their energies on antiquated issues of reputation, dress, status, and sexual outrage, they were in fact attempting to sustain the authority of the Spanish family, racial and social hierarchies, and even Spain's hold on the Americas. However fruitless, they believed these efforts were meaningful in defending the status quo in their changing world, especially in the face of threats from the Portuguese in the 1600s and the long-term colonial rivalry with the English. Tension that erupted into violence over sexual conduct or insults usually revealed more serious fears or political rivalries. Although it is impossible to know the entire back story, the incidents involving Captain Cornelio (as explored in chapter 9) and Gaspar (as explored in chapter 3) demonstrate the unrest associated with the Portuguese and English presence in the city. In the case of doña Luisa, war with the English in the mid-eighteenth century meant more Spanish soldiers in Cartagena. When military men such as don Francisco married into the local elite, confusion emerged out of changing social and familial dynamics at a time when upward mobility among Cartagena's nonwhite population also disrupted established custom.

Attacks on doña Luisa's sexuality, which incorporated both insults to her husband's honor and her demeaning associations with mulatas, were another way for some local residents to express their fears of changing values and social hierarchies. The efforts of the local military and clergy to bring down don Francisco and doña Luisa bring to life the domestic and personal side of an era of challenging social and political change and reveal how those who perceived new elements in their world and new threats might express their sense of instability by attacking what they interpreted as novel expressions of gender roles, sexuality, and honor. If the incidents of mulatas insulting her and calling her a puta actually happened, these also indicate that nonwhite women also feared a woman who did not fit accepted racial, sexual, and gender expectations. Some Carthaginians, including doña Luisa's friends and even her lovers, rightly or wrongly, felt both flexible and secure in their elite status at the top of the social and racial hierarchy and did not fear or feel threatened by an alliance with a bold, extroverted woman. Like Paula de Eguiluz, doña Luisa was an energetic, prepossessing woman capable of intimidating her local society into a repressive reaction, but her persecution happened far too late to effectively stop social change.

CONCLUSION

THE PURPOSE OF THIS BOOK HAS BEEN TO EXPLORE THE INTERACTION between private lives and the colonial courts, with a focus on the rhetoric of honor and the unclear boundaries between licit and illicit sex. I have also shown whenever possible that colonial women understood and manipulated sexuality in their private lives and in the court systems, expanding the narrow vision of the moralizing literature of the day. Risky sex could result in murder, imprisonment, or inquisition trials, but some married women dared to conduct affairs or intimate friendships with eligible men trusted by their husbands in the privacy of their own homes. Non-elite women organized their sex lives with economic goals in mind but also competed with their peers over eligible men of their choice. Immense scandals, such as the concerted attempt by local representatives of the church, state, and military to bring down doña Luisa Llerena for her association with don Juan de Arrechederreta, eventually died down. These cases prove that sex was not suppressed or secret in colonial Cartagena, from the seventeenth century when elite and poor women dabbled in sexual magic through to the eighteenth-century custom of the cortejo. Public sexual reputation remained of great importance throughout the entire period of Spanish rule, and on those occasions when private sexuality became public, it proved a matter of great civic concern.[1]

It may be argued that I have taken a far too optimistic view of female sexual agency in colonial Cartagena, that I have selected cases where women were in an unusually advantageous position, that I have deemphasized the violence and inequality inherent to this system, and that sex in the colonial era "constantly repeated the conquest."[2] Despite superb scholarship, the most common view still perceives violence as central to colonial sexuality, a focus that ignores the subtleties of day-to-day sexual interactions and how these interactions can reveal more about race, power, and gender relations. A popular generalization of colonial sexuality exposes a limited vision of race and gender roles: Spanish men taking their selfish pleasures at will from women of all races, a "rapacious" society "in which all women constituted objects of unbridled desire."[3] In this tired formulation, Spanish men are the sexual actors and nonwhite women are most often the victims of these acts. We hear very little about the sexuality of nonwhite men; instead we hear countless commentaries derived from proscriptive moralizers on the sexuality of Spanish, indigenous, African, and racially-mixed women.[4] Colonial sex as a subject of academic study always seems to be about misogyny or hierarchy-enforcing expressions of power, never enjoyment or emotional ties. A closer looks reveals the possibility of a more active role for all colonial subjects, even encompassing female or nonwhite male sexual desire. Secondly, virtually every case in this book demonstrates that strategic rhetoric of female sexuality could be an effective weapon in a judicial setting, especially useful in shaming political rivals. I have always made clear that these strategies existed but involved some risk for women.

When archival documentation offered an example of a sexually active woman, I did not interpret this as just another demonstration of official misogyny serving only to highlight the contemporary understanding of women as evil tempters or irrational sexual beings. As noted by Guido Ruggiero:

> there has been a virtually equal misogynist bias that female sexuality up to the modern period in the West was uniformly passive almost to the point of being asexual. . . . [However] women as well as men went outside their marriages to find sexual satisfaction often at considerable economic and social risk.[5]

In the study of colonial Latin American women, all historians should at least entertain the idea that women made choices when it came to their sexuality and that they actually experienced sexual desires, even if they were heavily influenced by economic necessity and social and gender hierarchies. As this book has shown, fulfilling sexual desires was challenging for elite women trapped in marriages with much older men, which was why they felt compelled to resort to love magic and consultations with diverse healers and experts in the erotic arts.

In the seventeenth century, the gendered terminology relating to love and sexual desire sometimes seems foreign to modern understandings, but even these narrow and heavily-mediated accounts can tell us about love and sex if we interpret them more broadly. In the early seventeenth century, the Cartagena doctor Juan Mendez Nieto wrote of his concerns about "love as a specific passion in the soul capable of producing erotic melancholy" as well as provoking a kind of physical illness in women.[6] He described one Cartagena widow who suffered "hysteria and illness in her womb" due to, in his view, the overabundance of the female version of semen. The widow's comadre helped her with a remedy that, although the doctor did not use these exact words, equated to masturbating her friend with her fingers covered in an unguent.[7] Mendez Nieto suggested that he cured other women with the same method but also remarked that when the widow remarried a "prudent and discreet" thirty-five-year-old man, she no longer needed medical care.[8]

The seventeenth-century doctor frames sexual needs differently than the way we might perceive them today, but his words also reveal actual experience and sympathy for women's sexuality and desire. Anecdotes describing women's sexuality have led scholars to focus too narrowly on early modern misogyny, neglecting some clear insights into women's actual sexual experiences or emotions. Thus, Berhend-Martínez assumes that simple misogyny underlays an apparently tolerant clerical attitude toward female sexual desires in seventeenth-century Spain, which he prefers to view as simply proving "a widely held assumption that defined lust, elicited by and directed at women, as a pervasive temptation that had to be guarded against at all times." His evidence comes from one woman who expressed her lustful feelings toward a friendly priest as "'a certain uneven pulse and sensual movement.'"[9] If we cease to focus exclusively on male domination or clerical misogyny, these examples can provide evidence for how widows and other women in this time had actual sexual desires that they discussed with their intimate friends and who, if at all possible, sought partners to satisfy their needs.

The study of sexuality in Latin America opens a window into Cartagena bedrooms and how women of different racial and social statuses interacted in the domestic sphere. Women from the time of doña Lorenzana through to the eighteenth century, especially doña Luisa and the proven adulteress doña Estefana, observed and understood the different kinds of sexual opportunities open to nonwhite women and, for this reason, turned to them as confidants and intimate assistants when they wanted to engage in illicit affairs.

In doña Lorenzana's circle, love magic served as a diversion, and women entertained the idea of adultery, even if some single or widowed women pursued lovers more desperately out of economic and social necessity. Of course, nearly all of the women of African descent mentioned in this book were not married but were sexually active. However, and especially in the case of free women, we should not assume their relationships were unwilling ones. It is possible that the sexuality of these women was not always "a matter of survival but of pleasure." Illicit sex did not always mean "exploitation of women based on their economic need or lower social status."[10] Even for enslaved women such as Diego López's lover Rufina, sex cannot be reduced to a simple story of victimization. Although colonial Latin American men in general expressed disdain for the alleged promiscuity of freedwomen, this attitude does not emerge as noticeably from women's testimonies in the cases cited in this book, at least until the mid-eighteenth century. The Spanish doñas who consulted Paula de Eguiluz envied her power over men. In an environment where the majority of sexual encounters took place outside the matrimonial bed, Spanish women consulted women, both nonwhite and Iberian, with more experience in romantic love and desire when they chose to explore their sexual options.

However, undoubtedly, women's sexual choices and attempts at exercising sexual agency caused disruption and violence. Women's strong sexual desires remained dangerous forces. But it was not always men who reacted with angry, apparently uncontrolled, brutality: sometimes women themselves wreaked their personal vengeance when passion descended into rage. Women, especially those of precarious and limited means, competed for desirable men. They channeled their desperation into violence against other women living in the same difficult conditions. A story about female fury illustrates the darker side of colonial women's experiences of sex and love, as well as the limitations of crown authorities and local judicial officials over these kinds of cases. In the early 1790s, two poor women of African descent lived and worked on the island of Tierrabomba in Cartagena's harbor (previously the site of a Jesuit brick making hacienda and the new location for the local leper colony). Unfortunately, both Antonia Abad Santamaría and Justa Manuela Cabezas had a sexual relationship with the same man, the slave Manuel del Rosario de Jesús.[11] Antonia said she was twenty-five years old, born and raised on another harbor island called Bocachica, and was working as a laborer. Justa was a native of Tierrabomba. The two women had a history of fighting over Manuel. As a result, Justa had been imprisoned in Cartagena for wounding Antonia on the arm. Upon her release, she was warned not to return to Tierrabomba, but she disobeyed the command, provoking a more serious fight between the rivals.[12] This fatal altercation started when Justa approached Antonia near the brickworks while the latter was slicing food over a fire. The two women started quarreling, according to the seventy-eight-year-old *moreno libre* witness named Nicolás Blanquiser. During the tussle, Antonia claimed that she stabbed Justa in the left thigh in self-defense. As the wound began to bleed copiously, Antonia ran away. No one on the hacienda was able to stop the bleeding, so Justa died quickly. The local residents took the issue to the lieutenant in charge of the harbor fortifications, who, after examining some Tierrabomba residents, passed the case on to Lieutenant Governor Sebastian Gaviria, noting that the witnesses were so poor that they could not feed themselves while making their statements on the mainland.[13]

Antonia fled the scene without knowing that her rival died from the wound.[14] She found her masters on the island and they helped transport her to the Media Luna entrance to the city (even though she could not remember their names when she testified in court). From there, she sought refuge in the Santo Toribio parish church. Gaviria had to negotiate with the bishop to arrest Antonia and incarcerate her in the royal jail.[15] Although she was removed from ecclesiastical immunity without dispute at first, in the following months, the governor, bishop, and audiencia expended a great deal of energy arguing for or against the legality of Antonia's imprisonment. The main concern was that if Antonia acted in self-defense and only committed a minor crime, she should have remained under the protection of the church. Although witness accounts proved that Antonia killed Justa, the homicide was probably not deliberate and if the fight had occurred in the city, a doctor or surgeon probably could have easily saved Justa's life. Documents presented to the audiencia cited papal bulls and royal decrees relating to the issue, submerging the human passions involved in a morass of jurisdictional squabbles.[16] As was often the case, the tension between various overlapping bureaucracies confused official reactions to a violent act inspired by passionate human emotions. As a result, the ultimate decision regarding Antonia's fate has disappeared.

Justa and Antonia's violent and vengeful rage proves the extremes some Cartagena women would go to in the name of love and/or lust. Both of these women suffered from the poverty and isolation typical of life on Tierrabomba, where they were virtual prisoners if they could not find a boat to the mainland.

Perhaps their extremely narrow occupational options and intolerable living conditions pushed them to more desperate acts in the name of sexual jealousy than were commonly documented in the city itself. Within Cartagena's walls, the Spanish crown and its imperial institutions did not actively seek to suppress female sexuality. Husbands or other family members attempted to control women's intimate lives by resorting to violence justified by the rhetoric and values of the honor code. Spanish authorities also tried to maintain gender roles and loosely monitor female sexuality by supporting men's private acts of violence through not prosecuting crimes relating to honor or enforcing very light punishments when the cases did come to trial. But as we have seen often in this book, legal disputes over sexuality or honor often intertwined with local politics or wider-ranging imperial worries and rivalries. Local officials used the language of sexuality and honor to bring down their political rivals, and competing overlapping judicial and institutional structures lessened male ability to rule women's sexuality, as did the paternalistic function of the courts themselves. Over the centuries, this was a far more effective way to rule a complex empire than the black legend of Spanish male sexual rapaciousness.[17]

NOTES

Introduction

1. AHN, *Querella de Lorenzo Martínez de Castro*, fojas 2–3.
2. Splendiani et al., *Cincuenta años*, 3:120–21. The *visita* mentions that Rufina's mother doña María de Rojas was also on trial for witchcraft, but no further information could be found on the possibility that she passed on knowledge to her daughter. Since Rufina was born in Seville, this further supports the idea that much of the local practice of magic had Spanish origins. Probably Rufina mentioned her mother's trial when she gave her family background, but I have not found the complete version of Rufina's trial.
3. AHN, *Querella de Lorenzo Martínez de Castro*, foja 6.
4. Ibid., fojas 4–5.
5. Ibid., fojas 11–12, 15–16.
6. Ibid., foja 8.
7. Ibid., fojas 13–14.
8. Ibid., foja 9.
9. Splendiani et al., *Cincuenta años*, 3: 121. A few years later, an inquisitor called Pedro Medina came from Spain to examine the Cartagena Holy Office, looking into the 1643 accusations that Ortiz had committed adultery along with the Cartagena tribunal's many other bureaucratic and moral shortcomings. However, by this time doña Rufina was already deceased.
10. Restrepo, *Brujería y reconstrucción*, concentrates on uncovering clues of African spiritual and supernatural beliefs and practices in Cartagena through inquisitorial documents. For colonial Brazilianists, the Afro-centric approach (especially in the works of James Sweet, Laura de Mello e Souza, and João José Reis) fits better with the evidence and historic conditions. In certain Cartagena cases not discussed in this book, African healing techniques and perceptions of the human body and health clearly played a critical role. See McKnight, "'En su tierra lo aprendió.'"
11. Dawdy, *Building the Devil's Empire*, 4–5, 141–42. While Cartagena history has been well served by scholars in the United States who focus on politics, military

history, and the economy (including Lance Grahn, Allan Kuethe, and Marixa Lasso), historians writing in Spanish provide much greater detail on society and social practices, architecture, and religious history. The classic historians of Cartagena include Nicolás del Castillo Mathieu, Eduardo Lemaitre, Manuel Tejado Fernández, Roberto Arrazola, and María Carmen Borrego Plá. Colombian scholars with an interest in gender include Borja Gómez, Carmen Castañeda García, Pablo Rodríguez Jiménez, and María Cristina Navarrete.

12. When exploring the diversity of local ethnic identities, English-language scholarship on Cartagena has emphasized the enslaved and Afro-descended residents of the city, although Africans were far from the only local inhabitants forced to live in the city. The indigenous population in the region of Cartagena was decimated in the 1500s and represented less than 1 percent of the urban population at any time in the post-conquest period. Historians also have thoroughly examined the New Christian population, mainly Portuguese *conversos* who were persecuted by the local Inquisition tribunal. Most recently, see Schorsch, *Swimming the Christian Atlantic*, 121–68, 186, 203, 247–48, 400–408.

13. All population figures taken from Roca and Díaz, "Cartagena de Indias en 1777" (this essay has also been published as *Tres siglos*). See also Greenow, *Family, Household, and Home*.

14. Vila Vilar, *Aspectos sociales en América colonial*, 4–13, and Garrido, "Vida cotidiana en Cartagena de Indias en el siglo XVII," 457–58.

15. Greenow, *Family, Household, and Home*, 7.

16. For the development of Cartagena's religious and military infrastructure from an architectural perspective, see the classic Dorta, *Cartagena de Indias*. More recent scholarship continues to cite Dorta as authoritative.

17. Vázquez de Espinosa, *Compendio y descripción de las Indias Occidentales*, 447–48.

18. Lux Martelo, *Las mujeres*, 86.

19. Ibid., 86–90, gives descriptions of these women and their establishments.

20. Guido Ruggiero notes a similar situation in Renaissance Venice, *The Boundaries of Eros*, 153.

21. Greenow, *Family, Household, and Home*, 25–26, 29–30. The rest of the households were run by Spanish or nonwhite men. Spanish men were almost always married when they held the role of head of household, which is logical given the local gender imbalance. Wealthier households generally had more residents, in the form of dependents, servants, and slaves. All three of these categories created the numeric predominance of single, nonwhite women in Cartagena.

22. Lane, *Pillaging the Empire*, 51. See also Lane, "Corsarios, piratas y la defensa de Cartagena de Indias en el siglo XVI."

23. Dorta, *Cartagena de Indias*, 10–11, 18–19, and Gerassi-Navarro, *Pirate Novels*, 22.

24. Díaz and Roca, *Tres siglos*, 13, and Lane, *Pillaging the Empire*, 27.

25. Lane, *Pillaging the Empire*, 38–39.

26. Dorta, *Cartagena de Indias*, 8, 29–30. Dorta's work includes maps and plans from this era, illustrating the beginnings of fortification projects in the late sixteenth

century. See also the beautifully-illustrated book by Redondo Gómez, *Cartagena de Indias*, 147–57.

27. Dorta, *Cartagena de Indias*, 37–39.

28. Accounts of the 1697 attack were written by the participants and many historians over the centuries. See Dorta, *Cartagena de Indias*, 99–111, for a summary. For literary analysis of contemporary accounts, including a useful historiographical overview, see Borrero Londoño, "De Pointis y la representación textual de la expedición a Cartagena en 1697."

29. Some of the Holy Office files are accessible online at the *Portal de Archivos Españoles*.

30. Greenleaf, *The Mexican Inquisition of the Sixteenth Century*, 1.

31. Ibid., 3.

32. Darnton, *The Great Cat Massacre*, 258.

33. Davis, *Fiction in the Archives*, 5.

34. Lavrin, "Sexuality in Colonial Mexico." At least as far back as Phelan's *The Kingdom of Three Quitos*, historians of Latin America have exposed the weak points in Spanish rule. Burkholder and Chandler revisited this idea in *From Impotence to Authority*. Herzog continued to prove this point in *Upholding Justice*. Although they deal mainly with the nineteenth century and later, I found Aguirre's *The Criminals of Lima* and Arrom's *Containing the Poor* to be helpful reminders of the weakness of apparently oppressive Latin American institutions. While scholars happily accept loopholes and ineffectiveness in the economy and politics, sexuality retains an image that suggests effective imperial and patriarchal domination. See Gonzalez-Casanovas, "Gender Models in Alfonso X's *Siete partidas.*"

35. Most notably, Poska, *Women and Authority*, and Barahona, *Sex Crimes, Honour, and the Law*.

36. Poska, *Women and Authority*, 2–4.

37. The essays in Saint-Saëns, *Sex and Love in Golden Age Spain*, highlight these opposing interpretations. See Barahona, "Courtship, Seduction and Abandonment," and Saint-Saëns, "'It is not a Sin!'"; versus Haliczer, "Sexuality and Repression in Counter-Reformation Spain."

38. Twinam, *Public Lives, Private Secrets*, 31, and Boyer, "Honor Among Plebeians," 152–54.

39. Foucault, *Histoire de la sexualité* and *Surveiller et punir*. Foucault's idea of an "individuated subject" hinges on a negation of full human consciousness before the advent of the modern state—and colonial Latin American historians often seem to negate the desires (especially sexual) of Spain's subjects in the New World in favor of emphasizing repression. Nancy F. Partner's analysis fits well with some understandings of colonial Latin America: the all-too-willing acceptance of "standardized prescriptive doctrines of official religious culture . . . as a literal and sufficient description of . . . human reality." The focus on discourse, following Foucault, "virtually ignores the psychological and physical dimensions of human experience . . . the role of emotion and embodiment." Partner, "Did Mystics Have Sex?," 299–300.

40. Mannarelli, *Private Passions*, 41.

41. Ruggiero, *The Boundaries of Eros*, 4.

42. A description used in reference to the exaggerated assessment of sex in Europe before the eighteenth century. Briggs, *Witches and Neighbors*, 223.

43. Murray, "Introduction" to *Desire and Discipline*, x.

44. Powers, "Conquering Discourses of 'Sexual Conquest,'" 7 and 26. Powers criticizes Gutiérrez's oft-cited book, *When Jesus Came*, as a "sexualization of Pueblo women" that "recolonizes them." She is also wary of Trexler's *Sex and Conquest*. Both of these books focus on sexual violence in colonial Latin America, although Trexler is more unique in his emphasis on the abuse of men (9–10). Socolow, in *The Women of Colonial Latin America*, states that in the seventeenth century, "the church was more and more successful in its campaign of sexual repression" (15).

45. For the Hispanic honor code, see Burkholder, "Honor and Honors in Colonial Spanish America," 19, 22–26, 28–29, 38–39; Shumway, *Ugly Suitor*, 25–26; and Taylor, *Honor and Violence*, 100–155.

46. See Martinez, *Genealogical Fictions*.

47. "Nobles and commoners alike strove to maintain honor, simply defined as one's self-esteem as well as the public esteem other members of society bestowed on an individual." In Burkholder, "Honor and Honors," 18, 43n2. See also Lipsett-Rivera, *Gender and the Negotiation of Daily Life*, 12–19.

48. Twinam, *Public Lives, Private Secrets*, 27–30, 49–50, 337–39.

49. Tamar Herzog discusses reputation in relation to Castilian law in her analysis of the case of an extended family living in colonial Quito. Due to their reputation, all of the residents of their region were convinced that every member of this family was a livestock thief. See Herzog, *Upholding Justice*, chap. 6, see esp. 208–11 and 213–14. Herzog also notes a difference between rumor, gossip, and reputation: reputation was a rumor elevated to the status of universal knowledge and indisputable truth. See Herzog, *Upholding Justice*, 214. She argues that rumors and gossip, unlike reputation, functioned on a social, not a legal level. See Herzog, *Upholding Justice*, 217.

50. Gutiérrez, *When Jesus Came*, 219, 242.

51. Peter Wade critiques the idea that colonial male sexual desire was "hydraulic," or required an outlet of some kind, as a "repressed biological instinct." Instead, sex in Spanish America was culturally constructed and complex, tied to particular historic family structures and moral values, just as we understand it to be in other settings. Wade, *Race and Sex*, 56–57.

52. Twinam, *Public Lives, Private Secrets*, 92–94, 98.

53. Sloan, *Runaway Daughters*, 112–14.

54. See Boyer, "Catarina María complains that Juan Teioa Forcibly Deflowered Her," 155–65, and Boyer, "Honor among Plebeians," 171–75.

55. See Nesvig, *Ideology and Inquisition*, 6–9, 20–47, 168–73, for a recent and erudite history of the medieval background to inquisitorial censorship, lists of cases before the New Spain tribunal from 1590 to 1639, as well as complete historiographic references and discussion of trends in the study of the Holy Office. The best

overview of the Cartagena tribunal, including plentiful statistical analysis, is Álvarez Alonso, *La Inquisición en Cartagena*. The other essential source for Cartagena is Splendiani et al., *Cincuenta años*, vols. 1–4. Another good summary of inquisitorial practice, including in Cartagena, is Ceballos Gómez, *Hechicería, brujería, e Inquisición*, esp. 115–24. Ceballos Gómez also provides the most detailed summary of a 1565 Cartagena witchcraft case. Schwartz's *All Can Be Saved* is another recent essential source on the Iberian tribunals and cites many examples of the persistence of iconoclastic popular beliefs regarding sex and religion during the Counter Reformation.

56. Berco, *Sexual Hierarchies*, 91–92.

57. Schwartz, *All Can Be Saved*, 129.

58. In Behar, "Sexual Witchcraft, Colonialism, and Women's Powers." Behar over-emphasizes the role of the Inquisition as inspiring female self-censorship, not considering that the women purposely designed their confessions to strike the expected repentant tone.

59. See Few, *Women Who Live Evil Lives*, 44, 52–53, and Lewis, *Hall of Mirrors*, 109–10, 118–20.

60. See Bristol, *Christians, Blasphemers and Witches*, 188–89.

61. Jaffary, *False Mystics*, 12–15.

62. Because my main case study of witchcraft included the rote rhetoric of demonology, I found studies of European witch-hunts to be very helpful, especially those done by Robin Briggs, Lyndal Roper, Brian Levack, and the essays in the collection *Early Modern European Witchcraft*, ed. Henningsen and Ankarloo.

63. Few, *Women Who Live Evil Lives*, 26. Some of the women *de mala vida* discussed in her book were probably at least occasional prostitutes, in line with the most common understanding of the term mala vida and the fact that many of them went by nicknames and aliases, a common practice for prostitutes. See also Gutiérrez, "Women on Top," 385–86. Although the Spanish governor dismissed the witchcraft accusations under discussion, Gutiérrez stresses that Spanish "aristocrats" were those most fearful of Indian women who overturned sexual and gender hierarchies.

64. Gauderman, "The Authority of Gender," 89.

Chapter One

1. AGN, *Causa seguida a Juan Ramírez*, fojas 165–317, and Barahona, *Sex Crimes, Honour, and the Law*, xiv, 5–7, 18. See also Castañeda García, *Violación, estupro y sexualidad*.

2. Poska, *Women and Authority*, 7, 41–74, 94–107, 144–53, discusses how "the Castilian legal system provided women and their families with a variety of mechanisms to restore their impugned reputations" (7). Gauderman, *Women's Lives*, 6–11, explains how investigating legal documentation for Spanish America illuminates the ineffectiveness of using a strictly patriarchal model to explain this society.

3. Lipsett-Rivera, "A Slap in the Face of Honor," 179.

4. Poska, *Women and Authority*, 106.

5. Arrom, *Women of Mexico City*, 62, 71–77.

6. Sloan, *Runaway Daughters*, 58, 114–17. Later in the colonial era, race labels were readily deployed to add insult to injury. See Lipsett-Rivera, "Scandal at the Church," 216–33.

7. Boyer, "Honor among Plebeians," 156, and Lipsett-Rivera, "A Slap in the Face of Honor," 180–92.

8. Shumway, *Ugly Suitor*, 28.

9. Arrom, *Women of Mexico City*, 63–64.

10. Twinam, *Public Lives, Private Secrets*, 79.

11. AGN, *Causa seguida a Juan Ramírez*, foja 170. Invoking God was common in medieval Venetian sex crimes. See Ruggiero, *The Boundaries of Eros*, 22.

12. Lavrin recounts a similar case in "Sexuality in Colonial Mexico," 59–60.

13. For a lengthy analysis of domestic geography and honor, see Lipsett-Rivera, *Gender and the Negotiation of Daily Life*, 31–136.

14. AGN, *Causa seguida a Juan Ramírez*, foja 193.

15. See Pike, *Penal Servitude in Early Modern Spain*, for a classic history on life as a convict/rower in this era.

16. See von Germeten, "Juan Roque's Donation."

17. AGN, *Causa seguida a Juan Ramírez*, fojas 180–89.

18. As will be seen in the story of doña Lorenzana de Acereto's life experiences in the next chapter.

19. Shumway, *Ugly Suitor*, 78–79. Age could be critical in these cases—*rapto* or elopement was not a crime (unless done with violence) if the girl was over sixteen, similar to our laws on statutory rape. Sloan, *Runaway Daughters*, 1.

20. Barahona, *Sex Crimes, Honour, and the Law*, 7–8, 183.

21. AGN, *Causa seguida a Juan Ramírez*, foja 170.

22. Sloan, *Runaway Daughters*, 160–61, 174–75.

23. Ruggiero, *The Boundaries of Eros*, 48–49, 62–63.

24. AGN, *Causa seguida a Juan Ramírez*, fojas 184–86, 190–92.

25. Ibid., fojas 198, 201, 220, 226.

26. The case continues on AGN, *Juicio seguido a Juan Ramírez*, fojas 320–48.

27. AGN, *Causa seguida a Juan Ramírez*, foja 267.

28. Ibid., fojas 235, 268.

29. Ibid., fojas 246–47.

30. Ibid., fojas 254, 297–98.

31. The University of Seville has digitalized this book and it can be read at http://blad14.us.es/fondos.

32. AGN, *Causa seguida a Juan Ramírez*, fojas 266–72.

33. Ibid., fojas 278–80.

34. Ibid., fojas 282–96, 298.

35. Ibid., fojas 318–19.

36. Ruggiero, *The Boundaries of Eros*, 26–28.

Chapter Two

1. Splendiani et al., *Cinquenta años*, 2: 35–104, reproduces three different inquisitors' reports of this auto.
2. Sánchez Ortega, "Sorcery and Eroticism," 59–61. Sánchez Ortega divided love magic into three subfields (divination, erotic magic, and incantations) that accurately correspond to the methods used by Cartagena practitioners. Sánchez Ortega mentions evidence of the use of beans in divination and conjuration, drawing from Iberian inquisition trials. The suerte de habas was commonly practiced in Cartagena, including by Iberian women. On the other hand, Maya Restrepo conjectures that the beans represent the African divine entity Exu. See *Brujería y reconstrucción*, 645–47. Because beans were common in Spanish cookery since at least the time of the Roman Empire, it seems likely that their magical associations were an ancient Spanish tradition (perhaps with very ancient African origins), rather than a more recent African introduction. See also Cirac Estopañán, *Los procesos*, articulo VIII.
3. Cirac Estopañán, *Los procesos*, 214, and Sánchez Ortega, "Sorcery and Eroticism," 61–62, 83–84. Sánchez Ortega found almost no references to marriage and husbands in her study of early modern Iberian witch trials.
4. Restrepo, *Brujería y reconstrucción*, 638–53; Few, *Women Who Live Evil Lives*; and Bristol, *Christians, Blasphemers, and Witches*, provides references for earlier studies of this kind on pages 152–59.
5. Proctor, *Damned Notions*, 77–90. In terms of the business side of magic and curing, Laura Lewis writes that the common practice of consulting *curanderos* in New Spain meant a Spaniard "had to gain entry into the Indian world of witchcraft." Lewis, *Hall of Mirrors*, 119.
6. Bristol, *Christians, Blasphemers, and Witches*, 168, 188–89.
7. See Soto Aparicio's novel, *Camino que anda*, 48, 84, 234; Solano Alonso, *Salud, Cultura y Sociedad*, 282; and Villa Gómez, *Vidas apasionadas*. For a fast-paced summary of her life, see Tejado Fernández, *Aspectos de la vida social*, 88–100.
8. During the early 1600s, Lorenzana's niece, also named Lorenzana, lived with her. The younger Lorenzana was described as the daughter of Marcelo de Espinoza, "killed by rebel blacks in New Spain" and an Indian woman called Rafaela who lived inland in a pueblo under the control of an *encomendero*. AGN, *Proceso de Lorenzana*, fojas 10–12.
9. Ibid., fojas 40–41.
10. Spanish American women could legally marry at age twelve and men at fourteen. See Shumway, *Ugly Suitor*, 76–77. Shumway observes that parents might use age difference to formally object to a marriage, especially for the opposite scenario—a woman twenty years older than her teenage groom.
11. AGI, *Francisco de Santander*.
12. AGI, *Cartas de Gobernadores*; AGI, *Carta de Francisco de Herrera Campuzano*; AGN, *Proceso de fe de Lorenzana*, foja 17; and AGI, *Carta de cabildo secular*.
13. AGN, *Proceso de Lorenzana*, fojas 78–79.

14. Álvarez Alonso, *La Inquisición en Cartagena*, 61; Greenleaf, *The Mexican Inquisition of the Sixteenth Century*, 193, 204–5; and Tavárez, *The Invisible War*, 90.

15. Álvarez Alonso, *La Inquisición en Cartagena*, 33.

16. Cirac Estopañán, *Los procesos*, 106–12; Sánchez Ortega, "Sorcery and Eroticism," 74–76; and AGN, *Proceso de Lorenzana*, foja 1.

17. Splendianni et al., *Cincuenta años*, 2: 89.

18. Ibid., 2: 85–89.

19. Ibid., 2: 42–43, 45, 75–76, 79, 88–89. In seventeenth-century Spain, dozens of women, including courtesans and unmarried lovers, also admitted to divining with beans. Cirac Estopañán, *Los procesos*, 51.

20. AGN, *Proceso de Lorenzana*, fojas 26–30. The inquisitors called in *calificadores* drawn from the local Dominicans, Franciscans, and Jesuits, in order to judge the spells mentioned in the confessions. After writing down several of them, the clerics labeled them heretical examples of blasphemy and sorcery, noting that some of the words of the spells implied pacts with the devil. However, they did not mention any of the demonological traditions of a witches' Sabbath.

21. Sánchez Ortega, "Sorcery and Eroticism," 72–73, 85–86, includes different versions of this spell. See AGN, *Proceso de Lorenzana*, foja 3.

22. A reference to the crippled demon Cojuelo. AGN, *Proceso de Lorenzana*, foja 28. The inquisition calificadores judged this spell to be sorcery and heretical.

23. AGN, *Proceso de Lorenzana*, fojas 45, 52, 53, and Splendianni et al., *Cincuenta años*, 2: 85.

24. Splendianni et al., *Cincuenta años*, 2: 85–87.

25. Sánchez Ortega, "Sorcery and Eroticism," 81–82.

26. AGN, *Proceso de Lorenzana*, foja 32.

27. Splendianni et al., *Cincuenta años*, 1: 36, and 2: 85–88.

28. AGN, *Proceso de Lorenzana*, foja 72, and Splendianni et al., *Cincuenta años*, 2: 42–43, 77–78.

29. A Madrid woman in the 1620s also worried about her husband and took part in a similar ritual. See Cirac Estopañán, *Los procesos*, 54. The Cartagena Holy Office tried two Spanish men and one Italian for attempting this divination method. See Splendianni et al., *Cincuenta años*, 2: 246, 248, 361.

30. Women also used this substance for divination in Toledo. Sánchez Ortega, "Sorcery and Eroticism," 60, 65–66.

31. Splendianni et al., *Cincuenta años*, 2: 42–43, 76, and Cirac Estopañán, *Los procesos*, 52.

32. Atondo Rodriguez, *El amor venal*, 123–133.

33. See Tausiet, *Abracadabra omnipotens*, 181; Perry, *Gender and Disorder*, 56; and Valbuena, "Sorceresses, Love Magic, and the Inquisition," 207–24.

34. Atondo Rodriguez, *El amor venal*, 31–33, 56–62.

35. Splendianni et al., *Cincuenta años*, 2: 42, 74–77.

36. AGN, *Proceso de Lorenzana*, foja 34. Doña Lorenzana's statements make it clear that a circle of women took part in these magical activities and often this was

a social activity. Juan Lorenzo had to put a halt to his attempt at a well-known Spanish divination involving bread because one of doña Lorenzana's friends was too *gorda* to sit on the floor and participate.

37. Ibid., fojas 15–16, 68.

38. Ibid., fojas 31–32.

39. In this era even convents were often embroiled in sex scandals. See, for example, Ruggiero, *The Boundaries of Eros*, 77–83.

40. AGN, *Proceso de Lorenzana*, fojas 9–10.

41. Ibid., foja 15, and Splendianni et al., *Cincuenta años*, 2: 40, 47.

42. Perhaps Lorenzana expressed this request to send the message of her interest in sorcery. The request could be a kind of coded suggestion that she needed containers for her potions.

43. Juan Lorenzo's confessions relating to Lorenzana are in AGN, *Proceso de Lorenzana*, fojas 5–8.

44. Ibid., fojas 10–12.

45. Ibid., foja 100.

46. For a brief summary of patriarchal rights in the Hispanic world, see Shumway, *Ugly Suitor*, 22. For more detail, see Boyer, "Women, *La Mala Vida*, and the Politics of Marriage," 252–56.

47. AGN, *Proceso de Lorenzana*, fojas 32–34, 55, 58.

48. Ibid., foja 82.

49. Ibid., fojas 42–43.

50. Ruggiero, *The Boundaries of Eros*, 163. As Ruggiero writes, "In Venice the sexuality of marriage faced great obstacles. Especially at the upper social levels, males had established a sexual identity and habits well before marriage in the culture of illicit sexuality. Young girls in their early teens when married to such men must have had trouble competing with those habits and that other culture of sexuality." Ruggiero stresses that we should not assume noble women then retreated into passive seclusion, rejecting sexuality and desire; he found evidence of elite women initiating adulterous relationships.

51. This example of illicit sexuality did not escalate into a public scandal for a variety of reasons. First, it was only discussed during purportedly secret testimonies before the Holy Office. Second, it involved individuals who could not rely on the rhetoric of the honor code to account for their sexual behavior. Therefore, no one reacted violently to the alleged act of "simple fornication." The act itself was not viewed as criminal or apparently even illicit enough to arouse the inquisitors' ire, so fornicators did not suffer further prosecution. See Schwartz, *All Can Be Saved*, 26–33, 130–32, 156–58, for early modern Iberian understandings of the sinfulness of "simple fornication."

52. AGN, *Proceso de Lorenzana*, fojas 18–19.

53. Another elderly Spanish beata was in charge of drying out the donkey head sent to her by doña Lorenzana. A slave carried the head on a tray covered with a cloth, and the beata dried the brain and used it to make some biscuits. Unfortunately,

her chickens ate some of the brains while they were drying. Again, the stated purpose was to improve Andres's disposition. See AGN, *Proceso de Lorenzana*, fojas 21–22.

54. This particular governor fought with the new inquisitors in town, resulting in his excommunication in 1612. Castillo Mathieu, *Los Gobernadores*, 44.

55. AGN, *Proceso de Lorenzana*, fojas 23–24.

56. Doña Lorenzana denied poisoning her husband's eggplant with spines or flowers of "pinipinig," but she admitted that she heard some eggplant seeds were good for improving a man's mood. She said that everyone ate this dish, but only her husband was mildly ill, and she cured him with her own homemade medicines. See AGN, *Proceso de Lorenzana*, fojas 50, 57.

57. Ibid., fojas 74–75. Given the thousands of words of gossip expended on all of the documentation cited in this book, especially the Llerena case analyzed below, it is surprising that anyone in this society would take special note of or view negatively the character trait of "speaking poorly of others."

58. Ibid., fojas 76–78.

59. Ibid., fojas 80, 83, 85. One of these scribes testified that Lorenzana's lover Francisco de Santander questioned him about his relationship with Pacheco, obviously in an attempt to help the case.

60. Ibid., foja 75.

61. Ibid., fojas 35, 57, 81.

62. Splendianni et al., *Cincuenta años*, 2: 95–96.

63. AGN, *Proceso de Lorenzana*, fojas 87–88, 92, 94, 97.

64. Ibid., fojas 38–40.

65. The latter illness may have referred to an attack of depression or even some kind of fit, since mal de corazón is a Spanish euphemism for epilepsy. See Kany, *American-Spanish Euphemisms*, 12. Geoffrey Parker interprets mal de corazón in discharged soldiers as "post traumatic stress disorder." See Parker, *The Army of Flanders*, 143.

66. AGN, *Proceso de Lorenzana*, foja 45.

67. The activities of the racially-mixed circle surrounding doña Lorenzana complicate the common emphasis on a widespread perception of Africans as especially erotic, due to their association with the devil. See Borja Gómez, *Rostros y Rastros*, 159–68.

Chapter Three

1. Taylor, *Honor and Violence*, 67–69.

2. Contrast this to doña Lorenzana's futile efforts to control sexual activity among her slaves and employees, as discussed in chapter 2.

3. This approach agrees with Barbara H. Rosenwein's dismissal of the idea that certain eras were emotional in essence while others can be summed up as emotionally uncontrolled. See *Emotional Communities*, 1–3. Rosenwein views emotions as an essential field of historical study and traces the use of the word "emotion" in a

modern sense only to around 1800. Before then, the proper terms for the feelings discussed in this Conclusion would be "passions, affections, and sentiments."

4. See Rosenwein, *Emotional Communities*, 5–11, for a discussion of the influence of Johan Huizinga and Norbert Elias on this historical vision of emotions. Rosenwein continues her critique of Elias in "Controlling Paradigms," 237–39. See also White, "The Politics of Anger," 128–31, on the ideas of Marc Bloch on immature medieval emotions.

5. Lipsett-Rivera, *Gender and the Negotiation of Daily Life*, 5–11, highlights the fact that colonial men knew that a well-understood code guided their acts of public violence, even if this is not always obvious in criminal cases.

6. Rosenwein, "Controlling Paradigms," 244.

7. AGN, *Causa seguida a Francisco Luis*, foja 427. This decree probably emanated from the metropolis, since a similar crackdown on slave sexuality took place in the archdiocese of Mexico in the early 1600s. See Bennett, *Colonial Blackness*, 37–44. I disagree with Bennett: these sporadic attempts to reign in sexuality (enforced with petty two peso fines) do not prove the church effectively disciplined individual sex lives on a day-to-day basis.

8. AGN, *Causa seguida a Francisco Luis*, fojas 397, 401, 435, 437, 439, 441, 462.

9. This word was a common insult in Spain. See Taylor, *Honor and Violence*, 165–71, for a wide range of typical violence-provoking insults in early modern Spain.

10. AGN, *Causa seguida a Francisco Luis*, foja 447.

11. Ibid., fojas 461–62.

12. AGN, *Causa seguida a Diego Cortes*, fojas 848–947.

13. Ibid., fojas 866–70. Each of the women testified, although Isabel refused to take an oath because she was pregnant and she feared this act might cause a miscarriage.

14. Ibid., fojas 932–38.

15. Ibid., fojas 866–91.

16. Ibid., fojas 859, 861, 872–73, 899, 931–32.

17. Ibid., fojas 872–74, 888–90.

18. Ibid., fojas 858, 967, 932, 943, 945, 969.

19. Castillo Mathieu, *Los Gobernadores*, 48–49.

20. AGN, *Causa seguida a Diego Cortes*, fojas 849–50, 911–12, 949.

21. AHN, *Testimonio de una causa criminal*, fojas 11–13.

22. Proctor, *Damned Notions*, 113.

23. Álvarez Alonso, *La Inquisición en Cartagena*, 45.

24. AHN, *Causa criminal contra Francisco Guerra*, fojas 22–23.

25. Ibid., foja 10.

26. Ibid., fojas 24–26.

27. Ibid., fojas 16–18.

28. Ibid., fojas 19–20.

29. Ibid., fojas 4–6.

30. Ibid., foja 2.

31. Ibid., fojas 9, 22, 28, 40.

32. Asserting this complex idea, limpieza de sangre, for the sake of immigrating to the New World was not uncommon among black Sevillans. See Garofalo, "The Case of Diego Suárez" (unpublished paper).

33. Proctor, *Damned Notions*, 107–9. Proctor provides a clear explanation of how slaves used the courts to negotiate their daily lives including workloads and punishments on 96–119 and 152–61.

34. See Fuente, "Slaves and the Creation of Legal Rights in Cuba," for more on late colonial negotiation of slaves' legal rights and how this worked within the confines of customary practices.

35. Proctor, *Damned Notions*, 118–19.

36. On the interaction between private rage/revenge and public justice elsewhere in colonial Latin America see Stern, *The Secret History of Gender*, 24, 89, 138–40; and Taylor, *Drinking, Homicide, and Rebellion*, 99–105. Georgina Dopico Black also summarizes the studies that explore the actual practice of wife murder in early modern Spain in *Perfect Wives*, 114. See also 115–63 for her analysis of a bloody theatrical uxorocide, with an emphasis on examining the woman's body and literally purging it of dishonorable blood.

Chapter Four

1. AGI, *María Nele contra Coronel*, 1644.

2. For information on the ethnic makeup of these settlements, see Landers, "*Cimarrón* Ethnicity in the Caribbean," 38–41. For a perceptive look at the communication between palenqueros and urban dwellers in Cartagena and the violent suppression of these late seventeenth-century revolts, see Landers, "The African Landscape of Seventeenth-Century Cartagena."

3. Taylor, *Honor and Violence*, 17–64.

4. AGN, *Causa criminal seguida por Benito Maldonado Millán*, fojas 67–122.

5. AGN, *María Juárez contra Juan Sanz*.

6. See Bakewell, "Mining in colonial South America," 125, 128, and Florescano, "The formation and economic structure of the hacienda in New Spain," 165.

7. In 1656, two male clients seduced and then killed a Spanish prostitute named doña Manuela with a drink at this price. See chapter 9.

8. AGI, *María Nele contra Coronel*, fojas 172–73, 202–3, 207, 216, 220. See Taylor, *Drinking, Homicide, and Rebellion*, 65, 67, 158, for Spanish attitudes toward drunks and violence.

9. Although the defense would not confirm that this insult caused the fight, enough witnesses mentioned it to make it seem likely. See AGI, *María Nele contra Coronel*, fojas 3, 4, 5, 7, 9, 14, 16, 28, 30, 65, for witness statements. These are classic insults to encourage a Spanish American fight. See Taylor, *Drinking, Homicide, and Rebellion*, 82. The interesting fact is that the Spanish-speaking witnesses testified to hearing the words *borracho cornudo* in *la lengua irlandesa*. This raises two questions:

what language was actually spoken? If it was not Spanish, how did some of the witnesses know what had been said?

10. AGI, *María Nele contra Coronel*, fojas 55–60, 77–78, 144, 202.

11. Ibid., fojas 56, 83, 201–2, 207. Quote taken from 174.

12. Ibid., fojas 3–6. Not long after, one of the young men was caught trying to leave the city by boat.

13. Ibid., fojas 6, 13, 18, 22, 228.

14. Perez Tostado, *Irish Influence*, narrates the rise and fall of Irish/Spanish cooperation, especially on 15–16, 20–25, 33–35, 146–83. For Spanish attitudes to the Irish, see 49–58. For more information on the political relationship between Spain and Ireland, see Recio Morales, *España y la pérdida*, and Casway, *Owen Roe O'Neill*, 12–63.

15. Block, *Ordinary Lives*, 102–6, 117–22.

16. AGI, *María Nele contra Coronel*, foja 3.

17. Ibid., foja 181.

18. Manning, *An Apprenticeship in Arms*, 117–18.

19. AGI, *María Nele contra Coronel*, fojas 66–74, duplicate an official document presented in Santo Domingo to the governor telling this story, along with statements made by several Irishmen living in Cartagena.

20. Ibid., fojas 73, 181.

21. Ibid., fojas 178, 181–82. The close connection with the Catholic Church was the norm for Irish aristocrats, possibly the captain's relatives. See Casway, *Owen Roe O'Neill*, 10–11.

22. For Protestant claims during the Irish rebellion, see Cope, *England and the 1641 Irish Rebellion*. For a suggestion to reject early modern Irish victimization stories, see Macinnes, "Connecting and Disconnecting," 6, 18, 19.

23. Pérez Tostado, *Irish Influence*, 15–16. Pérez Tostado notes that Irish aristocrats presented the 1607 "Flight of the Earls" (including the O'Neills and Tyrconnells) and its aftereffects to the Spanish crown "as an utter injustice," on 24–25, with a similar tone of English abuse of the Irish given in Captain Cornelio's statements.

24. Ohlmeyer, "Military Migration," 82.

25. AGI, *María Nele contra Coronel*, fojas 178, 181.

26. Ibid., fojas 176, 198.

27. Downey, "Catholicism, Milesianism, and Monarchism," 167, 169, 175, and Kidd, *British Identities Before Nationalism*, 64–65, 146–47, 150–51, 160–61.

28. The daughter was tried from 1662 to 1664 by the Spanish Inquisition tribunal in New Mexico. See Coll, "Doña Teresa de Aguilera," 89–108. In a politically motivated case, involving past governors and local friars, doña Teresa was tried (asserting her Catholic Christianity, she was found not guilty) for suspicions of Judaism, along with her husband (96–100). Doña Teresa was born in 1613 and was educated in a convent in Milan. She met her husband in Cartagena and also lived in Mexico City. See also Hordes, *To the End of the Earth*, 149–57. Doña Teresa's father, Governor Aguilera, held office during a successful expedition against the

English settlement on the Caribbean Providencia Island (not far from the coast of Nicaragua). See Castillo Mathieu, *Los Gobernadores*, 54.

29. See examples in Hazard, "'A New Company of Crusaders,'" 168.

30. Another example of the "Latinizing" of an Irish name is Florence Conry becoming Florentius Conrius. See Downey, "Catholicism, Milesianism, and Monarchism," 171. Of course Captain Cornelio's name could be something else entirely. See examples of falsified code names on Casway, *Owen Roe O'Neill*, 48.

31. Pérez Tostado, *Irish Influence*, 24.

32. Pestana, *English Atlantic*, 19.

33. The total number of Irish living in St. Christopher, Nevis, Monserrat, and Antigua numbered 3,446 in 1678. See Binasco, "The Activity of Irish Priests," 4.

34. Pestana, *English Atlantic*, 6, and Block and Shaw, "Subjects without an Empire."

35. Akenson, *If the Irish Ran the World*, 21–27, 35.

36. Pestana, *English Atlantic*, 16, 20. The earl of Marlborough captured St. Christopher, Montserrat, and the island of Santa Cruz in 1645. Pestana, *English Atlantic*, 47–48. Igor Pérez Tostado agrees that, "En el Caribe hispano tampoco podrá la comunidad irlandesa organizarse alredor de un O'Neil u O'Donnell." See Pérez Tostado, "La llegada de irlandeses," 306.

37. Akenson, *If the Irish Ran the World*, 26–27, 31.

38. See the entries for Sir Phelim O'Neill and Owen Roe O'Neill in Lee, *Dictionary of National Biography*. See also AGI, *María Nele contra Coronel*, foja 79.

39. Binasco, "The Activity of Irish Priests."

40. Pestana, *English Atlantic*, 26–27, 49–50.

41. Perceval-Maxwell, *The Outbreak of the Irish Rebellion*, 280–81.

42. Casway, *Owen Roe O'Neill*, 53.

43. Pestana, *English Atlantic*, 199–201.

44. Pestana, *English Atlantic*, 151, and Lane, *Pillaging the Empire*, 103.

45. Lane, *Pillaging the Empire*, 99–100, 104.

46. Block and Shaw, "Subjects without an Empire." In this article, Block and Shaw present a 1643 account of a very similar desperate escape by good Irish Catholics abused by the English who ended up in Hispaniola, seeking refuge and protection from the Spanish. These Irish were also said to have been ejected by the English, so it seems likely that they had some connection to or at least awareness of Captain Cornelio's group.

47. Macinnes, "Connecting and Disconnecting," 19.

48. AGI, *María Nele contra Coronel*, fojas 55–60, 77–78, 144, 183–91, 202. The claim that he was guiding a foreigner was not as unlikely as it might sound at first. Between 1643 and 1646, seven Englishmen and one Scot voluntarily presented themselves to the Holy Office to receive instruction in Catholicism. Block, *Ordinary Lives*, 120–22.

49. Castillo Mathieu, *Los Gobernadores*, 57–58.

50. AGI, *María Nele contra Coronel*, fojas 183–91.

Chapter Five

1. Penyak and Vallejo, "Expectations of Love," 564–65, 570.
2. Ibid., 577.
3. Ibid., 586.
4. Arrom, *Women of Mexico City*, 252–58.
5. Berhend-Martínez, *Unfit for Marriage*, xii, and Ruggiero, *The Boundaries of Eros*, 63–64.
6. Seed, *Love, Honor, and Obey*, 47–50, 56, 119.
7. See Socolow, "Acceptable Partners," 229.
8. Folger, *Escape from the Prison of Love*, 20.
9. Greer and Rhodes, *María de Zayas*, 21–22, 25.
10. Seed, *Love, Honor, and Obey*, 39, 51–52. For further explorations of love in early modern Spanish literature, see Stoll and Smith, *Gender, Identity, and Representation*, and Parker, *The Philosophy of Love*.
11. AGN, *seducción de Ana de Bolívar*, fojas 303–484.
12. Ibid., fojas 305–6.
13. Ibid., foja 335.
14. Ibid., fojas 307–10.
15. Ibid., fojas 335–38.
16. Ibid., fojas 311–15.
17. AGN, *Causa seguida a Juan Carillo*, fojas 351–562.
18. See Ruggiero, *The Boundaries of Eros*, 19–21, for a Venetian case along the same lines.
19. AGN, *Causa seguida a Juan Carillo*, foja 330.
20. Ibid., fojas 326–28, 355.
21. Ibid., fojas 473–74.
22. Barahona, *Sex Crimes, Honour, and the Law*, 41–58.
23. AGN, *Causa seguida a Juan Carillo*, foja 440.
24. Ibid., fojas 331–34.
25. Ibid., fojas 335–42. Very ineffective municipal jails were common in Spanish America. See Herzog, *Upholding Justice*, 192–94.
26. Ibid., fojas 397–400.
27. Ibid., foja 412.
28. Ibid., fojas 411, 426–28.
29. Ibid., fojas 444–46.
30. Ibid., foja 489.
31. Ibid., fojas 447–51.
32. Ibid., foja 558.
33. Ibid., foja 555.
34. A controlled and restrained or religious understanding of love is implied by the Latin root word *caritas*. See Rosenwein, *Emotional Communities*, 52, 142–45.
35. AGN, *seducción de Ana de Bolívar*, fojas 335, 339.
36. AGN, *Causa seguida a Juan Carillo*, foja 170.

37. Ibid., fojas 356, 482.

38. AGN, *Causa criminal contra Francisco Guerra*, fojas 24, 28.

39. Briggs, *Witches and Neighbors*, 377. Boyer's analysis of bigamy and "love matches" in the colonial era extends this hypothesis to Spanish America. See Boyer, *Lives of the Bigamists*, 79–84.

40. Ruggiero, *The Boundaries of Eros*, 65–66.

41. Hermes Tovar Pinzón duplicates a large number of affectionate letters sent between spouses during the Colombian independence movement, as well as providing many archival cases relating to love and sex in Nueva Granada. See Tovar Pinzón, *La batalla*. Ann Twinam also cites passionate love letters (between unmarried individuals) in Twinam, *Public Lives, Private Secrets*, 39, 105–6, 200.

42. AGI, *Autos sobre bienes de difuntos, Antonio Sigarra*.

43. *Hermano* was a common term of affection between lovers and spouses in this era's personal letters. Rebecca Earle rightly notes that this implies a kind of equality and companionship, actually *less* emphasized later when terms such as *hija* (which suggests an unequal relationship) became more popular. See Earle, "Letters and Love."

44. Although women frequently hired public letter writers, as seen in Arrom, *Women of Mexico City*, 60, the letters cited here use none of the standard conventions, such as *vuestra merced*, that might mark it as a professionally-written letter. James Lockhart, Emeritus Professor of History, University of California, Los Angeles, personal communication with author, June 21 and 23, 2010.

45. It is common to view letters, even those written as recently as the twentieth century, as public documents to be read aloud to an audience. This may not have been the case for this letter or most of the letters cited in chapter 10.

Chapter Six

1. See Medina, *Historia del tribunal*, 213, 225, and Lea, *The Inquisition in the Spanish Dependencies*, 464–65. Historians should take care with these sources, since Lea is often just a summary of Medina, and Medina himself depended on summaries written in the 1600s. Neither man actually read Paula's trial, at least as can be determined from their writings on the subject.

2. The entrepreneurial activities of Paula and other healers in Cartagena can be compared to the active and competitive markets presented by Mangan, *Trading Roles*. For the historiography of this topic, as well as how it helped forge or enforce market women's gender and ethnic identity, see 6–15.

3. Since Paula herself caused the arrests of other freedwomen, the role of race was more complicated than a simple desire to "control and acculturate" Afro-Caribbean women, as suggested by Ceballos Gómez in her analysis of earlier witch persecutions in Cartagena, *Hechicería, brujería, e Inquisición*, 85–6. This is cited in Proctor, *Damned Notions*, 92.

4. With its focus on Cartagena, this book will not cover Paula's first trial and life in Santo Domingo and Cuba. This trial is summarized by Sara Vicuña Guengerich in "The Witchcraft Trials of Paula de Eguiluz."

5. See chapter 8 for an inventory of Paula de Eguiluz's clothing at the time of her 1624 arrest.

6. Mantelillos, whose name means "small tablecloth," was also the demon named by a mestizo man named Juan Luis who came before the Mexico inquisition in 1595. This earlier version of Mantelillos also understood the art of seduction and was willing to help his human counterpart. Juan Luis confessed to inquisitors that he tattooed an image of Mantelillos on his arm at age thirteen while in a local jail, and from that day forward, the demon helped him with his agricultural work and in seducing over one hundred women. Juan Luis's Mantelillos was also a good-looking man, who had another ugly, "fiery" face. Lewis, *Hall of Mirrors*, 138–41.

7. AHN, *Proceso de Paula de Eguiluz*, bloque 3, fojas 5–7.

8. Ibid., fojas 4–5.

9. Ruggiero, *The Boundaries of Eros*, 34.

10. This anecdote and Paula's entire personality suggests that Paula does not fit the link often made between sex and violent conquest in colonial Latin American studies. Wade carefully notes after reading secondary sources that, "It is difficult to interpret such Inquisitorial records for motive and emotion, but clearly Paula had a number of sexual relationships in which she, despite her slave status, managed a certain amount of autonomous action." Wade, *Race and Sex*, 81.

11. One of the inquisitors during Paula's trial was Domingo Vélez de Asás y Argós, who, as a cathedral canon, helped defend doña Lorenzana twenty years earlier. Educated in Salamanca, he moved on the Mexican tribunal in 1637. See Álvarez Alonso, *La Inquisición en Cartagena*, 61–78.

12. Several factors help explain this new development. First, after over two decades in Cartagena, inquisitors must have known that Spanish husbands did not permit public humiliation of their wives and had the power to prevent punishment, even light ones such as fines and private penitence. Inquisitors may have hoped their persecutions would be more effective without rocking the established hierarchies.

13. Schorsch, *Swimming the Christian Atlantic*, 121–68.

14. AHN, *Proceso de Paula de Eguiluz*, bloque 2, fojas 29–34. Details will be discussed in chapter 7.

15. Ibid., fojas 36, 43–44.

16. Splendiani et al., *Cinquenta años*, 2: 270.

17. Barbara described a six-month sexual relationship with the Devil before she left Spain. See ibid., 307–10.

18. Ana de Fuente's initial confession in 1632 is recorded in AHN, *Proceso de Paula de Eguiluz*, bloque 2, fojas 6–13.

19. Ibid., foja 111, and Behar, "Sexual Witchcraft, Colonialism, and Women's Powers."

20. AHN, *Proceso de Paula de Eguiluz*, bloque 2, fojas 36–38.

21. Ibid., foja 109, and bloque 3, fojas 143–44. Barbola and Paula conferred on this request and decided that since Ana had asked them so many times, they should go to the couple's house. They put unguent on their bodies and flew over with their demon familiars and entered through the window. Neighbors heard a terrifying noise and commotion, although they did not consider it that odd since they were used to loud fights between doña Ana and don Francisco. Paula said that the slaves, in contrast to the neighbors, realized that witches were coming to the house. However, before entering the bedroom, the demons turned away from don Francisco because he wore a fragment of the true cross.
22. AHN, *Proceso de Paula de Eguiluz*, bloque 2, fojas 51–54, 107, 109–10.
23. In Cuba, Paula met the devil in the form of a woman and a handsome man. See Restrepo, *Brujería y reconstrucción*, 605–7.
24. Briggs, *Witches and Neighbors*, 30.
25. AHN, *Proceso de fe de Paula de Eguiluz*, bloque 2, foja 27.
26. See Ceballos Gómez, *Hechicería*, 97–98, for another attractive Cartagena devil.
27. AHN, *Proceso de fe de Paula de Eguiluz*, bloque 2, foja 69.
28. Ibid., foja 29.
29. Ibid., foja 44.
30. Ibid., foja 31.
31. Ibid., fojas 88–89.
32. See Maya, "Paula de Eguiluz" for more information on Paula's love life in Cuba.
33. AHN, *Proceso de fe de Paula de Eguiluz*, bloque 3, foja 93.
34. Ibid., foja 37.
35. Ibid., foja 14.
36. AHN, *Proceso de fe de Paula de Eguiluz*, bloque 2, foja 39, and AHN, *Proceso de fe de Diego López*, foja 15.
37. Cirac Estopañán, *Los procesos*, 216.
38. AHN, *Proceso de fe de Paula de Eguiluz*, bloque 2, fojas 49, 65. See Sánchez Ortega, "Sorcery and Eroticism," 74–76. Paula said she learned the conjuration of the star in Habana. Maya Restrepo has found that many of Paula's spells were written in a manuscript called the *Magia Salomonis*, confiscated by the Holy Office in 1527 in the Canary Islands. See Restrepo, *Brujería y reconstrucción*, 615–38. Restrepo makes the connection between the Canaries, Cartagena, and Paula's circle through a woman from the Canaries living in Cuba who was tried in Cartagena for using spells, possibly ones written down. It seems more likely that these were traditional Iberian spells that spread across the Atlantic and Caribbean by way of untold numbers of traveling women who lived lives not unlike the gypsies mentioned in Sánchez Ortega, "Sorcery and Eroticism."
39. AHN, *Proceso de fe de Paula de Eguiluz*, bloque 2, fojas 48–9, 61. Bernarda's auto de fe took place a few months before Paula's arrest in September of 1632. She was accused of using various spells and herbs in her love magic practice, as well as killing a man with powders. Her punishment was one hundred lashes, banishment

from Santo Domingo, and two years of service in the San Sebastian hospital. During the auto de fe, she had to wear a cord around her neck as a symbol of her crimes. Later, Bernarda was caught up in the witch-hunt since Paula mentioned her frequently in her confessions. This led to accusations of the more serious offense of a pact with the Devil. Her defense fought this accusation, noting that some of her accusers had retracted their confessions. She denied everything and was tortured. Bernarda broke down after the first "turn" and admitted everything but said Paula brought her to the witches' junta, a reversal of Paula's confession that it was Bernarda who had taught Paula conjurations. Her second punishment was two hundred lashes and ten years of banishment. See Splendiani et al, *Cincuenta años*, 291, 398, 423–24.

40. AHN, *Proceso de fe de Paula de Eguiluz*, bloque 2, fojas 48, 59.
41. Ibid., fojas 59–60.
42. Ibid., foja 60.
43. Cirac Estopañán, *Los procesos*, 116–33.
44. Schorsch tends to base his suppositions about Paula's maleficio on Diego López's statements, despite the fact that he was her archenemy. See Schorsch, *Swimming the Christian Atlantic*, 131, 139–140, 144–45.
45. Proctor, *Damned Notions*, 92–93.
46. AHN, *Proceso de fe de Paula de Eguiluz*, bloque 2, fojas 14, 23.
47. Ibid., foja 15.
48. Ibid., fojas 52–53.
49. Ibid., fojas 56–57.
50. Ibid., fojas 61–66, 133.
51. AHN, *Proceso de fe de Diego López*, foja 1.
52. Ibid., fojas 7, 37–50.
53. AHN, *Proceso de fe de Paula de Eguiluz*, bloque 3, fojas 101–13.
54. Ibid., fojas 141, 146.
55. Ibid., fojas 149–51. For this definition of gatatumba, see Borao, *Diccionario de voces aragoneses*, 247. Members of the H-Latam list suggested these translations of the seventeenth-century insults. The ideas volunteered by Christopher Conway, Giovanna Urdangarain, Marixa Lasso, and Rafael Tarrago were especially helpful.
56. Splendiani et al., *Cincuenta años*, 2: 375–79.
57. Ibid., 413.
58. AHN, *Proceso de fe de Diego López*, foja 15.
59. Schorsch, *Swimming the Christian Atlantic*, 248–49.
60. See Solano Alonso, *Salud, cultura y sociedad*, and Lux Martelo, *Las mujeres*.
61. Navarrete, *Practicas religiosas*, 115–17. López was later imprisoned for helping a slave escape.
62. Medina, *Historia del tribunal*, 225–26.
63. Proctor, *Damned Notions*, 1–35.

Chapter Seven

1. Sandoval, *Treatise on Slavery*, 189.
2. Rowland, "'Fantasticall and Devilishe Persons,'" 161.
3. Roper, *Witch Craze*, 107.
4. Splendiani et al., *Cinquenta años*, 2: 298.
5. Ibid., 303.
6. Ibid., 304.
7. Ibid., 310.
8. Ibid., 314–15.
9. Roper, *Witch Craze*, 98, and Briggs, *Witches and Neighbors*, 25.
10. Splendianni et al., *Cincuenta años*, 2: 302. The Spanish inquisition did not require evidence of the famous "devil's mark."
11. Splendianni et al., *Cincuenta años*, 2: 318.
12. Briggs, *Witches and Neighbors*, 26–28, quote on 28.
13. The women do not use the term "Sabbath."
14. AHN, *Proceso de fe de Paula de Eguiluz*, bloque 2, foja 33, and bloque 3, foja 95.
15. Splendianni et al., *Cincuenta años*, 2: 299.
16. AHN, *Proceso de Fe de Paula de Eguiluz*, bloque 3, foja 58.
17. Even though Luisa was one of the poorer women among those who took part in the 1633 auto de fe, she was far from wearing rags. She owned a good quality black taffeta skirt and bodice, as well as workday clothes, including a brown wool skirt, various shirts, and petticoats. She filled her Getsemaní room with simple bedding and linens, but had a few luxuries on hand, including chocolate and silver spoons. See chapter 8 for a full analysis of the accused witches' wardrobes.
18. Splendianni et al., *Cincuenta años*, 2: 317.
19. AHN, *Proceso de fe de Paula de Eguiluz*, bloque 2, fojas 33–34, and bloque 3, foja 96.
20. This misconception was common in the colonial era.
21. Roper, *Witch Craze*, 94–95.
22. Ibid., 82–89, 93–96.
23. Splendianni et al., *Cincuenta años*, 2: 299.
24. Ibid., 300.
25. Ibid., 302.
26. Ibid., 303, 319. This is not Rufina de Rafael Pérez, lover of Diego López.
27. Roper, *Witch Craze*, 92–93.
28. Splendianni et al., *Cincuenta años*, 2: 311.
29. Ibid., 313.
30. Ibid., 316.
31. Ibid., 315.
32. Restrepo, *Brujería y reconstrucción*, 568, and Sánchez Ortega, "Sorcery and Eroticism," 59.
33. Roper, *Witch Craze*, 32, and AHN, *Proceso de fe de Diego López*, foja 29. Some sections of López's trial are reproduced in Tejado Fernández, *Aspectos de la vida social*.

34. AHN, *Proceso de fe de Paula de Eguiluz*, bloque 2, foja 139, and bloque 3, foja 94.

35. Most, but not all, of Diego's case has survived in a 52 foja summary sent to Spain in 1634.

36. AHN, *Proceso de fe de Paula de Eguiluz*, bloque 3, foja 63.

37. AHN, *Proceso de fe de Diego López*, foja 4.

38. Ibid., foja 5.

39. Stephens, *Demon Lovers*, 20, 54–55, and Broedel, *Malleus Maleficarum*, 182.

40. Berco, *Sexual Hierarchies*, 9 and chapter 2.

41. Briggs, *Witches and Neighbors*, 25.

42. Roper, *Witch Craze*, 90–91.

43. AHN, *Proceso de fe de Diego López*, foja 5.

44. Gauderman, "It Happened on the way to the *Temescal*." This article analyzes contributions to the special issue edited by Pete Sigal and John Chuchiak, entitled *Sexual Encounters/Sexual Collisions: Alternative Sexualities in Colonial Mesoamerica*.

45. Tortorici, "'Heran Todos Putos,'" especially pages 49 and 56.

46. In his statements, he sometimes designated Rufina as "de Rafael Gómez" or "de Clara Núñez," in reference to the names of her owners at the time of their affair. López did this to avoid confusion with the other Rufina "de Amador Pérez," an older alleged witch who was clearly more involved in the social gatherings that may have sparked this witch hunt.

47. AHN, *Proceso de fe de Diego López*, foja 2.

48. Splendianni et al., *Cincuenta años*, 2: 399.

49. Schorsch explores this facet of López more deeply but misleadingly presents López as accurately quoting a very honest and believable Rufina in his audiences with inquisitors, perpetuating various fantasies (born in either Diego or Rufina's mind) including that Rufina was the only non-white member of Paula's circle of witches. Schorsch, *Swimming the Christian Atlantic*, 131–38, 140.

50. Splendianni et al., *Cincuenta años*, 2: 399.

51. AHN, *Proceso de fe de Diego López*, foja 8.

52. Ibid., foja 11.

53. Ibid., foja 12.

54. Ibid., foja 19.

55. Ibid., fojas 31–32.

56. Ibid., foja 33.

57. Ibid., foja 34.

58. Ibid., foja 50.

59. Ibid., foja 51.

60. Ibid., fojas 51–52.

61. Similarly, Roper sees realistic depictions of village festivals in some of the European confessions of taking part in a witches' Sabbath. See Roper, *Witch Craze*, 109. I simply cannot believe that these women actually believed they had sex with demons. As we see in Paula's testimony, more intense confessions and greater experience with inquisitors led to her absolute denial of sex with Mantelillos, although earlier in life

she had admitted it. Remember, Paula said she only *assumed* others had sex at the juntas, since she viewed this as the normal procedure.

62. AHN, *Proceso de fe de Diego López*, foja 6, and AHN, *Proceso de fe de Paula de Eguiluz*, bloque 3, foja 194.

63. AHN, *Proceso de fe de Paula de Eguiluz*, bloque 2, foja 17.

64. Splendiani and Aristizábal, *Proceso de Beatificación*, 191, 196.

65. Ibid., 190–91.

66. Ibid., 193; and Sandoval, *Treatise on Slavery*, 155.

67. AHN, *Proceso de Elena de la Cruz*, fojas 156–68. Thank you to Robert Ferry for giving me his notes on this file.

68. AHN, *Proceso de Paula de Eguiluz*, bloque 2, foja 50.

69. Bensusen, "Cartagena's Fandango Politics," 130.

70. AHN, *Proceso de fe de Paula de Eguiluz*, bloque 2, foja 113.

Chapter Eight

1. Although statistics are incomplete and it is difficult to determine if soldiers and convicts were counted, numerically, women dominated the local population. See Rodríguez Jiménez, "Composición y estructura," 237.

2. Lux Martelo, *Las mujeres*, 82–83.

3. See Haidt, "The Wife, the Maid, and the Woman in the Street," for an argument for focusing on textiles as a more revealing window into Spanish women's experiences than written sources (so often mediated by men).

4. Documents inventorying the possessions owned by women of African descent are difficult to find because they had no need or money to make last wills and testaments.

5. Comaroff, "The Empire's Old Clothes," 19–20.

6. Sandoval, *Treatise on Slavery*, 28, 41–42. Of course these descriptions offer a dramatic contrast to Sandoval's emotionally fraught descriptions of the nudity suffered by African slaves in Cartagena.

7. McFarlane, *Colombia before Independence*, 141–58.

8. Earle, "National Dress."

9. Earle, "Two Pairs of Pink Satin Shoes!!," 183. It is interesting to note that eighteenth-century travelers to Spain perceived madrileños dress as pathetically plain. By this time, the rest of Europe had caught up to Spanish America's ostentation.

10. Earle, "Luxury, Clothing, and Race," 223.

11. Martín Gaite, *Love Customs*, 19.

12. Comaroff, "The Empire's Old Clothes," 21.

13. Sandoval, *Treatise on Slavery*, 58–59, 69, 90, 97, and all of book 2, chapter 22.

14. Ibid., 96.

15. Splendiani and Aristazábal, *Proceso de beatificación*, 22, 169, 173, 344–45.

16. Martínez Reyes, *Cartas de los Obispos*, 264–65.

17. Walker, *Shaky Colonialism*, 132–38, 153–54.

18. Ibid., 134, 141.

19. Sennet, *Fall of Public Man*, 64–68.

20. Juan and Ulloa, *Voyage*, 1: 4.

21. Sennet, *Fall of Public Man*, 67.

22. Sennett explores the idea of street clothes and theater costumes merging in eighteenth-century Paris. When one actress appeared on stage dressed as a "real'" peasant, in sandals and with bare legs, "the audience was disgusted." Less wealthy viceregal (but not indigent) women, viewing their street appearances as a performance, probably feared such a reaction if they dressed in a downwardly mobile fashion. See *Fall of Public Man*, 71.

23. A handful of women's possessions are documented in the *bienes de difuntos* files located in Seville's Casa de Contratación. These records exist because bureaucrats inventoried possessions owned by foreigners, including Spaniards, who died in Cartagena with living, direct heirs across the Atlantic, in order to record the money that crossed on Spanish fleets and to fairly distribute it according to testamentary bequests. If a last will and testament did not exist, the officials made lengthy investigations to guarantee that the inheritances found their European owners. Hundreds of *bienes de difuntos* files came from Cartagena, concentrating in the 1600s. Many of these record deaths at sea, in battles, or soon after arrival in the port.

24. AGI, *Bienes de difuntos de Catalina Vasquez*, fojas 2–4, 22–23, 38–39.

25. Storey, "Clothing Courtesans," 96. See Karras, *Common Women*, 21–22, and Collier Frick, *Dressing Renaissance Florence*, 185–87.

26. Storey, "Fragments from 'Life Stories.'"

27. Maya, "Paula de Eguiluz."

28. AHN, *Proceso de fe de Paula de Eguiluz*, bloque 1, foja 37.

29. AHN, *Proceso de fe de Paula de Eguiluz*, bloque 2, fojas 1, 26.

30. Storey, "Clothing Courtesans," 97.

31. Comaroff, "The Empire's Old Clothes," 24.

32. Gage, *The English-American*, 85–87.

33. Storey, *Carnal Commerce*, 27–28.

34. For Juana's inquisition trial, see Splendianni et al., *Cincuenta años*, 2: 314, 330–33. For the inventory, see AHN, *Inventario y almoneda de los bienes*, fojas 1–4.

35. Splendianni et al., *Cincuenta años*, 2: 299–300, 335–36, 371–72.

36. Storey, *Carnal Commerce*, 175.

37. AHN, *Inventario y almoneda de los bienes secuestrados*, fojas 242–254.

38. Storey, *Carnal Commerce*, 175.

39. AHN, *Inventario y almoneda de los bienes secuestrados*, fojas 36–39.

40. AHN, *Proceso de fe de Paula de Eguiluz*, bloque 3, foja 60.

41. AHN, *Inventario y almoneda de los bienes secuestrados*, fojas 65–75.

42. Splendiani et al., *Cincuenta años*, 2: 304–5.

43. AHN, *Proceso de fe de Paula de Eguiluz*, bloque 3, fojas 33–34.

44. Splendianni et al., *Cincuenta años*, 2: 342–43.

45. Barbara Voss notes that geographical provenance was a critical descriptor in clothing inventories. See Voss, *The Archeology of Ethnogenesis*, 269.

46. AHN, *Inventario y almoneda de los bienes secuestrados*, fojas 43–52. It is interesting to note that the black town crier Joseph purchased much of the cheap clothing and other inexpensive items sold at these auctions. An unmarried mulata bought Ana María's house on the plot of land for 300 pesos.

47. AHN, *Proceso de fe de Paula de Eguiluz*, bloque 2, foja 71. The sisters' names derive from fourth-century Sevillan martyrs.

48. AHN, *Proceso de fe de Diego López*, fojas 5, 28.

49. Justa was described as a servant of María Ana de Armas Clavijo, the widow of Amador Perez, as was her sister. This is a different Rufina than Diego López's lover Rufina de Clara Núñez.

50. AHN, *Proceso de fe de Paula de Eguiluz*, bloque 3, fojas 42–43, 48–51.

51. Splendiani et al., *Cincuenta años*, 3: 298, 303–4.

52. The *Conjura de la Retractación* is documented in AGI, *Proceso de Paula*, bloque 3, fojas 51–53; AHN, *Proceso de Diego López*, 14–15; and Splendiani et al., *Cincuenta años*, 3: 341–42, 351–53, 380–87. Maya Restrepo provides a summary in *Brujería y reconstrucción*, 583–90.

53. Splendiani et al., *Cincuenta años*, 3: 380–81.

54. Ibid., 381–83.

55. As noted in chapter 8, Diego López had attended to Rufina after the birth of her child.

56. Splendiani et al., *Cincuenta años*, 3: 385–86.

57. Ibid., 415–16.

58. AHN, *Inventario y almoneda de los bienes secuestrados*, fojas 255–72.

59. Pablo Rodríguez, *Sentimientos y vida*, 274.

60. AHN, *Inventario y almoneda de los bienes secuestrados*, fojas 122–25.

61. Splendiani et al., *Cincuenta años*, 3: 212, 293–97.

62. For a superb introduction to race, ethnicity, and identity see Fisher and O'Hara, "Racial Identities and Interpreters." For more on clothing and identity in their edited volume, *Imperial Subjects*, see Mangan, "A Market of Identities," 71–77, and Tavárez, "Legally Indian," 91–93.

Chapter Nine

1. AGN, *Proceso de Felipe Chamburú*, fojas 396–97.

2. The file does not explain a specific course of events that led to identification of the body. As soon as doña Manuela was found, everyone seemed to know her identity, perhaps because of her reputation as a prostitute, or perhaps simply because this was a small city with only a few hundred elite Spanish women residents.

3. Historians have found that men of indigenous ancestry were especially likely to murder in revenge for adultery or at least to use this explanation to justify their violent acts. Taylor, in *Drinking, Homicide, and Rebellion*, found that 9.2 percent of homicides in his study of judicial records in central Mexican Indian villages related to female adultery. In the less Hispanized region of the Mixteca Alta, over 28 percent of men claimed that they murdered inspired by unfaithful wives. Offenders justified their behavior as done to protect their honor. This may have been a way to lessen the seriousness of their crime. See 94, 97, 104, 109–10. Murdering adulterous spouses in central Mexico, however well it seems to fit Hispanic honor codes, may have been a continuation of pre-colonial, indigenous justice. See Terraciano, "Crime and Culture," especially 724–29. Terraciano discusses native ideas of honor on 730, drawing from work by Taylor, Stern and Lavrín. Penyak and Vallejo did not find use of the word "honor" often in cases of domestic abuse. See Penyak and Vallejo, "Expectations of Love," 567–68.

4. Taylor, *Honor and Violence*, 6, 225.

5. White, "The Politics of Anger," 132–38.

6. See Dopico Black, *Perfect Wives*. Dopico Black points out that the popularity of wife-murder plays coincided with a proliferation of manuals on ideal wifely behavior. For her list of examples of both genres, see pages 16–19. Obviously controlling female sexuality was a huge concern, but perhaps because this was a time when men already perceived a loss of control?

7. See Twinam, "The Negotiation of Honor," 71–72.

8. Lanz, "Changing Boundaries," 170.

9. van Deusen, *Between the Sacred and the Worldly*. Historians of colonial India bring to life the complex culture of prostitution and its important effect on colonial rule and even sexuality in London. In her short summary of colonial prostitution, Powers cites only one monograph entirely dedicated to this topic: Ana María Atondo Rodriguez's *El amor venal*. This well-researched book points the reader to countless archival cases, but few historians working in English have pursued these leads, despite the thriving study of prostitution in Spain of the same era as well as well-received books on Latin America prostitution in the nineteenth and twentieth centuries. All of these books combine analysis of attempts at regulation with exploration of the culture and experience of prostitutes themselves. See the bibliography of Levine, *Prostitution, Race and Politics*. Also Atondo Rodríguez, *El amor venal*, cited in Powers, *Women in the Crucible of Conquest*, 136–41. For Spain, there is a large bibliography, including: López Beltrán, *La Prostitución*, and Atondo Rodriguez, *El amor venal*, 31, 38–39. For modern Latin America, see Guy, *Sex and Danger in Buenos Aires*, and Bliss, *Compromised Positions*.

10. Atondo Rodríguez, *El amor venal*, 23–24, 27, 29, and Pablo Rodríguez, "Las mancebías españoles," 39.

11. Atondo Rodríguez, *El amor venal*, 32–34, 41–42, and Jaramillo de Zuleta, "Las arrepentidas," 98. For the unusual relationship between the king and the nun,

see Fedewa, *María of Agreda*. For an entertaining account of the king's scandalous life, see Hume, *The Court of Philip IV*, 45, 54–56, 206–8, 347–52.

12. Davis, *Fiction in the Archives*, 3–4. As Davis observes, as soon as a witness for the defense portrays a woman as immoral in any way, it is clear that the testimony will end in her death.

13. AGN, *Proceso de Felipe Chamburú*, fojas 398–401.

14. Ibid., fojas 406–7.

15. Atondo Rodríguez, *El amor venal*, 186–87, lists several crude but humorous nicknames given to prostitute doñas in 1670s Mexico City, including "la Chinche," "las Priscas," "Cedacito" (sieve), "la Vende barato" (sold cheaply), "la Lorencilla," "la Díxome díxome" (tell me tell me), "la Manteca," "la Migajita" (the last, according to Atondo Rodríguez, probably referring to a large and a small woman), and "Mundo Nuevo."

16. AGN, *Proceso de Felipe Chamburú*, fojas 402–6.

17. Ibid., fojas 410–11.

18. Ibid., fojas 412–19. Don Felipe's testimonies blend together to form a self-exculpating narration that perfectly fits Davis's opinion that "the reader knows from the first mention of the lascivious wife who the victim is likely to be." She also observes that gentlemen usually needed to recount their life stories in much greater detail to exonerate themselves from criminal acts. The longer the story, the more guilty the nobleman. See Davis, *Fiction in the Archives*, 2–3, 39.

19. Probably in the famous sinking of the capitana or lead vessel (the *Jesús María de la Limpia Concepción*) of the Armada *del amar del sur*, the worst loss in the history of the Pacific flota.

20. Don Felipe sets the tone by emphasizing he is innocently going about his business. See Davis, *Fiction in the Archives*, 44–46, for more on this style of narration.

21. AGN, *Proceso de Felipe Chamburú*, foja 417.

22. Ibid., fojas 425–27.

23. Ibid., fojas 390, 426.

24. Ibid., foja 427.

25. This sum is not trivial—several times what a laborer would earn for a day's work—but it is humiliatingly small in contrast to the theoretically priceless commodity of an elite woman's honor.

26. AGN, *Proceso de Felipe Chamburú*, fojas 428–30.

27. Ibid., foja 431.

28. Ibid., fojas 517–20, 525, 532.

29. Ibid., fojas 485, 495.

30. Ibid., fojas 509–14.

31. Ibid., foja 442.

32. Ibid., foja 465.

33. Ibid., fojas 466–68.

34. Ibid., fojas 482–83, 490–93.

35. Ibid., foja 498, 558.

36. Ibid., fojas 551–53.

37. Ibid., fojas 554–55.

38. Ibid., fojas 558–59.

39. Ibid., fojas 560–61.

40. Ibid., fojas 561–62.

41. Storey, "Clothing Courtesans," 107.

42. AGN, *Proceso de Felipe Chamburú*, foja 396.

43. Ibid., fojas 400, 636–37.

44. Storey, *Carnal Commerce*, 174–75.

45. Fortini Brown, *Private Lives in Renaissance Venice*, 160. See also Storey, *Carnal Commerce*, 190–96, for descriptions of Roman prostitutes' living quarters.

46. AGN, *Proceso de Felipe Chamburú*, fojas 400–401.

47. Ibid., fojas 404–5, 438, 486, 529, 535, 634, 659.

48. Taylor, *Honor and Violence*, 196–99. Taylor observes that the simple fact that a wife murderer was on trial proves that this was illegal. Spanish jurists also suggested extremely harsh punishments for these men.

49. AGN, *Proceso de Felipe Chamburú*, foja 461–63.

50. Ibid., fojas 472–73.

51. Ibid., fojas 609–10.

52. In late fifteenth-century Venice, a husband received a sentence of decapitation (preceded by cutting off his hand and hanging it around his neck). The sentence was carried out at the scene of his uxoricide, where he actually had seen his wife having sex with her lover. Ruggiero, *The Boundaries of Eros*, 68.

53. AGN, *Proceso de Felipe Chamburú*, foja 629–31.

54. Ibid., foja 390.

55. Ibid., fojas 391–95.

56. Ibid., foja 479. Moxica's defense also argues that many people might have passed through Lucrecia's house that night, so she could not accurately identify his client (see foja 481).

57. Ibid., fojas 393–95.

58. Ibid., foja 677.

59. Doña María's husband was of Roman ancestry and served as the treasurer of Holy Crusade (a complex money making institution for the Spanish crown). The issues emerging from María Cabeza de Vaca's last will and testament are preserved in hundreds of pages of documents stored in the Archivo General de Indias (AGI), Seville, Escribanía, 775A, 775B, and 775C. The testament cited here is in piece 18 of Escribanía 775A.

60. A "loyal, intelligent" black man could help as majordomo, in charge of collecting the infirmary's income (drawn from the properties doña María bequeathed to her charitable foundation). AGI, escribanía 775A, pieza 18, *Testamento de María de Cabeza de Vaca*, subsections 14–20.

61. For the history of the notorious scandals and conflicts involving Piedrola and Cartagena's convents in the 1680s, see Groot, *Historia eclesiastica y civil*, 1: 385–97,

and Lea, *The Inquisition in the Spanish Dependencies*, 491–97. Research for this book could not encompass the complex and immense documentation on the 1680s church/state conflict known as the *cessatio a divinis*, or stoppage of church services in Cartagena, despite its possible importance for local understandings of honor, sex, and violence.

62. AGN, *Obispo y cabildo fundan*, fojas 250–69.

63. Ibid., foja 758.

64. Ibid., foja 260.

65. Ibid., fojas 268–69.

66. AGN, *Cabildo de Cartagena*, fojas 170–178.

67. Juan and Ulloa, *Noticias secretas*, 503–4. As quoted, "No es regular en aquellos países el haber mujeres públicas ó comunes, cuales las hay en todas las poblaciones grandes de Europa, y por el mismo respecto lo es, el que las mujeres no guarden la honestidad que es correspondiente á las que se casan; de suerte que sin haber mujeres rameras en aquellas ciudades, está la disolución en el mas alto punto á donde puede llegar la imaginación, porque toda la honradez consiste allí en no entregarse profanamente á la variedad de sujetos que las soliciten y haciéndolo señaladamente con uno ú otro no es ni desdoro, ni asunto para desmerecer."

68. A similar situation is presented in Elbl, "'Men without Wives,'" especially 74–75.

69. Pablo Rodríguez, "Servidumbre sexual," 87–88.

Chapter Ten

1. For the military side of the Bourbon reforms and their effect on Cartagena, see chapter 11. For general political and economic histories of the new viceroyalty of New Granada in the eighteenth century, see Phelan, *The People and the King*; Fisher et al., *Reform and Insurrection*; McFarlane, *Colombia Before Independence*; and Grahn, *The Political Economy of Smuggling*. See also the general sources on Cartagena architecture cited in the Introduction.

2. For historical sources on crime and punishment in Latin America, see Aguirre and Buffington, *Reconstructing Criminality in Latin America*; Salvatore et al., *Crime and Punishment*; Aguirre, *The Criminals of Lima*; Piccato, *City of Suspects*; Haslip-Viera, *Crime and Punishment*; Scardaville, "Crime and the Urban Poor"; Herzog, *La administración como un fenómeno social*; Johnson, *The Problem of Order in Changing Societies*; Lozano Armendares, *La criminalidad*, 35, 44; Aufderheide, "Order and Violence"; and Domínguez, "Delito y sociedad."

3. An interesting divorce case is AGN, *Doña Marcela de Llanos*, fojas 1–235. I have not examined this case in detail because although it was possible the couple was from Cartagena, all of the evidence comes from a rural area south of Barranquilla.

4. Sloan, *Runaway Daughters*, 119–21.

5. Seed, *Love, Honor, and Obey*, is the best known of this kind of study.

6. For more information on marriage, the church, and the real *pragmática*, see

Shumway, *Ugly Suitor*, 3, 68–69; Sloan, *Runaway Daughters*, 40–41, 145; and, for a fascinating discussion of the fluid aspects of personal honor, Büschges, "Don Manuel Valdivieso."

7. Arrom, *Women of Mexico City*, 66, 113, 208–17, 245.

8. Boyer, "Women, *La Mala Vida*, and the Politics of Marriage," 258–80.

9. Lipsett-Rivera, *Gender and the Negotiation of Daily Life*, 117–20.

10. See Bennett, *Colonial Blackness*, 137–40, for another example of a nonwhite woman's attempt to assert her honor in a marriage claim. Bennett also discusses the increasing church marriages among Afro-Mexicans along with the associated claims to honor over the course of the colonial era, 90, 183–84. See von Germeten, *Black Blood Brothers*, 124–37.

11. AGN, *Autos seguidos por Martina Francisca Morales*, fojas 673–761, quote from 679.

12. Ibid., fojas 683–84, 691.

13. Ibid., fojas 694–95, 729, 732–33.

14. Ibid., fojas 736–38, 759.

15. AGN, *Sumario instruido a José Joaquín Ampuria*, fojas 461–77.

16. Ibid., foja 464.

17. Ibid., fojas 476–77.

18. AGN, *Juicio sobre anulación*, fojas 511–23.

19. Ibid., foja 514. See Berhend-Martinez, *Unfit for Marriage*.

20. AGN, *Juicio sobre anulación*, foja 517, 519–23.

21. The surnames of these unsatisfactory medical men were Poyol, Gori, Buena, and the famous Gastelbundo.

22. This marriage dispute involved a married couple and a close male friend present in Cartagena due to his occupation as a bureaucrat carrying out one facet of the eighteenth-century Bourbon reforms. A similar situation sparked the major sex scandal involving doña Luisa Llerena, discussed in the next chapter. The 1778 case exposes a consummated affair that generated very little scandal, while, as we will see, doña Luisa possibly did not have sexual relationships outside marriage, but her behavior generated reams of rumors and gossip.

23. AGN, *Causa seguida por amancebamiento*, fojas 220–51. See Deans-Smith, *Bureaucrats, Planters, and Workers*.

24. Love letters could be critical pieces of evidence in cases involving sex and marriage. See Twinam, "The Negotiation of Honor," 70, for a reproduction of a colonial love letter and page 91 for love letter rhetoric of this era. Richard Boyer's essay, "Honor among Plebians," in the same book also discusses how an Indian woman supposedly used love letters to seduce a young man, 171–72. Lavrin quotes lines from eighteenth-century love letters in "Sexuality in Colonial Mexico." Nineteenth-century love letters are discussed in Sloan, *Runaway Daughters*, 94–96, and Shumway, *Ugly Suitor*, 73–75. For what I believe to be a fake love letter (but useful in its goal of narrating the problems of a forced marriage), see van Deusen, "'Wife of my Soul and Heart.'"

25. Arrom, *Women of Mexico City*, 242–44, and López-Cordon Cortezo, "Women in Society," 110.
26. Martín Gaite, *Love Customs*, 89–93.
27. AGN, *Causa seguida por amancebamiento*, fojas 226–27.
28. Ibid., foja 226.
29. Ibid., fojas 227–28.
30. The epistolary culture is more studied for France and England. See for example Goodman, *Becoming a Woman*.
31. The note in question simply says: "Hoy me han ofrecido contarme las piernas por un modo extrano, pero no digo que tienes pocos cojones el que lo ha pensado, es muy pendejo el que tiene miedo, pero yo como valiente, salgo al camino y no de miedo." Many thanks to Rachel Moore for the translation.
32. AGN, *Causa seguida por amancebamiento*, fojas 226, 230, 239.
33. Ibid., foja 231.
34. This is especially clear in chapter 11.
35. AGN, *Causa seguida por amancebamiento*, fojas 229–30.
36. Ibid., fojas 235–36.
37. Ibid., fojas 236–41.
38. Ibid., fojas 241–51.
39. Martín Gaite, *Love Customs*, x, 1, 9, 86, 99–103.
40. For domestic violence in colonial Mexico, see Stern, *The Secret History of Gender*, and Penyak and Vallejo, "Expectations of Love."
41. AGN, *Sumario instruido a Juan de Castro*, fojas 833–913. For dates and basic information on Cartagena's governors, see Castillo Mathieu, *Los Gobernadores*, 120–22.
42. AGN, *Sumario instruido a Juan de Castro*, foja 844.
43. Ibid., fojas 897, 900, 902.

Chapter Eleven

1. For a different approach to this case, see von Germeten, "Prostitution and the Captain's Wife." Documentation relating to the Llerena/Piñero scandal is stored at the Archivo General de Indias (AGI), Sevilla, Santa Fe, *Expediente sobre el adulterio*, expedientes 754, 755, and 756, dating from 1756 to 1760. The term lenocinio is only used in the AGI title for this case, not in the documentation itself. I believe a nineteenth- or early twentieth-century archivist applied this title, given its increasing use at this time. It is in line with moral stances and fears of pandering or "pimping," perceived as a greater concern than it had been in the colonial era. See Bliss, *Compromised Positions*.
2. Mannarelli, *Private Passions*, 70–71.
3. AGI, *Letter from Ignacio de Barragán y Messa*, fojas 15–16.

4. For a history of Polo Nieto, see González Suárez, *Historia General de la Republica*, 5: 168–200.

5. This is the rank between cadet and lieutenant. See Rivas, "The Spanish Colonial Military," 261.

6. Marchena Fernández, *La Institución Militar*, 114, 155, 325–26, and McFarlane, *Colombia Before Independence*, 196–97.

7. For information on this battle, see Robinson, "The English Attack on Cartagena," 62–71; Nowell, "The Defense of Cartagena," 477–501; Ogelsby, "Spain's Havana Squadron"; Ogelsby, "England vs. Spain"; and Mogollón et al., "Mesa Redonda." English pamphleteers and participants wrote extensively on this defeat—see for example Knowles, *An Account of the Expedition to Carthagena*.

8. AGI, *Carta de Braulio Herrera*, foja 105.

9. AGI, *Informas hecha a pedimiento del cuerpo de capitanes del batallón*, fojas 17–18.

10. Ibid., fojas 27, 32.

11. Ibid., foja 76.

12. "Digale a doña Luisa si soy yo putona como ella." AGI, *Carta de Braulio Herrera*, foja 107.

13. AGI, *Informas hecha a pedimiento del cuerpo de capitanes del batallón*, foja 52.

14. See Martin Gaite, *Love Customs*, 100–101.

15. AGI, *Informas hecha a pedimiento del cuerpo de capitanes del batallón*, fojas 27, 34–35, 48–49, 53, 57–58.

16. Don Juan petitioned three times between 1755 and 1765 for official permission to sell slaves in Cartagena. See AGN, *Negros y Esclavos*. In 1760, don Juan had 105 slaves in transit via Porto Belo. See AGN, *Negros y Esclavos*, and AGN, *Juan Arechederreta,*.

17. Sloan, *Runaway Daughters*, 123–24, and Martin Gaite, *Love Customs*, 88.

18. AGI, *Informas hecha a pedimiento del cuerpo de capitanes del batallón*, fojas 27, 38, 55–56, 73–74, 88.

19. Ibid., fojas 25, 27, 66–67, 72, 83.

20. AGI, *Carta de Fray Braulio Herrera*, fojas 100–125.

21. Martín Gaite, *Love Customs*, 32, 88.

22. Arrom, *Women of Mexico City*, 144.

23. The full name of the viceroy was José de Solis Folch de Cardona and he held this office from 1753 to 1761. Known as the "virrey fraile," he is a popular figure in Colombian history and literature as his own life was full of sex scandals. Even his deployment to New Granada has been viewed as a response to personal embarrassments at the highest level in Madrid. The Virrey Fraile had several children with his mistress but joined the Franciscan Order in 1762. For an introduction to this fascinating character, see Lyday, "History and Legend."

24. AGI, *Carta de Fray Braulio Herrera*, foja 121.

25. AGI, *Informas hecha a pedimiento del cuerpo de capitanes del batallón*, fojas 21, 31, 39–41, 63–65, 75, 84.

26. AGI, *Carta de Fray Braulio Herrera*, fojas 160–99, 237–63.

27. AGI, *Petition in the name of don Francisco Piñero*.

28. AGI, *Carta de Fray Braulio Herrera*, fojas 156–58.

29. Ibid., fojas 156–58.

30. AGI, *Informas hecha a pedimiento del cuerpo de capitanes del batallón*, fojas 34–35, 56–57.

31. Ibid., fojas 107–9.

32. Juan and Ulloa, *Voyage*, 1: 32–33.

33. Ibid., 31.

34. Ibid., 2: 60.

35. Lemoine, "El Vestido Criollo." The description of traje de mulata comes from 334–36.

36. Martín Gaite, *Love Customs*, xi.

37. Santa Gertrudis Serra, *Maravillas*, 1: 43.

38. AGI, *Carta de Fray Braulio Herrera*, foja 157.

39. Ibid., fojas 350, 354, 356, 367, 373, 396, 404, 410, 436, 446.

40. Walker, *Shaky Colonialism*, 132–38, 141, 153–54.

41. Martín Gaite, *Love Customs*, 40–50.

42. These statements were made on AGI, *Carta de Fray Braulio Herrera*, fojas 302–452.

43. See statements made on ibid., fojas 157–58, 360, 363, 370, 377, 391, 394, 396, 399, 402.

44. Juan and Ulloa, *Voyage*, 1: 39–40.

45. Martín Gaite, *Love Customs*, 22–24, 93–94.

46. For more on this new style of socializing, see López-Cordon Cortezo, "Women in Society," 103–14.

47. Women in early modern Spain also engaged in this kind of public shaming. See Taylor, *Honor and Violence*, 157–93. Church was a common location for public confrontations.

48. AGI, *Testimonio de las diligencias*, fojas 20–22.

49. Ibid., fojas 20–22.

50. Doña Luisa's witnesses speak on ibid., fojas 30–78.

51. Ibid., foja 35.

52. Ibid., fojas 45, 51.

53. Ibid., foja 69. The parenthetical explanation is in the original document.

54. Ibid., fojas 30, 37, 41, 51, 59, 67.

55. Clark, "Whores and Gossips," 235, 238.

56. AGI, *Testimonio de las diligencias*, fojas 30, 31, 33, 36, 53, 57, 64, 78.

57. Martín Gaite, *Love Customs*, 76–77; and López-Cordon Cortezo, "Women in Society," 108–10.

58. Castillo Mathieu, *Los Gobernadores*, 104–5.

59. Marchena Fernández, *La Institución Militar*, 328–30. According to the governor, constant desertions and low salaries also brought down the battalion. See also Marchena Fernández, "Sin temor de rey ni de dios." In this essay, Marchena Fernández also provides a brief summary of the scandal, describes the 1741 battle

and its after effects (including a rebellion by all of the non-officer class soldiers in Cartagena in 1745, which must have had lasting resonance for don Francisco and his colleagues), and provides an extensive bibliography. See 46–48, 57–68, 76–77.

60. AGN, *María Mercedes Piñero contra José de Vela*, fojas 456–57, 460–67.

61. AGS, *María Josefa Piñero, descuentos de pensión*, 1798.

Conclusion

1. Berhend-Martínez, *Unfit for Marriage*, xi.

2. Paraphrased from a comment made to me at the Rocky Mountain Conference of Latin American Studies, Park City, Utah, March 29, 2012.

3. Bennett, *Colonial Blackness*, 138.

4. Martínez, "The Black Blood."

5. Ruggiero, *The Boundaries of Eros*, 64.

6. Lux Martelo, *Las mujeres*, 72, 75, 98.

7. What a male cleric or doctor might interpret or present as masturbation can easily be understood instead as sex between women. See Velasco, *Lesbians*, 20, 24.

8. This is the only example of lesbian erotic activity that I have encountered in documentation from Cartagena, although scholars have proven that sexual relationships between early modern Iberian women were not ignored or unremarked, but in fact recognized and acknowledged. Velasco convincingly argues that both lesbian personal identity and sex between women were well known before the modern era. See Velasco, *Lesbians*, 2, 5, 13.

9. Berhend-Martínez, *Unfit for Marriage*, 123–24.

10. Ruggiero, *The Boundaries of Eros*, 81.

11. AGN, *Proceso de Antonia*, fojas 310–55. Antonia and Justa were not described as slaves in this documentation, although Antonia did say she had *dueños* or owners.

12. Ibid., fojas 289–91.

13. Ibid., fojas 279–81.

14. A tactic also seen frequently in the sixteenth-century requests for royal pardon. Davis, *Fiction in the Archives*, 7–8, 31, 34, 69, 92, 94.

15. AGN, *Proceso de Antonia*, fojas 284–86, 290–91.

16. Ibid., fojas 317–21.

17. As Kimberly Gauderman observes, "in many aspects of Spanish American life patriarchy is a modern creation." *Women's Lives*, 11.

Bibliography

Archives

Archivo General de Indias (AGI), Seville, Spain.

Contratación 303. Number 2. *Autos sobre bienes de difuntos, Antonio Sigarra, negro, difunto en Veracruz.*

Contratación 559B. Number 4. Rollo 2. 1679. *Bienes de difuntos de Catalina Vasquez.*

Contratación 5296. Exp. 1:36. *Francisco de Santander.*

Escribanía 573A. *Doña María Nele y el fiscal contra Gonzalo Jiménez Coronel teniente del Gobernador de Cartagena sobre la muerte de don Capitán Cornelio Cornelius.* 1644.

Escribanía, 775A, 775B, and 775C. *Pleitos de la Audiencia de Santa Fe,* 1691.

Expediente 754. Document 3. *Petition in the name of don Francisco Piñero,* 1757.

Expediente 754. Document 4. *Testimonio de las diligencias que instruye doña Luisa de Llerena y Polo contra la difamación que le ha sobrevenido a su honra.*

Expediente 754. *Letter from Ignacio de Barragán y Messa.*

Santa Fe 38. Exp. 3:79. *Cartas de Gobernadores.*

Santa Fe 56A. Exp. 50. *Carta de Francisco de Herrera Campuzano.*

Santa Fe 63. Exp. 2. *Carta de cabildo secular de Cartagena en desaprobación del sargento mayor.*

Santa Fe 754–756. *Expediente sobre el adulterio y lenocinio de Luisa de Llerena, mujer de Francisco Piñero, capitán del batallón fijo de Cartagena de Indias, que paso por el consejo de Indias,* 1756–1760.

Santa Fe 755. *Carta de Fray Braulio Herrera.* 1756.

Santa Fe 755. Duplicated on microfilm roll C-12896. *Carta de Braulio Herrera.*

Santa Fe 755. *Informas hecha a pedimiento del cuerpo de capitanes del batallón.*

Archivo General de la Nacion (AGN), Bogota, Colombia.

Cabildos. Tomo 76. Document 50. *Cabildo de Cartagena destina para Socorro de los expósitos.*

Colonia. Policia. Legajo 2. *Obispo y cabildo fundan una casa de reclusión para cortesanas.* 1790.

Criminales. Rollo 180. Document 13. *Proceso de Antonia Abad Santamaría, quien dio muerte a Justa Manuela Cabezas.*

Criminales. Rollo 182. Document 5. *Proceso de Felipe Chamburú, Andrés de Escalante y Gabriel de Butrino y Mojica sindicados de la degollación de dona Manuela de Andrade en un arrabal de Cartagena.*

Criminales. Rollo 183. *Causa seguida a Diego Cortes de Mesa y alteres por tentativa de homicidio en la persona de Gaspar Zúñiga de los Reyes.*

Criminales. Rollo 183. Document 29. *La curia de Cartagena y la causa seguida por amancebamiento a Juan José de Sagastuy.*

Criminales. Rollo 190. Document 2. *Causa seguida a Juan Ramírez por el estupro de María de Montemayor, hija de Francisco de Montemayor y María Adame, denunciantes de hecho.*

Criminales. Rollo 190. Document 4. *Causa seguida a Francisco Luis, sindicado del homicidio de Jerónimo de Serpa.*

Criminales. Rollo 191. Document 15. *Juicio sobre anulación del matrimonio de Nicolás de la Parra y Marcelina Martínez por defecto de la impotencia.*

Criminales. Rollo 192. Document 5. *Juicio seguido a Juan Ramírez por el estupro de María de Montemayor.*

Criminales. Rollo 192. Document 6. *Causa seguida a Juan Carillo de Albornoz por asalto a la casa de Pedro Soto de Altamirano y estupro de Agustina, negra esclava.*

Criminales. Rollo 193. Document 3. *Sumario instruido a Diego Ortiz de la Maza en virtud del denuncio de Pedro de Soto Altamirano y María Jiménez de la Torre de escalamiento de la casa de ella y seducción de Ana de Bolívar*

Criminales. Rollo 193. Document 5. *Sumario instruido a Juan de Castro en virtud de denuncio de Lorenza Leal su consorte de sevicia con ella.*

Criminales. Rollo 194. Document 1. *Doña Marcela de Llanos con su legítimo marido don Manuel Hernandez por adulterio.*

Criminales. Rollo 194. *Sumario instruido a José Joaquín Ampuria por haber violado la virginidad de María Josefa del Carmen del Oro, engañándola con promesa de matrimonio.*

Criminales. Roll 196. Document 8. *María Juárez ama de Catalina Angola contra Juan Sanz de Normant sobre la muerte de Catalina Angola.*

Criminales. Tomo 34. Document 4. *Autos seguidos por Martina Francisca Morales, samba libre, contra Felipe Santiago de Soto, por incumplimiento de promesa de matrimonio y otras cosas.*

Criminales. Tomo 122. Document 14. *Causa criminal seguida por Benito Maldonado Millán, alcalde de Cartagena, contra Juan de salinas, negro esclavo, por un pendencia de cuchilladas, alboroto, y escándalo que origino en dicha ciudad. La real audiencia confirma la sentencia pronunciada por el alcalde.*

Criminales. Tomo 183. *Nota sobre querella de María Mercedes Piñero contra José de Vela, su marido.*

Expedientes 114, 925, 1131. *Negros y Esclavos.*

Expediente 343. *Juan Arechederreta, comunicaciones sobre la cantidad de negros esclavos que por cuenta de el se introdujeron a Portobelo.*
Inquisición 1620. Expediente 1. *Proceso de fe de Lorenzana de Acereto.*

Archivo General de Simancas (AGS), Simancas, Spain.
Secretario del Despacho de Guerra Legajo 7231. Expediente 64. *María Josefa Piñero, descuentos de pensión.* 1798.

Archivo Histórico Nacional (AHN), Madrid, Spain.
Inquisición 1616. Expediente 5. *Testimonio de una causa criminal de oficio contra Francisco Guerra y Bonifacio de Treviño.*
Inquisición 1620. Expediente 7. *Proceso de fe de Diego López.*
Inquisición 1620. Expediente 8. *Proceso de Elena de la Cruz.*
Inquisición 1620. Expediente 10. *Proceso de fe de Paula de Eguiluz.*
Inquisición 4822. Expediente 2. *Inventario y almoneda de los bienes secuestrados a varias mujeres negras, reconciliadas por el tribunal de la Inquisición de Cartagena de Indias en el Auto de Fe celebrado el 26 de Marzo 1634.*
Querella de Lorenzo Martínez de Castro.

Unpublished Dissertations, Theses, and Papers

Almodóvar, Carlos Noel. "Escepticismo y vulnerabilidad en el Tribunal del Santo Oficio de la Inquisición de Cartagena de Indias ante los procesos de brujería y hechicería contra esclavos y libertos: un reflejo del impacto del choque ideológico y geográfico en la sociedad colonial caribeña, 1614–1634." Master's Thesis, Universidad de Puerto Rico, 2008.
Aufderheide, Patricia Ann. "Order and Violence: Social Deviance and Social Control in Brazil, 1780–1840." PhD diss., University of Minnesota, 1976.
Fleener, Charles Joseph. "The Expulsion of the Jesuits from the Viceroyalty of New Granada, 1767." PhD diss., University of Florida, 1969.
Garofalo, Leo. "The Case of Diego Suárez: Defining Empire through Afro-Iberian Incorporation and Movement in the Early Ibero-American World." Unpublished paper presented at the Atlantic World Workshop, New York University, NY, Fall 2009.
Graff, Gary Wendell. "Cofradías in the New Kingdom of Granada: Lay Fraternities in a Spanish-American Frontier Society." PhD diss., University of Wisconsin, 1973.
Guzzo, Peter Paul. "The Independence Movement and Failure of the First Republic of Cartagena de Indias, 1810–1815." PhD diss., Catholic University of America, 1972.
Little, Christopher Bradford. "The Changing Rose: The Spanish Romancero in Colonial New Granada, 1498–1717." PhD diss., University of Virginia, 1992.
Penyak, Lee. "Criminal Sexuality in Central Mexico, 1750–1850." PhD diss., University of Connecticut, 1993.

Price, Thomas. "Saints and Spirits: A Study of Differential Acculturation in Colombian Negro Communities." PhD diss., Northwestern University, 1955.

Scardaville, Michael. "Crime and the Urban Poor: Mexico City in the Late Colonial Period." PhD diss., University of Florida, 1977

Tortorici, Zeb. "*Contra Natura*: Sin, Crime, and 'Unnatural' Sexuality in Colonial Mexico, 1530–1821." PhD diss., University of California, Los Angeles, 2010.

Vidal Ortega, Antonino. "Cartagena de Indias en la articulación del espacio regional Caribe 1580–1640: la producción agrarian." PhD diss., Universidad Internacional de Andalucía, 1998.

Printed Sources

Acosta de Samper, Soledad. *Los piratas de Cartagena: Crónicas histórico-novelescas.* Bogota: Imprenta de la Luz, 1886.

Aguirre, Carlos. *The Criminals of Lima and Their Worlds: The Prison Experience, 1850–1935.* Durham, NC: Duke University Press, 2005.

Aguirre, Carlos, and Robert Buffington, eds. *Reconstructing Criminality in Latin America.* Wilmington, DE: Scholarly Resources, 2000.

Akenson, Donald Harman. *If the Irish Ran the World: Montserrat, 1630–1730.* Montreal: McGill-Queen's University Press, 1997.

Alcedo y Herrera, Antonio. *Diccionario geográfico e histórico de las Indias occidentales o América.* Volume 5. Madrid: Manuel González, 1789.

Álvarez Alonso, Fermina. *La inquisición en Cartagena de Indias durante el siglo XVII.* Alcalá: Fundación Universitaria Española, 1996.

Angerman, Arina, ed. *Current Issues in Women's History.* London: Routledge, 1989.

Angulo Bossa, Alvaro. *Aspectos sociales y políticos de Cartagena de Indias: Siglos XVI y XX.* Cartagena: Editorial Antillas, 2001.

Ankarloo, Bengt, and Gustav Henningsen, eds. *Early Modern European Witchcraft: Centres and Peripheries.* Oxford: Clarendon Press, 1989.

Anonymous. *A Journal of the Expedition to Cartagena with Notes in Answer to a Late Pamphlet Entitled an Account of the Expedition to Carthagena.* London: J. Roberts, 1744.

Anonymous. *An Account of the Expedition to Cartagena with Explanatory Notes and Observations.* London: M. Cooper, 1741.

Anonymous. "Los leprosos de Caño de Loro, 1806." Introduced and transcribed by Jorge Tomás Uribe Angel. *Boletín de Historia y Antigüedades* 90, no. 823 (October–December 2003): 865–72.

Aristizabel Giraldo, Tulio, S.J. *Iglesias, conventos y hospitales en Cartagena colonial.* Bogota: El Áncora, 1998.

———. *Retazos de Historia: los Jesuitas en Cartagena de Indias.* Cartagena: Ediciones Antropos, 1995.

Arrazola, Roberto. *Palenque: primer pueblo libre de América*. Cartagena: Ediciones Hernández, 1970.

——. *Secretos de la Historia de Cartagena*. Cartagena: Tipografía Hernández, 1967.

Arriaga Copete, Libardo. *Cátedra de estudios afrocolombianos*. Colombia: Contreras Hernández, 2002.

Arrom, Silvia Marina. *Containing the Poor: The Mexico City Poor House, 1774–1871*. Durham, NC: Duke University Press, 2000.

——. *The Women of Mexico City, 1790–1857*. Stanford, CA: Stanford University Press, 1985.

Atondo Rodríguez, Ana María. *El amor venal y la condicion feminina en el Mexico colonial*. Mexico: INAH, 1992.

Bakewell, Peter. "Mining in Colonial South America." In *Colonial Latin America*. Vol. 2 of *The Cambridge History of Latin America*, edited by Leslie Bethell, 105–51. Cambridge: Cambridge University Press, 1984.

Balestra, Alejandra, Glenn Martínez, and María Irene Moyna, eds. *Recovering the U.S. Hispanic Linguistic Heritage: Sociohistorical Approaches to Spanish in the United States*. Houston: Arte Público Press, 2008.

Barahona, Renato. "Courtship, Seduction and Abandonment in Early Modern Spain. The example of Vizcaya, 1500–1700." In *Sex and Love in Golden Age Spain*, edited by Alain Saint-Saëns, 43–55. New Orleans: University Press of the South, 1996.

——. *Sex Crimes, Honour, and the Law in Early Modern Spain: Vizcaya, 1528–1735*. Toronto: University of Toronto Press, 2003.

Barbier, Jaques A. and Lynda DeForest Craig. "Lepers and hospitals in the Spanish Empire: an aspect of Bourbon reform in health care." *Ibero-American Architecture* 11, no. 4 (1985): 383–406.

Barras de Aragón, Francisco de las. *Documentos referentes al Canal de Navegación construido en 1650 entre Cartagena de Indias y el Rio de la Magdalena*. Madrid: Imprenta de Ramona Velasco, 1931.

Behar, Ruth. "Sexual Witchcraft, Colonialism, and Women's Powers: Views from the Mexican Inquisition." In *Sexuality and Marriage in Colonial Latin America*, edited by Asunción Lavrin, 178–206. Lincoln: University of Nebraska Press, 1992.

Bennett, Herman L. *Colonial Blackness: A History of Afro-Mexico*. Bloomington: Indiana University Press, 2009.

Bensusen, Guy. "Cartagena's Fandango Politics." *Studies in Latin American Popular Culture* 5 (1984): 127–34.

Berco, Christian. *Sexual Hierarchies, Public Status: Men, Sodomy, and Society in Spain's Golden Age*. Toronto: University of Toronto Press, 2007.

Berg, Maxine, and Elizabeth Eger. *Luxury in the Eighteenth Century: Debates, Desires and Delectable Goods*. New York: Palgrave, 2003.

Berhend-Martinez, Edward J. *Unfit for Marriage: Impotent Spouses on Trial in the Basque Region of Spain, 1650–1750*. Reno: University of Nevada Press, 2007.

Bethell, Leslie, ed. *The Cambridge History of Latin America*. 11 vols. Cambridge: Cambridge University Press, 1984.

Binasco, Matteo. "The Activity of Irish Priests in the West Indies: 1638–1669." *Irish Migration Studies in Latin America* 7 (November 2011): 20–35.

Bledsoe, Thomas. *St. Peter Claver as Seen by a North American Writer*. Cartagena: Editorial San Pedro Claver, 1957.

Bliss, Katherine. *Compromised Positions: Prostituion, Revolution, and Social Reform in Mexico City, 1918–1940*. University Park: Penn State University Press, 2001.

Block, Kristen. *Ordinary Lives in the Early Caribbean: Religion, Colonial Competition, and the Politics of Profit*. Athens: University of Georgia Press: 2012.

Block, Kristen, and Jenny Shaw. "Subjects without an Empire: The Irish in a Changing Caribbean." *Past and Present* 210 (February 2011): 34–60.

Borah, Woodrow. "Trends in Recent Studies of Colonial Latin American Cities." *Hispanic American Historical Review* 61, no. 3 (1984): 535–54.

Borao, Jerónimo. *Diccionario de voces aragoneses*. Zaragoza: Imprenta de Hospicio Provincial, 1884.

Borja Gómez, Jaime Humberto. *Rostros y Rastros del demonio en la Nueva Granada: indios, negros, judíos, mujeres y otras huestes de Satanás*. Bogota: Editorial Ariel, 1998.

———, ed. *Inquisición, muerte y sexualidad en la Nueva Granada*. Bogota: Editorial Ariel-Ceja, 1995.

Borrego Plá, María del Carmen. *Cartagena de Indias en el siglo XVI*. Seville: Publicaciones de la Escuela de Estudios Hispano-Americanos de Sevilla, 1988.

———. *Palenques de Negros en Cartagena de Indias a fines del siglo XVII*. Seville: Publicaciones de la Escuela de Estudios Hispano-Americanos de Sevilla, 1973.

Borrero Londoño, Ricardo. "De Pointis y la representación textual de la expedición a Cartagena en 1697: Tipología discursiva, ambigüedad, y pragmatismo transcendental." *Fronteras de la Historia* 14, no. 2 (2009): 368–90.

Bossa Herazo, Donaldo. *Nomenclatura cartagenero*. Bogota: Banco de la República, 1981.

Boyer, Richard E. "Catarina María complains that Juan Teioa Forcibly Deflowered Her." In *Colonial Lives: Documents on Latin American History, 1550–1850*, edited by Richard Boyer and Geoffrey Spurling, 155–65. Oxford: Oxford University Press, 1999.

———. "Honor Among Plebeians: *Mala Sangre* and Social Reputation." In *The Faces of Honor: Sex, Shame, and Violence in Colonial Latin America*, edited by Lyman L. Johnson and Sonya Lipsett-Rivera, 152–78. Albuquerque: University of New Mexico Press, 1998.

———. *Lives of the Bigamists: Marriage, Family, and Community in Colonial Mexico*. Albuquerque: University of New Mexico Press, 1995.

———. "Women, *La Mala Vida*, and the Politics of Marriage." In *Sexuality and Marriage in Colonial Latin America*, edited by Asunción Lavrin, 252–86. Lincoln: University of Nebraska Press, 1992.

Boyer, Richard E., and Geoffrey Spurling, eds. *Colonial Lives: Documents on Latin American History, 1550–1850*. New York: Oxford University Press, 2000.

Bradley, Harriet. "The Seductions of the Archive: Voices Lost and Found." *History of the Human Sciences* 12, no. 2 (1999): 107–22.

Briggs, Robin. *Witches and Neighbors: The Social and Cultural Context of European Witchcraft*. New York: Penguin, 1996.

Bristol, Joan Cameron. *Christians, Blasphemers, and Witches: Afro-Mexican Ritual Practice in the Seventeenth Century*. Albuquerque: University of New Mexico Press, 2007.

Broedel, Hans Peter. *The 'Malleus Maleficarum' and the Construction of Witchcraft: Theology and Popular Belief*. Manchester: Manchester University Press, 2003.

Bronner, Fred. "Urban Society in Colonial Spanish America: Research Trends." *Latin American Research Review* 21, no. 1 (1986): 7–72.

Burkholder, Mark A. "Honor and Honors in Colonial Spanish America." In *The Faces of Honor: Sex, Shame, and Violence in Colonial Latin America*, edited by Lyman L. Johnson and Sonya Lipsett-Rivera, 18–44. Albuquerque: University of New Mexico Press, 1998.

Burkholder, Mark A., and D. S. Chandler. *From Impotence to Authority: The Spanish Crown and the American Audiencias, 1687–1808*. Columbia: University of Missouri Press, 1977.

Büschges, Christian. "Don Manuel Valdivieso y Carrion Protests the Marriage of his Daughter to Don Teodoro Jaramillo, a Person of Lower Social Standing." In *Colonial Lives: Documents on Latin American History, 1550–1850*, edited by Richard Boyer and Geoffrey Spurling, 224–35.Oxford: Oxford University Press, 1999.

Cabellos Barrairo, Enrique. *Cartagena de Indias: Mágica acrópolis de América*. Madrid: Colegio de Ingenieros de Caminos, Canales, y Puertos, 1991.

Caicedo Licona, Carlos Arturo. *Por qué los negros somos así: bases históricas para descifrar la psiquis del negro-pacífico de Colombia*. Medellín: Editorial Lealon, 2001.

Calvo Stevenson, Haroldo, and Adolfo Meisel Roca, eds. *Cartagena de Indias en el siglo XVII*. Cartagena: Banco de la República, 2007.

———. *Cartagena de Indias y su historia*. Bogota: Universidad Jorge Tadeo Lozano, Banco de la República, 1998.

Cañizares-Esguerra, Jorge, James Sidbury, and Matt D. Childs, eds. *The Black Urban Atlantic in the Age of the Slave Trade*. Philadelphia: University of Pennsylvania Press, Forthcoming.

Castañeda García, Carmen. *Violación, estupro y sexualidad: Nueva Galicia, 1790–1821*. Guadalajara: Editorial Hexágono, 1989.

Castillo Mathieu, Nicolás del. *Esclavos negros en Cartagena y sus aportes léxicos*. Bogota: Instituto Caro y Cuervo, 1982.

———. *La llave de las Indias*. Bogota: Ediciones El Tiempo, 1981.

———. *Los gobernadores de Cartagena de Indias (1504–1810)*. Bogota: Academia colombiana de la historia, 1998.

———. *El Puerto de Cartagena visto por algunos autores coloniales*. Bogota: Instituto Caro y Cuervo, 1965.

Casway, Jerrold I. *Owen Roe O'Neill and the Struggle for Catholic Ireland*. Philadelphia: University of Pennsylvania Press, 1984.

Ceballos Gómez, Diana Luz. *Hechicería, brujería e Inquisición en el Nuevo Reino de Granada: Un duelo de imaginarios*. Bogota: Editorial Universidad Nacional, 1994.

Cervantes, Fernando. *The Devil in the New World: The Impact of Diabolism in New Spain*. New Haven, CT: Yale University Press, 1994.

Chandler, David. "Health Conditions in the Slave Trade of Colonial New Granada." In *Slavery and Race Relations in Latin America*, edited by Robert Brent Toplin, 51–88. Westport, CT: Greenwood Press, 1974.

———. *Health and Slavery in Colonial Colombia*. New York: Arno, 1981.

Cirac Estopañán, Sebastian. *Los procesos de hechicerías en la Inquisición de Castilla la Nueva*. Madrid: Diana Artes Gráficas, 1942.

Clark, Anna. "Whores and Gossips: Sexual Reputation in London, 1770–1825." In *Current Issues in Women's History*, edited by Arina Angerman, 231–48. London: Routledge, 1989.

Cohen, Elizabeth. "Evolving the History of Women in Early Modern Italy: Subordination and Agency." In *Spain in Italy: Politics, Society, and Religion, 1500–1700*, edited by Thomas Dandelet and John Marino, 325–54. Leiden: Brill, 2007.

Coll, Magdalena. "Doña Teresa de Aguilera y Roche, una mujer en la Inquisición en Nuevo México, una voz en la historia del español de Sudoeste de los Estados Unidos." In *Recovering the U.S. Hispanic Linguistic Heritage: Sociohistorical Approaches to Spanish in the United States*, edited by Alejandra Balestra, Glenn Martínez, and María Irene Moyna, 89–108. Houston: Arte Público Press, 2008.

Collier Frick, Carole. *Dressing Renaissance Florence: Families, Fortunes, and Fine Clothing*. Baltimore: Johns Hopkins University Press, 2002.

Colmenares, Germán. *Cali, Terratenientes, Mineros, y Comerciantes, Siglo XVIII*. Bogota: TM, 1997.

———. *Historia económica y social de Colombia, 1537–1719*. 2 vols. 3rd ed. Bogota: Editorial la Carreta, 1978.

Comaroff, Jean. "The Empire's Old Clothes: Fashioning the Colonial Subject." In *Cross-Cultural Consumption: Global Markets, Local Realities*, edited by David Howes, 19–38. London: Routledge, 1996.

Conde Calderón, Jorge. *Espacio, Sociedad y Conflictos en La Provincia de Cartagena, 1740–1815*. Barranquilla: Fondo de Publicaciones de la Universidad del Atlántico, 1999.

Cook, Alexandra Parma, and Noble David Cook. *Good Faith and Truthful Ignorance: A Case of Transatlantic Bigamy*. Durham, NC: Duke University Press, 1991.

Cope, Joseph. *England and the 1641 Irish Rebellion*. Rochester, NY: Boydell, 2009.

Cueto, Marcos. "Social Medicine and Leprosy in the Peruvian Amazon." *Americas* 61, no. 1 (July 2004): 55–80.

Cunin, Elisabeth. *Identidades a flor de piel: lo "negro" entre apariencias y pertenencias: categorías raciales y mestizaje en Cartagena, Colombia*. Bogota: Instituto Colombiano de Antropología e Historia, 2003.

Cushner, Nicholas P. *Soldiers of God: The Jesuits in Colonial America, 1565–1767.* Buffalo, NY: Language Communications, 2002.

Dandelet, Thomas, and John Marino, eds. *Spain in Italy: Politics, Society, and Religion, 1500–1700.* Leiden: Brill, 2007.

Darnton, Robert. *The Great Cat Massacre: And Other Episodes in French Cultural History.* New York: Basic Books, 1984.

Davis, Natalie Zemon. *Fiction in the Archives: Pardon Tales and Their Tellers in Sixteenth-Century France.* Stanford, CA: Stanford University Press, 1987.

Dawdy, Shannon Lee. *Building the Devil's Empire: French Colonial New Orleans.* Chicago: University of Chicago, 2008.

Deans-Smith, Susan. *Bureaucrats, Planters, and Workers: The Making of the Tobacco Monopoly in Bourbon Mexico.* Austin: University of Texas Press, 1992.

Díaz de Paniagua, R. A., and R. Paniagua Bedoya. *Getsemaní: Historia, patrimonio y bienestar social en Cartagena.* Cartagena: Coreducar, 1993.

Díaz de Paniagua, R. A., ed. *Cartagena popular: Aproximación al análisis socio-cultural.* Cartagena: Centro de Cultura Afrocaribe-Coreducar, 1994.

Díaz Díaz, Fernando, ed. *Historia documental de Colombia: Siglos XVI, XVII, XVIII.* Tunja: Universidad Pedagógica y Tecnológica de Colombia, 1974.

Diaz Diaz, Rafael Antonio. *Esclavitud, region y ciudad: El sistema esclavista urbano-regional en Santafe de Bogota, 1700–1750.* Bogota: Centro Editorial Javeriano, 2001.

Domínguez, Zoila Gabriel de. "Delito y sociedad en el Nuevo Reino de Granada período virreinal, 1740–1810." *Universitas Humanistica* 8–9 (1974, 1975): 281–398.

Dopico Black, Georgina. *Perfect Wives, Other Women: Adultery and Inquisition in Early Modern Spain.* Durham, NC: Duke University Press, 2001.

Downey, Declan. "Catholicism, Milesianism, and Monarchism: The facilitators of Irish Identification with Habsburg Spain." In *Extranjeros en el Ejercito: Militares irlandeses en la sociedad Española, 1580–1818,* edited by Enrique García Hernán and Óscar Recio Morales, 164–85. Madrid: Ministerio de Defensa, 2007.

Duffy, Christopher. *Fire and Stone: The Science of Fortress Warfare, 1660–1860.* New York: Hippocrene Books, 1975.

———. *Siege Warfare: The Fortress in the Early Modern World, 1494–1660.* New York: Barnes and Noble Books, 1977.

Earle, Rebecca. "Letters and Love in Colonial Spanish America." *The Americas* 62, no. 1 (July 2005): 17–46.

———. "Luxury, Clothing, and Race." In *Luxury in the Eighteenth Century,* edited by Maxine Berg and Elizabeth Eger, 219–27. New York: Palgrave, 2003.

———. "National Dress in Spanish America." In *The Politics of Dress in Asia and the Americas,* edited by Mina Roces and Louise Edwards, 163–81. Portland, OR: Sussex Academic Press, 2007.

———. "Two Pairs of Pink Satin Shoes!! Clothing, Race, and Identity in the Americas, seventeenth to nineteenth Centuries." *History Workshop Journal* 52 (2001): 175–95.

Elbl, Ivana. "'Men without Wives': Sexual Arrangements in the Early Portuguese Expansion in West Africa." In *Desire and Discipline: Sex and Sexuality in the*

Premodern West, edited by Jacqueline Murray and Konrad Eisenbicher, 61–86. Toronto: University of Toronto Press, 1996.

Escobar Quevedo, Ricardo. *Inquisición y judaizantes en América Española (siglos XVI–XVII)*. Bogota: Editorial Universidad del Rosario, 2008.

Eslava, Sebastian de, Virrey de Santa Fe. *Diario en todo lo ocurrido en la expugnación de los fuertes de Bocachica, y sitio de la ciudad de Cartagena de las Indias: formado de los pliegos remitidos a Su Magestad. . . .* Madrid, 1741.

Faber, F. W., ed. *The Life of the Venerable Father Claver, S.J., Apostle of the West Indies*. London: Thomas Richardson and Son, 1849.

Farnum, Mabel. *Street of the Half-moon: An Account of the Spanish Noble, Pedro Claver*. Milwaukee, WI: Bruce Publishing Company, 1940.

Fedewa, Marilyn. *María of Agreda: Mystical Lady in Blue*. Albuquerque: University of New Mexico Press, 2010.

Fernández de Piedrahita, Lucas. *Historia general del Nuevo Reyno de Granada*. Bogota: Editorial ABC, 1942.

———. *Noticia historial del Nuevo Reyno de Granada (1688)*. Bogota: Editorial Kelly, 1973.

Fernández, Díaz de Lamadrid. "Informe del Obispo de Cartagena sobre el estado de la religión y la iglesia en los pueblos de la Costa, 1781." In *Cartagena de Indias: de la colonia a la república*, edited by Gustavo Bell Lemus, 62–69. Bogota: Fundación Simón y Lola Gubereck, 1991.

Fernández, Josef. *Apostólica y penitente vida de V.P. Pedro Claver de la Compania de Jesús. . . .* Zaragoza: Diego Dormer, 1666.

Few, Martha. *Women Who Live Evil Lives: Gender, Religion, and the Politics of Power in Colonial Guatemala*. Austin: University of Texas Press, 2002.

Finotti, Joseph. *Peter Claver: A Sketch of his Life and Labors in behalf of the African Slave*. Boston: Lee and Shepard, 1868.

Fisher, Andrew B., and Matthew D. O'Hara. "Introduction: Racial Identities and Their Interpreters in Colonial Latin America." In *Imperial Subjects: Race and Identity in Colonial Latin America*, edited by Andrew Fisher and Matthew O'Hara, 7–23. Durham, NC: Duke University Press, 2009.

———, eds. *Imperial Subjects: Race and Identity in Colonial Latin America*. Durham, NC: Duke University Press, 2009.

Fisher, John, Allen Kuethe, and Anthony McFarlane. *Reform and Insurrection in Bourbon New Granada and Peru*. Baton Rouge: Louisiana State University Press, 1990.

Florescano, Enrique. "The Formation and Economic Structure of the Hacienda in New Spain." In *Bibliographic Essays*. Vol. 11 of *The Cambridge History of Latin America*, edited by Leslie Bethell, 153–188. Cambridge: Cambridge University Press, 1984.

Folger, Roger. *Escape from the Prison of Love: Caloric Identities and Writing Subjects in Fifteenth-century Spain*. Chapel Hill: University of North Carolina Press, 2009.

Fortini Brown, Patricia. *Private Lives in Renaissance Venice: Art, Architecture, and the Family*. New Haven, CT: Yale University Press, 2004.

Foucault, Michel. *Histoire de la sexualité*. Paris: Gallimard, 1976.

———. *Surveiller et punir: naissance de la prison*. Paris: Gallimard, 1975.

Franklin, Vincent P. "Bibliographical Essay: Alonso de Sandoval and the Jesuit Conception of the Negro." *Journal of Negro History* 158 (1973): 349–60.

Friede, Juan. *Fuentes documentales para la historia del Nuevo Reino de Granada*. 10 vols. Bogota: Banco Popular, 1975.

Friedemann, Nina de. "Cabildos negros: refugios de Africanía en Colombia." *Montalbán* 20 (1988):121–34.

———. *La Saga del Negro: Presencia Africana en Colombia*. Bogota: Instituto de Genética Humana, Facultad de Medicina, Pontificia Universidad Javeriana, 1993.

Fuente, Alejandro de la. "Slaves and the Creation of Legal Rights in Cuba: *Coartación* and *Papel*." *Hispanic American Historical Review* 87, no. 4 (2007): 659–92.

Gage, Thomas. *The English-American: A New Survey of the West Indies*. Edited by Arthur Percival Newton. London: Routledge, 1928.

Gagliano, Joseph and Charles E. Ronan, eds. *Jesuit Encounters in the New World: Jesuit Chroniclers, Geographers, Educators, and Missionaries in the New World, 1549–1767*. Rome: Institutum Historicum, 1997.

García de Proodian, Lucía. *Los judíos en América*. Madrid: Consejo Superior de Investigaciones Científicas, 1966.

García Hernán, Enrique and Óscar Recio Morales, eds. *Extranjeros en el Ejercito: Militares irlandeses en la sociedad Española, 1580–1818*. Madrid: Ministerio de Defensa, 2007.

Garrido, Margarita. "Vida cotidiana en Cartagena de Indias en el siglo XVII." In *Cartagena de Indias en el siglo XVII*, edited by Haroldo Calvo Stevenson and Adolpho Meisel Roca, 455–70. Cartagena: Banco de la República, 2007.

Gauderman, Kimberly. "The Authority of Gender: Marital Discord and Social Order in Colonial Quito." In *New World Orders: Violence, Sanction, and Authority in the Colonial Americas*, edited by John Smolenski and Thomas J. Humphrey, 71–91. Philadelphia: University of Pennsylvania Press, 2005.

———. "It Happened on the Way to the *Temescal* and Other Stories: Desiring the Illicit in Colonial Spanish America." *Ethnohistory* 54, no. 2 (2007): 181–84.

———. *Women's Lives in Colonial Quito: Gender, Law, and Economy in Spanish America*. Austin: University of Texas Press, 2003.

Geggus, David P., ed. *The Impact of the Haitian Revolution in the Atlantic World*. Columbia: University of South Carolina Press, 2001.

Gerassi-Navarro, Nina. *Pirate Novels: Fictions of Nation Building in Spanish America*. Durham, NC: Duke University Press, 1999.

Ginzburg, Carlo. "Deciphering the Sabbath." In *Early Modern European Witchcraft: Centres and Peripheries*, edited by Gustav Henningsen and Bengt Ankarloo, 121–38. Oxford: Clarendon Press, 1990.

Gómez Pérez, María del Carmen. "Los extrajeros en la América colonial: su expulsión de Cartagena de Indias en 1750." *Anuario de Estudios Americanos* (1983): 37, 279–311.

———. *Pedro de Heredia y Cartagena de Indias*. Sevilla: Escuela de Estudios Hispano-Americanos, 1984.

———. "La población de Cartagena de Indias a principios del siglo XVIII." *Temas americanistas* 2 (1983): 14–18.

Gonzalez-Casanovas, Roberto J. "Gender Models in Alfonso X's *Siete partidas*: The Sexual Politics of 'Nature' and 'Society.'" In *Desire and Discipline: Sex and Sexuality in the Premodern West*, edited by Jacqueline Murray and Konrad Eisenbichler, 42–60. Toronto: University of Toronto Press, 1996.

González Suárez, Federico. *Historia General de la Republica del Ecuador.* 7 vols. Quito: Imprento del Clero, 1901.

Goodman, Dena. *Becoming a Woman in the Age of Letters.* Ithaca, NY: Cornell University Press, 2009.

Grahn, Lance. *The Political Economy Of Smuggling: Regional Informal Economies in Early Bourbon New Granada.* Boulder, CO: Westview Press, 1997.

Greenleaf, Richard. *The Mexican Inquisition of the Sixteenth Century.* Albuquerque: University of New Mexico Press, 1969.

Greenow, Linda L. *Family, Household and Home: A Micro-geographic Analysis of Cartagena (New Granada) in 1777.* Syracuse, NY: Department of Geography Discussion Paper Series, 1976.

Greer, Margaret and Elizabeth Rhodes, eds. *María de Zayas y Sotomayor: Exemplary Tales of Love and Tales of Disillusion.* Chicago: University of Chicago Press, 2009.

Groot, José Manuel. *Historia eclesiástica y civil de Nueva Granada.* 5 vols. Bogota: Ministerio de Educación Nacional, 1953.

Gutiérrez Azopardo, Ildefonso. "El comercio y Mercado de negros esclavos en Cartagena de Indias (1533–1850)." *Quinto Centenario* 2 (1987): 187–210.

———. *Historia del negro en Colombia.* Bogota: Nueva América, 1980.

———. "Los libros de registro de pardos y morenos en los Archivos parroquiales de Cartagena de Indias." *Revista española de Antropología Americana* 13 (1983): 121–41.

Gutiérrez, Ramón A. *When Jesus Came, the Corn Mothers Went Away: Marriage, Sexuality, and Power in New Mexico, 1500–1846.* Stanford, CA: Stanford University Press, 1991.

———. "Women on Top: The Love Magic of the Indian Witches of New Mexico." *Journal of the History of Sexuality* 15, no. 2 (2006): 373–90.

Guy, Donna. *Sex and Danger in Buenos Aires: Prostitution, Family, and Nation in Argentina.* Lincoln: University of Nebraska Press, 1991.

Haidt, Rebecca. "The Wife, the Maid, and the Woman in the Street." In *Eve's Enlightenment: Women's Experience in Spain and Spanish America, 1726–1839*, edited by Catherine M. Jaffe and Elizabeth Lewis, 115–27. Baton Rouge: Louisiana State University Press, 2009.

Hale, Lindsay. *Hearing the Mermaid's Song: The Umbanda Religion in Rio de Janeiro.* Albuquerque: University of New Mexico Press, 2009.

Haliczer, Steven. "The Jew As Witch: Displaced Aggression and the Myth of the Santo Niño de La Guardia." In *Cultural Encounters: The Impact of the Inquisition in Spain and the New World*, edited by Mary Elizabeth Perry and Anne J. Cruz, 146–55. Berkeley: University of California Press, 1991.

———. "Sexuality and Repression in Counter-Reformation Spain." In *Sex and Love in Golden Age Spain*, edited by Alain Saint-Saëns, 81–94. New Orleans: University Press of the South, 1996.

Harding, Richard. *Amphibious Warfare in the Eighteenth Century: The British Expedition to the West Indies, 1740–1742*. Suffolk: Boydell Press, 1991.

Haring, Clarence. *The Buccaneers in the West Indies in the XVII Century*. New York: Dutton, 1910.

Haslip-Viera, Gabriel. *Crime and Punishment in Late Colonial Mexico City, 1691–1810*. Albuquerque: University of New Mexico Press, 1990.

Hazard, Benjamin James. "'A New Company of Crusaders Like That of St. John Capstran': Interaction Between Irish Military Units and Franciscan Chaplains, 1579–1654." In *Extranjeros en el Ejercito: Militares irlandeses en la sociedad Española, 1580–1818*, edited by Enrique García Hernán and Óscar Recio Morales, 181–97. Madrid: Ministerio de Defensa, 2007.

Helg, Aline. "A Fragmented Majority: Free 'Of All Colors,' Indians and Slaves in Caribbean Colombia During the Haitian Revolution." In *The Impact of the Haitian Revolution in the Atlantic World*, edited by David P. Geggus, 157–75. Columbia: University of South Carolina Press, 2001.

———. "The Limits of Equality: Free People of Color and Slaves during the First Independence of Cartagena, Colombia (1810–15)." *Slavery and Abolition* 20 (1999): 1–30.

Henao, Jesús Mará, and Geraldo Arrubla. *History of Colombia*. Translated and edited by J. Fred Rippy. Chapel Hill: University of North Carolina Press, 1938.

Henningsen, Gustav. *The Salazar Documents: Inquisitor Alonso De Salazar Frías and Others on the Basque Witch Persecution*. Leiden: Brill, 2004.

Henningsen, Gustav, and Bengt Ankarloo, eds. *Early Modern European Witchcraft, Centres and Peripheries*. Oxford: Oxford University Press, 1990.

Hernández Blázquez, Benjamín. "Piratas y corsarios en Cartagena de Indias." *Historia y Vida* Año XXIX, no. 337 (1996): 36–45.

Herráez S. de Escariche, Julia. *Don Juan Zapata de Mendoza, gobernador de Cartagena*. Seville: Escuela de Estudios Hispano-Americanos de la Universidad de Sevilla, 1946.

Herrera Ángel, Martha. *Poder Local, Población y Ordenamiento Territorial en La Nueva Granada, Siglo XVIII*. Bogota: Archivo General de la Nación, 1996.

Herrera, Carlos. "Infidelity and the Presidio Captain: Adultery and Honor in the Lives of María Rosa Tato Y Anza and José Antonio Vildósola, Sonora, New Spain, 1769–1783." *Journal of the History of Sexuality* 15, no. 2 (2006): 204–27.

Herzog, Tamar. *La administración como un fenómeno social: La justicia penal de la ciudad de Quito (1650–1750)*. Madrid: Centro de Estudios Constitucionales, 1995.

———. *Upholding Justice: Society, State, and the Penal System in Quito (1650–1750)*. Ann Arbor: University of Michigan Press, 2004.

Higgins, Kathleen J. *"Licentious Liberty" in a Brazilian Gold-Mining Region: Slavery, Gender, and Social Control in Eighteenth-Century Sabará, Minas Gerais*. University Park: Penn State University Press, 1999.

Hordes, Stanley M. *To the End of the Earth: A History of the Crypto-Jews of New Mexico.* New York: Columbia University Press, 2005.

Howes, David, ed. *Cross-Cultural Consumption: Global Markets, Local Realities.* London: Routledge, 1996.

Hume, Martin Andrew Sharp. *The Court of Philip IV: Spain in Decadence.* New York: Eveleigh Nash, 1907.

Jaffary, Nora. *False Mystics: Deviant Orthodoxy in Colonial Mexico.* Lincoln: University of Nebraska Press, 2004.

Jaffe, Catherine M., and Elizabeth Franklin Lewis, eds. *Eve's Enlightenment: Women's Experience in Spain and Spanish America, 1726–1839.* Baton Rouge: Louisiana State University Press, 2009.

Jaramillo de Zuleta, Pilar. "Las *arrepentidas.*" In *Placer, dinero, y pecado: historia de la prostitución en Colombia,* edited by Aída Martínez and Pablo Rodríguez. Bogota: Aguilar, 2002.

Jaramillo Uribe, Jaime. *Ensayos de historia social colombiana.* Bogota: Universidad Nacional de Colombia, 1968.

———. "Esclavos y Señores en la sociedad colombiana del siglo XVII." *Anuario Colombiano de Historia Social y Cultural* I (Bogota, 1963).

Johnson, Lyman L., ed. *The Problem of Order in Changing Societies: Essays on Crime and Policing in Argentina and Uruguay, 1750–1940.* Albuquerque: University of New Mexico Press, 1990.

Johnson, Lyman L., and Sonya Lipsett-Rivera, eds. *The Faces of Honor: Sex, Shame, and Violence in Colonial Latin America.* Albuquerque: University of New Mexico Press, 1998.

Juan, Jorge, and Antonio Ulloa. *Noticias secretas de America.* London: Taylor, 1826.

———. *A Voyage to South America.* Vol. 1. Translated by John Adams. London: Stockdale, 1806.

Kany, Charles Emil. *American-Spanish Euphemisms.* Berkeley: University of California Press, 1960.

Karras, Ruth. *Common Women: Prostitution and Sexuality in Medieval England.* Oxford: Oxford University Press, 1998.

Kidd, Colin. *British Identities Before Nationalism: Ethnicity and Nationhood in the Atlantic World, 1600–1800.* Cambridge: Cambridge University Press, 1999.

King, James. "Slavery in New Granada." In *Greater America: Essays in Honor of Herbert Eugene Bolton,* edited by Adele Ogden and Engel Sluiter, 295–318. Berkeley: University of California Press, 1945.

Knowles, Sir Charles. *An Account of the Expedition to Carthagena, With Explanatory Notes and Observations.* London: M. Cooper, 1743.

Kuethe, Allan James. *Military Reform and Society in New Granada 1773–1808.* Gainesville: University Press Florida, 1978.

Lamet, Pedro Miguel. *Un Cristiano Protesta: Pedro Claver (1580–1654).* Barcelona: Biblograf, 1980.

Landers, Jane. "The African Landscape of Seventeenth-Century Cartagena and its Hinterlands." In *The Black Urban Atlantic in the Age of the Slave Trade*, edited by Jorge Cañizares-Esguerra, James Sidbury, and Matt D. Childs. Philadelphia: University of Pennsylvania Press, 2013.

———. "*Cimarrón* Ethnicity in the Caribbean." In *Identity in the Shadow of Slavery*, edited by Paul Lovejoy, 30–54. London: Continuum, 2000.

Lane, Kris. "Corsarios, piratas y la defensa de Cartagena de Indias en el siglo XVI." In *Cartagena de Indias en el siglo XVI*, edited by Haroldo Calvo Stevenson and Adolfo Meisel Roca, 3–28. Cartagena: Banco de la República, 2006.

———. *Pillaging the Empire: Piracy in the Americas, 1500–1750*. New York: M.E. Sharpe, 1998.

Lanz, Eukene Larkara. "Changing Boundaries of Licit and Illicit Unions: Concubinage and Prostitution." In *Marriage and Sexuality in Medieval and Early Modern Iberia*, edited by Eukene Larkara Lanz, 158–94. New York: Routledge, 2002.

———, ed. *Marriage and Sexuality in Medieval and Early Modern Iberia*. New York: Routledge, 2002.

Lasso, Marixa. "Haiti as an Image of Popular Republicanism in Caribbean Colombia." In *The Impact of the Haitian Revolution in the Atlantic World*, edited by David P. Geggus, 176–90. Columbia: University of South Carolina Press, 2001.

Laures, John, S. J. *The Friend of the Colored Man, with an Afterword on the Race Problem in the United States*. Brooklyn: International Catholic Truth Society, 1928.

Lavrin, Asunción. "Sexuality in Colonial Mexico: A Church Dilemma." In *Sexuality and Marriage in Colonial Latin America*, edited by Asunción Lavrin, 47–95. Lincoln: University of Nebraska Press, 1992.

———, ed. *Sexuality and Marriage in Colonial Latin America*. Lincoln: University of Nebraska Press, 1992.

Lea, Henry Charles. *The Inquisition in The Spanish Dependencies*. New York: Macmillan Company, 1922.

Lee, Sidney, ed. *Dictionary of National Biography*. 63 vols. London: Smith & Elder, 1895.

Lemaitre, Eduardo. *Breve Historia de Cartagena, 1501–1901*. Bogota: Ediciones del Banco de la República, 1979.

———. *A Brief History of Cartagena*. Translated by Dennis Lynch. Cartagena: Editora Bolívar, n.d.

Lemaitre Noero, María Clara. *Getsemaní: El Último Cono Donde Desembocan Los Vientos*. Cartagena: Instituto Distrital de Cultural, 2001.

Lemoine, Martina. "El Vestido Criollo en las Antillas Francesas (1848–1950)." *Anales del Museo de América* 14 (2006): 327–50.

Lemus, Gustavo Bell, ed. *Cartagena de Indias: de la colonia a la república*. Bogota: Fundación Simón y Lola Gubereck, 1991.

Lepore, Jill. "Historians Who Love Too Much: Reflections on Microhistory and Biography." *Journal of American History* 88, no. 1 (June 2001): 129–44.

Levine, Philippa. *Prostitution, Race, and Politics: Policing Venereal Disease in the British Empire*. New York: Routledge, 2003.

Levison, Julie H. "Beyond Quarantine: A History of Leprosy in Puerto Rico, 1898–1930s." *História, Ciências, Saúde; Manguinhos* 10, Supplement 1 (2003): 225–45.

Lewis, Laura A. *Hall of Mirrors: Power, Witchcraft, and Caste in Colonial Mexico.* Durham, NC: Duke University Press, 2003.

Lipsett-Rivera, Sonya. *Gender and the Negotiation of Daily Life in Mexico, 1750–1856.* Lincoln: University of Nebraska Press, 2012.

———. "Scandal at the Church: José de Alfaro Accuses doña Teresa Bravo and Others of Insulting and Beating his *Castiza* Wife, Josefa Cadena." In *Colonial Lives: Documents on Latin American History*, edited by Richard Boyer and Geoffrey Spurling, 216–33. Oxford: Oxford University Press, 2000.

———. "A Slap in the Face of Honor: Social Transgression and Women in Late-Colonial Mexico." *The Faces of Honor: Sex, Shame, and Violence in Colonial Latin America*, edited by Sonya Lipsett-Rivera and Lyman Johnson, 179–200. Albuquerque: University of New Mexico Press, 1998.

List, George. "Mambira en Cartagena." *Revista Colombiana de Antropología* (1966): 14, 267–76.

López Beltrán, Maria Teresa. *La Prostitución en el Reino de Granada a finales de la Edad Media.* Malaga: Diputación Provincial de Malaga, 2003.

López-Cordon Cortezo, María Victoria. "Women in Society in Eighteenth-Century Spain, Models of Sociability." In *Eve's Enlightenment: Women's Experience in Spain and Spanish America, 1726–1839*, edited by Catherine M. Jaffe and Elizabeth Franklin Lewis, 103–14. Baton Rouge: Louisiana State University Press, 2009.

Lovejoy, Paul, ed. *Identity in the Shadow of Slavery.* London: Continuum, 2000.

Lozano Armendares, Teresa. *La criminalidad en la ciudad de México, 1800–1821.* Mexico: Universidad Nacional Autónoma de México, Instituto de Investigaciones Históricas, 1987.

Lualdi, Katharine Jackson, and Anne T. Thayer, eds. *Penitence in the Age of Reformations.* Aldershot: Ashgate, 1999.

Lucena, Juan de and Alonso de Sandoval. *Historia de la vida del Padre Francisco Xavier y de lo que en la India Oriental hizieron los religiosos de la Compania de Jesús.* Seville: Francisco de Lyra, 1619.

Lunn, Arnold. *A Saint in the Slave Trade.* New York: Sheed and Ward, 1935.

Lux Martelo, Martha Elisa. *Las mujeres de Cartagena de Indias en el Siglo XVIII: Lo que hacían, les hacían y no hacían, y las curas que les prescribían.* Bogota: Universidad de los Andes, 2006.

Lyday, Leon. "History and Legend in 'El Virrey Solís' of Antonio Álvarez Lleras." *Hispania* (1969): 13–20.

Macinnes, Allan I. "Introduction: Connecting and Disconnecting with America." In *Shaping the Stuart World, 1603–1714; The Atlantic Connection*, edited by Allen Macinnes and Arthur H. Williamson, 1–32. Leiden: Brill, 2006.

Macinnes, Allen I., and Arthur H. Williamson, eds. *Shaping the Stuart World, 1603–1714; The Atlantic Connection.* Leiden: Brill, 2006.

Malavassi Aguilar, Ana Paulina. "Cotidianidad marginal: la lugubre y frugal vida al interior del lazareto general del estado de Costa Rica, 1833–1850." *Revista de Historia* 38 (July–December 1998): 143–65.

Mangan, Jane E. "A Market of Identities: Women, Trade, and Ethnic Labels in Colonial Potosí." In *Imperial Subjects: Race and Identity in Colonial Latin America*, edited by Andrew Fisher and Matthew O'Hara, 61–80. Durham, NC: Duke University Press, 2009.

———. *Trading Roles: Gender, Ethnicity, and the Urban Economy in Colonial Potosi.* Durham, NC: Duke University Press, 2005.

Mannarelli, María Emma. *Hechiceras, beatas y expósitas: mujeres y poder inquisitorial en Lima.* Lima: Ediciones del Congreso del Perú, 1998.

———. *Private Passions and Public Sins: Men and Women in Seventeenth-Century Lima.* Translated by Sidney Evans and Meredith D. Dodge. Albuquerque: University of New Mexico Press, 2007.

Manning, Roger B. *An Apprenticeship in Arms: The Origins of the British Army 1585–1702.* Oxford: Oxford University Press, 2006.

Mantilla R., Luis Carlos. *Los Franciscanos en Colombia.* 4 vols. Bogota: Nelly, 1984.

———. *Las Últimas Expediciones Franciscanas Al Nuevo Reino de Granada: Episodios de Criollismo Conventual o de Rivalidad Hispano-Criolla, 1756–1784.* Bogota: Kelly, 1995.

Marchena Fernández, Juan. *La Institución Militar en Cartagena de Indias en El Siglo XVIII.* Sevilla: Escuela de Estudios Hispano-Americanos, 1982.

———. "Sin temor de rey ni de dios. Violencia, corrupción y crisis de autoridad en la Cartagena colonial." In *Soldados del Rey: el ejército borbónico en América colonial en vísperas de la Independencia*, edited by Juan Marchena Fernández and Allan J. Kuenthe, 31–100. Castello de la Plana, Spain: Publicación de la Universidad Jaume I, 2005.

Marchena Fernández, Juan, and Allan J. Kuenthe, eds. *Soldados del Rey: el ejército borbónico en América colonial en vísperas de la Independencia.* Castello de la Plana, Spain: Publicación de la Universidad Jaume I, 2005.

Marchena Fernández, Juan, and María del Carmen Gómez Pérez. *La Vida de Guarnición en las Ciudades americanas de la Ilustración.* Madrid: Ministerio de Defensa, 1992.

Marco Dorta, Enrique. *Cartagena de Indias, la Ciudad y sus Monumentos.* Seville: Escuela de Estudios Hispanoamericanos, 1951.

———. *Cartagena de Indias: Puerto y plaza fuerte.* Cartagena: Amado, 1960.

Markoe, William M., S. J. *The Slave of the Negroes.* Chicago: Loyola University Press, 1920.

Martin, Dale B. *Slavery as Salvation: The Metaphor of Slavery in Pauline Christianity.* New Haven, CT: Yale, 1990.

Martínez, Aída, and Pablo Rodríguez. *Placer, dinero y pecado: historia de la prostitución en Colombia.* Bogotá: Aguilar, 2002.

Martínez Fajardo, E. *Cuentas y leyendas de Cartagena.* Cartagena: Mundo Nuevo, 1948.

Martínez, María Elena. "The Black Blood of New Spain: Limpieza De Sangre, Racial Violence, and Gendered Power in Early Colonial Mexico." *The William and Mary Quarterly* 61, no. 3 (2004): 479–520.

————. *Genealogical Fictions:* Limpieza de sangre, *Religion, and Gender in Colonial Mexico.* Stanford, CA: Stanford University Press, 2008.

Martínez Osorio, Eliana Margarita, and María Claudia del Pilar Méndez Muñoz. "Tejar de San Bernabé de los Jesuitas, Isla de Tierra Bomba, Una Propuesta de Rescate del Patrimonio." Trabajo de Grado, Fundación de Universidad de Bogota Jorge Tadeo Lozano, Facultad de Arquitectura, 1998.

Martínez Reyes, Gabriel, ed. *Cartas de Los Obispos de Cartagena de Indias Durante El Período Hispánico, 1534–1820.* Medellín: Editorial Zuluaga, 1986.

Martínez Valverde, Carlos. "La marinería en la defensa de Cartagena de Indias, en 1741." *Revista General de Marina* 191 (1976): 121–32.

Martín Gaite, Carmen. *Love Customs in Eighteenth-Century Spain.* Translated by Maria G. Tomsich. Berkeley: University of California Press, 1991.

Matta, Enrique de la. *El asalto de Pointis a Cartagena de Indias.* Seville: Escuela de Estudios Hispano-Americanos de Sevilla, 1979.

Maya, Adriana. "Paula de Eguiluz y el arte de bien querer: apuntes para el estudio de la sensualidad y del cimarronaje femenino en el Caribe, siglo XVII." *Historia Critica* 24 (2003): 1–23.

McCormack, Brian. "Conjugal Violence, Sex, Sin, and Murder in the Mission Communities of Alta California." *Journal of the History of Sexuality* 16, no. 3 (2007): 391–415.

McFarlane, Anthony. "*Cimarrones* and *palenques*: Runaways and Resistance in Colonial Colombia." *Slavery and Abolition* 6 (1985): 131–51.

————. *Colombia before Independence: Economy, Society, and Politics under Bourbon Rule.* Cambridge: Cambridge University Press, 1993.

McKnight, Kathryn Joy. "'En su tierra lo aprendió': An African *Curandero's* Defense before the Cartagena Inquisition." *Colonial Latin American Review* 12, no. 1 (2003): 63–84.

McKnight, Kathryn Joy, and Leo Garofalo, eds. *Afro-Latino Voices: Narratives from the Early Modern Ibero-Atlantic World, 1550–1812.* Indianapolis, IN: Hackett, 2009.

Medina, José Toribio. *Historia del tribunal del Santo Oficio de la Inquisición de Cartagena de las Indias.* Santiago de Chile: Imprenta Elzeviriana, 1899.

————. *La imprenta de Cartagena de Indias.* Santiago: Elzeviriano, 1904.

————. *La Inquisición en Cartagena de Indias.* Bogota: Valencia Editores, 1978.

Meisel Roca, Adolfo. "Esclavitud, mestizaje, y haciendas en la Provincia de Cartagena, 1533–1810." *Desarrollo y Sociedad* 4 (July 1980): 237.

————, ed. *Historia económica y social del Caribe Colombiano.* Bogota: Ediciones Uninorte, Ecoe Ediciones, 1994.

Meisel Roca, Adolpho, and María Aguilera Díaz. "Cartagena de Indias en 1777: Un análisis demográfico." *Boletín cultural y bibliográfico* 34, no. 45 (1997): 21–57.

————. *Tres siglos de la historia demográfica de Cartagena de Indias.* Cartagena: Banco de la República, 2009.

Mercado, Pedro de, S. J. *Historia de la Provincia del Nuevo Reino y Quito de la Compania de Jesús.* Bogota: Empresa Nacional de Publicaciones, 1957.

Mesa, Carlos E. "Debates concepcionistas en Santa Fe de Bogotá." *Bolívar* 44 (October 1955): 758–88.

Mogollón, José Vicente, Rodolfo Segovia Salas, and Anthony McFarlane. "Mesa Redonda: El sitio de Vernon de 1741." In *Cartagena de Indias en el siglo XVIII*, edited by Haroldo Calvo Stevenson and Adolfo Meisel Roca, 451–74. Cartagena: Banco de la República, 2005.

Monsieur de Pointis to Cartagena being a particular relation of the taking and plundering of that city, by the French, in the year 1697 English'd from the original publish'd at Paris by Monseiur de Pointis himself. And illustrated with a large draught of the City of Cartagena, its harbour and forts. London: S. Crouch, 1699.

Mora de Tovar, Gilma Lucía. *Aguardiente y Conflictos Sociales en La Nueva Granada Durante El Siglo XVIII.* Bogota: Universidad Nacional de Colombia, Centro Editorial, 1988.

Morgan, Ronald J. "Jesuit confessors, African slaves and the practice of confession in seventeenth-century Cartagena." In *Penitence in the Age of Reformations*, edited by Katharine Jackson Lualdi and Anne T. Thayer, 222–39. Aldershot: Ashgate, 1999.

Morillo, José. *Muros invictos, glorificación literaria de Cartagena.* Cartagena: Editorial Bolívar, 1947.

Mörner, Magnus, ed. *The Expulsion of the Jesuits from Latin America.* New York: Knopf, 1965.

Morse, Robert. "Trends and Issues in Latin American Urban Research, 1965–1971." *Latin American Research Review* 6, no. 1 (1971): 3–52.

Muchembled, Robert. "Satanic Myths and Cultural Reality." In *Early Modern European Witchcraft: Centres and Peripheries*, edited by Gusá Henningsen and Bengt Ankarloo, 139–60. Oxford: Clarendon Press, 1990.

Múnera, Alfonso. *El Fracaso de La Nación: Región, Clase y Raza en El Caribe Colombiano (1717–1821).* Bogota: Banco de la República, El Ancora Editores, 1998.

Muriel, Josefina. *Los Recogimientos de mujeres: respuesta a una problemática social novohispana.* México: Universidad nacional autónoma de México, Instituto de investigaciones históricas, 1974.

Murray Cestero, Walter S. "Lepra, exilio ritual y confinamiento en *La historia de la locura en la época clásica* de Michel Foucault." *Homines* 11, no. 1–2 (March 1987–February 1988): 361–68.

Murray, Jacqueline. "Introduction." In *Desire and Discipline: Sex and Sexuality in the Premodern West*, edited by Jacqueline Murray and Konrad Eisenbicher, ix–xxv. Toronto: University of Toronto Press, 1996.

Murray, Jacqueline, and Konrad Eisenbicher, eds. *Desire and Discipline: Sex and Sexuality in the Premodern West.* Toronto: University of Toronto Press, 1996.

Navarrete, María Cristina. "Cotidianidad y cultura material de los negros de Cartagena en el siglo XVII." *América Negra* 7 (1994): 65–79.

———. *Génesis y Desarrollo de la Esclavitud en Colombia, siglos XVI y XVII.* Cali, Colombia: Universidad del Valle, 2005.

——. *Historia Social del Negro en La Colonia: Cartagena, Siglo XVII*. Santiago de Cali: Universidad del Valle, 1995.

——. *Prácticas religiosas de los negros en la Colonia, Cartagena Siglo XVII*. Santiago de Cali: Universidad del Valle, 1995.

Nesvig, Martin. *Ideology and Inquisition: The World of the Censors in Early Mexico*. New Haven, CT: Yale University Press, 2009.

Nowell, Charles E. "The Defense of Cartagena." *Hispanic American Historical Review* 42 (November 1962): 477–501.

Nye, Mary Jo. "Scientific Biography: History of Science by Another Means?" *Isis* 97, no. 2 (June 2006): 322–29.

Nye, Robert A. *Masculinity and Male Codes of Honor in Modern France*. New York: Oxford University Press, 1993.

——, ed. *Sexuality*. Oxford: Oxford University Press, 1999.

Obregón Torres, Diana. "De 'árbol maldito' a 'enfermedad curable': los médicos y la construcción de la lepra en Colombia, 1884–1939." In *Salud, cultura y sociedad en América Latina*, edited by Jairo Solano Alonso, 159–178. Lima: Instituto de Estudios Peruanos, 1996.

——. *Batallas contra la lepra: estado, medicina y ciencia en Colombia*. Medellín: Banco de la República, Fondo Editorial Universidad EAFIT, 2002.

——. "Medicalización de la lepra: una estrategia nacional." *Anuario Colombiano de Historia Social y de la Cultura* 24 (1997): 139–65.

Oddi, Longaro degli. *Vita Di Sánto Pietro Claver della Compagnia Di Gesu Apostolo Dei Negri*. Roma: Armanni, 1888.

Ogden, Adele, and Engel Sluiter, eds. *Greater America: Essays in Honor of Herbert Eugene Bolton*. Berkeley: University of California Press, 1945.

Ogelsby, J. C. M. "England vs. Spain in America, 1739–1748: The Spanish Side of the Hill." *Historical Papers* 5, no. 1 (1970): 147–57.

——. "Spain's Havana Squadron and the Preservation of the Balance of Power in the Caribbean, 1740–1748." *Hispanic American Historical Review* 49, 3 (August 1969): 473–88.

Ohlmeyer, Jane. "Military Migration and the Stuart Kingdoms." In *Extranjeros en el Ejercito: Militares irlandeses en la sociedad Española, 1580–1818*, edited by Enrique García Hernán and Óscar Recio Morales, 65–85. Madrid: Ministerio de Defensa, 2007.

Olsen, Margaret M. *Slavery and Salvation in Colonial Cartagena de Indias*. Gainesville: University Press of Florida, 2004.

Ortega Lázaro, Luis, O. H. *Para la Historia de la Orden Hospitalaria de San Juan de Dios en Hispanoamérica y Filipinas*. Madrid: Hermanos de San Juan de Dios, 1992.

Ortega Noriega, Sergio. *De la santidad a la perversión: o de porqué no se cumplía la ley de Dios en la sociedad novohispana*. México: Grijalbo, 1986.

Ortega Ricaurte, Carmen. *Negros, Mulatos y Zambos en Santafé de Bogotá: Sucesos, Personajes y Anécdotas*. Bogota: Academia Colombiana de Historia, 2002.

Ortega Torres, José J. *La obra salesiana en los lazaretos*. Bogota: Escuelas Gráficas Salesianas, 1938.

Pacheco, Juan Manuel, S. J. *Los Jesuitas en Colombia*. 3 vols. Bogota: Editorial San Juan Eudes, 1962.

Palacios de la Vega, Joseph. *Diario del Viaje del P. Joseph Palacios de la Vega entre los indios y negros de la provincia de Cartagena en el Nuevo reino de Granada, 1787–1788*. Edited by Gerardo Reichel Dolmatoff. Bogota: Editorial ABC, 1955.

Palacios Preciado, Jorge. *La Trata de negros por Cartagena de Indias*. Tunja: Universidad Pedagógica y Tecnológica, 1973.

Parker, Alexander A. *The Philosophy of Love in Spanish Literature, 1480–1680*. Edinburgh: Edinburgh University Press, 1985.

Parker, Geoffrey. *The Army of Flanders and the Spanish Road, 1567–1659*. Cambridge: Cambridge University Press, 2004.

Partner, Nancy F. "Did Mystics Have Sex?" In *Desire and Discipline: Sex and Sexuality in the Premodern West*, edited by Jaqueline Murray and Konrad Eisenbichler, 296–313. Toronto: University of Toronto Press, 1996.

Pastor, Lince Restrepo. *Genealogías de Cartagena*. Bogota: Instituto Colombiano de Cultura Hispánica, 1993.

Penyak, Lee and Veronica Vallejo. "Expectations of Love in Troubled Mexican Marriages during the Late Colonial and Early National Periods." *The Historian* 65, no. 3 (2003): 563–86.

Perceval-Maxwell, M. *The Outbreak of the Irish Rebellion of 1641*. Montreal: McGill-Queen's University Press, 1994.

Perez Tostado, Igor. *Irish Influence at the Court of Spain in the Seventeenth Century*. Dublin: Four Courts Press, 2008.

———. "La llegada de irlandeses a la frontera caribeña hispana en el siglo XVII." In *Extranjeros en el Ejercito: Militares irlandeses en la sociedad Española, 1580–1818*, edited by Enrique García Hernán and Óscar Recio Morales, 298–312. Madrid: Ministerio de Defensa, 2007.

Perry, Mary Elizabeth. *Gender and Disorder in Early Modern Seville*. Princeton, NJ: Princeton University Press, 1981.

Perry, Mary Elizabeth, and Anne J. Cruz, eds. *Cultural Encounters: The Impact of the Inquisition in Spain and the New World*. Berkeley: University of California Press, 1991.

Pestana, Carla Gardina. *The English Atlantic in an Age of Revolution, 1640–1661*. Cambridge, MA: Harvard University Press, 2004.

Phelan, John Leddy. *The Kingdom of Three Quitos*. Madison: University of Wisconsin Press, 1967.

———. *The People and the King: The Comunero Revolution in Colombia, 1781*. Madison: University of Wisconsin Press, 1978.

Piccato, Pablo. *City of Suspects: Crime in Mexico City, 1900–1931*. Durham, NC: Duke University Press, 2001.

Pike, Ruth. *Penal Servitude in Early Modern Spain*. Madison: University of Wisconsin Press, 1983.

Pita Pico, Roger. "Aventuras y desventuras de extranjeros en las provincias de Cartagena y Santa María durante el periodo colonial." *Aguaita* 15–16 (December 2006–June 2007): 16–26.

Picón-Salas, Mariano. *Pedro Claver, El Santo de los Esclavos*. México: Fondo de Cultura Económica, 1950.

Pointis, Jean-Bernard-Louis Desjean, baron de. *Monsieur de Pointi's Expedition To Cartagena*. London: Crouch, Mount, and Feltham, 1699.

Porras Troconis, Gabriel. *Cartagena hispánica*. Bogota: Biblioteca de Autores Colombianos, Editorial Cosmos, 1954.

——. *Historia de la cultura en el Nuevo Reino de Granada*. Seville: Escuela de Estudios Hispano-Americanos, 1952.

Posada, E., and P.M. Ibáñez, comps. *Relaciones de mando: memorias presentadas por los gobernantes de Nuevo Reino de Granada*. Bogota: Imprenta Nacional, 1910.

Poska, Allyson M. *Women and Authority in Early Modern Spain: The Peasants of Galicia*. Oxford: Oxford University Press, 2005.

Powers, Karen Vieira. "Conquering Discourses of 'Sexual Conquest': Of Women, Language and *Mestizaje*." *Colonial Latin American Review* 11, no. 1 (2002): 7–32.

——. *Women in the Crucible of Conquest: The Gendered Genesis of Spanish American Society, 1500–1600*. Albuquerque: University of New Mexico Press, 2005.

Proceso de beatificación y canonización de San Pedro Claver. Translated by Anna María Splendiani and Tulio Aristizábal. Bogota: Pontificia Universidad Javieriana, 2002.

Procter, John, O. P. *St. Peter Claver of the Society of Jesus: "The Apostle of the Negroes."* London: Burns and Oates, 1888.

Proctor, Frank T. *"Damned Notions of Liberty": Slavery, Culture, and Power in Colonial Mexico, 1640–1769*. Albuquerque: University of New Mexico Press, 2010.

Quevedo, Emilio V. *La Ilustración y la enseñanza de la medicina en el Nuevo Reino de Granada*. Madrid: CSIC, 1985.

Rama, C. M. *Los afro-uruguayos*. Montevideo: Siglo Illustrado, 1969.

Ramsey, Russell W. "The Defeat of Admiral Vernon at Cartagena in 1741." *Southern Quarterly* 1 (July 1963): 332–55.

Recio Morales, Óscar. *España y la pérdida del Ulster: Irlanda en la estrategia de la Monarquía hispánica (1602–1649)*. Madrid: Ediciones del Laberinto, 2003.

Redondo Gómez, Maruja. *Cartagena de Indias: Cinco siglos de evolución urbanística*. Bogota: Fundación Universidad de Bogota Jorge Tadeo Lozano, 2004.

Restrepo, Luz Adriana Maya. *Brujería y reconstrucción de identidades entre los Africanos en la Nueva Granada, Siglo XVII*. Bogota: Ministerio de Cultura, 2005.

Retegui Bensusan, Mariano de. *Viaje de Cádiz a Cartagena de Indias de José Celestino Mutis y Bosio: 7 de Septiembre/29 de Octubre de 1760*. Cádiz: Jiménez-Mena, D. L., 1978.

Rey Fajardo, José del. *Los Jesuitas en Cartagena de Indias, 1604–1767*. Bogota: Centro Editorial Javierano, 2004.

Richardson, Catherine, ed. *Clothing Culture, 1350–1650*. Hampshire: Aldershot, 2004.

Rivas, Christine. "The Spanish Colonial Military: Santo Domingo 1701–1779." *The Americas* 60, 2 (October 2003): 249–72.

Robinson, James Alexander. "The English Attack on Cartagena in 1741." *The Hispanic American Historical Review* 2, no. 1 (February 1919): 62–71.

Roces, Mina and Louise Edwards, eds. *The Politics of Dress in Asia and the Americas*. Portland, OR: Sussex Academic Press, 2007.

Rodríguez, Pablo. "Las mancebías españoles." In *Placer, dinero y pecado historia de la prostitución en Colombia*, edited by Aída Martínez and Pablo Rodríguez, 23–66. Bogota: Aguilar, 2002.

Rodríguez-Bobb, Arturo. *Exclusión e Integración del Sujeto Negro en Cartagena de Indias en Perspectiva Histórica*. Madrid: Iberoamericana, 2002.

Rodríguez Freile, Juan. *The Conquest of New Granda*. Translated by William C. Atkinson. London: Folio Society, 1961.

Rodríguez Jiménez, Pablo. "Composición y estructura de las familias neogranadinas, Siglo XVIII." In *Inquisición, Muerte y Sexualidad en la Nueva Granada*, edited by Jaime Humberto Borja Gómez, 199–241. Bogota: Editorial Ariel-Ceja, 1995.

———. *Seducción, amancebamiento y abandono en la Colonia*. Bogota: Fundación Simón y Lola Guberek, 1991.

———. *Sentimientos y vida familiar en el Nuevo Reino de Granada, Siglo XVIII*. Bogota: Editorial Ariel, 1997.

———. "Servidumbre sexual: La prostitución en los siglos XV–XVIII." In *Placer, dinero y pecado historia de la prostitución en Colombia*, edited by Aída Martínez and Pablo Rodríguez, 67–88. Bogota: Aguilar, 2002.

Rodríguez Plata, Horacio. "Origen de la lepra en la antigua provincia del Socorro." *Boletín de Historia y Antigüedades* 74, no 759 (October–December 1987): 751–54.

Roncancio Parra, Andrés. *Índices de Documentos de La Inquisición de Cartagena de Indias*. Bogota: Instituto Colombiano de Cultura Hispánica, 2000.

Roos, Ann. *Peter Claver: Saint Among Slaves*. New York: Vision Books, 1965.

Roper, Lyndal. *Witch Craze Terror and Fantasy in Baroque Europe*. New Haven, CT: Yale University Press, 2004.

Rosenwein, Barbara H., ed. *Anger's Past: The Social Uses of an Emotion in the Middle Ages*. Ithaca, NY: Cornell University Press, 1998.

———. "Controlling Paradigms." In *Anger's Past: The Social Uses of an Emotion in the Middle Ages*, edited by Barbara Rosenwein, 233–47. Ithaca, NY: Cornell University Press, 1998.

———. *Emotional Communities in the Early Middle Ages*. Ithaca, NY: Cornell University Press, 2006.

Rowland, Robert. "'Fantasticall and Devilishe Persons': European Witch Beliefs in a Comparative Perspective." In *Early Modern European Witchcraft: Centres and Peripheries*, edited by Bengt Ankarloo and Gustav Henningsen, 161–90. Oxford: Clarendon Press, 1989.

Ruggiero, Guido. *The Boundaries of Eros: Sex Crime and Sexuality in Renaissance Venice*. Oxford: Oxford University Press, 1985.

Safford, Frank, and Marco Palacios. *Colombia: Fragmented Land, Divided Society*. New York: Oxford University Press, 2002.

Saint-Saëns, Alain. "'It is not a Sin!': Making Love According to the Spaniards in Early Modern Spain." In *Sex and Love in Golden Age Spain*, edited by Alain Saint-Saëns, 11–26. New Orleans: University Press of the South, 1996.

———, ed. *Sex and Love in Golden Age Spain*. New Orleans: University Press of the South, 1996.

Saint-Saëns, Alain, and Maria Jose Delgado, eds. *Lesbianism and Homosexuality in Early Modern Spain: Literature and Theater in Context*. New Orleans: University Press of the South, 2000.

Salcedo Salcedo, Juan. *Urbanismo hispano-americano, Siglos XVI, XVII y XVIII*. Bogota: CEJA, 1998.

Salvatore, Ricardo, Carlos Aguirre, and Gil Joseph, eds. *Crime and Punishment in Latin America: Law and Society Since Late Colonial Times*. Durham, NC: Duke University Press, 2001.

Sánchez, Ana. *Amancebados, hechiceros y rebeldes: Chancay, siglo XVII*. Cusco, Perú: Centro de Estudios Regionales Andinos Bartolomé de las Casas, 1991.

Sánchez Ortega, María Elena. "Sorcery and Eroticism in Love Magic." In *Cultural Encounters: The Impact of the Inquisition in Spain and the New World*, edited by Mary Elizabeth Perry and Anne J. Cruz, 58–92. Berkeley: University of California Press, 1991.

Sandoval, Alonso de. *De Instauranda Aethiopum Salute; El Mundo de La Esclavitud Negra en América*. Bogota: Empresa Nacional de Publicaciones, 1956.

———. *Treatise on Slavery*. Translated and edited by Nicole von Germeten. Indianapolis, IN: Hackett, 2008.

Santa Gertrudis, Fray Juan de. *Maravillas de la Naturaleza*. Bogota: Biblioteca de la Presidenciade Colombia, 1956.

Sauer, Carl. *The Early Spanish Main*. Berkeley: University of California Press, 1969.

Schorsch, Jonathan. *Swimming the Christian Atlantic: Judeoconversos, Afroiberians and Amerindians in the Seventeenth Century*. Leiden: Brill, 2009.

Schwartz, Stewart. *All Can Be Saved: Religious Tolerance and Salvation in the Iberian Atlantic World*. New Haven, CT: Yale University Press, 2009.

Seed, Patricia. *To Love, Honor, and Obey in Colonial Mexico: Conflicts Over Marriage Choice, 1574–1821*. Stanford, CA: Stanford University Press, 1988.

Segovia Salas, Rodolfo. *The Fortifications Of Cartagena de Indias: Strategy And History*. Bogota: Carlos Valencia, 1982.

Sennet, Richard. *The Fall of Public Man*. New York: Vintage Books, 1977.

Serrano y Sanz, Manuel, ed. *Cedulario de las provincias de Santa Marta y Cartagena de Indias: (siglo XVI)*. Madrid: Librería General de Victoriano Suárez, 1913.

Sevilla Casas, Elías. *Los mutilados del oprobio: estudio sobre la lepra en una region endémica de Colombia*. Bogota: Colcultura, 1995.

Sharp, William Frederick. *Slavery on the Spanish Frontier: The Colombian Chocó, 1680–1810*. Norman: University of Oklahoma Press, 1976.

Shumway, Jeffrey M. *The Case of the Ugly Suitor and Other Histories of Love, Gender, and Nation in Buenos Aires, 1776–1870*. Lincoln: University of Nebraska Press, 2005.

Sigal, Peter Herman. *Infamous Desire: Male Homosexuality in Colonial Latin America*. Chicago: University of Chicago Press, 2003.

Silverblatt, Irene Marsha. *Moon, Sun, and Witches: Gender Ideologies and Class in Inca and Colonial Peru*. Princeton, NJ: Princeton University Press, 1987.

Simposio de Historia de las Mentalidades. *Familia y poder en Nueva España: memoria del Tercer Simposio de Historia de las Mentalidades*. Mexico, D.F.: Instituto Nacional de Antropología e Historia, 1991.

———. *Familia y sexualidad en Nueva España: Familia, matrimonio y sexualidad en Nueva España*. Mexico: Fondo de Cultura Económica, 1982.

Simposio sobre Bibliografía del Negro en Colombia. *El Negro en La Historia de Colombia: Fuentes Escritas y Orales*. Bogota: Fondo Interamericano de Publicaciones de la Cultura Negra de las Américas-UNESCO-F.C.I.F., 1983.

Slattery, John R. *The Life of Saint Peter Claver, the Apostle of the Negroes*. Philadelphia: H.L. Kilner, 1893.

Sloan, Kathryn A. *Runaway Daughters: Seduction, Elopment, and Honor in Nineteenth-Century Mexico*. Albuquerque: University of New Mexico Press, 2008.

Socolow, Susan Migden. "Acceptable Partners: Marriage Choice in Colonial Argentina, 1778–1810." In *Sexuality and Marriage in Colonial Latin America*, edited by Asunción Lavrin, 209–51. Lincoln: University of Nebraska Press, 1992.

———. *The Women of Colonial Latin America*. Cambridge: Cambridge University Press, 2000.

Solano Alonso, Jairo, ed. *Salud, Cultura y Sociedad: Cartagena de Indias, Siglos XVI y XVII*. Barranquilla: Universidad del Atlántico, 1998.

Soriano Llera, Andrés. *La medicina en el Nuevo Reino de Granada durante la conquista y la colonia*. Bogota: Imprenta Nacional, 1966.

Soto Aparicio, Fernando. *Camino que anda*. Bogota: Plaza y Janés Editores, 1980.

Splendiani, Anna María, José Enrique Sánchez Bohórquez, and Emma Cecilia Luque de Salazar, eds. *Cincuenta Años de Inquisición en El Tribunal de Cartagena de Indias, 1610–1660*. 4 vols. Bogota: Centro Editorial Javierano, 1997.

Stephens, Walter. *Demon Lovers: Witchcraft, Sex, and the Crisis of Belief*. Chicago: University of Chicago Press, 2002.

Stern, Steve J. *The Secret History of Gender: Women, Men, and Power in Late Colonial Mexico*. Chapel Hill: University of North Carolina Press, 1995.

Stoll, Anita, and Dawn L. Smith, eds. *Gender, Identity, and Representation in Spain's Golden Age*. Cranbury, NJ: Bucknell University Press, 2000.

Storey, Tessa. *Carnal Commerce in Counter-Reformation Rome*. Cambridge: Cambridge University Press, 2008.

———. "Clothing Courtesans: Fabrics, Signals, and Experiences." In *Clothing Culture, 1350–1650*, edited by Catherine Richardson, 95–107. Hampshire: Aldershot, 2004.

———. "Fragments from the 'Life Stories' of Jewelry Belonging to Prostitutes in Early Modern Rome." *Renaissance Studies* 19, no. 5: 648–57.

Streicker, Joel. "Policing Boundaries: Race, class and gender in Cartagena, Colombia." *American Ethnologist* 22, no. 1 (1995): 54–74.

———. "Rethinking Race, Class and Region in a Tourist Town." *Identities* 3, no. 4 (1997): 523–55.

Tausiet, Maria. *Abracadabra omnipotens: magia urbana en Zaragoza en la Edad Moderna*. Madrid: Siglo XXI de España Editores, 2007.

Tavárez, David. *The Invisible War: Indigenous Devotions, Discipline, and Dissent in Colonial Mexico*. Stanford, CA: Stanford University Press, 2011.

———. "Legally Indian: Inquisitorial Readings of Indigenous Identity in New Spain." In *Imperial Subjects: Race and Identity in Colonial Latin America*, edited by Andrew Fisher and Matthew O'Hara, 81–100. Durham, NC: Duke University Press, 2009.

Taylor, Scott K. *Honor and Violence in Golden Age Spain*. New Haven, CT: Yale University Press, 2008.

Taylor, William B. *Drinking, Homicide, and Rebellion in Colonial Mexican Villages*. Stanford, CA: Stanford University Press, 1979.

Tedeschi, John. "Inquisitorial Law and the Witch." In *Early Modern European Witchcraft: Centres and Peripheries*, edited by Gustav Henningsen and Bengt Ankarloo, 83–119. Oxford: Clarendon Press, 1990.

Tejado Fernández, Manuel. *Aspectos de la vida social en Cartagena de Indias durante el seiscientos*. Seville: Escuela de Estudios Hispano-americanos, 1954.

Terraciano, Kevin. "Crime and Culture in Colonial Mexico: The Case of the Mixtec Murder Note." *Ethnohistory* 45, no. 4 (Fall 1998): 709–45.

Terrall, Mary. "Biography as Cultural History of Science," *Isis* 97, no. 2 (June 2006): 306–13.

Toplin, Robert Brent, ed. *Slavery and Race Relations in Latin America*. Westport, CT: Greenwood Press, 1974.

Tortorici, Zeb. "'Heran Todos Putos': Sodomitical Subcultures and Disordered Desire in Early Colonial Mexico." *Ethnohistory* 54, no. 1 (2007): 35–67.

Tovar Pinzón, Hermes. *La batalla de los sentidos: infidelidad, adulterio y concubinato a fines de la colonia*. Bogotá: Ediciones Fondo Cultural Cafetero, 2004.

Trexler, Richard C. *Sex and Conquest: Gendered Violence, Political Order, and the European Conquest of the Americas*. Ithaca, NY: Cornell University Press, 1995.

Twinam, Ann. *Merchants and Farmers in Colonial Colombia*. Austin: University of Texas Press, 1982.

———. "The Negotiation of Honor." In *The Faces of Honor: Sex, Shame, and Violence in Colonial Latin America*, edited by Lyman Johnson and Sonya Lipsett-Rivera, 68–102. Albuquerque: University of New Mexico Press, 1998.

———. *Public Lives, Private Secrets: Gender, Honor, Sexuality, and Illegitimacy in Colonial Spanish America*. Stanford, CA: Stanford University Press, 1999.

Urueta, José. *Documentos para la historia de Cartagena*. 6 vols. Cartagena: Tipografía Araujel, 1887–1891.

Valbuena, Olga Lucia. "Sorceresses, Love Magic, and the Inquisition of Linguistic Sorcery in *Celestina.*" *Publications of the Modern Language Association of America* 109, no. 2 (1994): 207–24.

Valtierra, Ángel, S. J. *Pedro Claver: El Santo Redentor de los negros: Cuarto centenario de su nacimiento.* 2 vols. Bogota: Banco de la Republica, 1980.

——. *Peter Claver, Saint of the Slaves.* Translated by Janet Perry and L. J. Woodward. London: Newman Press, 1960.

——. *Santo Que Libertó Une Raza, San Pedro Claver.* Bogota: Banco de la República, 1980.

van Deusen, Nancy. *Between the Sacred and the Worldly: The Institutional and Cultural Practice of* Recogimiento *in Colonial Lima.* Stanford, CA: Stanford University Press, 2002.

——. "'Wife of my Soul and Heart, and All my Solace': Annulment Suit between Diego de Arenas and Ysabel Allay Suyo." In *Colonial Lives: Documents on Latin American History, 1550–1850,* edited by Richard E. Boyer and Geoffrey Spurling, 130–40. New York: Oxford University Press, 2000.

Vásquez de Espinosa, Antonio. *Compendio y descripción de las Indias Occidentales.* Edited by Balbino Velasco Bayón. Madrid: Ediciones Atlas, 1969.

Vega Umbasia, Leonardo Alberto. *Pecado y delito en la Colonia: la bestialidad como forma de contravención sexual, 1740–1808.* Bogota: Instituto Colombiano de Cultura Hispánica, 1994.

Velandia, Roberto. *Historia documentada de la fundación de Agua de Dios.* Bogota: Biblioteca de Autores Cundinamarqueses, 2002.

Velasco, Sherry. *Lesbians in Early Modern Spain.* Nashville, TN: Vanderbilt University Press, 2011.

Vicuña Guengerich, Sarah. "The Witchcraft Trials of Paula de Eguiluz, a Black Woman, in Cartagena de Indias, 1620–1636." In *Afro-Latino Voices: Narratives from the Early Modern Ibero-Atlantic World, 1550–1812,* edited by Kathryn Joy McKnight and Leo Garofalo, 175–93. Indianapolis, IN: Hackett, 2009.

Vidal Ortega, Antonio. *Cartagena de Indias y la región histórica del Caribe, 1580–1640.* Sevilla: Escuela de Estudios Hispano-Americanos, 2002.

Vila Vilar, Enriqueta. *Aspectos sociales en América colonial de extranjeros, contrabando y esclavos.* Bogota: Instituto Caro y Cuervo, 2001.

——. "Extranjeros en Cartagena (1593–1630)." *Jahrbuch für Geschichte* 16 (1979): 146–77.

Villa Gómez, Jimena. *Vidas apasionantes: heroínas, artistas y amantes en la historia de America Latina.* Bogota: Intermedio Editores, 2002.

Von Germeten, Nicole. *Black Blood Brothers: Social Mobility for Afromexicans.* Tallahassee: University Press of Florida, 2006.

——. "Juan Roque's Donation of a House to the *Zape* Confraternity, Mexico City, 1623." In *Afro-Latino Voices: Narratives from the Early Modern Ibero-Atlantic World, 1550–1812,* edited by Kathryn Joy McKnight and Leo Garofalo, 83–104. Indianapolis, IN: Hackett, 2009.

———. "Prostitution and the Captain's Wife." *Studies in Eighteenth-Century Culture* 39 (Spring 2010): 263–78.

Voss, Barbara. *The Archeology of Ethnogenesis: Race and Sexuality in Colonial San Francisco*. Berkeley: University of California Press, 2008.

Wade, Peter. *Race and Sex in Latin America*. New York: Pluto Press, 2009.

Walker, Charles. *Shaky Colonialism: The 1746 Earthquake in Lima, Peru, and Its long Aftermath*. Durham, NC: Duke University Press, 2008.

West, Robert. *Colonial Placer Mining in Colombia*. Baton Rouge: Louisiana State University Press, 1952.

———. *The Pacific Lowlands of Colombia: A Negroid Area of the American Tropics*. Baton Rouge: Louisiana State University Press, 1957.

White, Cassandra. "Carville and Curupaiti: Experiences of Confinement and Community." *História, Ciências, Saúde; Manguinhos* 10, supplement 1 (2003): 123–41.

White, Stephen D. "The Politics of Anger." In *Anger's Past: The Social Uses of an Emotion in the Middle Ages*, edited by Barbara Rosenwein, 127–52. Ithaca, NY: Cornell University Press, 1998.

Wood, Peter. *The Spanish Main, the Seafarers*. Virginia: Time Life Books, 1979.

Zabaleta Jaspe, Horacio. *Réquiem por un viejo hospital*. Bogota: Ediciones Tercer Mundo, 1976.

Zamora, Alonso de, O. P. *Historia de la Provincia de San Antonio de Nuevo Reino de Granada*. 4 vols. Bogota: Editorial A. B. C., 1945.

Zapata Olivella, Manuel. *El Árbol Brujo de La Libertad: África en Colombia: Orígenes, Transculturación, Presencia, Ensayo Histórico Mítico*. Valle: Universidad del Pacifico, 2002.

Zapatero, Juan Manuel. *Historia de las fortificaciones de Cartagena de Indias*. Madrid: Ediciones Cultura Hispánica del Centro Hispanoamericano, 1979.

Zea, Adolfo de Francisco. "La sociedad ante la lepra." *Boletín de Historia y Antigüedades* 91, no. 825 (April–June 2004): 327–40.

INDEX

adultery, 1, 35, 132–40, 198–204, 207–31
passim; gifts as evidence, 193, 200, 202,
215–16, 223; as justification for murder,
167, 172–73, 176–79; letters as evidence,
199–200; in literature, 167, 213; love
magic and, 32, 44–47; prosecution of,
10–11, 198–204; with slaves, 48–49

archival narratives, as fiction or
performance, 22–25, 59, 76–80, 111,
126, 169, 192–93. *See also* Davis, Natalie
Zemon

archives, 8–9, 10

audiencia (court of appeal in Bogota),
57–58, 83–84, 98, 185; in marriage
disputes, 196–97, 205, 216

bishop of Cartagena, 57–58, 186–87, 210;
adjudicating marriage disputes and
breach of promise cases, 192, 194–95;
love magic cases, 35–36, 42; moral
proclamations, 56, 142, 149; proposals
to enclose prostitutes, 188–89

Bourbon Reforms, 191, 198, 202, 206, 230–31

Bristol, Joan, 14–15, 34

Caribbean: English and Irish in, 79–82;
and love magic, 33–34, 116, 122–3; and
witchcraft, 132

Catholic Church, 6; judicial sanctuary and,
25, 90, 96, 170–72, 236; as a setting for
disputes, 58, 226, 229; as a setting for
seduction, 92

Claver, Peter, 98, 140–41, 148–49, 161

clothing, 144–165 passim, 220–23; attempts
to regulate, 148–50, 151–52; and elite
women, 148–49, 150–51, 220–23; gender
appropriate, 137, 212; given to seduce
women, 92; and prostitutes, 151–52,
156–57, 181–82; and sexual reputation,
27, 28, 164–65, 223; and status, 144–46,
150; *traje de mulata* (typical "mulata"
clothing) 213, 220–22

confession, sacrament of, 63

cortejo (paramour for married women),
198–204, 206, 213–16, 226

courtship, 86–90; public gossip about, 89–90;
use of gifts, 90, 92; use of letters, 22

Cuba, 32, 104, 107, 113, 152–53

cuckoldry, 49, 59, 73, 214–15, 224, 228

curanderas (healers), 105, 110, 114, 103–23
passim; community of, 110, 114–19, 143

Davis, Natalie Zemon, 9, 169, 264n12,
264n18

demonology, 125–27, 129–30, 134

demons: appearance, 113–14, 130; as a
companion and helper, 111–14, 128,
255n6; invoked in spells, 37–38, 41, 43,
115–16; names, 131–32; sex with, 112–13,
126–31, 134–35, 138–39, 159, 259n61

devil: pacts with, 38, 126–31, 133–35, 159;
promising wealth, 125, 128–31, 159

divorce, 191–206 passim, 230; for adultery,
198–204; court procedures, 192–94; for
drunkenness, 204–5; for impotence,
196–97

Drake, Francis, 8

drunkenness: binge drinking, 72–73; Irish
vs. Spanish culture of, 72–75; and
untrustworthiness in court, 48

dueling, 57, 59–60, 72, 73

emotions, 248n3; anger, 45–46, 54–69
passim, 101, 119, 140, 167; fear, 107–8;
jealousy, 63–67, 167, 235–36; love, 86–90,
98–101; shame and guilt, 128, 132–33,
137–38, 143. See also honor; masculinity

English in Cartagena, 75, 82–83

English Parliament, 76–77, 81

estupro (defloration), 19–30 passim, 90–95,
98; compensation for, 29. See also
seduction

fortifications and military defense, 6, 8, 191,
205, 210–11, 230, 240n26. See also pirates

Foucault, Michel, 10–11, 241n39

Gage, Thomas, 154–55

Getsemaní, Cartagena neighborhood, 7, 118,
129, 159, 173, 174, 180

gossip, 12, 55–56, 170, 242n49; clerics as
spreading, 209–11, 214–16, 220; refusing
to spread, 217, 227; and women's sexual
reputation, 20–21, 26–27, 28–29, 58,
201–2, 207–31 passim

governor of Cartagena: adjudicating
breach of promise cases, 20, 25, 196; as
protector of slaves, 62–67

Haiti, 77

honor, 11–13, 189–90; displayed through
wealth, 145, 147; family protection
of, 27, 85–102 passim, 177, 214–15; of
foreigners, 78, 82; as a justification for
violence, 54–69 passim, 73, 167, 171–73,
176–79, 212–13; negotiated within the
military, 207–31 passim; plebian idea of
honor, 20–21; and slaves, 58–69 passim;
as used in court, 4–5, 68–69, 78, 94–97,
166–86 passim, 201–2, 217–19, 224;
women's understanding of, 20–21, 186,
202, 209, 227–30

husbands, 45–49, 58–61, 109–11, 171–79,
198–204

hysteria, 234

imperialism, 5, 69, 156, 241n34; and
clothing, 146–47; competing
institutions, 61–67, 236–37; materialism
of, 125

impotence, 196–97

imprisonment: negotiation of conditions,
3, 51, 95–96, 107–9, 122, 175–76, 197;
rivalries and factions, 120–2, 160–61

Inquisition, Holy Office of the Spanish,
13–14, 61–67; arrival in Cartagena, 36;
autos de fe, 31, 128; criticism of, 164;
inventories of confiscated property,
156–59, 162–63; judicial immunity of,
62–67; prosecuting love magic, 103–24
passim; as a source for historians, 9;
special treatment for elite, 31–32, 49–52;
voluntary confessions, 14, 36–37, 43, 45,
106, 117–18, 252n48

inquisitors, seducing 1–4

Ireland and Spain, 74–75; Irish in Cartagena,
70–84 passim, 251n28; military service
for Spain, 76, 77; nobility, 79; rebellions,
74, 79, 80–81; resisting Protestantism,
77

Jesuits, 125, 146, 148–49, 217, 226, 235

jewelry, 44, 45, 76, 145, 147; given by lovers,
216; owned by prostitutes, 154, 181–82,
186; and sexual reputation, 27, 223;
worn by freedwomen, 150–62 passim;
worn by slaves, 222

Lima, Peru, 10, 149–50, 209, 221, 223–24

limpieza de sangre (blood purity) 11, 62, 67,
78, 177, 187, 194

love: causing madness and disorder, 86, 98;
in literature, 87; and witchcraft, 106;
within marriage, 86–90, 98–101, 195.
See also emotions

love letters, 100–101, 199–200

Madrid, 75